INTERNATIONAL MIGRATION AND GLOBAL JUSTICE

Law and Migration

Series Editor:
Satvinder Singh Juss
King's College London

Migration and its subsets of refugee and asylum policy are rising up the policy agenda at national and international level. Current controversies underline the need for rational and informed debate of this widely misrepresented and little understood area.

Law and Migration contributes to this debate by establishing a monograph series to encourage discussion and help to inform policy in this area. The series provides a forum for leading new research principally from the Law and Legal Studies area but also from related social sciences. The series is broad in scope, covering a wide range of subjects and perspectives.

International Migration and Global Justice

SATVINDER SINGH JUSS
King's College London, UK

ASHGATE

Published by
Ashgate Publishing Limited
Gower House
Croft Road
Aldershot
Hampshire GU11 3HR
England

Ashgate Publishing Company
Suite 420
101 Cherry Street
Burlington, VT 05401-4405
USA

Ashgate website: http://www.ashgate.com

British Library Cataloguing in Publication Data
Juss, Satvinder S. (Satvinder Singh)
    International migration and global justice. – (Law and migration)
    1. Emigration and immigration 2. Emigration and immigration –
    Government policy 3. Emigration and immigration law
    4. Refugees 5. Refugees – Government policy 6. Refugees –
    Legal status, laws, etc.
    I. Title
    325

Library of Congress Cataloging-in-Publication Data
Juss, Satvinder S. (Satvinder Singh)
    International migration and global justice / by Satvinder Juss.
        p. cm. -- (Law and migration)
    Includes index.
    ISBN 978-0-7546-4671-6
    1. Emigration and immigration--Government policy. 2. Emigration and immigration--
Moral and ethical aspects. 3. Emigration and immigration--Social aspects. 4.
Globalization. I. Title. II. Series.

    JV6038.J87 2006
    325--dc22

                                                    2005037636

Hardback edition reprinted 2007

ISBN 13: 978-0-7546-4671-6 (hbk)
ISBN 13: 978-0-7546-7289-0 (pbk)

Typeset by Manton Typesetters, Louth, Lincolnshire, UK.
Printed and bound in Great Britain by MPG Books Ltd, Bodmin, Cornwall.

Contents

Preface

International migration today is as controversial as ever. Yet, migration today has to be viewed as a feature of global change and development. It is part of the process of international globalization. It is a gross mistake to see it as an isolated phenomenon which some commentators and policy analysts still do. International migration has been hastened by a number of factors, such as, the reduction in the cost of international movement, the spread of international communications media, and the internationalization of commerce, all of which have led to a transnational system of political organization where space/time differences have collapsed and the nation state is deterritorialized. The rise in international travel alone has been remarkable with direct implications for immigration. When the Geneva Convention on Refugees was drafted in 1951 only 7 million people flew internationally. Only 15 years later, by 1967, the figure stood at 51 million. By 1993, the number of airline travellers had shot up to 500 million. That represented a staggering 3,500 per cent increase over a 50 year period since 1951. These factors have tended to the recognition of a global infrastructure; a global harmonization or convergence; an increased sense of borderlessness; a global diffusion of localized phenomena and characteristics; and a breathtakingly fast geographical dispersal of core competences in some leading state activities.

Although, even an isolated event like the devaluation of the Thai bhat in July 1997 can spark off a global financial crisis, globalization is more than just the flow of money and trade. As the amount of space and time available to people decreases, the world's population becomes ever more interdependent. Although, the paradigm example of globalization is the integration of financial markets on a global basis – because capital flows are becoming denationalized and national sovereignty is becoming increasingly irrelevant in this area – it is now abundantly clear that other key areas of national competences are also affected, such as the regulation of immigration controls (seen through the adoption of a series of Conventions in Europe), environmental protection, public health, information, and the very idea of a national culture itself. This suggests that policy-making increasingly has to address wider global concerns. The focus is therefore not on some narrow state interest but on the 'public interest' of the world community. Indeed, the wider public interest of the world community has already been addressed in the field of environmental pollution. Ever since the Stockholm Declaration of 1972 there have been a series of international treaties on ozone depletion, climate change, endangered species, and ocean pollution. But more needs to be done across a range of policy areas.

The wider public interest of the world community will have to be addressed because of the internal contradictions of globalization. Already, there are tensions apparent between the forces of localization and globalization which look set to become an emerging new battleground in the twenty-first century. Seattle, Washington, Prague and Gleneagles have already concentrated our minds on this tension with protesters from all over the world setting out to challenge the inequity and instability of the financial system, the degradation of the environment, and the denial of basic human rights to people everywhere in the world. These dissenters of globalization would know that the biggest beneficiaries of globalization are the organized criminal gangs trafficking in drugs, arms and prostitutes because they can so easily exploit worldwide markets. Thus, if in the twentieth century the battleground of political ideas was between the Left and the Right it is now between 'localists' and 'globalists'. While the globalists pitch for higher profits through the maximization of trade and money flows, the localists would allegedly seek to wrest back the control of their economies from the rapacious international competitiveness of multinationals, who would subject them in their own countries to the environmentally and socially damaging effects of globalization.

No doubt, economic globalization is responsible for the dangerous polarization between multi-billionaires and the millions who are living on less than two dollars a day. Thus, the combined GDP of the 48 poorest countries in the world is still less than the combined wealth of the three richest people in the world – Microsoft's Bill Gates, Walmarts' Walton family, and the Sultan of Brunei. The rich mostly benefit from globalization. It is no use saying that breakthroughs like the internet offer everyone a ready route to growth, when over 80 per cent of the net's users live in the West. The inequality gap is widening through the spiral of debt and poverty. Thirty years ago, the per capita incomes in Africa were three times those in East Asia. Today, they are less than half. Since the early 1960s, life expectancy in developing countries has actually risen from 46 to 62 years whereas in sub-Saharan Africa it is just 50 years. According to the British Prime Minister, Tony Blair, 'Africa is a scar on our conscience'. But it is important to understand how this refugee-producing Continent has come to this calamitous state. Prolonged famine, such as in the Horn of Africa, has disrupted the delicate balance of Africa's environment; Geographical lines defining states artificially, regardless of tribal affiliations, have cast a long shadow from the legacy of Colonialism; Political systems, without civil institutions necessary to support them, transposed by Western Colonial powers withdrawing hastily in the 1950s and 1960s; The Cold War fought for many decades in such large parts of the Continent as the Horn of Africa, Zaire, and Angola; the scourge of Apartheid affecting the development of the whole of Southern Africa because it affected front-line states like Mozambique, Angola and Namibia; economic mismanagement by African leaders who set up ill-conceived and dissolute projects; a debt crisis caused by the receipt of western loans to finance projects with the result that poor states were in no position to repay loans. Africa today spends twice as much on debt payments than on health. Tanzania – described once by its President, Julius Nyerere, as a Fourth World country – spending a staggering nine times as much. Debt bondage is a modern form of slavery, with western countries owed, until a few years ago, £138 billion, working out to £231 for every man, woman and child. A burgeoning population growth in circumstances where, although per capita incomes have been falling because growth has not matched the forces of demography, sub-Saharan Africa has a rising population of over 600 million people. Small wonder then, that people who are as impoverished as this want to seek a better existence elsewhere. Small wonder then, that immigration from the poorer world to the richer countries has been on the increase in the last 30 years.

It is unsurprising then, that the world is awash with refugees. Currently, standing at 125 million, this population, already immense, is growing remorselessly – driven by refugee-producing and migration-facilitating conditions: such as political repression, armed conflict, civil strife, environmental disaster, famine, social and economic disintegration, wretched government policies, and improvements in communication and transportation opportunities. The purpose of this book is not to look at the suffering of these people. It is to provide a lens through which these phenomena may be understood in the interests of international peace and security. Migration is a major political and economic issue of our time. There is an urgent need for a fact-based, non-partisan assessment of the impact of migration. This is because facts and figures are often distorted to meet different agendas.

The *UN Convention on Refugees* was written for a different era when the Iron Curtain was still hanging across Europe and before cheap travel became an everyday reality. There is an evident need for a new international treaty which clearly defines a refugee and better sets out the burden-sharing obligations of European countries. Never in recent times has there been a situation in the democratic world that has more urgently needed brave moral leadership. Humanity, justice and decency have to override political expediency. In many cases from where refugees are fleeing resources have been pillaged and plundered for decades and the people are now being turned away. They are fleeing from oppression and the oppression is poverty. The number of applicants for asylum in Britain is less than 1 per cent of the world's refugee population. Yet, the hysteria over refugees reaches ever more new heights. Trained journalists rarely ask refugees what they are fleeing from or why they are seeking asylum. Yet, this is surely as important a question as the numbers applying for refugee status. The Press has consistently failed to report the very conditions and events that create refugees. When they fail to report these events the media not only fail to report why refugees flee their homes but also allow the offending regime to continue its human rights abuses unchallenged: witness Charles Taylor's Liberia or the Sudanese government's onslaught in Darfur. This failure only creates more refugees.

The *United Nations Annual Human Development Report* in 1999 called for a rewriting of global economic rules to avoid inequalities between poor countries and wealthy individuals. The UN wants a more representative system of global governance. Its recommendations include an international forum of business, trade unions, and environmental/development groups to consider the dominance of the G7 countries in global decision-making; a Code of Conduct for the multi-nationals; and the creation of an international legal centre to help poor countries conduct global trade negotiations. This book explains why this alone is not enough. The liberalization of immigration controls must also follow. The distinction between voluntary and involuntary immigrants should cease to be the cornerstone of international refugee policy. Immigration should be recognized as a moral and economic imperative as much for the developed as for the under-developed world. This is not just in the interests of humanity, justice and decency. It is also in the global public interest – although few yet recognize it.

Acknowledgements

This book focuses on freedom of movement as one of the necessary goods of life. Historically, the free movement of people across the Globe has helped to under-pin ideas of international morality, all the way from the pursuit of humanitarian objectives, to the redistribution of economic resources, to the enrichment of national cultures. Today, globalization has led to an even greater inter-dependency of nations making free movement rights even more important. Accordingly, this book also argues for a new conception of a humanitarian refugee whereby those in the northern hemisphere can think in terms of solidarity with those in the South and work towards a right to development throughout the whole world. Ultimately, therefore, the facilitation of free movement also impacts on questions of international justice. Not everyone in the developed world, of course, sees free movement in quite this way. In his masterly *Microcosmorphia Academica*, F.N. Cornford, once noted the frequent conservative objection that 'one should not act justly now, for fear of raising expectations that one will act still more justly in the future'. But justice is important because restrictions on free movement are the single biggest obstacle to the alleviation of world poverty, impacting on international justice, and damaging the prospects for international peace and stability in some of the most vulnerable parts of the world. This is to say nothing of the burdens on the developed world of maintaining rigid immigration control, in terms of both huge financial and labour costs. This book is not about the abandonment of all immigration controls. It is about having a rational policy based on a careful calculus of costs and benefits to the developed world.

I have had the good fortune over the years of benefiting from the camaraderie and friendship of a number of people renowned in the fields of immigration and refugee law. They have both wittingly and unwittingly helped me develop the views expressed in this book. In academic circles, there have been Professors James Hollifield, Steven Legomsky, Kay Hailbronner, Geoff Gilbert, Nigel Harris, Werner Menski, James Hathaway, and Guy S. Goodwin-Gill. All have played a role, and not least through their writings. James Hathaway and Alexander Neve's, *Making International Refugee Law Relevant Again: A Proposal for Collectivised and Solution-Oriented Protection* (10 Harv. Hum. Rts. J., 115 (1997)) provided me with an opportunity for intellectual tussle by enabling me, as a Human Rights Fellow at Harvard Law School from 1996-1997, to first engage in a detailed critique of modern refugee law (see *Towards a Morally Legitimate Reform of Refugee Law*, 11 Harv. Hum. Rts. J., (1998) Spring, pp.311-354). I am grateful to Professor Hathaway for his generosity of soul in now reviewing the manuscript of this book and contributing an endorsement. Professor Guy Goodwin-Gill has found the time to contribute a sparkling and insightful Foreword to this work, despite being extremely busy and abroad. He has been especially supportive and always responsive to my e-mail requests. His *The Refugee in International Law* (2ⁿᵈ edn., Oxford, 1996) is now an established classic and a standard text for my refugee law classes. Sadly, the 3ʳᵈ edition of this work does not arrive in time for me to avail myself of it. Professor Geoff Gilbert has always been close at hand and ever-helpful (and not just as the General Editor of the *International Journal of Refugee Law*) in providing assistance over my Masters courses at King's College London.

In practitioner and judicial circles, I am exceedingly grateful to members of the *Asylum & Immigration Appeals Tribunal* ('AIT'), especially at Birmingham for providing a wonderfully collegiate environment for the practice of immigration and refugee law. In particular, I am greatly appreciative of the help and support of Mr. John McCarthy, always generous with his time, and willing to intellectually eviscerate all manner of refugee issues ranging from the 'burden of proof' to 'persecution'. His regular discussions with me about how refugee law works, (or ought to work) in a practically meaningful way, has always been like a ballast of fresh air. I am also grateful to Messers, Nick Renton and Ian French. In their own relaxed ways, they have striven to make this jurisdiction a model of efficiency and effectiveness, and thereby helped me to combine my scholarship with my practice of refugee law. Dr. Hugo Storey has corresponded regularly with me as a Senior Immigration Judge and supported my scholarly endeavours.

King's College Law School at London University has provided me with unrivalled academic ambience that has been wonderfully conducive to the best kinds of research. The Law Department is a testament to present and past heads of school who have helped foster a collegiality in the School that is second to none. Colleagues here have been great sources of encouragement and intellectual support. The *Centre of European Law* at King's College London made a generous award to provide financial support for the research undertaken in this book. King's College Law School afforded me with a Sabbatical for much of 2006. I have had the privilege of being a Course Director in three Masters level degree courses, and those students who I have taught 'International Refugee Law' on the MA in *International Peace and Security* and the *London University LLM* have often taught me as much as I have taught them. This book is tribute to them and it is hoped that in the years to come they will find it as helpful as it is challenging.

Outside King's College, I was engaged between 2004-2005 in charitable work as a Migration Commissioner with colleagues at the *Royal Society of Arts* on a major project. This culminated in our report in November 2005 on 'Migration: A Welcome Opportunity' (www.migrationcommission.org) which was commended to the British Government. Those that think that the ideas expressed in this book are little short of heresy may want to look at our recommendations there. Finally, no intellectual endeavour on my part can be complete without my recording the enormous debt that I owe to Professor Paul O'Higgins, who taught me at Cambridge in the 1980s and left an indelible mark on me. In the quarter of a century that has since passed, he has always remained in touch leaving me to aspire to his standards of rigorous scholarship and intellectual generosity.

This book may never have been published when it was, were it not for the keen interest in its subject-matter expressed by my publishers at Ashgate. In particular, I would like to single out for praise Alison Kirk, for her dedication, care and patience and Gemma Lowle, my Desk Editor, and Nigel Farrow, and Dymphna Evans for their professionalism. It is to be hoped that this work will be a fitting start to the series on 'Law and Migration' which I have been asked to head by Ashgate Publishing.

I dedicate this work to my long suffering family who patiently waited for their holiday during the long summer days of 2005 while I wrote furiously. I hope this book is at least a tiny consolation for the holiday they missed.

Satvinder Singh Juss
King's College London
Easter 2006

Foreword

Given what has been achieved with regard to refugees, even if not as much as many would like, the almost total absence of international regulation is one of the most intriguing aspects of migration in its ordinary sense. Nearly everywhere, immigration law and policy are driven by local perceptions and characterized by controls intended to serve national goals, which in turn tend to be narrowly defined or framed.

There is no doubt that the pressure to migrate will continue, or that globalization will play its role. In part, movements will be for demographic reasons, such as population or environmental pressures; in part, because of economic pressures, such as unemployment or underemployment; and in part, because of political conditions creating refugees, such as coercion resulting from conflict or persecution. In this unexceptional scenario, the developed world will continue to attract the politically and economically displaced, no matter how tough or deterrent it presents itself. Experience shows, moreover, that unilateral measures and strict policies on admission are difficult to maintain at a constant level of consistency, particularly in the face of complex changing conditions and the ever-present drive to competitiveness.

The line between voluntary and forced migration is increasingly blurred and indeterminate. People have a greater number of choices today, communications have expanded, information is readily available, and transport is cheaper; those in search of work join those in search of refuge. One result is the growth in people smuggling and trafficking, an industry itself driven also by the demand in developed and developing economies for both skilled and unskilled labour.

One bright point is that the complexity and cross-sectoral dimensions of migration questions are now beginning to be recognized, and that this book is part of that urgent debate. The author, Dr Juss, argues persuasively for States finally to wake up to the global dimensions of migration. Progress will only come when they step away from outmoded conceptions of sovereignty, which stand in the way of coherent policy and practice, and when they recognize that the full benefits of migration will only be tapped when individual rights and interests are factored in.

In this complicated and highly mobile world, the voice of the migrant and the interests of transnational communities are heard as infrequently as the call for social justice and equity in international order. Stability and order, though, will depend on these issues being integrated into policy- and decision-making on migration, while States locally will also need to face up to the reality of multiculturalism, to all the questions of 'assimilation' and cultural identity, as well as to basic rights issues, such as community membership and community claims.

In its present formulation, neither international law nor human rights law contains all the answers. Notwithstanding the developing international discourse, neither States nor international organizations may yet be able to learn from experience and to move on to an era marked by effective commitment to global justice. Migration offers one of the most exciting challenges for the twenty-first century, and what Dr Juss does is to prepare the ground for that debate, identifying the most pressing questions, and highlighting the approach from principle.

Guy S. Goodwin-Gill
All Souls College, Oxford
16 January 2006

Select List of Cases

Abdalla v Immigration and Multicultural Affairs, 51 A.L.B.11 (1998) (Federal Court of Australia).
Acero Garces [1999] INLR 460.
Adan v Secretary of State for the Home Department, 2 W.L.R 702 (1998) H.L.
AE and FE v Secretary of State for the Home Department [2003] INLR 475.
Aguirre-Cervantes v. Immigration and Naturalization Service, 273 F.3d 120 (9th Cir. 2001).
Ahmed v Austria, 24 Eur. H.R. Rep. (Ser.B) at 278, 279-80 (1996).
Ammani v Sweden Application No 60959/00 (unreported) 22 October 2002.
Apthekar v Secretary of State, 378 U.S. 500, 519 (1964).
Applicant A v Minister for Immigration & Ethnic Affairs (1997) 190 CLR 225.
Arriaga-Barrientos v INS, 937 F.2d 411 (9th Cir. 1991).

Bastanipour v Immigration and Naturalisation Service 980 F.2d 1129 (7th Cir. 1990).
Bensaid v United Kingdom (2001) 33 EHRR 205.

Canada (Attorney-General) v. Ward (1993) 2 SCR 689.
Case 75/63, *Unger v Bestuur Ter. Pedriifsvereniging Voor Detailhandel en Ambachten*, 3 C.M.L.R. 319 (1964).
Case 7/75, *Fracas v Belgian State*, 2 C.M.L.R. 442, 450 (1975).
Case 48/75, *State v Royer*, 2 C.M.L.R. 619 (1976).
Case 53/81, *Levin v Staatssecretaris van Justitie*, 1982 E.C.R. 1035, (1982).
Case 59/85, *The State (Netherlands) v Reed*, 2 C.M.L.R. 448 (1987).
Case 370/90, *Regina v Immigration Appeal Tribunal and Surinder Singh ex parte Secretary of State for the Home Department*, 3 C.M.L.R. 358 (1992).
Chahal v United Kingdom (1996) 23 EHRR 413.
Chan v Canada (Minister of Employment & Immigration) [1995] 3 S.C.R 593.
Cheung v Canada (Minister of Employment & Immigration) [1993] 102 D.L.R 4th 214 (Can.).
Cruz Varas v Sweden (1991) 14 EHRR 1.

D v United Kingdom (1997) 24 EHRR 423, 447, at para 49.
Demirkaya v Secretary of State for the Home Department [1999] Imm Ar 498; [1999] INLR 441, CA, per Stuart-Smith LJ at para 18.
Desir v Ilchert 840 F.2d 723 (9th Cir. 1998).

To my Family

'Migration is the oldest action against poverty. It selects those who most want help. It is good for the country to which they go; it helps break the equilibrium of poverty in the country from which they come. What is the perversity in the human soul that causes people to resist so obvious a good.'

J.K. Galbraith

1 Rediscovering International Morality

Freedom of movement is 'the first and most fundamental of man's liberties'.[1] Without it, other rights are precarious. Universally recognized values, such as mutual aid, humanity, hospitality, comity, mutual intercourse, and good faith, all depend on the right to free movement for their efficacy. The world order depends on freedom of movement. Whether one is looking at the encouragement of peace by the easing of demographic pressures, or the enrichment of national cultures, or the redistribution of economic resources, or the pursuit of humanitarian objectives, freedom of movement has a central role to play in the modern global order.[2] All are fundamentally interconnected and indivisible from one another.

Freedom of movement is enshrined in the foundation document of the human rights movement. The *Universal Declaration of Human Rights 1948* affirms that 'Everyone has the right to freedom of movement and residence within the borders of each state'[3] and that 'Everyone has the right to leave any country, including his own, and to return to his country'.[4] More specifically, it declares that 'Everyone has the right to seek and to enjoy in other countries asylum from persecution'.[5] The Preamble of the 1948 *Declaration* proclaims this Charter of Rights 'as a common standard of achievement for all peoples and all nations' and goes on to declare that 'the rights and freedoms' therein are to be enjoyed 'without any distinction of any kind, such as race, colour, sex, language, religion, political or other opinion, national or social origin, property, birth or other status'.[6]

The economist J.K. Galbraith, once said, migration is 'the oldest action against poverty'.[7] The history of peoples' struggle to survive and to prosper is rooted in the history of migration.[8] Their struggle to escape insecurity and poverty is also best epitomized in the history of migration. And their readiness to move in response to opportunity is also most clearly reflected in migratory movements. Migration has caused 175 million people today, or just under 3 per cent of the total population of the world, to live outside their country of birth.[9] Freedom of movement has come to be seen as one of the necessary goods of life. Free movement begets a free life. A free life means better life chances for the individual. Where an individual lives determines a person's

1

life, liberty, and well-being. Free movement as a fundamental right recognizes 'the ageless quest of individuals for a better life everywhere'.[10] The access to a foreign territory is a necessary component of the right to free movement. This is because it enables individuals everywhere to have the essential alternative of participating in the social processes of another state in an effort to develop their own freedom and appreciation of life.[11]

Freedom of movement, and particularly the freedom to move to another territory, can therefore be said to be a basic human right, like the right to be free from 'arbitrary interference with a person's privacy, family, home' or to be free from attacks on his 'honour and reputation';[12] or 'the right to marry and to found a family';[13] or the right not to be discriminated against,[14] all of which are also enshrined in the *Universal Declaration of Human Rights*. More than 30 years ago, Roger Nett wrote that:

> [w]hereas, in the past, civil rights were defined largely as devices by which people might escape from tyranny and direct abuse, *the right of people to equal opportunities is rather clearly the underlying theme of all civil rights today*. We still talk about free speech, religion, and the right to vote as though they were ends in themselves, and indeed they can be. But people have become conscious that their purpose in seeking or maintaining them is to equalize opportunities, to make possible a life that would otherwise be denied, and that it is in this sense that we are most likely to define justice today.[15]

In the words of Michael Dummett, the Emeritus Professor of Logic at the University of Oxford, there is a distinction to be made between what a person 'deserves' and what is his 'due'. As he explains, 'There are some things which are everybody's due. The basic conditions that enable someone to live a fully human life are due of every human being, just in virtue of being human: these are what are nowadays called "human rights"'.[16] It seems to me that these are all 'dignity rights' inherent in a meaningful human existence predicated on the moral equality of all human beings. But I propose to argue here that it is less well recognzied that the right to free movement is integral to the enduring existence of liberal democracies. It is central to how democratic states conceive of, and sustain themselves. This is because liberal democracies extol the virtues of civic equality. As Ruth Rubio-Marin states if 'liberal democracy is to remain alive' then affluent and industrialized Western society must critically question its policies of the 'degrees and kinds of exclusion of non-national residents'.[17] One may be driven to the conclusion, as Christian Joppke is, that 'accepting unwanted immigration is inherent in the liberalness of liberal states' given that today '[u]nder the hegemony of the United States, liberalism has become the dominant Western idiom in the postwar period, indicating a respect for universal human rights and the rule of law'.[18] Paradoxically, liberal scholars recognize the existence of a post-national order. Yet, they still start from the premise of closed societies rather than the democratic concepts of civic equality. Liberal scholars, it seems to me, need to be more intellectually robust and less intellectually hamstrung in this. Indeed, according to Professor Rubio-Marin, discrimination against non-nationals cannot be right because the commitment to a liberal and democratic legal order must be measured by inclusiveness, to which the concept of closed so-cieties is anathema.[19]

A similar point has been rather refreshingly made by Professor Kevin John-son who argues that legal scholarship generally treats closed borders as the assumed state of immigration law, with the law facilitating the efficient, fair and rational administration of a comprehensive system of immigration con-trols. In an eloquent analysis of US law, Johnson makes a case for 'open borders' and articulates arguments for eliminating the border as a legal con-struct that impedes the movement of people into the US declaring that politicians, activists, and scholars have not seriously considered opening the borders to all comers.[20]

Whether or not borders should be thrown open, in my view the case for an open system of immigration controls is unassailable simply because the con-cept of closed societies is repugnant to the very idea of international mutuality, communality and solidarity. This may sound polemical. It is not. It is forgotten that in 1892, in the heyday of European restrictionism, the *Institute of Interna-tional Law* proposed the *International Regulations on the Admission and Expulsion of Aliens*,[21] a liberal instrument designed to establish a state's duty to admit aliens. The legal right of a state to control the admission of aliens, as 'a logical and necessary consequence' of its sovereignty and independence, was tem-pered by the obligations of 'humanity and justice'.[22] Sovereign states, while protecting their security, had to have regard to the right and liberty of foreign-ers wishing to enter its territory. Its key provisions are worth recounting. They are even more relevant to the international community today than they were over a hundred years ago in a fractious, unstable and uncertain world, that is in dire need of re-discovering the principles of international morality:

> ARTICLE 6. Free entrance of aliens to the territory of a civilized state, may not be generally and permanently forbidden except in the public interest and for very seri-ous reasons, for example, because of fundamental differences in customs or civilization or because of a dangerous organization or gathering of aliens who come in great numbers.

> ARTICLE 7. The protection of national labor is not, in itself, a sufficient reason for non admission.

> ARTICLE 12. Entrance to a country may be forbidden to any alien individual in a condition of vagabondage or beggary, or suffering from a malady liable to endanger the public health, or strongly suspected of serious offences committed abroad against the will or health of human beings or against public property or faith, as well as to aliens who have been convicted of the said offences.

The reference to 'free entrance of aliens' by 'a civilized state' in a way that is not 'generally and permanently forbidden' is refreshing in the light of the subsequent failure of twentieth century international instruments to match such values, let alone develop them any further; as is the principle that the 'protection of national labor is not, in itself, a sufficient reason for non admis-sion'. Of course, restrictions may be imposed by a sovereign state but only if this is 'in the public interest and for very serious reasons', and the examples of 'public health' and the suspected commission of 'serious offences' serve to highlight the bases upon which exclusion of aliens may be properly justifiable.

Exclusion on the grounds 'of fundamental differences in customs or civilization' is anachronistic today in an era of anti-discrimination laws and increased international inter-dependency and the globalization of culture, although it is accepted that some would disagree. Even so, it is difficult not to conclude that this is racially discriminatory and inherently inconsistent with the very idea of 'free entrance of aliens' which is 'not [to] be generally and permanently forbidden' by 'a civilized state'. This was an issue that the international community could have more imaginatively tackled in the twentieth century. Unfortunately, the *Eighth Commission* of the Institute decided, having drafted the regulations, not to adopt them in favor of a more limited sovereign right of the state to exclude individuals, so as to have a set of stable principles for the future. In the event, twentieth century international instruments did not even follow through these fundamental precepts in later enactments, let alone develop them in a realistic and meaningful way. Nevertheless, these 1892 proposals help me to advance my argument that the international system needs to be based on fundamental values of international mutuality, communality and solidarity if it is to be just, stable and durable. It is significant, as far as the search for a new international morality is concerned, that the *Eighth Commission* rejected a proposed amendment to allow states to exclude individuals on the grounds of 'race, customs, or civilization'.[23] If this was anathema then, it should be anathema now one hundred years later. The international community should, accordingly, determine to concretize the fundmental values of international morality in the promulgation of clear international rules of conduct.

The right to free movement is one such right. This does not mean that it cannot be subject to restriction by states. It is well known that most human rights today are subject to principles of legitimate restriction and proportionality. It simply implies the recognition that the free movement right is so fundamental that the realization of human aspiration depends upon it. It has already been suggested that the global community must 'by the operation of law' seek to 'facilitate natural processes of human migration as a means of accommodating basic human needs and human dignity'.[24] It seems to me that it is here that the distinction between refugees and other migrants breaks down yet again since, once again, one is looking at fair opportunity. To quote, Roger Nett:

> What is implied in the right to free movement as it relates to fair opportunity? One dimension is material, the right of people who are trapped in overcrowded areas or areas without sufficient resources to go where resources are not so taken up. The other, more purely political, is the right of people to move away from oppression, persecution, unfair restriction, or even disagreeable social environments and social orders. One involves the right to come; the other, the right to go.[25]

Despite this eloquent reasoning, and even though the right to free movement has normative force, it is not unequivocally recognized as a fundamental human right by positive law.

How far then, I ask, can the normative commitment to free movement be practically relevant? The law on free movement rights is a classic illustration of the gulf between the 'is' and the 'ought'. What 'ought' to be is very different from what 'is' the case. In this chapter, I set out to take a critical look at this paradox inherent in the phenomenon of free movement. In human rights discourse 'rights' are derived from 'claims'. A rights approach offers a normative vocabulary that facilitates both the framing of claims and the identification of the rights holder. Indeed, as Jacqueline Bhabha, a foremost liberal thinker on refugee and human rights issues, has argued recently, 'In today's world, the experience of serious human rights violations is closely linked to the act of migration'.[26] At the same time, there have been in human rights work:

> fundamental changes in the approach to children's rights, environmental rights, indigenous rights, and to group rights more generally, changes that have altered the landscape for considering the appropriate objects of rights-protective intervention and the legitimate targets for accusations of human rights abuse.[27]

These have made the application of human rights arguments to migration and asylum law all the more relevant.

The power of rights dialogue lies in its use of a normative language to make moral claims.[28] As a form of rights-dialogue, human rights are no-where more important than when the state is dealing with vulnerable populations and individuals. As the Secretary-General to the United Nations, Kofi Annan, once said that:

> Human Rights are what make us human. They are the principles by which we create the sacred home for human dignity, are the expression of those traditions of tolerance in all cultures that are the basis of peace and progress properly understood and justly interpreted are foreign to no culture and native to all nations.[29]

The paradox is that throughout the twentieth century, despite the rising 'claim' to the exercise of free movement rights, the 'right' to free movement in law has, if anything, been subject to ever more restrictions in the developed world. In this chapter, I set out to show that notwithstanding this paradox, the lack of a legal right to freedom of movement across borders is remarkable lacuna in the typography of international human rights law. Accordingly, this chapter adopts an empirical approach to demonstrate the proposition that whatever positive law says there is empirical evidence for a fundamental right to freedom of movement in western culture. This empirical evidence comes in the form of the records of classical publicists, the historical practice of the affluent nations of the North, the legal affirmation of that practice in the judicial dicta of the leading liberal legal systems in the world, and the writings of modern publicists.

From this empirical evidence, I would contend that it is possible to conclude that, twentieth century restrictions on free movement rights should be seen not as a norm. They are a departure from what has been the historical norm in human society. The argument that I present here is controversial, but not without foundation. In the broad sweep of history, mankind's human experience was not the restriction on free movement rights, but the relentless expansion of those rights in the pursuit of basic fundamental rights. In the words of Roger Nett:

> ... people have always recognized this right [ie the right to free movement] de facto, and ancient as well as modern history is full of instances of migration to avoid persecution and in search of better opportunities.[30]

The evidence that I present, I believe, thus leads to the conclusion that there is a compelling case for the legalisation of free movement rights. The way in which this can be done is as follows. For those, facing a flagrant violation of their fundamental rights, I believe that one can begin by adopting a more expansive definition of refugee status. For those seeking to flee conditions of poverty and destituition, one can begin with enshrining a right to work,[31] without an automatic entitlement to settle in the receiving countries. In fact, for those countries that are facing labour shortages (which includes the whole of Western Europe and the USA) steps should be taken to legalize illegal immigration.

When Malaysia expelled 380,000 foreign labourers in 2005, most of them from impoverished Indonesia, following an amnesty between October 2004 and February 2005, those who did not leave before the deadline were hunted by 300,000 vigilantes recruited and armed by the government and forcibly expelled. The Malaysian government, in the face of mounting international criticism, argued that it was protecting Malaysian jobs and cracking down on illegal immigration. Within months Malaysia faced chronic labour shortages. Plantations, construction sites and factories ground to a halt. Illegal immigrants made up 10 per cent of the Malaysian workforce and the Malaysian economy relied upon them to do the menial jobs that most Malaysians would not do. Despite attempts to entice them back, most have been unwilling to return. Of the 380,000 who left, fewer than 40,000 have been willing to come back. This is 'a salutary warning to Europe's vocal anti-immigration lobby' because Malaysia has now 'been forced to beg the illegal immigrants it chased out only months ago to return to solve severe labour shortages ...'.[32] Thus attempts to legalize immigration would, in my considered opinion, be a step towards 'rational' policy formulation. It would recognize what is already taking place. A rational policy on migration would eliminate waste, aid both developing and developed societies, and bring attendant benefits to voluntary migrants and involuntary refugees alike.

THE UN CHARTER AND FREE MOVEMENT RIGHTS

To the extent that refugees are also migrants, and part of the mass movement of people, the analytical distinction between the two ceases at some point to be a meaningful one. Accordingly, I believe that any attempt to devise a new international migration regime must take into account the fact that refugees are immigrants into a country. Leading reform proposals on refugee law will founder otherwise. Thus, the late Arthur C. Helton argued that 'a new international regime concerning forced migration is needed'.[33] Zolberg, Suhrke and Aguayo have argued that all victims, and not just activists and targets, of violence should be given asylum.[34] But if the developed countries of the North are concerned about increased immigration, these proposals will not be supported by them unless placed in the context of overall immigration faced by them and the expectation in liberal democratic societies that they be resolved through the application of democratic principles.

Freedom of movement may be one of the tolerant traditions common to all cultures based on peace and progress, but even in the UDHR, refugees alone have the right to seek and to enjoy asylum from persecution in other countries,[35] for they are involuntary migrants and deserve especial consideration. Immigrants generally, who are voluntary migrants, do not have the right to enter another country, but only the right 'to leave any country … and to return'.[36] For these migrants, the freedom of movement is only half a right because it privileges the state's right over the individuals, including the state's right to pass laws to exclude her or him. It does not privilege the individual's right over the state, including her or his right to demand entry. In human rights terms, this is an anomaly that is all the more remarkable given that many other individual rights of dignity and personhood (such as to be free from attacks on honour and reputation) are posited as fully-fledged human rights. It is also anomalous given the modern phenomenon of world-wide migration where large numbers of people move, and manage to secure admission, to other countries.

The anomaly of lack of legal rights, in relation to an activity so largely participated in by so many people, is not questioned because of the absence of a significant challenge to the legitimacy of current immigration controls, and the emotive context in which immigration and refugee policy are currently discussed and presented. Legitimacy cannot be assumed simply because there is a high degree of congruity between state practice in western immigration control. Human rights can, and increasingly do, prioritize themselves over state sovereignty. In western democracies most immigration and asylum appeals before state authorities involve an immigration/asylum decision followed by a human rights decision in respect of each claim. In Britain, in June 2004, the House of Lords held that human rights under the ECHR are capable of being engaged in expulsion cases where the expellee would suffer a denial of human rights in the receiving.[37] In one of the two cases, the House held that the claimant's right to respect for private life protected by Art. 8 of the ECHR could be engaged by the forseeable consequences for health of removal from the United Kingdom pursuant to an immigration decision.[38] Lord Bingham further held that if '*return to Germany would violate Mr Razgar's rights under Article 8*' then '*the Secretary of State could not properly certify this claim to be manifestly unfounded*',[39] even the Secretary of state had the clear power to certify a claim under domestic legislation duly passed by Parliament.[40]

Yet, it is plain that the UDHR's statement of principle on free movement rights is not practically useful. In normative terms, the right to leave a country cannot be fully exercised without a corresponding right to enter another country. In fact, Articles 15, 23, and 25 of the UDHR establish basic rights to change one's nationality, to work freely under favorable conditions, and to secure an adequate standard of living. These are the very rights that are integral to the maintenance of an international order. Accordingly, it has been argued that there must thus be a corresponding right to admit a person who has left his own country because:

> the right to leave a country cannot be fully exercised unless there is a right of entry into another country. If there is an obligation upon a state to let every one leave it, there must be a corresponding obligation on other states to let people enter it without discrimination. Barriers imposed by states on entry, such as quota systems or racial and religious requirements, must be lifted.[41]

Plainly, the conferment of such a right is practically meaningless unless liberally interpreted. Implicitly, this imposes an obligation on territories not to entirely deny entry to foreign nationals.[42]

It is nevertheless, significant that the right was not unequivocally formulated as such and significant as to why it was not. The failure to properly expound this right has meant that the international right to freedom of movement has not been fully developed. Why it was not is a more interesting question. It is submitted that it was not because of considerations of culture and community. Free movement as a fundamental right has remained incomplete because of the perceived need by communities to protect themselves from the influx of the 'other' who is culturally different. This perceived need has distorted free movement rights. The failure to be clear has distorted the right of the individual to assert a claim on the state of another. The result is that this right is not positively enshrined. And, it has distorted the right of the refugee to seek sanctuary in another country because that right, although expressly formulated as a legal right in the UDHR, has, over the years, become linked with the right to migrate generally. Thus, the current development of international law does not evince, even at the beginning of the new millennium in the twenty-first century, a general right of freedom of movement in individuals. When 171 states gathered at the World Conference on Human Rights in Vienna in June 1993,[43] the United Nations Secretary-General, Boutros Boutros-Ghali, in opening the Conference, observed that:

> I believe that in this point in time it is less urgent to define new rights than to persuade states to adopt existing instruments and apply the effectively.[44]

Indeed, even the right to asylum has yet to fully evolve in international law. The 171 states, in adopting the Vienna Declaration and Program of Action, did not expand the existing concept of the right of asylum and simply re-iterated the provisions of the Universal Declaration of Human Rights:

the World Conference on Human Rights re-affirms that everyone, without distinction of any kind is entitled to the right to seek and to enjoy in other countries asylum from persecution.[45]

Thus, although the implementation of the *UN Declaration of Human Rights 1948* has gradually been undertaken through the adoption of binding international agreements the limitations on the right to free movement remain. *The International Covenant on Economic Social and Cultural Rights 1966* (ICPPR) protects 'the right to liberty of movement' but only of 'everyone lawfully within the territory of a state';[46] the *International Convention on the Elimination of All Forms of Racial Discrimination 1966* (CERD) protects the 'right to freedom of movement and residence within the border of the state',[47] but expressly states that the *Convention* 'shall not apply to distinctions, exclusions, restrictions, or preferences made by a state party to this Convention between citizens and non-citizens';[48] the *Convention for the Elimination of All Forms of Discrimination against Women* (CEDW) affirms the 'equality of men and women, of human rights and fundamental freedoms in the political, economic, social cultural, civil or any other field'[49] but contains no right to free movement itself; the *Convention against Torture and other Cruel, Inhuman or Degrading Treatment or Punishment 1984* prevents non-refoulment by asserting that 'No State Party shall expel, return ('refouler') or extradite a person to another State where there are substantial grounds for believing that he would be in danger of being subjected to torture'[50] but otherwise contains no provision for freedom of movement; the *Convention on the Rights of the Child 1989* expressly declares that:

> States Parties shall take appropriate measures to ensure that a child who is seeking refugee status or who is considered in accordance with applicable international or domestic law and procedures shall … receive appropriate protection and humanitarian assistance in the enjoyment of applicable rights set forth in the present Convention[51]

but again carries with it no right to free movement for children; the *International Convention on the Protection of the Rights of All Migrant Workers and Members of their Families 1990*, in a wide-ranging and generous catalogue of rights, whilst recognizing that '[m]igrant workers and members of their families shall be free to leave any state, including their State of origin' and 'shall have the right at any time to enter and remain in their State of origin'[52] does not contain a free-standing right to enter into any other state; and finally, the *Vienna Declaration and Programme of Action from UN World Conference on Human Rights 1993* comes full circle and 'stresses the importance of the Universal Declaration of Human Rights, the 1951 Convention relating to the status of Refugees, its 1967 Protocol and the regional instruments' so that it simply 'reaffirms that everyone, without distinction of any kind, is entitled to the right to seek and to enjoy in other countries asylum from persecution, as well as the right to return to one's own country'[53] with no further rights, including not even the right to secure asylum, which is exactly the situation that pertained nearly half a century ago when the UDHR was proclaimed. It is as if the world has stood still in that time.

International instruments on migration make a distinction between two kinds of rights. The right to migrate and the right to seek asylum are technically different rights.[54] One is voluntary, the other is involuntary. One is a matter of state practice; the other is a matter of international law. Yet, both are migrants and the distinction between voluntary and involuntary migrants is not observed in the European Community where the Treaty on European Union adopts in a single framework, matters of foreign policy, national security, justice, immigration and home affairs[55] (and has been criticized as such by bodies such as ECRE and Amnesty International). As a result, the term immigration is synonomous with asylum.[56] This does not mean that the technical distinction between refugees and other immigrants is invalid.[57] Certainly the express recognition in international law of refugees as persons with minimum rights and protections, who by virtue of the distinctive concepts of asylum and non-refoulement, are different from other aliens who seek entry, is not without legal basis. That legal basis, however, is increasingly subject to question. Even half a century ago, Jacques Vernant observed that an individual's 'economic situation is no longer looked on as a "natural" phenomenon, but as a responsibility of the State'. He rightly went onto to explain how '[I]n a great many States any measure, whatever its nature, is a political event'.[58] Zolberg pointed out how the undermining of the economic position of Russian Jews at the end of the nineteenth century made their survival impossible and making flight the only viable alternative.[59] Shacknove argued that even natural disasters like drought and floods could trigger refugee flows where State action is inadequate.[60] Emma Haddad writes that:

> economic and political causes of flight are inextricably linked, and any clear separation of the two between (voluntary) migrants and (involuntary) refugees respectively remains far from satisfactory.[61]

In fact, for more than a quarter of a century now, there have been 'involuntary' flows of people who are, as Santos in his seminal work notes:

> still more at odds with international and domestic refugees legislation: hundreds of thousands of people fleeing from famine, starvation and natural disasters (droughts, earthquakes, volcanic eruptions). In many cases of extreme poverty and environmental crises have acted together with civil war or political repression to provoke massive displacements of people, as in Haiti or Eritria, in Mozambique or Cambodia. These are dramatic situations, apparently ever more recurrent, in which the distinction between economic and political factors have been blurred, if not totally dissolved; situations in which the calamitous deterioration of native survival system turns the question of the voluntary or involuntary nature of the migration into a macabre exercise.[62]

Thus, how we define 'refugees' is highly contested. But the resistance to change is also deep-seated. When faced with the influx of Haitians into the USA, Teitelbaum referred to the arguments of one lawyer, Kurzban, representing the Haitians, who, 'asserts that they have as much right to stay as Cubans who fled Castro or Nicaraguans who fled the Sandinistas. The government's efforts to expel the Haitians, he says come from a blend of racism and loyalty to Duvalier's regime'. Teitelbaum described the response of the General Counsel of the Immigration and Nationality Service ('INS') for the USA, one by the name of Inman, who, 'dismisses these statements with an angry wave. "This is *war*", he declares. "The war is to in effect eliminate the definition of refugee and to open our borders to anybody that wants to come in and have a worldwide equalization of wealth and property"'.[63] But, why should the refugee status not be used to equalize wealth and opportunity? In the words of Santos,[64] '[i]t is today widely recognized that national boundaries are a major political device to maintain inequality across the world system …'. The question then is one of international justice and morality. As such, it brings into ever-more sharper relief the observation of Debra Satz that 'neither nationality or state boundaries, as such, have moral standing with respect to questions of justice'.[65] At one level, justice for the poorer world would require better and more effective rights in the international system. Roger Nett has asked:

> If the set of rights is not functionally complete, what needs to be added to the rights we now recognize in order to make a working set? What rights might we expect some future Magna Carta to include? We suggest that one other 'right' relates directly to opportunity and would go a long way, virtually all the way, to close the existing set of rights and make it functionally much more viable. At some future point in world civilization, it may well be discovered that the right to free and open movement of people on the surface of the earth is fundamental to the structure of human opportunity and is therefore basic in the same sense as is free religion, speech, and the franchise.[66]

Mignolo, on the other hand, eschews a template approach. He calls for 'critical and dialogical cosmopolitan conversations, rather than blue-prints or master plans imposed worldwide'.[67] In these circumstances, is it really meaningful to rigidly distinguish between forced migration and voluntary migration? Are there really strict categories of asylum-seekers and economic migrants? What indeed, is the conceptual, empirical, and theoretical basis of this distinction? And, can we employ it meaningfully in policy terms for a new world order?

FREE MOVEMENT FROM CLASSICAL ANTIQUITY TO MODERNITY

There is an unbroken line of international morality that favours the right to free movement that western policy-makers need to heed. International morality requires that the right to free movement can be restricted only subject to certain well-known limitations. This tradition is worth recalling. It is faithfully recorded in the writings of classical and modern publicists. The doctrine of sovereignty did not prevent the belief in positive international morality. Even classical publicists who propounded sovereignty as a doctrine did not see it as an obstacle to positive morality in international law. It is true that sovereignty is directly linked to the independence of states. It is true it stands for freedom from external interference. However, a closer analysis between the two propositions shows that the doctrine of international morality and the doctrine of municipal sovereignty are not necessarily separate and discrete doctrines. The point has been well made in an excellent study by Nafziger in a seminal article, 'The General Admission of Aliens under International Law' in 1983, which is to be taken as the starting point.[68] Nafziger considers the proposition that a state has the right to exclude all aliens from its territory unless required to do so by treaty obligation with some scepticism. He considers, amongst other things, the origins of the modern proposition by tracing the practice of international states back to ancient principles. He also considers arguments of 'inherent power' of 'sovereignty' and of 'domestic jurisdiction'[69] that states employ to justify exclusionary policies. He concludes, however, that the 'the proposition appears to be instrumental in shaping exclusionary provisions of municipal law and policy and in forestalling the emergence of human migration as a comprehensive topic on the international agenda'.[70] In fact, international morality and municipal sovereignty do not stand opposed to one another. There is more affinity between the two than is commonly assumed. The sixteenth century writer, Jean Bodin, to whom the doctrine of sovereignty is often traced, while defining sovereignty as 'the absolute and perpetual power'[71] nevertheless, held it to be bound by divine law and others like Grotius,[72] Vattel,[73] Pufendorf,[74] and even Hobbes, and Locke allowed for similar limitations.[75] These limitations allow for an idea of positive morality in international law. Before we consider this, however, it is necessary to look at how the right to exclude aliens arose in states.

Nafziger explains that the proposition is, in fact, of remarkably recent origin. Those writers who have supported this proposition have often cited no authority for it.[76] The proposition has been given simply as a maxim. Often, the only authority cited is Anglo-American case law from the period 1889 to 1893 and selected citations from classic publicists.[77] The proposition arose at a time when the American and other European settled territories, such as Australasia and Southern Africa, were reaching their peak of emigration and the frontier was fast disappearing in the newly acquired territories. Nafziger explains that it was during the nineteenth century that, in the common-law countries of anglo-saxon heritage, the right to exclude aliens assumed a pre-eminence over a right of the alien to seek admission in a foreign territory, 'because these historical circumstances developed during the heyday of Austinian and Hobbesian positivism, with its peculiar limitation of law for sovereign commands', during this period the 'nativistic pronouncements of courts became engraved in stone'.[78] However, in non-common law countries, the tradition of free movement rights remained alive much longer. For example, Latin American jurists still tended to espouse the principles of interdependence and freedom of movement, even during this period, although their pronouncements became less important in the common law world.[79]

The exclusion of aliens was, therefore, only supported to a large extent in the nineteenth century. But this has to be noted in the context of the fact that the state itself was an alien concept. States could hardly exclude individuals if there were no states in the modern sense. Prior to the nineteenth century, closed cities and closed territories had been rare. Nafziger shows that Biblical injunctions favored free transboundary movement.[80] The Greeks also sharply distinguished between 'citizens' and 'barbarians' and later distinguished among citizens, naturalized aliens, public guests, domicile aliens, non-domicile aliens, and strangers.[81] The Romans were less exclusive than the Greeks.[82] They had a liberal policy of naturalization so long as assimilation was from within the vast Empire. Early church doctrine and stoic tradition helped shape the openness of Romans to foreigners. In turn, this helped fashion medieval universalism, which allowed considerable freedom of movement for specified classes of travelers.[83] It is the classic publicists, however, that when faced with the growing tension between traditional freedom of movement practices and the emerging concept of the sovereign state, denied the state an absolute right to exclude aliens.

Nafziger then gives a brisk account of these classical publicists. Hugo Grotius declared that, 'Of things which belong to Men in Common', there was the right to temporary sojourn, the right to permanent residence for those 'expelled from their homes', the right of foreigners to be free of discrimination on the basis of nationality, the right of foreigners to possess deserted and unproductive soil, and the right of foreigners to the necessities of life, such as food, clothing, and medicines.[84] Grotius quoted Strabo who had concluded that it was 'characteristic of barbarians to drive away strangers'.[85] Francisco De Vitoria applied also a sense of *noblesse oblige* to confirm the right of Spaniards to travel and life freely in Indian-held lands of the New World, 'provided they do no harm to the Natives'. Freedom to migrate freely, had been established 'from the beginning of the world', according to De Vitoria, and to deny admission to foreigners might even constitute an act of war.[86] Samuel Pufendorf went further and held that aliens could migrate for lawful reasons, including economic ones, and decried the sovereign right of a nation to exclude aliens.[87] However, it is Vattel who is more interesting. He is better known for his synthesis of natural law and positivism and his writings have strongly influenced the development of modern migration law. His writings have been widely misinterpreted as supporting the proposition that states may legitimately exclude all aliens. In fact, Vattel adopted and refined many of the principles of Grotius and Pufendorf. His contribution lies in distinguishing the internal law of nations, which was rooted in natural law, from the 'external law', which was rooted in positivism. Matters of conscience and principles were established by internal law, whereas matters of will were determined by external law. The first was a sovereign duty, the second a sovereign right. Vattel's fusion of these two principles is seen in his treatment of rights of passage. Whereas, on the one hand he recognizes that 'every nation has a right to refuse admitting a foreigner into her territory, when he cannot enter it without exposing the nation to evident danger, or doing her a manifest injury', he also, on the other hand, observes that:

> however … no nation can, without good reason, refuse even a perpetual residence to a man driven from his country. But, if particular substantial reasons prevent her from affording him an asylum, this man has no longer any right to demand it.[88]

Vattel, in fact, even elaborated upon the right of procuring provisions by force:

> The earth was designed to feed its inhabitants; and he who is in want of everything is not obliged to starve, because all property is vested in others … Extreme necessity revives the primitive communion, the abolition of which ought to deprive no person of the necessaries of life … The same right belongs to individuals, when if foreign nations refuse them a just assistance.[89]

Vattel thought that sovereignty was subject to internal law and he referred to the internal law of free passage and residence as 'the line of conduct which a nation is, by her duty to other nations, bound to observe in the exercise of her rights'.[90] It is clear from a comprehensive analysis of Vattel's works that concepts of 'conscience', and 'duties of humanity' were vital to his order of things. The inter-relationship between external and internal law has been ignored in modern times because modern positivism views internal law as no more binding than a moral obligation. Sir William Blackstone has demonstrated the tension between sovereign rights theory and actual practice, precisely in the arena of migration rights:

> [b]y the law of nations no member of one society has a right to intrude into another … those being ever excepted were driven on the coast of necessity, or by any quest that deserves pity or compassion. Great tenderness is shown by our laws … with regard … to the admission of strangers who come spontaneously: for so long as their nation continues at peace with ours, and they themselves behave peaceably, they are under the King's protection …[91]

To conclude, the classical publicists provide no basis for the proposition that a sovereign has an unfettered right to exclude all aliens. However, when by the end of the nineteenth century, most geographical frontiers of the Western world had been reached, increased economic and political tensions arose. It was at this time that nationalism and protectionism began to be embraced as popular policies. For the first time, governments began to systematically deny admission to particular kinds of aliens. Nafziger's historical survey ends by recognizing that this practice was intensified during the First World War and the Great Depression of the 1930s when nation-state cleavages led to the imposition of comprehensive restrictions. Restrictions, however, were applied only to specific classes of aliens and they should not be read as providing a basis for a general right of exclusion for all aliens. Most significantly, Oriental labor was targeted during this period in the United States, Australia, New Zealand and Canada and new racially discriminatory laws were put in place.[92]

The landmark decisions of this period are characterized by a nativism which has become the definitive hallmark of migration policies in the developed world. It is important to recognize however, that these policies essentially served an instrumentalist purpose. When the US Supreme Court decided the leading immigration cases of this period, it even referred, for its purpose, to the leading treatise by Sir Robert Phillimore who had formulated 'a received maxim of International Law, that the government of a state may prohibit the entrance of strangers into the country'. Phillimore's only authority for the 'received maxim' was limited British practice. However, he had observed that the maxim only came into effect 'during periods of revolutionary disturbances'. The policy of 'wise states', according to Phillimore, including Rome, was to 'open wide the door for the reception and naturalization of foreigners'.[93] However, the die of restrictionist state practice in immigration control had been cast by the end of the nineteenth century. Its baleful influence was to extend far, wide, and long. It is still with us. As late as 1973, one of the reputedly greatest English judges of the twentieth century was able to make the dubious declaration that, 'I have always held the view that in common law no alien has any right to enter this country except by leave of the Crown: and the Crown can refuse leave without giving any reason'.[94]

Nafziger's early illuminating account does, however, leave us with three inter-related questions to consider. First, is there a model of free movement rights available in the world today? What is it based upon? Can we learn from it? And, what are its shortcomings? Second, if there is such a model and it is flawed or incomplete, can the illustrious tradition of the classical publicists realistically be extended into the world as it is today, or is that tradition outdated? The question is important in the light of the writings of more modern publicists, given that international law has always been receptive to the writings of publicists who have often exercised a formative influence in this area. If so, what do the modern publicists have to say about such a right? Third, if historically, in the nineteenth and twentieth centuries, nativism has served to restrict free movement rights, what grounds are there for assuming that such nativism will not be equally decisive in shaping the migration policies of the twenty-first century? What about the asserted right of communitarians to shape their own societies by choosing who to admit and who to reject? We will consider all three questions.

Sovereignty, Security and the European Union

The freedom to live and work anywhere in Europe is the single most important principle of the European Union (EU) project. It is, therefore, natural to look to the EU for developing new standards of international morality in the field of international migration. Of course, the European migration system is treaty-based and only allows free admission to nationals of member states. Nearly a quarter of a century ago, Nafziger had already argued that 'the global practice of admitting special classes of aliens under treaty and municipal law sheds further doubt, though inconclusive, on the validity of the exclusionary proposition'.[95] Under the *Treaty of Rome*, all members of the European Communities must abolish 'any discrimination based on nationality between workers of the Member States as regards employment, remuneration, and other conditions of work and employment'.[96] Under Article 48(3) all workers are bestowed with rights of free movement within the Common Market nations.[97] The right is such as would be of value to the nationals of non-European countries as well, because fundamentally it is predicated on the right to work. The principle of mutuality is in play here because work provides economic benefits to both the worker and the country in which the worker is working. Thus, the provision provides workers within the Common Market (a) to accept offers of employment actually made; (b) to move about freely for this purpose within the territory of Member States; (c) to stay in any Member State in order to carry on an employment in conformity with the legislative and administrative provisions governing the employment of the workers on that state; and (d) to 'live…in the territory of a Member State after having been employed there'. Other articles then help enforce these rights.[98] There is no reason why nationals of non-European Third World countries could not also be extended these same rights for there would be mutual benefit here also. A continent like Africa could be lifted out of its shaming poverty and Europe would get the workers it needs.

Under the *Treaty of Rome*, the admission of aliens from nearby affiliated countries is the more interesting exception, particularly given that it is an area of gradual expansion today. In 1994, I had already pointed out how Sweden, whilst formally recognizing the status of 'guest workers' for some immigrants, nevertheless aspires to a sense of community with other Nordic countries so that over half of Sweden's foreign subjects come from adjoining territories.[99] Nafziger had suggested that more formal regional agreements have been reached in order to accommodate the flow of human migration and this helps to confirm the state practice of admitting well defined classes of aliens. As far as the admission of relatives of resident aliens is concerned, there is widespread practice for the reunion of family members in the immigration laws of nearly all liberal democracies. Nafziger pointed out that the *European Court of Justice* has supported intra-regional migration and has effectively eliminated severely the sovereign discretion over the admission of aliens by holding that the exclusion of aliens can only be undertaken for reasons or *ordre public*, security, or public health, and these exceptional limitations on the general right to free movement are to be subject to strict interpretation.[100] In addition, the *Final Act of the Conference on Security and Co-operation in Europe* (Helsinki Accords) provides an important qualified right of migration. The Accords confirm an obligation to admit aliens for purposes of family unification, especially to accommodate workers and marriage.[101] Nafziger's view is that '[a]lthough arguably not legally binding in themselves, the Accords provide a comprehensive, morally compelling expression of norms that, by influencing State behavious, amy constitute *lex ferranda'*.[102] Legal restrictions on the obligation to help reunite families and prospective marriage partners are also to be made subject to the strict scrutiny of the human rights provisions of the *United Nations Charter*.[103]

Yet, even though the elimination of internal frontiers to freedom of movement is the lynchpin of the evolving union within Europe.[104] The European Community's founding *Treaty of Rome 1957* promoted freedom of movement for workers within the Community.[105] The *Single European Act 1986* extended this freedom of movement to all EC citizens.[106] The Maastricht Treaty on the European Union further established the concept of European Union citizenship.[107] But these developments also made national governments nervous. A person who succeeds in entering a common territory is unlikely to be inspected again[108] this can be seen as a threat to security, especially where immigration from outside the European Union is concerned.[109] Paradoxically, member states have been reluctant to cede sovereignty over immigration to the European Community even though they know that sovereign control over domestic immigration policy is now impossible. This means that there is an inherent conflict between national and supranational competence because:

> [the] conflict between the Treaty of Rome and the Single European Act, on the one hand and the goal of an integrated Europe, on the other, stems from the fact that the Treaties allow each country to continue its immigration policy, but the goal of an integrated Europe would seem to require a common immigration policy to ensure freedom of movement of all persons within the EC.[110]

This conflict translates itself into immigration policy generally and refugee and asylum policy more specifically. The result is that European governments have attempted to reach agreement on a common policy with regard to the admission of foreigners into a common territory.[111] The process of harmonization, however, involves a double standard of freedom of movement principles. Members of national states have had their rights expanded to partake in the social and economic benefits of all European Union countries. Non members, by contrast, have had their rights diminished to the lowest acceptable level for a European Union country. This is discriminatory. It is not an ideal basis for the establishment of a new international morality in the era of globalization and increased inter-dependency and inter-action in the world today.

What is remarkable is that when the Single European Act 1986 amended the Treaty of Rome to create a single European market, its purpose was not only to remove barriers to free trade and commerce and strengthen Europe as a trading bloc in a competitive world economy. There was also a broader social and political vision. These exalted ideas were confined to members of European national states only. They were so with the creation of an interconnected and inter-dependant European social community. As Jacqueline Bhabha observed that:

> [I]n this unified European social space, national, cultural and legal differences were not to preclude a quality of treatment and access for all European Community nationals with respect to employment, remuneration and other conditions of work.[112]

All member states had to comply with the European Convention on Human Rights and individuals had the right to petition if they did not. Yet, today the European Union itself has not signed up to the European Convention even though the European Commission observed as long ago as 1979 that it should.[113] Community policy was concerned with the Community worker as a human being, not a 'mere source of labour'.[114]

Even so, the overall program of the European Community was, compared to its North American counterpart, NAFTA, highly ambitious in its social and political orientation. NAFTA, by comparison, is only directed to non-immigrants who are involved in 'business activities at a professional level'; the purpose is not to create free movement between the three NAFTA countries, but to reduce such movement.[115] In many respects, the ambitious social agenda of the European Community has been impressively achieved. The free movement provisions have been extended, in the last 20 years, from workers[116] and self-employed persons[117] and their families[118] to students,[119] retired persons[120] and those who are self supporting,[121] in a scheme which covers a person's life from infancy to death. Where member states have been reluctant to implement their Treaty obligations under Community law, it has been possible to use the individual right of petition compel compliance. The European Court of Justice has acted to supervise the observance of European Community law.[122] It has used non-discriminatory norms to harmonise European Community law in areas of major social concern, such as maternity rights,[123] the rights of part time workers,[124] and immigration rights.[125] Most notable have been the enfranchising of immigration rights in the European Community with respect to non-European spouses[126] and unmarried partners.[127]

Nevertheless, the European system does not shore up the standards of international morality. The enfranchising of immigration rights in respect to nationals of member states of the European Union stands in stark contrast to the diminution of such rights for people from outside Europe. The truth is that where foreign non-European nationals are concerned individual state sovereignty has figured more prominently than regional concerns in policy making here. Thus, the abolition of border controls has been much more difficult in relation to non-union European immigration.[128] Border controls have always been the essence of statehood for they:

> provide(s) a measure of physical protection to the national society, the efficacy of which is enhanced by the fact that a border crossing is one of the few situations in which a person is required to identify himself in the absence of any criminal suspicion.[129]

Thus, even though the deadline for border control removals was January 1, 1993, two years after that date, complaints were still being lodged against member states for their failure to do so.[130] The position of non-European nationals remain problematic. It is still unclear whether the 'persons' referred to in the phrase 'free movement of persons'[131] covers non-EU nationals, or which frontiers count as external borders.[132] The decision of the European Court of Justice is still awaited on whether article 7(a) is directly applicable or not.[133] What seems clearer is that the failure to abolish border controls is unlawful.[134]

How did the European Union get itself into this state? The earlier years after all, had been promising. The answer lies in the rise of Eastern European immigration in the 1980s. This gave serious concern to national governments in the European Union because an individual who succeeds in gaining admission into the common territory was unlikely to be inspected again. Governments, concerned to protect their own domestic interests, sought, therefore, to agree upon common criteria that would regulate the flow of foreigners into the Community. It was, after all, their Community because, as Whitaker explains:

> [D]espite the move toward an integrated Europe, the citizens of the EC want to re-tain their culture and nationality.[135]

It is this indeed, that explains the historical absence in Europe of immigrant policies, since:

> [T]he desire to preserve a unique, national culture goes a long way to explaining why the majority of countries in Western Europe did not establish immigrant poli-cies which integrated immigrants into society as a whole, but rather treated immigrants as temporary residents.[136]

The new arrivals into Western Europe in the mid-1980s resulted from seismic geo-political changes in the world. These changes were interpreted as a threat to national security and this in turn reinforced a securitarian approach to im-migration both within individual Member States and within Europe generally.[137] It is not difficult to see why this happened. In the 1970s, with the end of the economic boom that followed the post-war period, European coun-tries had already seen it 'fit to restrict immigration in the slump that followed the first oil crisis of the early 1970s'.[138] Thus, primary immigration ended in Northern Europe in the 1970s and Southern Europe ended it in the 1980s. Not only was immigration politically unpopular but it was also felt that there were structural limits to integration in the form of a shortage in housing, schools and language training, although a country like the Netherlands 'still managed to relax the rules for family reunification to protect human rights'.[139] The In-terior Ministries of most European Countries felt a gradual but unmistakable sense of borderlessness. In the words of Randall Hansen:

> [B]orders within the EU are long and pass through territories, including waters, forests, and mountains, that are not easily controlled. Part of the Franco-Belgian border, for instance, weaves around an easily traversed river; an effective border control would require guards every few dozen meters.[140]

In addition to this, there was a strong belief in the North that the countries of Southern Europe, such as Greece and Italy, were not controlling their borders as effectively as they might otherwise do, so that immigrants who could not directly get into Northern European countries, such as Britain, France and Germany, could routinely do so by crossing the borders of Europe in the South. These concerns remained and festered coming to the boil with the fall of the Iron Curtain and the liberation of the Eastern Bloc countries at the beginning of the 1990s.

Prior to the collapse of the Soviet Union, the basis of refugee policy in the Cold War era was the grant of sanctuary to anyone fleeing the oppression of Communism. This basis shifted dramatically when Communism fell. The fall of the Berlin Wall in 1989 was hailed as the dawn of a new era, ending half a century of repression in the Communist regimes of Eastern Europe and the Soviet Union. It led to three direct effects, which are worth recalling. First, the fall of Communism led to the lifting of exit controls in Eastern European countries. This began on September 10, 1989. East Germans, who had sought refuge at the West German Embassy in Budapest, were permitted to reach the West when Hungary opened its border with Austria. President Erich Honecker of East Germany then allowed refugees in the Prague and Warsaw Embassies to board trains for West Germany. However, fearing that East German citizens would also flee the country, he banned visa-free travel to Czechoslovakia. About the same time, the Tory dominated Home Affairs Committee on Immigration, looking at predicted growths in applications of up to 150 per cent in 1990 caused by recent political changes in Eastern Europe, advocated the removal of visa restrictions upon immigrants from Eastern Europe.[141] Following a number of large political protests, the East German government eased travel restrictions on October 24, 1989 allowing East German citizens to enter Czechoslovakia. As 500,000 people demonstrated for democracy in the streets of East Berlin, Czechoslovakia opened its borders with East Germany on November 4. In less than five days, East Germany officially opened its Western borders. The Berlin Wall fell and the largest movement of populations across the borders of nation states began in Europe since the Second World War.[142]

Second, the opening of borders led to mass refugee movements in a way that led Western European countries to question their liberal asylum and immigration policies. Thus, the fall of Communism meant that immigration was taking place from areas of extreme poverty on a mass scale. There was huge disparity between industrialized nations and what were little better than Third World nations. Western nations were faced with handling a new phase in international migration. Eastern Europeans discontented with the hardships of a transition to capitalist or free market economies were keen to take advantage of their proximity with the West. Third, and most importantly, the ethnic conflict in Bosnia-Herzegovina, resulting directly from the fall of Communism in Eastern Europe,[143] produced hundreds of thousands of *bona fide* refugees.[144]

Of all the three reasons, it was this third reason that caused the most immediate concern for western governments because the War in Yugoslavia that followed the collapse of Communism reflected broader political changes and created the largest flows of population into Western Europe since the Second World War. European nations became immediately concerned to stem the flow of new immigrants. There was an important reason for this. The new immigrants were not Western Europeans. They were, it was felt, not easy to absorb. They came from the East. Yet, what started as a concern over the arrival of Eastern Europeans, such as Kosovans and Albanians, quickly spread to a general concern over immigrants form the Third World, in particular from Africa and the Middle East. This was inevitable as it followed on from the geo-political changes that accompanied the Fall of the Iron Curtain. As Loescher explains:

[w]hat concerns policy makers more is the kind of asylum seeker who is appearing at their borders, and the fact that this arrival is totally unregulated. Many of the 'new' refugees originate in the Third World, whereas in the past there were few large scale spontaneous arrivals from distant countries.[145]

The Economist observed that:

[r]ightly or wrongly, the community is less in a panic over immigrants from the east. They are, after all, fellow Europeans, often with useful skills to offer and many of them anyway likely to return home when economic circumstances permit.[146]

Often, there was concern that the new migrants were not fleeing state oppression or gross human rights violations but simply looking to improve their economic status. Why this should have mattered when Western Europe itself desperately needed new workers was never explained by western governments. Instead, as Egan and Storey observed:

[m]any Western governments now perceive asylum applications to be a smoke screen for the 'economic migration' which they had attempted to end.[147]

Thus it was that the word 'economic migrants' became a term of abuse rather than a term of endearment that deserved to have been. Here were people prepared to lift themselves by their boot-straps and make a go of life away from kith and kin in some foreign country. Yet, the unfolding climate of opinion in Europe was such that *The Economist* was forced forced to accuse Western Europe of xenophobia, observing that:

[t]he healthy feeling that binds together the societies of Europe's nation states now seems to be breeding something far from healthy, a mindless intolerance of outsiders.[148]

Such an opinion was not confined to the respectable news outlets. The leading human rights advocate, Professor James Hathaway complained about a new 'popular xenophobia' that was regarding immigrants as 'threats to regional stability' by assuming that 'immigrants will neither adjust to nor be accepted within European society'. He too, abhorred the tendency to view them as 'unwelcome competition for scarce jobs and housing'.[149] The lack of sophistication was such that all new immigrants from the East and the Third World were seen as threats to security because:

[G]overnments have decided to treat migrants from the less developed world as an undifferentiated evil: refugees, economic migrants, drug traffickers, and terrorists are officially categorized as presenting a unified threat, and will all confront a common policy of deterrents.[150]

When it comes to international migration, therefore, the countries of the European Union have prioritized and privileged sovereignty and security concerns over the principles of international solidarity and support. The history of European integration does not show otherwise. European integration has been achieved by three major treaties over a period of 20 years: the *Single European Act 1986*,[151] the *Maastricht Treaty 1992*,[152] and the *Amsterdam Treaty 1997*.[153] In 2000, the *Nice Treaty* made little change,[154] except for augmenting the Amsterdam Third Pillar by reference to Eurojust; and in 2005 the hapless *Draft Constitution*,[155] which was intended to enlarge the EU's powers in the area of both asylum and immigration (making these areas subject to voting by a qualified majority vote in Council), fell by the wayside, when it failed to be ratified in France. The Single European Act set out to facilitate the free movement of capital, persons, and goods within the EU but did not concern itself with individuals outside the EU. The Maastricht Treaty set out to complete the single market by creating a tripartite pillar structure for the proper governing of the EU. Matters concerning supra-national EU institutions came under the First Pillar.[156] Matters concerning common issues relating to foreign affairs came under the Second Pillar.[157] Matters concerning Justice and Home Affairs came under the Third Pillar.[158] Immigration and asylum policy came to be dealt with inter-governmentally because whereas issues falling within the purview of the First Pillar were clearly determined through the supra national institutions of the EU because the Commission would propose legislation and the European Court of Justice could then consider questions of State compliance with Treaty obligations, issues relating to the Third Pillar could only be developed if there was an agreement with all the EU members (which now number 25), failing which there could be no progress. Thus, when it came to questions of Justice and Home Affairs (JHA) each sovereign state in the EU had to negotiate and agree with others as an equal partner. The JHA officials coming from within the Member states naturally favoured a securitarian approach to immigration and asylum policy. The EU treaties themselves had no countervailing humanitarian provisions in them. In the event, the securitarian approach prevailed over the humanitarian approach. This was hardly surprising. The EC had after all been created as an economic enterprise. As such, its founding treaties were silent on the issue of the human rights protections for third-country nationals who were not resident in a Member State. On the other hand, both the UNHCR and the Council of Europe had a specific mandate for human rights and refugee protections. Under the Third Pillar, therefore, the organizational set-up for member state co-operation strongly promoted the securitarian model advocating restrictive asylum policies.

This inter-governmental Third Pillar approach changed with the *Amsterdam Treaty* which transferred asylum and immigration matters to the supranational First Pillar. Technically speaking, security concerns would not predominate this policy area to the exclusion of humanitarian considerations. The EU was now under an explicit obligation to respect 'fundamental rights'.[159] In 1997, in anticipation of the EU being enlarged with the first wave of new Eastern Europe members from Hungary, Poland, and the Czech Republic joining up, it was decided to reform the Third Pillar by limiting policy-making by inter-governmentalism, and transferring some of its competences to the First Pillar. The Treaty establishing the European Communities (TEC) brought under the ambit of the First Pillar matters relating to visas, asylum, immigration and freedom of movement, under a new Title IV.[160] The question remains, however, as to how effective this transformation will be in terms both of increased EU competence and human rights protections. The EU heads of State had called at the Tampere European Council, in October 1999 for a 'common European asylum system' but the European Council in Nice, barely 14 months later in 2000, rejected a call for qualified majority voting (QMV) in the Council of Ministers, which is surely one of the requirements for a common system. This raises the question whether 'a predominantly economic actor such as the European Union has the institutional capacity to act' in the field of human rights.[161]

Notwithstanding the Treaty of Amsterdam, which has transferred the asylum policy making from the intergovernmental Third Pillar to the Community Pillar, the existence of intensive transgovernmentalism at several levels will mean that there will be little agreement between member states about how to move forward in this policy area. On 1st May 2004, the five-year transitional period for the first work programme ended under Tampere. The Communication from the Commission on 2nd June 2004 on its Assessment of the Tampere Programme[162] generally painted a positive picture of the 'undeniable and tangible'[163] progress made since 1999, but there serious concerns over 'the legal and institutional constraints of the current Treaties, where unanimity in the Council generally remains the rule, [and which] partly explain these difficulties'. Clearly, this was to have grave serious implications for the development of a common asylum (and immigration) policy in Europe, because as the Commission explained:

> [T]he Member States are sometimes reluctant to cooperate within this new European framework when their interests are at stake.[164]

On 4th November 2004 the *Hague Programme* was approved by the European Council. This resulted from a public consultation process which was launched by the Commission, the so-called *Tampere II Process*, calling for a debate in the final evaluation of the *Tampere Process*,[165] the aim of which was to define a new programme.[166] The new programme has as its objective:

> the improvement of the common capability of the Union and its Member States to guarantee fundamental rights, minimum procedural safeguards and the access to justice to provide protection in accordance with the Geneva Convention ...

but it also aims

> to regulate flows and to control the external borders of the Union, to fight organized cross-border crime and repress the threat of terrorism ...

The multi-annual programme states that:

> [T]his is an objective that has to be achieved in the interests of the European citizens by the development of a Common Asylum System ... and the development of common policies.[167]

On 1st September 2005, EU Commissioner Frattini announced that the European Commission had adopted, 'an important and comprehensive package of concrete measures in the field of immigration and asylum', which represented 'an important step towards achieving the balanced approach to migration called for by the Hague Programme'.[168] However, this does not obscure the evolving difficulties in the emergence of a common asylum policy because the proposals also emphasize 'the need for a proper EU return policy and the issue of integration of third country nationals in our societies'.[169]

Whatever the economic imperatives of accepting new immigrants, the arrival of ever more entrants is considered to be politically problematic by the governments of Northern Europe. The opening in October 2005 of the accession process for Turkey's membership of the EU may 'kill off the EU's credibility deficit in the Muslim world' because 'it would strengthen the claim of Europe's 15 million Muslim to home in Europe' but the decade long process will not obscure the fact that the arrival of '80 million Turks within the EU' is something that 'vast swathes of Europe don't buy' at the moment because 'they fear it requires such a dilution of European identity that they don't want it'.[170] Europeanization of immigration policy is likely to be especially difficult given that there is little agreement between the supranational and trans-governmental agencies about the factual categorization of the immigration problem as well as the normative orientation of the common policy.

NOTES

1   M. Cranston, *What are Human Rights?*, 33, at 31 (1973).
2   For a consideration of some of these issues, see: James A.R. Nafziger, 'A Policy Framework for Regulating the Flow of Undocumented Aliens into the United States', 56 *Or. L. Rev.* 63, at 86–7 (1977).
3   Article 13(1) of the UDHR.
4   Article 13(2).
5   Article 14(1).
6   Article 2.
7   J.K. Galbraith, *The nature of mass poverty*, Harvard University Press (1979, p.7).
8   For a particularly poignant illustration of this, see the recent documentary Film by the Canadian film-maker, Ali Kazimi, *Continuous Journey* (86 min. 38 sec, video, colour, 2004). It recounts how in 1914, Gurdit Singh, a Sikh entrepreneur based in Singapore, chartered a Japanese ship, the *Komagata Maru*, to carry Indian immigrants to Canada. On May 23, 1914, the ship arrived in Vancouver Harbour with 376 passengers aboard: 340 Sikhs; 24 Muslims and 12 Hindus. Many of the men on-board were veterans of the British Indian Army and believed that it was their right as British subjects to settle anywhere in the Empire they had fought to defend and expand. They were refused permission to land. The film has been held to world-wide acclaim, being described as '… brilliant … rarely has a documentary been so beautifully directed and rendered, shot for shot, image by image, pan by pan, zoom by zoom, by Peter Wintonick, POV Magazine. Leah McLaren said of it that, 'Through archival footage, vintage photographic montage and inventive voice-over performance, Kazimi documents the story of the 340 Sikhs, 24 Muslims and 12 Hindus held on the boat a half mile from Canadian

shores without provisions for more than two months. Continuous Journey is the work of an experienced story-teller and image-maker. Kazimi's own journey from India (which he recounts here and in is previous films) has been a fortuitous event for Canada' (see, *The Globe & Mail*, January 21, 2005). The fact that the film won so many awards is a telling tribute to how the human instinct for survival still touches people so deeply. The film was Winner of the Audience Award for Best Feature Documentary at the San Francisco International Asian American Film Festival; the Winner, Second Place of the Audience Award and Honourable Mention for Best Director, Hot Docs 2004; and was Nominated by FOCAL International for Film Researcher of the Year Award.

9 See *Select Committee on International Development* (Sixth report; Session 2003–04) Published by the House of Commons on 29th June 2004. See http://www.publications.parliament.uk/pa/cm200304/cmselect/cmintdev/79/7902.htm Ev 211 [International Organization for Migration (IOM) memorandum].

10 James A.R. Nafziger, 'The General Admission of Aliens Under International Law', 77 *AJIL* (1983) 804–47 at p.846. The writer pays tribute to this work from which he has benefited for the formulation of his own arguments in this article.

11 N. McDougal and W. Reisman, *International Law in Contemporary Perspective*, 925 (1981).

12 Article 12.

13 Article 16.

14 Article 2.

15 Roger Nett, 'The civil right we are not ready for: The Right to Free Movement of People on the Face of the Earth', 81 *Ethics* 212, at 216 (1971).

16 Michael Dummett, *On Immigration and Refugees* (London, Routledge, 2001) at p.26. He states that 'Justice does not consist in giving each what he deserves … it consists in giving each his due'.

17 Ruth Rubio-Marin, *Immigration as a Democratic Challenge: Citizenship and Inclusion in Germany and the United States* (CUP, 2000) at p.1. The author is a professor of constitutional law at the University of Seville.

18 Christian Joppke, 'Why Liberal States Accept Unwanted Immigration' http://muse.jhu.edu/journals/world_politics/v050/50.2joppke.html (pp.266–93), at pp.292–3. which is why, as he writes, '[o]nly liberal states are plagued by the problem of unwanted immigrants', ibid. at p.269.

19 Ibid., at p.1.

20 Kevin R. Johnson, 'Open Borders?', 51 *UCLA Law Review* 193 (2003) pp.193–265.

21 12 *Inst. Droit Int'l Annuaire* 218 *et seq* (1892–94) [hereinafter referred to as *Proces-verbal des séances*]. For an English translation of the Regulations, see *Resolutions of the Institute of International Law* 104 *et seq* (J. Scott ed. 1916).

22 Ibid., see, the Preamble, to the *Resolutions of the Institute of International*, at p.104 *et seq* (J. Scott (ed.) 1916).

23 *Proces-verbal des séances, op. cit.*, at p.192.

24 Nafziger, 'The General Admission of Aliens Under International Law', at p.846.

25 Roger Nett, ibid., at p.218.

26 Jacqueline Bhabha, 'Internationalist Gatekeepers?: The Tension Between Asylum Advocacy and Human Rights', *Harv. Hum. Rts Jnl.* (vol. 15, Spring 2002) p.155 at p.156.

27 Jacqueline Bhabha, 'Internationalist Gatekeepers?'; ibid., at p.157.

28 See for example, Karl Klare, 'Legal Theory and Democratic Reconstruction: Reflection on 1989', *U. Brit. Colum. L. Rev.* (1991) Vol. 35, 69 at p.100. Also see, 'The

Coming of Communitarian Rights: Are Third-Generation Human Rights Really First-Generation Rights?', *International Journal of Discrimination & the Law* (1998) Vol. 3, pp.159–80.

29　Speech in Iran at the University of Tehran on 10 December 1995: see, *Report on the Situation of Human Rights in the Islamic Republic of Iran*, 28th January 1998; Quoted from the *Iran Country Assessment Report* (October 2002), Country Information and Policy Unit, Immigration and Nationality Directorate, Home Office, United Kingdom, at para 5.1.

30　Roger Nett, ibid., at p.219.

31　The UK has expanded the work permit scheme and adopted a category of sector-based employment for low and unskilled employees.

32　Justin Huggler, 'Malaysia begs expelled immigrant workers to return', *The Independent*, 27th May 2005 at p.32.

33　Arthur C. Helton, 'The Role of International Law in the 21st Century: Forced International Migration: A Need for New Approaches by the International Community', 18 *Fordham Int'l L.J.* 1623 (May 1995), at 1627.

34　Aristide R. Zolberg, Astri Zuhke, and Sergio Aguayo, *Escape from Violence: Conflict and the Refugee Crisis in the Developing World* (Oxford, 1989) where the authors at the outset observe that the number of refugees are 'widely perceived as an unprecedented crisis': see, Preface at p.v.

35　See fn., 5.

36　See fn., 3.

37　*R v. Secretary of State for the Home Department, ex parte Ullah & Do* [2004] UKHL 26 (d.17 /06/2004) and *R v. Secretary of State for the Home Department*, ex parte Razgar [2004] UKHL27 (d. 17/06/04).

38　*R v. Secretary of State for the Home Department, ex parte Razgar* [2004] UKHL27 (d. 17/06/04) at para. 10. The judgment of the House was itself based on the judgment of the *European Court of Human Rights in Bensaid v. United Kingdom* (2001) 33 EHRR 205. The outstanding question is what the level of severity should be for the anticipated breach to be shown before the interests of the state are outweighed in an expulsion case. The court has answered this holding that the interests of the state in maintaining a firm and orderly immigration control are to be overruled only where the anticipated breach is a flagrant denial or gross violation of the Convention right. This means showing a 'real risk' of harm.

39　At para. 24.

40　See section 72(2)(a) of the *Immigration and Asylum Act 1999*, which allows a claim to be certified on grounds that it is 'manifestly unfounded'.

41　Hussein A. Hassouna, *Remarks*, 67 ASIL BROC 135, 136 (1973).

42　Nafziger, 'The General Admission of Aliens Under International Law', *supra.*, at p.842.

43　United Nations, *World Conference on Human Rights* No.1 (1993).

44　Boutros Boutros-Ghali, *Human Rights: The Common Language of Humanity, Opening Statement of the World Conference on Human Rights* (June 14, 1993), in United Nations, *World Conference on Human Rights* 13 (1993).

45　*The Vienna Declaration and Program of Action,* June 25, 1993, in United Nations, *World Conference on Human Rights*, 36 (1993), Article 23.

46　6 *I.L.M.* (1967) 368: see Article 12. 136 Parties, entered into force on 23rd March 1976.

47　660 *U.N.T.S.* 195: see Article 5 (d)(i). 148 Parties, entered into force on 4th January 1969.

48　Article 1(2).

49 1249 U.N.T.S. 13: see Article 1. 155 Parties, entered into force on 3rd September 1981.

50 Doc. A /RES/39/46: see Article 3(1). 101 Parties, entered into force on 26th June 1987.

51 Dec. A/RES/44/25: see Article 22(1). 189 Parties, entered into force on 2nd September 1990.

52 Doc. A/RES/45/158: see Article 8 (1) and Article 8(2) respectively. 8 parties, will enter into force with 20th ratification or accession.

53 UN Document A/CONF. 157/24 (Part 1) 13th October 1993, pp.220–46, 32 I.L.M. 1661 (1993) 14 H.R.L.J. 352 (1993), 1 I.H.R.R. 240 (1994). Adopted by the World Conference on Human Rights at its 22nd plenary session on 25th June 1993. The Conference was convened by the United Nations and attended by representatives of 171 States.

54 The distinction is forcefully drawn by James C. Hathaway and R. Alexander Neve, 'Making International Refugee Law Relevant Again: A Proposal for Collectivized and Solution Oriented Protection', *Harvard Human Rights Journal*, Vol. 10, 152 (1997).

55 Giuseppe Callovi of the Commission of the European Communities has observed that 'the removal of restriction on freedom of movement of persons enshrined in the Paris Charter, occasional misuse of the right of asylum, and increasingly interdependent economies of the community have caused immigration to move up the agenda'. Guiseppe Callovi, 'Regulation of Immigration in 1993: Pieces of the European Community Jig-Saw Puzzle', 26 *Int'l. Migration Rev.* 353–4 (1992).

56 This could be because more accurate data is available on asylum applicants than on unlawful entrants: see, Commission of the European Communities, *Foreword to the Communication from the Commission to the Council and the European Parliament on Immigration and Asylum Policies*, COM (94) 5 at para. 13.

57 Professor Hathaway maintains that 'when refugees are grouped together with all other manner of migrants, be they legal or illegal, skilled or unskilled, law-abiding or undesirable, the fundamental distinction between refugees and other migrants, namely the involuntary nature of the refugees journey is lost': see, 'Making International Refugee Law Relevant Again', at p.152.

58 Jacques Vernant, *The Refugee in the Post-War World* (London, Allen & Unwin, 1953), at p.5.

59 Zolberg, Aristide R., Suhrke, Astri and Aguayo, Segio, *Escape from Violence: Conflict and the refugee crisis in the developing world* (Oxford, OUP, 1989).

60 Andrew Shacknove, 'Who is a refugee?', *Ethics* (Vol. 95, 1985), pp.274–84 at p.279.

61 Emma Haddad, 'Who is (not) a Refugee?' (European University Institute, Florence; EUI Working Paper SPS No. 2004/6; 2004) at p.23.

62 Boaventura de Sousa Santos, *Toward a New a Legal Common Sense* (2nd edn., 2002, London, Butterworths, LexisNexis), at p.226.

63 Teitelbaum, 'Political Asylum in Theory and Practice', 76 *The Public Interest*, 74, at pp.77–8 (1984).

64 Santos, ibid., at p.234, para 7.4.3.2.

65 Debra Satz, 'Equality of What among Whom? Thoughts on Cosmopolitanism, Statism, and Nationalism', in Shapiro and Brilmayer (eds), *Global Justice* (New York, NYU Press), pp.67–8.

66 Roger Nett, ibid., at p.218.

67 Walter Mignolo, 'The Many Faces of Cosmo-Polis: Border Thinking and Critical Cosmopolitanism', in Breckenridge, Pollock, Bhabha and Chakrabarty (eds), *Cosmopolitanism* (Durham, Duke Univ. Press), pp.157–87, at p.182.

68   James A.R. Nafziger, 'The General Admission of Aliens Under International Law', *77 AJIL* 804 (1983) at pp.804–47.
69   See pp.816–23.
70   See p.845.
71   See J. Allen, *A History of Political Thought in the Sixteenth Century* (Methuen (ed.) 1960) at pp.412–13.
72   H. Grotius, *De Jure Belli Ac Pacis*, bk. II, Ch. II (Carnegie Endowment trans., 1925) at pp.186–205.
73   E. De Vattel, *The Law of Nations* (J. Chitty (ed., 1839). See also, P. Remec, *The Position of the Individual in International Law According to Grotius and Vattel* (1960).
74   S. Pufendorf, *De Jure Naturae Gentium*, bk. VIII (Oxford ed. 1934) at p.365.
75   M.S. Rajan, *United Nations and Domestic Jurisdiction* (2nd ed. 1961) at pp.1–20.
76   For example, see, Aybay, 'The Right to Leave and the Right to Return: The International Aspect of Freedom of Movement', 1 *Comp. L.Y.B.* (1978) at p.121, 122; J. Brierly, *The Law of Nations* (6th edn., 1963) at p.276; L. Oppenheim, *International Law* (8th edn., Lauterpacht, 1955) at pp.675–6; S. Sinha, *New Nations and the Law of Nations* (1967) at p.97; P. Weis, *Nationality & Statelessness in International Law* (1956) at p.45; and G. Hackworth, *Digest of International Law* (1942) at pp.692–4, 717.
77   Although the publicists are often misinterpreted. For example, E. Borchard refers to the 'Ultimate power' of the state to exclude aliens, but then declares that this 'would violate the spirit of international law and endanger [a state's] membership in the international community': see, *The Diplomatic Protection of Citizens Abroad or the Law of International Claims* (1915) at pp.46–8.
78   Nafziger, *op. cit.* at p.808.
79   For example, I.P. Fauchille, *Traite De Droit International Public* (8th edn., 1926) at pp.894–5. Also see, P. Fiore, *International Law Codified and its Legal Sanction* (E. Borchard trans. 1918) at p.42.
80   See *Leviticus* 19:33–4 which is the most widely quoted today. Also see, A. Zimmerman, *Pius XII and International Migration: A Report of the Committee on Social Questions of the Catholic Association for International Peace* (1959) at pp.3–4.
81   J. Jones, *The Law and Legal Theory of the Greeks* (1956) at p.49.
82   C. Phillipson, *The International Law and Custom of Ancient Greece and Rome* (1911) at pp.213, 256.
83   H. Henriques, *The Law of Aliens and Naturalization* (1906) at pp.9–10.
84   H. Grotius, *De Jure Belli Ac Pacis*, bk. II, Ch. II (Carnegie Endowment trans. 1925), at pp.186–205.
85   At p.202.
86   F. De Victoria, *De Indis Et De Iure Belli Relectiones* (E. Nys ed. 1917), at p.151.
87   S. Pufendorf, *De Jure Naturae Gentium*, bk. VIII (Oxford edn. 1934), at p.365.
88   E. De Vattel, *The Law of Nations* (J. Chitty edn. 1839), at pp.107–108.
89   At p.178.
90   At pp.183–4.
91   W. Blackstone, *Commentaries on the Laws of England* (1783) at p.259.
92   See, Nafziger at p.816.
93   R. Phillimore, *International Law* (3rd edn., 1879) at p.320.
94   Lord Denning in *R v. Governor of Pentonville Prison, ex parte Azam* [1973] 2 All ER 741, at p.747.
95   Nafziger *op. cit.* at pp.839–40.
96   *Treaty Establishing the European Community*, Article 48(2) *done* 25th March 1957, 298 UNTS 3. Article 3(c) provides that the Community shall include within activities 'the abolition, as between member states, of obstacles to freedom of movement for persons'.

97   Satvinder Juss, *Immigration, Nationality, and Citizenship* (Mansell, London, 1993), at p.2.
98   Under Article 49 the *Treaty of Rome* prescribes procedures for implementing the free movement of workers. Under Article 50 it requires that 'Member States shall, within the framework of a joint programme, encourage the exchange of young workers'. Under Article 51 it provides for the adoption of 'such measures in the filed of social security as are necessary to provide freedom of movement for workers ...'.
99   Nafziger, *op.cit.*, at o.838, referring to Turack, 'Freedom of Transnational Movement: The Helsinki Accord and Beyond', 11 *VAND.J. TRANSNAT'l L.*585, pp.603–604.
100 Nafziger, 'The right of Migration under the Helsinki Accords', 1980 5 *ILL. L. J.* 395.
101 *Conference on Security and Cooperation in Europe: Final Act*, reprinted in 14 *ILM* 1292 (1975).
102 Nafziger, 'The General Admission of Aliens ...', *op. cit.*, at p.838 at fn. 182.
103 See the Accords, *op. cit.*, at p.1314.
104 See E.G. Loescher, *supra.*, at 617.
105 Treaty establishing the European Economic Community, article 3(C) [hereafter EEC Treaty].
106 Article 8(A) amends the Treaty of Rome to establish 'an without internal frontiers in which the free movement of goods, persons, services and capital is ensured'. Not later than Dec. 31, 1992. Further, Regulation 1612/68 requires equality of treatment for EC nationals in member states in relation to eligibility for employment, tax and social benefits, and family reunion.
107 Under article 8 every citizen of the Union is granted the right to move and reside freely within the territory of any of the member states: see, Ronald Kaye, 'British Refugee Policy in 1992: The Breakdown of A Policy Community', 5(1) *J. Refugee Stud.* 47, 57 (1992).
108 W.R. Bohning, 'Integration and Immigration Pressures in Western Europe', 130(4) *Int'l. Labor Rev.* 445, 451–2 (1991).
109 E. Whitaker, 'The Schengen Agreement and its Portent for the Freedom of Personal Movement in Europe', 6 *Geo. Immigr. L.J.*, 191, 219 (1992).
110 James C. Hathaway, 'Harmonizing for Whom? The Devaluation of Refugee Protection in the Era of European Economic Integration', 26 *Cornell Int'l L.J.*, 719, at 722, fn. 21.
111 See 'Europe's Immigrants: Strangers Inside the Gates', *The Economist*, Feb. 15, 1992 at 21.
112 Jacqueline Bhabha, 'European Harmonization of Asylum Policy: A Flawed Process', 35 *Va. J. Int'l. L.* 101 at 102.
113 Henry G. Schermers, 'Human Rights and Free Movement of Persons: The Role of the European Commission and Court of Human Rights', in *Free Movement of Persons in Europe, Legal Problems and Experiences*, 235, 237 (Henry G. Schermers *et al.* (eds), 1991).
114 Case 7/75, *Fracas v. Belgian State*, 2 C.M.L.R. 442, 450 (1975).
115 See 'Congress Approves NAFTA Legislation', 70 *Interpreter Releases*, 1546, 1547 (Nov. 22, 1993).
116 EC Treaty, *supra.*, article 48.
117 *Id.* article 52.
118 Council Directive 68/360, 1968 O.J. (L257) 13 (for families of workers); Council Directive 73/148, 1973 O.J. (L172) 14 (for families of self-employed).
119 Council Directive 90/366, 1990 O. J. (L180) 30.

120   Council Directive 90/365, 1990 O.J. (L180) 28.
121   Council Directive 90/364, 1990 O.J. (L180) 26.
122   The definition of workers' families has been no more liberal by the E.C.J. than that in any individual member states national laws: see, Council Regulation 1612/68, 1968 O.J., article 10(1) and (2).
123   Case 75/63, *Unger v. Bestuur Ter. Pedriifsvereniging Voor Detailhandel en Ambachten*, 3 C.M.L.R. 319 (1964).
124   Case 53/81, *Levin v. Staatssecretaris van Justitie*, 1982 E.C.R. 1035, (1982).
125   Case 48/75, *State v. Royer*, 2 C.M.L.R. 619 (1976).
126   Case 370/90, *Regina v. Immigration Appeal Tribunal and Surinder Singh ex parte Secretary of State for the Home Department*, 3 C.M.L.R. 358 (1992).
127   Case 59/85, *The State (Netherlands) v. Reed*, 2 C.M.L.R. 448 (1987) involving the co-habitation rights of opposite sex unmarried partners.
128   Ever since the Tindemans Report in 1972, nearly a quarter of a century ago, the abolition of internal border controls has been on the European Agenda. See, J. P.H. Donner, 'Abolition of Border Controls', in *Free Movement of Persons in Europe, Legal Problems and Experiences*, at p.5 (Henry G. Schermers *et al.* (eds), 1991).
129   *Id.*, at 6.
130   *Regina v. Secretary of State ex parte Flynn*; *Migration Newssheet*, CCME Brussels Official Report, April 1995, at 3.
131   Article 7A of the EC Treaty (as amended by the Maastricht Treaty of Feb. 7, 1992) provides for 'an area without internal frontiers in which the free movement of goods, persons, services and capital is ensured in accordance with the provisions of the Treaty'.
132   See Donner, *supra.*, at 22.
133   *Migration Newssheet*, CCME Brussels, Official Report Jan. 1995, at 1.
134   See, Andrew Marshall and Colin Brown, 'UK to Face Challenge Over Customs Checks', *The Independent*, Feb. 13, 1995, at 3.
135   E. Whitaker, 'The Schengen Agreement and its Portent for the Freedom of Personal Movement in Europe', 6 *Geo. Immigr. L.J.* 191, 214 (1992).
136   *Id.* at 215.
137   See D. Bigo, 'Polices en resaux. L' experience europe'enne' (1996, Paris, Presses de Science Po); J. Huysmans, 'The European Union and the Securitization of Migration', *Journal of Common Market Studies* (2000, vol., 38, No. 5), at pp.751–71; and T. Kostakopoulou, 'The "Protective Union": Change and Continuity in Migration Law and policy in Post-Amsterdam Europe', *Journal of common Market Studies* (2000, vol. 38, No. 3), at pp.497–518.
138   See S. Juss, *Immigration, Nationality and Citizenship* (London, 1993) at p.7.
139   See Juss *op. cit.*, at p.7.
140   Randall Hansen, 'Asylum Policy in the European Union', *Geo. Immgr. L.J.* (Vol. 14, 2000, pp.779–800), at p.793.
141   See 'The Home Affairs Committee Report' on *Administrative Delays in the Immigration and Nationality Department*, 1989–90 (H.C. 319), at p.XI, para.30. See also, Satvinder Juss, *Discretion and Deviation in the Administration of Immigration Control*, London, 1997, at p.49.
142   See Ferdinand Protzman, 'Thousands Swell Trek to the West by East Germans', *New York Times*, Sept.12, 1989, at A1; 'Clamour in the East: A Singular Month Produces an Exodus', *New York Times*, Nov.10, 1989, at A16.
143   Gil Loescher, 'Refugee Movements and International Security', 28 (Adelphi Papers No.268, 1992).
144   'Refugees: Keep Out', *The Economist*, Sept. 19, 1992, at 64.

145 Gil Loescher, 'The European Community and Refugees', 65 *Int'l. Affairs*, 617, 619 (1989).

146 *The Economist*, June 1, 1991.

147 *The Guardian*, June 28, 1991, cited in S. Egan and A. Storey, 'European Asylum Policy: A Fortress Under Construction', *Trociare Development Review*, 49, 55 (1992).

148 See 'Europe's Immigrants: Strangers Inside the Gates', *The Economist*, February 15, 1992 at 21.

149 '... Europeans have come to see "foreigners" as threats to regional stability and security. There is a pervasive belief that the cultural and racial heterogenity, which accompanies immigration jeopardizes European identity and solidarity. There is concern that and that they will offer unwelcome competition for scarce jobs and housing. Governments have sustained this popular xenophobia ...'. See, James C. Hathaway, 'Harmonizing for whom? ...', *op.cit.*, at 720, in 1997, in the *Harvard Human Rights Journal*.

150 'Governments have decided to treat migrants from the less developed world as an undifferentiated evil: refugees, economic migrants, drug traffickers, and terrorists are officially categorized as presenting a unified threat, and will all confront a common policy of deterrents. States have elaborated an absolutely blunt legal response to the alleged menace of "foreigners" which effectively buries any concern for the human rights principles ...'. James Hathaway, ibid., at p.723.

151 *Single European Act*, June 29th, 1987, O.J. (L 169) (1987).

152 *The Treaty on European Union*, February 7th, 1992, O.J. (C 191) (1992), 31 I.L.M. 247 [hereafter, *The Maastricht Treaty*] at Tit, I-IV.

153 *Treaty Establishing the European Communities* (TEC) as amended by the Treaty of Amsterdam, October 2nd. 1997, O.J. (C 340) (1997) [hereinafter *The Amsterdam Treaty*] 204.

154 See Article 31(2) of the TEU after Nice.

155 *Treaty Establishing Council of Europe* (published 16th December 2004) O.J. (310) (vol.47, 2004) ISSN 1725–2423, approved by the Heads of State or Government on 18 June 2004 and signed on 29 October 2004, the treaty has yet to be ratified by the 25 Member States of the European Union before it enters into force.

156 See *The Maastricht Treaty*, supra., note 9, at Title I-IV.

157 Ibid., at Title V.

158 Ibid., at Title VI.

159 See Art. 6(") of the *Treaty of European Union 1997*.

160 See Schengen (Agreement and Convention) (visited Mar. 18th, 2000) http://europa.cu.int/scadplus/leg/en/cig/g4000s. htm#s 1. The transfer of the "Schengen Acquis" under this Treaty contains four components: (1) the June 14th, 1985 Schengen Agreement between France, Germany, and the Benelux Economic Union; (2) the June 19, 1990 Convention signed between the above five countries, Luxembourg, and the Netherlands, implementing the 1985 Agreement; (3) the Accession Protocols in the 1985 Agreement and the 1990 Implementation Convention signed with Italy (November 27, 1990). Spain and Portugal (June 25th, 1991), Greece (November 6th, 1992), Austria (April 28th, 1995), Denmark, Finland, and Sweden (December 19th, 1996) with related final acts and declarations; and (4) the decision and declarations adopted by the Executive Committee established by the 1990 Convention as well as acts adopted for the implementation of the Convention (Amsterdam Treaty, Annex, Schengen Acquis) Protocol Integrating the Schengen Acquis into the Framework of the European Union, October 2nd, 1997, O.J. (C 340) 93–7.

161 Sandra Lavenex, 'The Europeanization of refugee Policies: Normative Challenges and Institutional Legacies', *Journal of Common Market Studies* (2001, vol. 39, No. 5, pp.851–74), at p.869.

162 COM (2004) 4002 [final].

163 Ibid., at p.3.

164 Ibid., at p.4.

165 COM (2004) 4002 [final].

166 The main contributions – ranging from NGO dissatisfaction with the preoccupation with economic growth to the concern of Sweden over the documentation of many asylum-seekers – is set out at http://www.europa.eu.int/comm/justice_home/news/consulting_public/tampere_ii/news_tampereii_en.htm.

167 EU Press Release (25–26th October 2004) 13759/04 (Presse 302) at p.8. Adopted 22nd December 2004, taking effect on 1st January 2005: see Council doc. 15226/04, 15 Dec. 2004.

168 EU Commissioner Fratini on migration and asylum policies: see 'Press conference 1st September 2005' at http://www.statewatch.org/news/newsfull.htm According to EU Commissioner Frattini, 'The package adopted today comprises of measures constituting the two sides of the same coin: coherent, fair, efficient and credible European asylum and immigration policies'.

169 EU Commissioner Fratini on migration and asylum policies: see 'Press conference 1st September 2005' at http://www.statewatch.org/news/newsfull.htm.

170 Madeline Bunting, 'Regime Change, European-style, is a measure of our civilisation', *The Guardian*, 26th September 2005: see m.bunting@guardian.co.uk. For a more scholarly discussion of European identity in this context, see Elspeth Guild, *The Legal Elements of European Identity: EU Citizenship and Migration Law* (Kluwer Law International, The Hague, 2004).

2 Recognizing Free Movement

As in nineteenth century Europe, so also in the twentieth century, it was the affluent industrialized countries of the northern hemisphere who were at the forefront of developing restrictionist policies. The irony is that in so doing, the affluent North and West, have ignored the fact that their own basic rights and liberties were developed when they were once themselves the major beneficiaries of free movement rights in the West. They were once migrants themselves. The story of migration is accordingly a story of human development. In an age of global development, it deserves at long last to be recognized as that. Only then can rational, logical and affordable immigration and refugee policy be developed.

Nafziger's account was written at a time, more than 20 years ago, before the widespread acceptance of free movement as a component of human rights. Since then there has been a sea-change in perception and analysis. When it comes to free movement rights, as Harvey reminds us, '[i]t is generally accepted now that … interpretation should be tied to human rights norms'.[1] Indeed, as he explains, '[n]ew paradigms are emerging which present very different pictures of the future and are based on distinct understandings'.[2] To that extent, in considering whether or not free movement rights accrue to everyone everywhere, recent empirical approaches to the exercise of free movement rights are worth considering. This is especially so in an era when everyone everywhere wants to travel and partake in the goods of life.

In a recent book, *The Global Community*, W.M. Spellman, has argued that international migration is not a new and problematic issue at all. On the contrary, it is a basic instinct. He explains that:

> [t]ogether with unpredicatable shifts in climate, natural disasters and threats from hostile neighbours, a life of movement was the norm for most people and, as a result, fixed notions of territory and resource appropriation, the 'mine and thine', were largely absent from the collective assumptions of the group or kinship community.[3]

Spellman reminds us that '[p]rior to 1500 all great migrations were land-based affairs, most often associated with warfare and the violent displacement of agricultural labourers by cruel, mobile strangers'[4] but that '[t]he age of sail and, even more dramatically (after 1850), the advent of steam transport, forever altered basic migration patterns the world over. Now, for the first time in history, large numbers of women and men – as individuals, as family units, as whole communities – departed their countries … for a variety of transoceanic destinations'.[5] What happened is truly remarkable:

> The scale and diversity of the process had never been witnessed before. By the last decade of the nineteenth century, for example, two out of every five persons who had been born in British-controlled Ireland were living elsewhere, often an ocean away. Communities of North Indians were settling as indentured labourers in Caribbean sugar islands and on South African plantations. Over 60,000 Japanese labourers and their families were relocating to independent Hawaii … . Today more than 350 million people of African descent live outside Africa, compared with 540 million resident in that vast continent. Close to 30 million Chinese … live beyond the borders of mainland China. And, almost 9 million South Asians reside elsewhere … .[6]

As a result of transoceanic migration:

> No longer would major cultural traditions live in isolation from each other; thanks to transoceanic migration, the intermingling of faces and values, of preferences and traditions, of understanding and its opposite, would shrink the intellectual world to the point where knowledge of the 'other' culture often required no more than getting to know one's immediate neighbour.[7]

What is most interesting about Spellman's account, however, is the way in which he refers to the central players in the diaspora of world-wide communities. He explains that:

> The role of Europeans in the overall process of global transformation was, for good or ill, absolutely central; even the involuntary and brutal transatlantic diaspora of 12–15 million African women and men between 1500 and 1808 cannot be accounted for without a reference to European ambitions, European problems and European priorities. Only after 1500 was the entire globe brought into regular and sustained communication and trade contact, a network initiated and later dominated by ambitious Europeans. Again, only after 1500 did the inhabitants of one continent, Western Europe, begin the dynamic and often destructive process of overseas colonization which was to stamp the impress of a Christian and commercial civilization onto the varied templates of non-Western cultures.[8]

Spellman reminds us of the four distinct eras of international migration over the past half millennium identified by Douglas Massey.[9] Thus, the first era was from 1500–1800 when European colonization transformed the Americas, Africa, Asia, and Oceania.[10] The second era was the industrial period of the early nineteenth century which 'again, involved Europeans, but instead favoured free white labour seeking new opportunities outside'[11] their homelands. This period of migration was no less remarkable. Between 50–60 million people left Europe's industrial cities from 1800 to 1925 and 85 per cent of these settled in just five countries, namely, Australia, Argentina, Canada,

New Zealand, and the United States. The migration was disproportionately that of Europeans because during the entire 400-year period from 1500–1900 only 15 million Africans and Asians became intercontinental migrants.[12] The result was that '[i]n the process of resettlement these nineteenth-century Europeans successfully superimposed key aspects of their culture on a variety of native peoples'. The disparity had long-term consequences for the global community in the modern age. According to Alfred Crosby:

> [n]one of the major groupings of humankind is as oddly distributed about the world as European, especially western European Whites.[13]

The First World War brought to an end this era of large-scale European migration when receiving nations like the USA and Canada began to pass restrictive immigration laws. It is at this stage that forced migration, in the form of millions of war refugees, began to define Europe. The third era of migration began in the 1960s with the age of post-industrial 'Global Migration' in which 'a much wider array of sending and receiving countries'[14] participated. This is where people moved from densely settled industrialized regions to sparsely settled industrializing areas. The fourth era of international migration arose, however, when people from densely settled countries which are undergoing the early stages of industrialization and entry into the global economy, are moving to already highly urbanized, industrialized and densely settled countries.[15] These groups are largely non-European and largely unskilled. They have met with the increased rigour of immigration controls from the receiving countries of the West. According to Spellman:

> [t]he advent of plural sending areas, instead of ameliorating the economic and political challenges faced by sending nations, has in many cases actually exacerbated the problem of development, as receiving nations tend to favour the admission of skilled professionals.[16]

In a recent review of Spellman's book, Robert Winder has explained how the empirical evidence presented by Spellman only confirms that '[m]igration is an old impulse; what is new is the desire to prevent it'. However, what is unfair about it is that the story of migration 'begins and ends in Europe'. This is because whereas European navigators first explored and settled distant parts of the world, in an age of globalization it seems that 'the one thing that must be blocked at all costs is people'. What is ironic is that '[i]n the whole of the nineteenth century, not a single person was refused entry to the United Kingdom. Things have certainly changed'.[17]

   The account above, nevertheless, raises questions about how we view, or should view, immigration and asylum applications. During the era of empires many Europeans set out to work and settle in territories across the world. They set out to escape strong, centralized, authoritarian governments that suppressed basic civil and political rights. They set out as non-Conformists to secure somewhere else the right to religious freedom. They set out as impoverished squatters to escape famine and hunger. Were they genuine refugees or were they economic migrants? Was the distinction a meaningful one? In the words of Claire Palley, in *The United Kingdom and Human Rights*:

> To Third World eyes the United Kingdom does not appear humane. Instead, it appears hypocritical when United Kingdom emigration of the poor to the under developed world in the nineteenth and early twentieth centuries is contrasted with current attempts of the poor in Asia and Africa to emigrate to the developed world. Recent United Kingdom governments treatment of immigrants and those seeking political asylum is particularly criticized.[18]

The truth is that there is no logical or necessary distinction to be made between political and economic migrants. Both are forced to leave their homelands in search of a better life. Indeed, Saskia Sassen, one of the most lucid and imaginative social scientists of the last two decades, has drawn attention to 'the relative normality of the pursuit of work across borders during the emergence of the European nation-states'. In *Guests and Aliens,* she gives a detailed account of the economic and political mass migrations of Italians and Eastern European Jews during the nineteenth and early twentieth centuries.[19] Recently, Father Patrick Lynch wrote to the British Press expressing a sentiment that is worth reflecting on in full. He wrote:

> … I live and work in an area with a large immigrant population. I am regularly asked to write to the Home Office supporting applications to stay in this country, and occasionally I am requested to visit people in detention centers or police cells as they await deportation. They are economic not political refugees. They are very ordinary people who simply want to be able to work and thus support their families, and the reality is that there is work available in this country. They are desperate. By and large they work hard in low-paid jobs, live in poor conditions and ultimately contribute to society (financially and otherwise) far more than they receive. It is important to remember that for most of Europe emigration was the norm during the latter part of the nineteenth and the first half of the twentieth century. It was only after the second world war that the situation began to change and now because of economic development and smaller families the norm for northern and western Europe, including Italy, Spain, and Ireland, is immigration, not emigration … [20]

For those lucky enough to live in the West, the right to travel remains, even today, a basic human right. Indeed, the right to travel both within and without the territory has been judicially endorsed by the United States courts, though not fully developed. In *Kent v. Dulles* in 1958, the US Supreme Court held that:

> the right to travel is part of the 'liberty' of which the citizen cannot be deprived … Freedom of movement across frontiers in either direction, and inside frontiers as well, was part of our heritage. *Travel abroad like travel within the country [is] basic in our scheme of values.*[21]

Lawrence Tribe, argues that the right of a person to leave a territory in which he lives is the corollary of the right of a person to enter a territory in which he does not live. He argues that if it is wrong for the state to restrict exit, it is also wrong of the state to restrict entry of others. In international law, the right of nationals to leave is well recognized. The right of non-nationals to enter is, of course, is not. Yet, Tribe justifies the entry of 'those who might alter the status quo' as follows:

> [C]lose surveillance and control of travel … has always been a central technique of the totalitarian state, but centuries of experience should suffice to mark as especially suspect, any governmental measure designed to prevent the emigration of those dissatisfied with the existing order, *or the immigration of those who might alter the status quo*. Just as governments should be forbidden to expel the citizen who has become a source of unrest, so it cannot be permitted to imprison the citizen *who seeks freedom in another land*.[22]

In *Apthekar v. Secretary of State* in 1964, the Supreme Court while holding, in the words of Douglas J., that 'free movement by the citizen is … dangerous to a tyrant … and it is therefore controlled … in the interests of security',[23] appears to have upheld free movement rights as an aspect of free speech right, holding that:

> I see no way to keep a citizen from traveling within or without the country [unless] he has been convicted of a crime [or] there is probable cause for issuing a warrant [to arrest him]. *Freedom of movement [is] the very essence of our free society, setting us apart*. Like the right of assembly and the right of association, it often makes all other rights meaningful – knowing, studying, arguing, exploring, conversing, observing and even thinking.[24]

If individual self-fulfillment and self-realization is a basis for free movement rights, then this surely applies equally to voluntary migrants, moving for reasons of economic betterment, as much as it does to involuntary migrants, moving for reasons of persecution. Free movement makes other rights more meaningful. Jeanne N. Woods, in an article, 'Travel that talks', has argued that 'freedom of movement, like freedom of speech, promotes the values of individuals self realization and self determination'.[25] Indeed, Justice Brennan had no doubt that 'just as the Constitution protects both popular and unpopular speech, it likewise protects both popular and unpopular travelers'.[26] According to his formulation, free travel may just as well be an aspect of free speech. In fact, there would appear to be international law authority for this position adopted by the US Supreme Court.[27] John Hart Ely, in an attempt to rationalize the US Supreme Court decisions, states:

> The right at issue in the modern cases [is] not simply the right to travel to or through a state *but rather a right to move there – the right, if you will, to relocate*. [To] a large extent America was founded by persons escaping from environments they found oppressive. Mobility was quite free during the colonial period, and '[a]s a result, most colonials who dissented from their own communities conception of right and justice could move without great difficulty to a more congenial community'. [I think this tradition] *points us in the right direction*, one that associates the right to relocate not with the idea that it is some kind of handmaiden of majoritarian democracy but, quite to the contrary, with the notion that *one should have an*

option of escaping an incompatible majority. [A dissenting member of a community] should have the *option of exiting and relocating in a community whose values he or she finds more compatible.* … It is an old idea dating back at least as far as Rousseau's 'droit d'emigration' …[28]

Ely is suggesting here that the option to move should be available not only to those who fear persecution because they are with an 'incompatible majority' but also open to those who just want to live with those 'whose values he or she finds more compatible'. Ely's rationalization of the American cases answers an important question. Whereas these cases provide for a right to travel, including travel in order to work, they also imply a right to settle in a country of one's choice in Ely's 'right to move there – the right, if you will, to relocate'. There appears to be an attempt here to give this right the sort of legal basis that free speech has in the First Amendment of the American Constitution. If this is right then these rights clearly cannot just be intended for people of the Northern or the Western hemisphere. What is needed is a more comprehensive recognition of these rights on a global scale at a time when demographic pressures changing geopolitical alignments are making the world increasingly unstable. What is needed in immigration and refugee policy-making is an approach that eschews international instability and embraces global order over disorder.

There is, as seen above, compelling empirical evidence, not only that that free movement across national borders is, normatively speaking, a basic human right, because it has a long and illustrious history; but that it has been a *de facto* right in every practical sense, because it was exercised freely by anyone who had historically chosen to so exercise it. In the annals of international morality, it was recognized freely long before the development of modern international law. Indeed, Europeans exercised the right long before they thought of restricting it for others. Today, in an era of globalization the collective interest the world community is such that the normative and *de facto* right to free movement needs to be given a clear legal basis in the asylum and immigration laws of domestic legal systems.

FREE MOVEMENT AND THE MODERN PUBLICISTS

A second important question that Nafziger forces us to confront is whether modern publicists, writing for the modern era, have followed in the spirit of the classical publicists and endorsed freedom of movement as a normative principle. The question is important for two reasons. First, because globalization of immigration controls is today at its peak in the developed world; and secondly, because given that the doctrine of state sovereignty allegedly allows for the etermination by the state of its constituent population. Modern publicists wrote at a time when immigration restrictions were at their peak in most western countries. Yet, it is remarkable that they do not differ in this respect from the classical publicists. One contemporary philosopher, Joseph Carens has put forward an eloquent thesis in defense of free movement rights.[29]

Carens calls in the aid theories of modern liberal philosophers today to argue for a theory of free movement rights. First, he considers Robert Nozick who has argued that the state has no right to do anything other than enforce the rights which individuals already enjoy in the state of nature (e.g. property rights). This being so, Nozick argues that because the state enjoys a *de facto* monopoly of power or the enforcement of rights within its territory, it is obliged to protect the rights of its citizens and non-citizens equally.[30] Second, Carens considers John Rawls, who propounded a theory of the State that was more activist. Under Rawls' theory the state has positive responsibility for social welfare. Rawls believes that if people were asked behind a 'veil of ignorance' they would chose two things: (1) equal liberty for everyone; and (2) the acceptance of social and economic inequalities only so long as they were advantageous to the least well-off and attached to positions open to all under fair conditions of equal opportunity.[31] Carens draws upon this to argue that these principles, in particular the second principle, do not necessarily just apply to a population within the state. There is no reason why it cannot extend across states to apply to different societies and communities. We only think about the state because liberalism always presupposes the existence of the state as it sets out to explore the relationship between the individual and the state, in an effort to posit a doctrine of individual rights.

Michael Dummett takes an even more robust line. He states that philosophers from Plato to Rawls have only enquired into the foundations of justice in the context of a bounded society: 'they have rarely overstepped the boundaries of a society'. Consequently, 'they have seldom asked what obligations a state has towards those who are not its citizens'. This is an important question because '[a] just society … is not merely one whose members act justly: it is one that functions justly as a whole'. He then suggests that 'Egalitarianism is the belief that within a just society every individual must be accorded absolutely equal treatment; this is difficult to describe, let alone achieve'. Nevertheless, '[f]or the egalitarian, it is the duty of the state to correct for inherited inequalities as much as can be done, as in a card game which awards a premium to a player for having no trumps or no court cards in his hand'.[32] He is critical of Nozick for suggesting that that the natural forces of individual self-interest should be allowed to operate unchecked and that a just society need have no collective ideal at all.

This *laissez-faire* view rests 'on a prior presumption that justice is only an individual virtue: that no question arises whether a whole society functions justly'. But a society cannot be just if it allows every unequal transaction to take place unchecked, reasons Dummett, since it is well known how 'accidental advantages can lead over time to grotesque disparities of wealth and power' with the result that 'almost all societies are disfigured by such inequities'.[33] Inequalities, therefore, have to be justified. It is here that Rawls has a contribution to make for he has proposed that inequality within a society is legitimate only if the least well-off group is better off for it, than it would be without it. Dummett extends this reasoning to groups *outside* a bounded society. He reasons that:

What is apparent is that we can no longer regard justice as bearing only on the functioning of a single society, considered as that compared within a single sovereign state. The horrifying inequalities that often exist within any one such society are outstripped by the yet more horrifying inequalities between rich and poor ones – a disparity with the most powerful effect on migration between them.[34]

A state has a duty, argues Dummett, 'to come to the aid of other states when disasters strike them, such as floods, earthquakes, volcanic eruptions and famine' and although these are underpinned by 'a great many principles' in international law that govern one state's responsibility to another state 'to offer help … in moments of sudden and severe need' the reality is that 'these are largely unenforced'. This raises a further question: 'what duties … does a state have towards individuals seeking to enter the land over which it rules? The initial answer has to be that it must deal with them justly: it must give them their due'.[35] Dummett appears to imply here that this makes out a case for the right to migrate.

The arguments above – and especially those of Dummett – stretches the limits of liberal theory. Liberalism presupposes the existence of the state. Without the state there are no human rights. The liberal state is only so-called because it protects the human rights of its citizens within its borders. What these arguments accordingly point to, is a new way of thinking about human rights. One that allows for recognition of rights outside the state. Globalization, or what is sometimes called the second phase of modernity, shows that the state is increasingly obsolete as a sovereign entity. Ironically, the state is even more determined to control that which it thinks it can control, namely, population movements to and from its borders. However, globalization makes the sustenance of closed and insular states much more difficult. That is the lesson both of the uprisings of 1989 and of the horrifying attacks on the Twin Towers on 11th September 2001. The opening up of the world through trade, travel and television[36] suggests that so-called sovereign states are subject to the forces of internationalism in which the understanding of individual human rights must extend beyond borders.[37] In an era of the internationalization and globalization of environmental, resource, and rights issues new normative principles of appropriate state conduct and rights recognition have to be developed. Should we, therefore, be intellectually hamstrung by the limiting constraints of liberalism when considering the future development of free movement rights? Globalism[38] suggests that we should not.

Yet, even liberals today are arguing that there is a limit to the expression of solidarity with others in the international community. Recently in Britain, David Goodhart,[39] suggested that there may be a conflict between national solidarity and ethnic diversity that developed societies will have to resolve: 'Thinking about the conflict between solidarity and diversity is another way of asking a question as old as human society itself: who is my brother, with whom do I share mutual obligations?'. As he explained:

The traditional conservative, Burkean view is that our affinities ripple out from our families and localities to the nation, and not very far beyond. That view is pitted against a liberal universalist one that sees us in some sense equally obligated to all human beings, from Bolton to Burundi – an idea that is associated with the universalist aspects of Christianity and Islam, with Kantian universalism and with left-wing internationalism. Science is neutral in this dispute, or rather it stands on both sides of the argument. Evolutionary psychology stresses both the universality of most human traits and – through the notion of kin selection and reciprocal altruism – the instinct to favour our own. Social psychologists also argue that the tendency to perceive in-groups and out-groups, however ephemeral, is innate. In any case, Burkeans claim to have common sense on their side. They argue that we feel more comfortable with, and are readier to share with and sacrifice for, those with whom we have shared histories and similar values. To put it bluntly – most of us prefer our own kind.

Goodhart was keen to emphasize what preferring 'our own kind' does not mean: 'It does not mean that we are necessarily hostile to other kinds or that we cannot empathize with outsiders'. Yet, there was no doubt that '[g]reater diversity can produce real conflicts of values and interests, but it also generates unjustified fears' and that in Britain, '31 percent of people still admit to being racially prejudiced'. The reasons why this is important is that the welfare state, the distinguishing feature of Western European countries, is only sustainable if society is broadly homogenous, otherwise:

> [i]f values become more diverse, if lifestyles become more differentiated, then it becomes more difficult to sustain the legitimacy of a universal risk-pooling welfare state. People ask: 'Why should I pay for them when they are doing things that I wouldn't do?'. This is America versus Sweden. You can have a Swedish welfare state provided that you are a homogeneous society with intensely shared values.

Goodhart's analysis was both novel and unique as it came from the Left and was presented in well-reasoned, measured and moderate tones. In so doing, he was able to point out:

> one of the central dilemmas of political life in developed societies: sharing and solidarity can conflict with diversity. This is an especially acute dilemma for progressives who want plenty of both solidarity (high social cohesion and generous welfare paid out of a progressive tax system) and diversity (equal respect for a wide range of peoples, values and ways of life). The tension between the two values is a reminder that serious politics is about trade-offs.

In my view, Goodhart's eloquent and intuitively appealing thesis over-states the case for control on immigration. Solidarity is not threatened because some people 'are doing things that I wouldn't do?'. In an age of diversity and pluralist co-existence, with hardly any society being untouched by multiculturalism, most people are sophisticated enough to tolerate such minority practices as the killing of conscious animals by Jews and Muslims or the practice of arranged marriages by South Asians, without feeling resentful about having to pay for their medical treatment on the national health service. If they are resentful they are not any more so than a middle class London-based professional, who is having to pay his tax pounds for the welfare costs of a teenage single mother, on a deprived, drug-ridden, and largely unemployed, council estate in the North-East of England. What threatens national solidarity and cohesion are not the cultural practices of individual multi-ethnic communities, but differences in the political allegiances that they owe. For that we need not less integration, but more integration, which will achieve national solidarity. Goodhart's 'America versus Sweden' alleged dichotomy is wrong in this respect. What America surely proved more than anything is how a multi-layered and multi-faceted society of different races can merge into a melting-pot that is America provided only that they are absolutely un-equivocal about their assumed American identity. If Goodhart were right about diverse values and lifestyles becoming a threat to national solidarity, the Olympic silver-medallist, Pakistani boxer from Bolton, Amir Khan, with his family's traditional Punjabi dresses and religious views, would not have become such a celebrity, and won over the hearts of the British nation, as easily as he did.[40] No-one could argue that there would be a resentment to such a person benefiting from a 'universal risk-pooling welfare state'. The truth is that the welfare state is in decline in Britain and in much of European society for reasons unconnected to immigration and has been for many years now. Those '31 percent of people' that Goodhart found as 'still admit[ing] to being racially prejudiced' will remain racist come what may, whether or not immigrants hold dearly to their cultural beliefs. A country like Britain needs more integration not less, if there is to be a new all-inclusive British identity. What the terrible London bombings of 7th July 2005[41] tragically highlight is a failure of national integration and a consequent allegiance to a single political authority within a polity. Those immigrants who have successfully integrated have gone onto to lead productive lives and to become leading entrepreneurs and professionals in their adopted country. Those who have not, have remained cocooned and isolated in their own communities. Integration is not assimilation. So both immigrant communities and host communities can still remain distinct communities. Yet, it is integration that is the glue of national social solidarity. It is a two-way process in which both sides must participate. Immigrants are attracted by the democratic and participatory processes of western societies that lead to higher standards of living for them. Host western communities want immigrants from the developed world today, because of unfilled jobs and skills shortages and because the welfare state is floundering without the tax revenue generated by immigrants going into a universal risk-pooling system, that can secure the pensions of the native-born aged. For both sides, integration is vital for the maintenance of a healthy social fabric in national society.

Nevertheless, the argument that even developed societies are in reality distinguished by their cultural identity has been taken a stage further by another distinguished publicist across the Atlantic. Michael Walzer states that elite States must discriminate in order to preserve themselves in their choice of rules as to who they admit and who they reject, and he uses culture as the discerning discriminatory tool. This is the third important question that Nafziger leaves us to confront, namely, whether nativism properly can be the basis of migration policy today. Walzer identifies the problem as follows:

Since human beings are highly mobile, large numbers of men and women regularly attempt to change their residence and their membership, moving from unfavoured to favoured environments. Affluent and free countries are, like elite universities, besieged by applicants. They have to decide on their own size and character. More precisely, as citizens of such a country, we have to decide: whom should we admit? Ought we to have open admission? Can we choose amongst applicants? What are the appropriate criteria for distributing membership?[42]

Walzer states that the 'conventional answer' is that:

we who are already members do the choosing, in accordance with our own under-standing of what membership means in our community and of what sort of a community we want to have. Membership as a social good is constituted by our understanding; its value is fixed by our work and conversation; and then we are in charge (who else could be in charge?) of its distribution.[43]

Walzer propounds a communitarian thesis in defence of the rights and desires of the existing community. He states that for a State when it comes to choosing an admissions policy:

it is not merely a matter of acting in the world, exercising sovereignty, and pursuing national interests. At stake here is the shape of the community … Admission and exclusion are at the core of communal independence. They suggest the deepest meaning of self-determination. Without them, there could not be communities of character, historical stable, ongoing associations of men and women with some special commitment to one another … .[44]

It could be argued, however, that it is precisely because some societies are so affluent and free that they should not be allowed to deny admission to those less fortunate than themselves. Such an expectation arises from the principles of international morality, so that even though national polities must answer these questions for themselves, they must take account of the fact that for all international purposes all distinctions between different kinds of subjects have neither theoretical nor practical value. Michael Walzer's communitarian thesis of exclusionary rights is open to question. It is based on an idea of community or ethnicity that has a doubtful basis in the modern world. Michael Walzer, nevertheless, does also assert that just as liberal societies have choices, they also have constraints. Accordingly, for him:

… self-determination in the sphere of membership is not absolute. It is a right ex-ercised, most often, by national clubs or families, but it is held in principle by territorial states. Hence, it is subject both to internal decisions by the members themselves (*all* the members, including those who hold membership simply by right of place) and to the external principle of mutual aid. Immigration, then, is both a matter of political choice and moral constraint.[45]

The principle of self-determination used in this way, however, is deeply problematic. As a practical principle, self-determination applies mostly to cases of de-colonization where it is asserted as a right of people within the

State. As a normative principle it may have wider application beyond de-colonization. However, if so, it should be used with caution. One may happily recognize, in the words of Hurst Hannum, that:

> Ethnicity is an even more obvious basis on which to assert political power when one considers that, under the guise of the 'nation state', ethnicity (or linguistic affinity or religion) became the foundation of political organisation in the late nineteenth century.[46]

One may even recognize the powerful potency of the right to self-determination today. In the words of Walker Connor:

> [T]he self determination principle holds that any people, simply because it considers itself to be a separate national group, is uniquely and exclusively qualified to determine its own political status, including, should it so desire, the right to its own state. The concept, therefore, makes ethnicity the ultimate standard of political legitimacy.[47]

However, surely, this is where the problem lies. Self-determination can be a tyrannical exercise. It can become exactly the form of tyranny that Walzer eschews. If every person has a right in community, with others of his own choosing, to his own state, someone somewhere is going to be deprived of the right to community of his choice. This is especially so where community rights are linked with territorial rights, as is often the case. Not everyone can seek membership to a community and not everyone can seek admission to a territory because territory is scarce and resources are limited. Moreover, why should a people who arrived first on a territory have the right to exclude others if there is enough resources and territory to go around? Dummett rejects the argument that 'every nation deserves to inhabit a state exclusively reserved for it. This was an absurdity from its very introduction; for we have no way of saying what constitutes a nation'. For him, 'the principle of national self-determination is circular: if we recognize a group of people as forming a nation according to whether it has a territory it can call its own, the principle that a group is entitled to belong to a separate state if it constitutes a nation is no guide at all'.[48]

Since this so-called ethnic principle of self determination is so difficult to define and even more difficult to implement without causing grave injustice to another, it is unsurprising that it has never been seriously considered by the international community to be the sole, or even the primary, factor in assessing claims to statehood.[49] If ethnic claims to a bounded community, to the exclusion of others, is given full vent then, in words of Hannum, as frontiers are shifted and new populations move into new territories, 'a new age of intolerance is more likely to follow than is an era of mutual respect and tolerance for all'.[50] This is because, as Ernest Gellner, has explained:

> Some people romanticize their real or supposed ancestral community, and at the same time oppose ethnic prejudice and wish to be fair to everyone. But you can't really have it both ways. The cosy old community *was* ethnocentric, and if you wish

to love and perpetuate it as it truly was, prejudice against outsiders must be part of the romantic package-deal. The trouble about Nazis was that they were only too consistent on this point.[51]

As Gellner himself recognizes, in the late 20th century, the identification of a culture by a people has paradoxically today assumed a powerful significance that could augur badly for the future. Gellner's words are worth stating at length:

[M]odern society [is] literate, mobile, formally equal with a merely fluid, continuous, so to speak atomized inequality, and with this shared, homogenous, literacy-carried, and school-inculcated culture. It could hardly be more sharply contrasted with a traditional society, within which literacy was a minority and specialized accomplishment, and where stable hierarchy, rather than mobility was the norm, and culture was diversified and discontinous, and in the main transmitted by local social groups rather than by special and centrally supervised educational agencies. In such an environment, a man's culture, the idiom within which he was trained and within which he is effectively employable, is his most precious possession, the real entrance-guard to full citizenship and human dignity to social participation ... The wrong and alien culture becomes menacing. Culture, like prose, becomes visible, and a source of pride and pleasure to boot. The age of nationalism is born.[52]

It is certainly right, in the words of Roger Nett, that 'nationalism [is] the dominant and perhaps most effective institution of our time'. Yet, as he argues:

One certain benefit is that a system of open migration would further remove the unrealistic ideas that people have about others and enable their governments to focus more on real rather than imagined problems of human intention and welfare. Once the pain of giving up a bunker/siege mentality subsided in the privileged nations, a number of beneficial effects could be expected to ensue. People in more ordinary circumstances would discover or rediscover that humans on the surface of the earth are indeed one species not too different from themselves. As generations with hardened attitudes died out, new generations would soon come to feel that the right to movement about the surface of the earth is normal and beneficial. The incentive for war could possibly be greatly lowered.[53]

It remains deeply ironic, therefore, that culture and community are to be used as tools of discrimination in deciding membership of a society. If anything, all the indications are that states should adopt measures to avoid cultural discrimination. Walzer arguably fails to take full account of this. Monolithic cultural communities are rare to find today for as Hannum explains:

There are few, if any, nation-states in the world whose population reflects an entirely homogenous ethnic, cultural community to the exclusion of all others ... the search for homogeneity may, in fact, be more likely to lead to repression and human rights violations than to promote the tolerance and plurality which many would claim to be essential values in the twentieth century and beyond. As an artificial legal creation, the state continues to serve a purpose as the primary interlocuteur among those who possess organized military power in the world.[54]

Walzer, nevertheless, remains emphatic that '[t]he citizens are free, of course, to set up a club, make membership as exclusive as they like, write a constitution, and govern one another'. The only restriction on this right is that 'they can't claim territorial jurisdiction and rule over the people with whom they share the territory' since this would be 'a form of tyranny'.[55] Yet, the freedom to deny membership to others less fortunate, even in cases where one does not exercise dominion over them, purely on the basis of community is surely open to question. The implications for humanity and for the international order are clear. Humanity will remain divided between 'Us' and 'Them' and the international order will remain unstable as those who are excluded will fight to partake in the goods of life. Santos denounces Walzer's 'sophisticated defence of liberal political territoriality' as 'a politics that in fact excludes the great of the world population from the goods that Walzer's national community is capable of delivering'.[56]

Earlier, we saw the argument of Ruth Rubio-Marin that even for the 'liberal democracy' of individual Western countries 'to remain alive' there had to be a solid commitment to the democratic concept of civic equality.[57] The existence of liberal democracy, with its liberal constitutional order, depends on inclusiveness. In her words, 'fairness considerations may actually undermine the legitimacy of the exclusion of immigrants'.[58] Thus, any derogation from inclusiveness damages and undermines the principle of civic equality without which liberal democracy would cease to exist. Dummett goes further. He suggests that inclusiveness is also critically relevant to the enduring stability of the international order:

> The ever widening gulf between rich countries and poor countries presents the gravest problems facing the world at the beginning of the twenty-first century. Closing that gulf is the most urgent necessity that presses upon us; failure to achieve this not only maintains gross injustice, but threatens the stability of the world.[59]

Writing at the turn of the twentieth century, Michael Dummett points out the sheer inanity of discriminatory practices as well as their potentially harmful effects for a world that is both mobile and cosmopolitan:

> The world at the turn of the twentieth century is one in which there has long been no possibility of crossing any, but a very few, frontiers unhindered, but in which travel is swifter and easier than ever before, and there are manifold calamities – persecution, violence, war, hunger – pressing people to flee the lands in which they are living. We can therefore say with assurance that, in the world as it now is, and as it will doubtless be for many centuries yet, no state ought to take race, religion or language as essential to its identity. If it does, it will inevitably find living within its borders minorities not of the favoured one, speaking languages different from the majority tongue. These minorities will be liable to persecution or discrimination, whether by laws of the state or by the actions of those who belong to the dominant group ...[60]

In attacking the notion of 'identity', Dummett is emphatic that '[t]here is no country in today's world that does not have racial, religious or linguistic minorities; even if it lacked them, they would soon arrive'.[61] The irony is that these matters have been recognized by thoughtful and prescient officials for a long time. As long as a quarter of a century ago, the legal system of a leading contemporary liberal democracy had no difficulty in recognizing that the proposition that common law countries had an absolute right to exclude others was 'xenophobic'. The New Zealand Supreme Court observed that:

> the Royal prerogative to keep foreigners at bay has been superseded by the modern transportation and the mass population movements of the twentieth century.[62]

The legal right of a State to exclude people is often asserted as an expression of its sovereignty. As such, this concept needs to be analyzed here. Sovereignty implies absolute power. All power, however, is necessarily limited. State power cannot be described in terms of sovereignty. Sovereignty, indeed, is not a state of affairs. It is not a fact. It is simply a doctrine. As a doctrine, the primitive caricatures of Bodin, Hobbes and Austin, are now firmly discredited. At the beginning of the twenty-first century, sovereignty has never been weaker. Indeed, in an original and path-breaking work recently, Professor Dan Sarooshi has analyzed the various ways in which national powers are being conferred, transferred or delegated to international organizations, such as the United Nations, the World Trade Organization, and the European Union, making the doctrine of sovereignty questionable today.[63] The attacks on Afghanistan and Iraq by coalition forces to root out terrorism took place notwithstanding the doctrine of state sovereignty. So, why do states still rely on it? As a doctrine, sovereignty allows political activists to advance claims that further their political objectives.[64] Its history provides the key to its nature. Sovereignty had its origins in Europe during the political developments of the Middle Ages. At that time, the Pope was supreme in spiritual matters. The Emperor supreme in temporal matters. At first, the concept could not flourish because sovereignty was shared and divided. In the sixteenth century, however, individual states challenged the authority of the Pope and the Emperor and asserted 'independence from their supremacy in spiritual and temporal matters'.[65] It is in this context that sovereignty emerged as being seen as the supreme authority in an independent political society that was both indivisible and illimitable. Yet, the doctrine was fictitious from the start. Sovereignty is limited externally by the possibility of general resistance. Internally, it is limited by the very nature of power itself. Today sovereignty 'cannot be either the basis or the source of the law of nations'.[66] It is simply a term used to refer to the institutionalized independence of states who are subject to international law.[67] As applied to issues of migration and freedom of movement, sovereignty is both undefined and undefinable,[68] particularly in an era of mass movement and globalization. In fact, Deng has redefined sovereignty as 'responsibility' recently. As he states:

> I approach sovereignty not as a negative concept by which states barricade them-
> selves against international scrutiny and involvment, but rather as a positive
> concept entailing responsibility for the protection and general welfare of the citizens
> and those falling under state jurisdiction.[69]

Thus, the notion that a state may exclude all aliens is no more than a maxim.
It lacks concrete justification. The philosophical justification is the sovereign's
inherent powers to determine all activity within its territorial jurisdiction.
Sometimes the notion is reformulated, as Michael Walzer and the communitarians do, on the basis of an autonomous, communal self-determination of a
people to choose all other members of a national polity. These justifications,
whether philosophical or otherwise, do not bear closer scrutiny.

First, Vattel had suggested that a state has 'inherent powers' to take all
necessary measures, for its self-preservation, provided that these do not offend
against the laws of nature.[70] States often use this principle to act contrary to
international law so as to 'preserve its independence, and give security against
foreign aggression and encroachment' as a matter of its 'highest duty'.[71] However, if the self preservation of the state is not at stake, then the concept of
inherent powers is redundant in international law. In any event, the territorial-
ist presumption is of dubious validity in the global world. As Chief Justice
Marshall said in the US Supreme Court, 'The world being composed of distinct
sovereignties, possessing equal rights and equal independence, whose mutual
benefit is promoted by intercourse with each other and by an interchange of
those good offices which humanity dictates' sovereign states 'have consented
to a relaxation in practice … of that absolute and complete jurisdiction within
their respective territories which sovereignty confers'.[72] The concept of a
sovereign's inherent powers is, moreover, dangerous in the globalized community for it can easily become a function of brute force by a state if it is used
in circumstances other than a sovereign's self preservation or necessity.

Second, sovereignty which 'is described as a supreme and independent
authority of states over all persons and things in that territory' is no less easy
to dispose of today as a sole basis for the determination of the admission and
expulsion of aliens, even though it is 'very deeply rooted' in 'national sentiment and in the psychology of people'.[73] Sovereignty has served as a source
of major confusion in international law and it is high time that homage ceased
to be paid to it in the globalized world. It has been said that:

> [T]he notion that the validity of international law raises some peculiar problem
> arises from the confusion which the doctrine of sovereignty has introduced into
> international legal theory. Even when we do not believe in the absoluteness of state
> sovereignty we have allowed ourselves to be persuaded that the fact of their sov-
> ereignty makes it necessary to look for some specific quality, not to be found in
> other kinds of law, in the law to which states are subject.[74]

Hence, whilst it is possible to say in one breath that when it comes to questions
of immigration and nationality '[i]t is still common to find expressed the view
that such matters are for the local state alone to decide, in the plenitude of its
sovereignty',[75] in the next breath it becomes necessary to acknowledge that

'it is practically impossible to define sovereignty in isolation from any particular context'.[76]

Even outside the field of international relations, sovereignty has been contested for a very long time. For example, Harold Laski[77] regarded sovereignty as a legal fiction. He was deeply concerned with the legitimacy of the claims made upon the citizen by the State and, therefore, viewed political obligation as a moral problem. Laski could see no moral superiority in the claims of the State to regulate conduct and enforce obedience. He regarded all society, and political authority along with it, as necessarily federative in principle. Absolute sovereignty is a dream and a delusion of certain power holders. Thus there is a case for saying that the State by its very nature is federative and separate and that sovereignty is simply juxtaposed on what is actually a conglomeration of interests that we call the State. This is clear from Maitland's constitutional history. It is not sovereignty but pluralism that is of contemporary relevance today. Legal discourse must take that into account and ignores it at its peril. Pluralism addresses contemporary debates on the nature and future of democratic government and it adds an important missing ingredient to this debate. Pluralism is not as fashionable as it once was. It reached its height in the 1920s in Britain. In the 1920s, even the Fabian activists, Sidney and Beatrice Webb adopted it. Pluralism's decline was then rapid and dramatic, as was that of guild socialism as a political movement. By the late 1920s, pluralism's influence had declined to university teaching, to critical asides, and to footnotes in other people's books, and the leading pluralists were either already dead, in the case of Figgis (in 1919), or had abandoned pluralist propositions more or less explicitly, like Cole and Laski. The fact is that the theories of Bodin, Hobbes, and Austin have long been obsolete and their conceptions of the sovereign state are now primitive caricatures.

All power is necessarily limited simply by the very means of its exercise. Sovereignty is not a mere description of State power. Sovereignty is not, and never has been, a state of affairs. Sovereignty is less a fact than a doctrine. It is a politically highly consequential doctrine, if political activists subscribe to it and if it is not replaced by other doctrines that enable different political consequences to predominate. Sovereignty is a doctrine that allows political activists to advance claims and to utilize these claims to further their political objectives. There are three reasons why sovereignty is a problem. Firstly, it is undermined by autonomous associations. Secondly, the doctrine of sovereignty treats the State as if it were a single agent, with a single will, like an absolute monarch. However, the State is a complex amalgam of agencies and persons of different objectives and means of position. The notion of a single legitimate 'will' is central to the doctrine of sovereignty but there is no such will in society. And thirdly, a State in which all individuals are equally citizens and in which there is nothing between them and the State power, and in which they are obliged to obey the commands of their power, would be tyrannical to the point of intolerability were the power not subjected to some legitimation.

Communitarians often imply that they have the right to exclude individuals from their membership. The sovereign right to do so may well prevent the normal functioning and development of international law and organization. This is because it presents itself as 'the internal law of the state, namely, as the highest underived power' of the State.[78] This cannot be right because sovereignty is in reality a 'bundle of competences conferred by international law' itself making it 'essentially a relative notion' so that 'its content depends on the stage of development of international law'.[79]

Third, sometimes the doctrine of exclusive domestic jurisdiction is used today to re-assert the sovereign's inherent power to exclude aliens. But this doctrine too, suffers from the same inherent limitations. In fact, this doctrine has been described as 'one of the last refuges of the dogma of absolute sovereignty'.[80] The concept is worth referring to because it was precisely the concern over sovereign control of immigration matters that led to the permanent interposition of this concept under article 15(8) of the Covenant of the League of Nations.[81] It is now Article 2(7) of the *Charter of the United Nations 1948*.[82] However, the concept is still difficult because it is still international law that determines what lies within the domain of domestic jurisdiction.[83] Whereas it is still the case that under the current state of international law, admission of an alien to state remains within the domestic jurisdiction of the state, what is domestic jurisdiction in any given case, is still worth considering. As Lawrence Preuss has observed, 'Matters of domestic jurisdiction do not qualify themselves' because ultimately, '[t]heir boundaries are traced by international law' which has the jurisdiction to decide whether a matter has 'entered the domain guaranteed *au fond* by international law'[84] so as to limit domestic competence. There is a practical application of this limitation in Article 55 of the *Charter* which states that in order to create 'conditions of stability and well being which are necessary for peaceful and friendly relations among nations' the United Nations shall promise 'universal respect for and observance of human rights and fundamental freedoms for all without distinction as to race, sex, language or religion'.[85] Article 56 underpins this commitment by adding that 'all members pledge themselves to take joint *and separate action*, in co-operation with the organization, for the achievement of the purposes set forth in Article 55'. It seems that the normative commitment to upholding human rights has fundamentally and irrevocably changed doctrine of domestic jurisdiction. Thus, Professor Rosalyn Higgins has argued that:

> the claim ... human-rights questions cannot be essentially within the domestic jurisdiction ... seems justified, for Articles 55 and 56 impose specific legal obligations by which all states are bound, Article 2(7) nothwithstanding.[86]

Indeed, in 1955 the International Court of Justice rejected the determination of nationality as a basis for diplomatic protection, from the reserve domain of domestic jurisdiction of states. Whereas it may be uncertain to what extent the question of alien admission or exclusion is solely within the reserve domain of states under the present condition of international law, there should be no doubt that the racial, ethnic and cultural distinctions for the determination of these questions, are outlawed by international law. This is particularly so where this has an impact on the global order. Even three quarters of a century ago Brierly wrote that even questions of immigration, tariffs, and naturalization can 'shade off into others of a more contentious kind, such as the treatment of racial or linguistic or religious minorities, [and] misgovernment producing repercussions in other states'.[87]

What we can clearly say, therefore, is that whereas all states operate controlled borders, and have the right so to do under international law, there are certain limitations on what states can do. State action must be undertaken on the basis of universal respect for all human beings and without distinction as to race, sex, language or religion. State action also must not endanger conditions of stability and well being for peaceful and friendly relations among nations. Whether or not this implies a right to acquire, seek, and be granted entry, can only be determined in particular cases with due regard to these principles and the principles of international public morality. We should not, however, persist in dealing with these issues in a doctrinaire and dogmatic way. If we do so that will inevitably inhibit the normal processes of policy-making in the context of a changing world. Thus, it was the UN former Secretary-General Boutros-Ghali who noted in his *Agenda for Peace*, 'the time of absolute and exclusive sovereignty … has passed; its theory was never matched by its reality'.[88] When President Bush Sr attacked Iraq in 1990 for invading Kuwait the UN had never before approved the use of force to counter an invasion against a sovereign state. A further challenge to the post-second-world war order was posed by the Nato attack on Yugoslavia in 1999, and the US and UK attack on Iraq in 2003. Both were carried out without UN support. Both were justified, to a greater or lesser degree, as humanitarian wars. Both were of dubious legality. In the case of the attack on Yugoslavia, this was outside Nato's own remit as a defensive organization. Indeed, its mission statement was subsequently rewritten to allow for such actions. In the case of the attack on Iraq, there was no evidence of the possession of weapons of mass destruction, to justify the attack. Yet, in both cases, the ultimate goal of such intervention was regime change for a more stable and secure world. There is, of course, no evidence at all that such violent intervention has led to a stable and peaceful society in either of those countries, or in the world at large for that matter. Quite the contrary, in fact. In the case of Yugoslavia, half the Kosovan Serb population, numbering about 100,000 were driven out by the bombing, more than 200,000 minority populations, including the Roma, are now estimated to have left the country, and the most pro-western politician in the country, the Serbian Prime Minister Zorean Djindjic, was assassinated.[89]

Yet, like it or not, what remains clear from this challenge to the post Cold-War Order is that the framework of international law has changed. The chief casualty is state sovereignty. Intervention on allegedly humanitarian grounds can now take place even if the aggressor is not threatened by attack. Like it or not, there is an increased use today of the language of human rights as basis for legal action and inaction. If we ignore this change, we will obscure the realities of the current international order, and the ever-increasing interdependency in international relations, because 'sovereignty today … is an extraordinarily flexible, manipulative concept'.[90] In the face of these changes, rigid dogmatism and a failure to take human rights seriously will strain, and lead to the collapse of, the global order whose preservation is the *raison d'etre* of international law. In the circumstances, legal arguments can be deployed to expand the right to migrate in this changing global order. For example, we have so far noted the following legal rights: there is a right to seek refuge from persecution; there is a right to free movement (but no right to migrate indefinitely); and there is, technically speaking, the sovereign right in states to restrict entry. However, the ICESCR (unlike the ICCPR and the ECHR) provides for the right to work in a way that is not limited to those within the jurisdiction,[91] whereas the ICCPR makes a distinction between those lawfully and unlawfully within the territory.[92] Inasmuch as most migrants to the West – whether voluntary or involuntary – want sooner or later to work the right to free movement can best and most easily be developed on the basis of a legal right to work. This can then pave the way to a more permanent immigration.

There is, however, one argument in the modern world that is being used increasingly to restrict entry of new immigrants. This is found in Michael Walzer's communitarian approach. He raises the compelling and pressing question of self-determination. As he states, 'communal independence' goes to the 'deepest meaning of self-determination' without which there could be no enduring community. He is assisted in this by Dummett who recognizes that there is one right that any community has: 'The right is one possessed by groups united by race, religion, language or culture: such groups have a right not to be submerged' adding, however, that it has an 'extremely limited application'.[93]

Dummett asserts this right because:

> We each need to be able to feel at home somewhere; not just in some locality, but within the institutions and among the groups of those we are bound to by common endeavours and concerns.[94]

Restrictions of new immigrants can be contemplated because 'cultures are fragile: they can be dissipated by the impact of other cultures'.[95] For Dummett, 'That is why it is an injustice that immigration should ever be allowed to a size that threatens the indigenous population with being submerged' but adding that 'It is very seldom that there is a genuine danger of this'. Dummett gives two clear examples where this may be so. One example is where unrestricted immigration of its own people is allowed 'under a colonial regime indifferent to the wishes of the inhabitants of a territory it governs'. Another is 'when a government is determined to obliterate a minority, and sets about it ... by systematically settling large numbers in its territory' and of this, the 'examples from recent times are East Timor and Tibet'.[96] Thus, although Dummett asserts freedom from cultural subjugation as a basis for immigration control, it is highly significant that the examples he gives are of a subjugated people who deserve every right to preservation of their own way of life. It is doubtful, in my opinion, if the principle can ever properly be extended to people who are in a dominant position without leading to precisely the sort of cultural discrimination that Dummett so rightly rejects. Certainly, it is not clear from Dummett's analysis, in my view, as to how such a discriminatory policy can be carried out without being morally offensive.

One distinguished writer has written about Europe's recent immigration experience in terms that 'there is a pervasive belief that the cultural and racial heterogeneity which accompanies immigration jeopardizes European identity and solidarity'.[97] Spellman himself has reminded us that 'Talk of an emerging 'global village' may be difficult to accept in light of regional conflicts which have claimed the lives of over 25 million people since the end of the Second World War'.[98] Yet, this is all the more reason why cultural discrimination should be staunchly resisted.

What is worse is that cultural discrimination affects the processing of genuine immigration and asylum cases. Mary Coussey, during her recent investigation of the work of immigration officers at Heathrow, Gatwick and Stansted airports, did not find that a passenger's colour triggered further checks by immigration officers. What she did find was 'case-hardened officials' who had 'a cynical attitude towards some nationals'. In deciding upon refusals, case officials would use 'more subjective tests' of behaviour and dress. They would focus on subtle mistakes in dress such as wearing base-ball caps in too young a manner. She reported that 'some immigration officers said to me that they could distinguish a Roma by appearance, especially because of the style of dress' and that this was informally known as 'white shoes syndrome'. As a result, Ms Coussey, recommended that the government must do more to dispel the emotive and hostile climate about asylum seekers. She warned that this affects not only asylum caseworkers but also people in a position to practice racial discrimination.[99]

It does not need reiterating that such practices offend against the principle of the equal moral worth of all human beings enshrined in such legally binding instruments as the ECHR, ICCPR and CERD (including the non-binding seminal instrument, the UDHR). The latter, for example, is one of the most widely ratified instruments in the field of human rights and is in a broad sense the most important treaty regarding discrimination (even though it has not been ratified by the United Kingdom on grounds of national security).[100] Even the ICCPR is meant to be applied more robustly to protect the rights of aliens than it currently has been. Under a 1986 General Comment there was criticism that State Parties had failed to recognize that 'the rights in the Covenant [applied] to "all individuals within its territory and subject to its jurisdiction"',[101] which suggests that once an applicant for entry arrives in the jurisdiction he or she will not be denied the benefits of the Covenant. The guarantee of Covenant rights 'applies to aliens and citizens alike' as expressly provided for in the ICPPR, except where it is 'expressly' stated not to apply to aliens.[102] Accordingly, the General Comment re-affirmed the principle that '[T]he Covenant gives aliens all the protection regarding rights guaranteed therein, and its requirements should be observed by States parties in their legislation and in practice as appropriate'.[103] It is remarkable that Ms Coussey's research has needed to remind the government that discriminatory practices are wrong and unlawful. International law already outlaws such practices. A recent work by Matthew Gibney has focused on the ethics of asylum by drawing upon political theory and weaving it with a detailed account of the asylum policies of four leading western countries, before concluding that liberal states can only justifiable implement morally defensible responses to refugees.[104]

What is needed today is a not just the legal affirmation of equality and non-discrimination norms. What is needed is a society's legal commitment to cultural diversity. It is not enough to stipulate that:

> Immigration Officers, Entry Clearance Officers and all staff of the Home Office Immigration and Nationality [Directorate] will carry out their duties without regard to the race, colour or religion of persons seeking to enter or remain in the United Kingdom.[105]

A government official who carries out his duties 'without regard to the race, colour or religion' of applicants before him, is still likely to offend against the rights of cultural minorities if there is no obligation on him to show a commitment to culturally diverse rights. Formally neutral, and generally applicable, rules will only catch express breaches of non-discrimination or equality principles of law. They will not catch violations of cultural rights that do not amount to an express breach of the law. There is, therefore, necessarily a dimension to cultural rights that is not addressed by legally neutral law that is applied to communities that are necessarily diverse and different form the host community.

At a broader level, officials need to be not only culturally cognizant, in a culturally diverse and interdependent world, but they also need to be culturally competent, so that discrimination in the decision-making and policy-making process, is avoided.[106] Culturally cognizant systems recognize their weaknesses in serving minorities and attempt to improve their services to specific populations by hiring minority staff, initiating training for their workers on cultural sensitivity, and entering into needs assessments concerning minority communities. Culturally competent agencies are characterized by acceptance and respect for difference, continuing self-assessment regarding culture, careful attention tot he dynamics of difference, continuous expansion of cultural knowledge and resources, and a variety of adaptations to service models in order to meet the needs of minority populations better. Such agencies view minority groups as being distinctly different from one another and as having numerous subgroups, each with important cultural characteristics.[107] Cultural cognizance and competence can be more easily learnt and applied if government and officials recognize that when it comes to immigration 'the strength of the migratory impulse has doubtless enhanced the creation of culturally diverse societies in a number of developed countries'[108] which has been a laudable aim of government policy in recent years.

Communities must learn, therefore, to legislate against cultural discrimination. Communities must even learn to legislate to promote cultural diversity.[109] How a community does this depends very much upon its history, its cultural heritage, and its perception of its future interests. Yet, it is significant that leading liberal societies have managed to make this commitment to varying degrees. The Canadian Charter of Rights and Freedoms 1982 affirms that 'Every individual is equal before and under the law and has the right to the equal protection and equal benefit of the law without discrimination, and in particular, without discrimination based on race, national or ethnic origin, colour, religion' and various other grounds.[110] It expressly recognizes the existence of affirmative action programs for 'the amelioration of conditions of disadvantages groups including those that are disadvantaged because of race, national or ethnic origin, colour religion [and] sex'.[111] It is declared that:

> [t]he guarantee in this Charter shall not be construed so as to abrogate ... from any aboriginal ... or other rights nor freedoms that pertain to the aboriginal peoples of Canada ... .[112]

A stronger statement of principle is to be found in the New Zealand Bill of Rights 1990 which sets out to 'affirm, protect, and promote human rights and fundamental freedoms'[113] by protecting the rights of minorities, so that:

> A person who belongs to an ethnic, religious, or linguistic minority in New Zealand shall not be denied the right, in community with other members of that minority, to enjoy the culture, to profess and practice the religion, or to use the language, of that minority.[114]

But perhaps the strongest statement is to be found in the *Constitution of the Republic of South Africa 1996* which, reflecting upon its own racist past, affirms its 'Founding Provisions' as 'Human dignity, the achievement of equality and the advancement of human rights and freedoms' as well as 'Non-racialism and non-sexism'. The Constitution protects the right of 'Cultural, religious and linguistic communities' to exist and to develop by stipulating that:

> Persons belonging to a cultural, religious or linguistic community may not be denied the right, with other members of that community (a) to enjoy their culture, practice their religion and use their language; and (b) to form, join and maintain cultural, religious and linguistic associations and other organs of civil society.[115]

Yet, the most remarkable commitment to cultural rights comes, not from a State's own domestic affirmation of its fundamental rights, but from a supranational body, namely, the European Union's Charter of Fundamental Rights of the European Union 2000.[116] The Preamble of the Charter states that 'The peoples of Europe ... are resolved to share a peaceful future based on common values' and recognize that 'the Union is founded on the indivisible, universal values of human dignity, freedom, equality and solidarity' which 'Union contributes to the preservation and to the development of these common values while respecting the diversity of the cultures and traditions of the peoples of Europe as well as the national identities of the Member States ...'. It then states that 'To this end, it is necessary to strengthen the protection of fundamental rights in the light of changes in society, social progress and scientific and technological developments ...'. At the outset, there is an affirmation of what must be the ultimate right. The Charter states that 'Human dignity is inviolable. It must be respected and protected'.[117] The Charter affirms the traditional equality and non-discrimination norms by stating that 'Any discrimination based on any ground such as sex, race, colour, ethnic or social origin' etc. 'shall be prohibited'.[118] However, it then goes further and confirms a wider commitment so that 'The Union shall respect cultural, religious and linguistic diversity'.[119]

What is remarkable, however, in a instrument that has been criticized for giving 'the impression that the EU regards itself and its members as worthy of different treatment from the remaining members of the Council of Europe, a club of 'well-off' democracies',[120] is that the Charter gives the most resounding affirmation to the right to asylum into the countries of the European Union:

> The right to asylum shall be guaranteed with due respect for the rules of the Geneva Convention of 28 July 1951 and the Protocol of 31 January 1967 relating to the status of refugees and in accordance with the Treaty establishing the European Community.[121]

In so stating the Charter has squared the circle of refugee rights by ensuring, not only that there is the right to *seek* asylum as the *Universal Declaration of Human Rights* has stipulated, but the right to be 'guaranteed' asylum in the territories of the European Union, subject to the requirements of the Geneva Convention. The Charter demonstrates that it is possible for a human rights instrument for a particular people – in this case the 'peoples of Europe' – to guarantee rights for those who are not amongst them. It remains true that the Charter is non-binding. It is also subject tot he 1950 Convention that limits eligibility for asylum status. Further, the various Directives on definition and procedure firmly relocate decision-making and protection to areas beyond the EU borders. Yet, the statement of principle in law that has been articulated here is highly significant. What is needed now is for domestic human rights instruments to follow suit.

The communitarian assumptions of current immigration control cannot be endorsed for at least four reasons. First, we cannot, given the principle of preferential discrimination based on inherited characteristics of birth and geography, endorse the idea that some people are more entitled to have access and residence in a territory because of ethnic and cultural affinities than others, notwithstanding the fact that there is, in law, no right to choose a nationality. But then, nationality is a concept of law and what we are talking about here is membership of a community. Second, we cannot endorse the idea that restrictions can be introduced against some classes of immigrants because they reduce the current well-being of citizens, given the priority in roles of liberty, which must apply to everyone who is morally equal, everywhere. Third, we cannot endorse the commonly held belief that the effect on the culture and history of a society is an important criterion in determining the eligibility for entry of one class of persons as against the other, given the fact that this is not a relevant moral consideration. Fourth, we cannot ignore moral arguments in law. International law in particular must take cognizance of principles of international morality if it is to command respect and have any efficacy. Witness the ruling in the *East African Asians Case* by the European Commission that the European Convention on Human Rights, like the Convention on Genocide, has a humanitarian character whose object was to 'safeguard the very existence of certain human groups' and to 'endorse the most elementary principles of morality'.[122]

These principles suggest to us that if people want to sign the social contract and become full contributing members of a society, they should, where ever possible, be permitted to do so, because this is compatible with the idea of equal moral worth of all individuals. The social contract between the individual and his chosen society at large will make that individual subject to the same rights and obligations, without prejudice or preference, to which the entire community is subject. If the individual's membership of such a community is shown, however, on the evidence to be detrimental, such as on grounds of public health, public security, and public order, then the individual may be deprived of the right to enter into such a contract. However, such a withdrawal of membership must be subject to exacting standards in a liberal society.

NOTES

1   C.J. Harvey, 'Talking about Refugee Law', *JRS* (vol. 12, No.2, 1999) pp.101–33, at p.101, although it is noteworthy that in so stating the Professor Harvey is essentially concerned about the interpretation of international refugee law in the treaties.
2   At p.102.
3   W.M. Spellman, *The Global Community* (Sutton Publishing Limited, 2002) at p.1.
4   At p.2.
5   At p.3.
6   At pp.3–4.
7   At p.4.
8   At pp.4–5.
9   Douglas S. Massey, *et al.*, *Worlds in Motion: Understanding International Migration at the end of the Millennium* (Oxford, 1998).
10   See Spellman, at p.5.
11   See Spellman, at p.6.
12   See Spellman, at p.6.
13   See Spellman, at p.6.
14   See Spellman, at p.7.
15   See Massey *et al.*, *Worlds in Motion*, at pp.1–2.
16   See Spellman at p.7.
17   Robert Winder, 'A place of greater safety', *New Statesman*, 7th April 2003, at p.50.
18   Claire Palley, *The United Kingdom and Human Rights* (London, 1991), at p.134.
19   Saskia Sassen, *Guests and Aliens* (New Press, 1999).
20   See Fr. Patrick Lynch, 'Desperate Refugees who Merely Want to Work', *The Independent*, 15th May 2003, at p.19.

21   *Kent vs. Dulles*, 357 U.S. 116, 78 S. Ct. 1113, 2 L. Ed. 2d 1204 (1958) (emphases added).
22   Lawrence Tribe, *Constitutional Law*, 1383–84 (emphases added).
23   See *Apthekar vs. Secretary of State*, 378 U.S. 500, 519 (1964). This is the only case in which the US Supreme Court invalidated on a constitutional basis a congressionally imposed restriction that burdened the right to travel.
24   378 US 500 (emphases added) (1964).
25   Jeanne N. Woods, 'Travel That Talks: Towards First Amendment Protection of Freedom of Movement', *George Washington Law Review* (Vol.65, 1996) pp.106–29, at p.108.
26   *Haig vs. Agee*, 453 US 280, 319 (1981).
27   Article 19 of the ICCPR protects, *inter alia*, the right 'to seek, receive and impart information and ideas of all kinds regardless of frontiers'.
28   John Hart Ely, *Democracy and Distrust* (Harvard, 1980), 178–9 (emphases added).
29   Joseph Carens, 'Aliens and Citizens: The Case for Open Borders', *Review of Politics*, 47 (1987) 251.
30   Robert Nozick, *Anarchy, State and Utopia* (Oxford; Basil Blackwell, 1974).
31   John Rawls, *A Theory of Justice* (Cambridge, Mass. Harvard Uni. Press, 1971).
32   Dummett, *op cit.*, at p.23.
33   Dummett, at p.24.
34   Dummett, at p.25.
35   Dummett, at p.27.
36   Mary Kaldor, 'Armageddon Myths', *New Statesman*, 26th May 2003, pp.48–9, at p.48.
37   In this respect, see also, David Jacobsen, *Rights Across Borders* (1996, Baltimore, John Hopkins University Press) where he argues that since World War II citizenship has been increasingly devalued as governments extend rights to foreign populations and how, in turn, international human rights law has become increasingly important.
38   Globalism may, however, end sooner than we think. In a chilling new book, *The Long Emergency* (Atlantic Books, 2005), James Howard Kunstler argues that 'Globalism as we know it will end when the cheap oil runs out'. His argument is that, 'It is no exaggeration to state that reliable supplies of cheap oil and natural gas underlie everything we identify as a benefit of modern life. All the necessities, comforts luxuries, and miracles of our time – central heating, air-conditioning, cars, airplanes, electric lighting, cheap clothing, recorded music, movies, supermarkets, power tools, hip replacement surgery, the national defences, you name it – owe their origins or continues existence in one way or another to cheap fossil fuels'. The problem, however, is that there is no immediate viable replacement for such fuels at present. As he explains, '[t]hese days, even people who ought to know better are wishing ardently that a smooth, seamless transition from fossil fuels to their putative replacements – hydrogen, solar power, whatever – lies just a few years ahead. This is dangerous fantasy. The true best-case scenario may be that it will take decades to develop some of these technologies – meaning that we can expect an extremely turbulent interval between the end of cheap oil and whatever comes next'. The problem for the West is that '[t]he western way of life – which is now virtually synonymous with suburbia – can only run on reliable supplies of dependably cheap oil and gas' and given that fossil fuel reserves 'tend to be concentrated in places where the native peoples don't like the west', we are in for a period that 'is certain to ignite chronic strife between nations contesting the remaining supplies. These resource wars have already begun.

There will be more of them'. See an edited extract from Kunstler's book, NS Essay, *New Statesman* (1st August 2005), pp.23–5, at p.23.

39 David Goodhart is the editor of the left of centre, *Prospect Magazine*. His essay challenged liberals to rethink their attitudes to diversity and the welfare state, and in so doing it provoked a bitter debate among progressive thinkers in Britain. His full essay was later published in *The Guardian* newspaper on Tuesday 24th February 2004: see, unlimited@guardianunlimited.co.uk.

40 See Simon Barnes, 'Good guy punching well above his weight in time of trouble', *The Times* 16th July 2005, where he writes, 'Good family, lovely people. And there was Amir's Dad, like a walking symbol of the Britain we want to live in – brown face above a union jack waistcoat, bursting with pride and anxiety for his son. No ambiguities: we were on the same side, all wanting the same thing'.

41 On 7th July 2005, four bombs exploded on London's public transport system killing over 50 people and injuring 700 people. Three of the bombers came from South Leeds and the fourth from Luton. All four were killed in the attacks on the capital. At the time, it was commented that this was 'the work of people brought up in our multi-racial society of which policy-makers were rightly proud. This is not just a challenge for government but for civic society too'. Yet, many of the victims themselves would 'have come from the Muslim community'. Similarly, many of the people involved in the rescue exercises and the medical teams, were Muslim.' Indeed, 'the Muslim Council of Britain announced plans to hold protest marches against the bombing in half a dozen large towns with large Muslim communities including London, Manchester, Birmingham, Bradford, and Leeds.' See, 'Challenge to Civic Society', *The Guardian*, 13th July 2005 (see the Leader), at p.23.

42 Walzer, Michael, *Spheres of Justice: A Defence of Pluralism and Equality* (Oxford, 1983), at p.32.

43 Walzer, at p.32.

44 Walzer, at pp.61–2.

45 Walzer, Michael, *Spheres of Justice: A Defence of Pluralism and Equality* (Oxford, 1983), at p.62.

46 Hurst Hannum, *Autonomy, Sovereignty, and Self Determination: The Accommodation of Conflicting Rights* (Rev. Ed. 1990).

47 Walker Connor, 'The Political Significance of Ethno-Nationalism Within Western Europe', in Abdul Said and Luiz R. Simmons (eds), *Ethnicity in an International Context* (New Brunswick, N.J.: Transaction Books, 1976), at 111–12.

48 Dummett, *op. cit.*, at pp.9–10.

49 Hurst Hannum, *loc.cit.*

50 Hurst Hannum, *op.cit.*, at 455.

51 Ernest Gellner, *Culture, Identity, and Politics* (CUP, 1987).

52 Ernest Gellner, *op.cit.*, at 15–16.

53 Roger Nett, ibid, at p.225.

54 Hurst Hannum, *supra.*, at 26.

55 Walzer, at p.62.

56 Santos, ibid., at p.235.

57 Ibid., at p.1.

58 Ibid., at p.9.

59 Dummett, *op cit* at p.25.

60 Dummett, at p.6.

61 Dummett, at p.6.

62 [1978] 2 N.Z.L.R at 568. It also observed that there was a long custom of alien

admissions under the New Zealand Immigrant Act, which made such a proposition untenable.

63   Dan Sarooshi, *International Organisations and Their Exercise of Sovereign Powers* (OUP, Oxford Monographs in International Law, 2005).

64   Satvinder Juss, 'Abdandoning Vires-Based review', *The King's College Law Journal* (Vol. 13, Part 2, 2002), pp.239–53, at pp.244–5.

65   M.S. Rajan, *United Nations and Domestic Jurisdiction* (2nd edn., 1961), at pp.1–2.

66   Hersch Lauterpacht, *The Function of Law in the International Community* (London, 1933), at p.96.

67   *Customs Regime between Germany and Austria*, 1931 PCIJ, Ser. A/B, No. 41, at 57 (individual Opinion by Judge Anzilotti).

68   See C. Gordon and H. Rosenfeld, *Immigration Law and Procedure* (1978), at pp.2–16.

69   See Francis Madding Deng, 'The Global Challenge of Internal Displacement', *Journal of Law & Policy* (Vol. 5, 2001), p.144.

70   E. De Vattel, at pp.19–20.

71   *The Chinese Exclusion Case* 130. U.S. at 606.

72   *Schooner Exchange v. M'Faddon*, 11 U.S. (7 Cranch) 116, 136 (1812).

73   *The Corfu Channel Case*, [1949] ICJ Rep.1 (individual Opinion by Judge Alvarez), at p.43.

74   J. Brierly, *The Law of Nations* (6th edn. 1963) at p.54.

75   Guy S. Goodwin-Gill, *International Law and the Movement of Persons Between States* (1978), at pp.52–3.

76   Guy S. Goodwin-Gill, at p.51.

77   Who followed on from a group of distinguished legal pluralists at the London School of Economics, such as J.H. Cole, J.N. Figgis.

78   See L. Oppenheim, *International Law* (8th Edn. 1955), at pp.122–3.

79   J.L. Kunz, 'The Nottebohm Judgment', 54 *AJIL.* (1960) 536 at p.545. It is for this reason that, even 50 years ago, the Permanent Court of Justice, declared that the concept of sovereignty has today 'become an institution, an international social function of a psychological character which has to be exercised in accordance with a new international law'. In consequence, leading international lawyers have been led to observe that the essential question for international law is 'what is the maximum area of autonomy which the rules allow to states'.

80   M.S. Rajan, at p.1. Quoting Eduard Hambro.

81   Article 15(8) reads as follows: 'If the dispute between the parties is claimed by one of them, and is found by the Council to arise out of a matter which by international law is solely within the domestic jurisdiction of the party, the Council may in any case under this article refer the dispute to the Assembly'. See also, Helen Hart Jones, 'Domestic Jurisdiction – From the Covenant to the Charter', 46 *ILL. L. Rev.* (1951–52) p.219 at p.219. See also, C.H.M. Waldock, 'The Plea of Domestic Jurisdiction Before International Legal Tribunals', 31 *Brit. Y.B. Int'l L.* (1954), p.96, at p.100.

82   Article 2(7) reads: 'Nothing contained in the present Charter shall authorize the United Nations to intervene in matters which are essentially within the domestic jurisdiction of any State or shall require the members to submit such matters to settlement under the present Charter …'.

83   Waldock asserts that '[t]he criterion of the scope of the reserved domain under the Charter must still be found in international law and the only relevant inquiry … is whether international law contains any criterion determining the matters which are in essence matters of domestic jurisdiction'. See, Waldock, at p.129.

84 L. Preuss, 'The International Court of Justice, the Senate, and Matters of Domestic Jurisdiction', 40 *AJIL*. (1946) p.720 at pp.726–7.
85 The full text of Article 55 reads as follows:

> With a view to the creation of conditions of stability and well being which are necessary for peaceful and friendly relations among nations based on respect for the principle of equal rights and self-determination of peoples, the UN shall promise: higher standards of living , full employment , and conditions of economic and social progress and development; solutions of international, economic, social, health and related problems; and international cultural and educational co-operation; and universal respect for and observance of human rights and fundamental freedoms for all without distinction as to race, sex, language or religion.

86 Rosalyn Higgins, *The Development of International Law through the Political Organs of the United States* (1963), at p.128. Also see, Ian Brownlie, *Principles of Public International Law* (4th edn. 1990), at p.552.
87 J.L. Brierly, 'Matters of Domestic Jurisdiction', 6 *Brit. Y.B. Int'l L*. (1925), p.8, at p.14.
88 *An Agenda for Peace*, Report of the Secretary-General to the Security Council, UN Doc. A/47/277-S/24111 (1992), para.17.
89 Kate Hudson, *Breaking the South Slav Dream: The Rise and Fall of Yugoslavia*; also see her, 'A Pattern of aggression', *The Guardian*, 14th August 2003, at p.23.
90 Richard B. Lillich, 'Sovereignty and Humanity: Can They Converge?', in Atle Grahl-Madsen and Jiri Doman (eds), *The Spirit of Uppsala* (Berlin and New York: De Gruyter, 1984), at 413.
91 Article 6 reads:

> The States Parties to the present Covenant recognize the right to work, which includes the right of everyone to the opportunity to gain his living by work which he freely chooses or accepts, and will take appropriate steps to safeguard this right.
>
> The steps to be taken by a State Party to the present Covenent to achieve the full realization of this right shall include technical and vocational guidance and training programmes, policies and techniques to achieve steady economic, social and cultural development and full and productive employment under conditions safeguarding fundamental political and economic freedoms to the individual.

92 Article 12(1) reads: Everyone lawfully within the territory of a State shall, within that territory, have the right to liberty of movement and freedom to choose his residence.
93 Dummett, at p.14.
94 Dummett, at p.18.
95 Dummett, at p.19.
96 Dummett, at p.20.
97 See James C. Hathaway, 'Harmonizing For Whom? The Devaluation of Refugee Protection in the Era of European Economic Integration', 26 *Cornell Int'l L.J.*, at p.720.
98 Spellman, at p.8.

99   Alan Travis, 'Clothes Test for Asylum Seekers', *The Guardian*, 9th July 2003, at p.6.
100 Discrimination is defined in the International Convention on the Elimination of all Forms of Discrimination 1969 as follows:

> '... any distinction, exclusion, restriction or preference based on race, colour descent, or natural or ethnic origin which has the purpose or effect of nullifying or impairing the recognizition, enjoyment or exercise, on an equal footing, of human rights and fundamental freedoms in the political, economic, social, cultural or any other field of public life'.

101 *International Covenant on Civil and Political Rights* (ICCPR), *General Comment on the Position of Aliens Under the Covenant*, 1986: see Article 1. General Comment 15(27) under Article 40, Paragraph 4, of the *International Covenant on Civil and Political Rights*, 'on the position of aliens under the Covenant', 9th April 1986. Article 1 reads:

> 'Reports from States parties often failed to take into account that each State party must ensure the rights in the Covenant to "all individuals within its territory and subject to its jurisdiction" (art 2(1)). In general, the rights set forth in the Covenant apply to everyone, irrespective of reciprocity, and irrespective of his or her nationality or statelessness' (emphasis added).

102 Article 2 of the General Comment read as follows:

> 'Thus, the general rule is that each one of the rights of the Covenant must be guaranteed without discrimination between citizens and aliens. Aliens receive the benefit of the general requirement of non-discrimination in respect of the rights guaranteed in the Covenant, as provided for in article 2 thereof. This guarantee applies to aliens and citizens alike. Exceptionally, some rights recognized in the Covenant are expressly applicable only to citizens (art. 25), while article 13 applies only to aliens. However, the Committee's experience in examining reports shows that in a number of countries other rights that aliens should enjoy under the Covenant are denied to them or are subject to limitations that cannot always be justified under the Covenant' (emphasis added).

103 Article 4 of the General Comment read as follows:

> 'The Committee considers that in their reports States parties should give attention to the position of aliens, both under their law and in actual practice. The Covenant gives aliens all the protection regarding rights guaranteed therein, and its requirements should be observed by States parties in their legislation and in practice as appropriate. The position of aliens would thus be considerably improved. States parties should ensure that the provisions of the Covenant and the rights under it are made known to aliens within their jurisdiction'.

104 Matthew Gibney, *The Ethics and Politics of Asylum* (CUP, 2004). The four countries chosen are Germany, the UK, the USA, and Australia.
105 See *Statement of Changes in Immigration Rules* (HC 395) at paragraph 2. These are departmental ministerial rules setting out the way in which the day-to-day ad-

ministration of immigration control is to be implemented in the United Kingdom.

106 See S. Juss, *Discretion and Deviation in the Administration of Immigration Control* (London, 1997), at p.5.

107 For a more detailed discussion see, Satvinder Juss, 'Cultural Competence and the Law of Mental Health', in Bhui and Olajide, *Mental Health Service Provision for a Multi-Cultural Society* (Saunders, London, 1999), at pp.102–17, at p.110–11. For an understanding of how the legal system should develop a theory of 'cultural jurisprudence' for the proper determination of due process rights of minority populations see, Satvinder Juss, *Discretion and Deviation in the Administration of Immigration Control* (Modern Legal Studies, Sweet & Maxwell, 1997), at pp.10–12.

108 Spellman, at p.8.

109 Consider, in particular, the development of 'Charter Rights' in Canada described by F.L. Morton and Rainer Knopff, *The Charter Revolution and the Court Party* (Broadview Press, Peterborough, Ontario, 2000).

110 Article 15(1) which comes under the heading of 'Equality Rights'.

111 Article 15(2).

112 Article 25.

113 Preamble, Para (a).

114 Article 20.

115 Section 33(1).

116 2000/C 364/01. See, P. Alston and J. Weiler, 'An EU Human Rights Policy', in P. Alston (ed.), *The EU and Human Rights* (1999), Cap.1. Also see, S. Fredman, C. McCrudden, and M. Freedland, 'An E.U. Charter of fundamental rights' [2000], *Public Law*, pp.178–86.

117 Article 1.

118 Article 21.

119 Article 22.

120 Fredman, McCrudden and Freedland, at pp.180–81, who set out the arguments both from the opponents and the proponents of the *EU Charter of Fundamental Rights*.

121 Article 18.

122 *East African Asians vs. The United Kingdom – Applications Numbers.* 4403/70-4419/70, 4422/70, 4423/70, 4434/70, 4443/70, 4476/70-4478/70, 4486/70, 4501/70 and 4526/70-4503/70.

3 Common Utility and Justice

In this chapter, I want to argue for a rational policy in immigration control. This is because mass international migration is here to stay. The distinguished legal scholar and sociologist, Santos, has observed that three main factors are likely in the future to lead to an increase in 'subordinate transnational migration'. These are 'the increasing inequality between the North and the South; the growing instability in the interstate system – including civil wars, ethnic infrastate nationalisms, boundary disputes and threat of nuclear holocaust – directly or indirectly related to the renewed struggle for supremacy among core states; [and] the likelihood of a global environmental disaster due to uncontrolled reproduction of anarchy in investment decision-making and anti-ecological consumption habits and lifestyles'. All of these, in his view, would eventually 'challenge in fundamental ways the principle of territorial sovereignty, as well as its satellite concepts of national community, citizenship and membership'.[1] International migration is therefore, likely to increase in the coming decades. In Britain, Nigel Harris, in a ground-breaking book, *The New Untouchables*, has demonstrated that rising immigration was a response to changes in the economy, and that despite tighter controls, increasing numbers of workers are moving, whether legally or not, between countries. Unskilled immigrant workers, he suggested, play a vital role in improving standards of living in the developed world. However, in turn the countries from which they have come benefit in a major way from the earnings sent back home. Harris argued that few of the fears about immigration are justified, and that increased immigration tends to mean that jobs and incomes expand. Harris concluded that governments would eventually just have to ensure that people have the freedom to come and go as they choose.[2]

In this chapter, I make a case for a rational policy in immigration control. A rational policy is one that achieves 'maximum social gain'. Rational policy-making implies that governments choose only those policies that result in net gains to society, and which exceed costs by the greatest amount, and they should refrain from policies if costs are not exceeded by gains. Rationalism is not to be viewed in a narrow pounds-and-pence framework. Rationalism requires there to be a calculation of all social, political, and economic values which is either sacrificed or achieved by the adoption of a public policy. A rational immigration policy will accordingly, consider the needs of the domestic labour market alongside inimical public opinion; national security concerns alongside the observation of human rights obligations, questions of social absorption alongside the expenditure in increased regulation, and domestic interests alongside international solidarity with developing countries. It could pave the way for an understanding of how migration can best be managed. A rational policy may allow new paradigms for effective and fair immigration 'policy' to be developed, in a way that no other policy could. It may yet be possible to show that the developed world can have a policy that is fair, both to sending and receiving immigration countries, because it is able to factor in both economic and ethical principles.

Political scientists refer to a number of models of policy analysis that governments use to make policy. These can be referred to variously as the institutional model, the process model, the incremental model, the group model, the elite model, the public choice model and the game theory model. For example, institutionalism occurs where public policy is authoritatively determined, implemented, and enforced by the institutions of government, such as Parliament, Whitehall and the Courts, as these have the biggest monopoly of legitimacy, universality and coercion. Policy process occurs where there is a general outline of problem identification, agenda setting, and then policy formulation takes place. Incrementalism views public policy as a continuation of past government activities with only incremental modifications. Group theory recognizes that individuals with common interests club together to make more effective demands on the government, and so the theory emphasizes interaction among groups as the central fact of politics. And so on. Immigration policy, on the other hand, has probably all too often in the past fallen prey to the elite theory of politics, which views public policy as the preferences and values of a governing elite. Elite theory suggests that since most people are apathetic and ill-informed about public policy, it is the elites that actually shape mass opinion on policy questions rather than the masses who shape elite opinion.

Immigration policy, however, has just as much fallen prey to the game theory model. Game theory occurs where there is no independently 'best' choice that one can make. The 'best' outcomes depend on what others do. The notion of the 'game' arises from the fact that the 'players' have to adjust their conduct to reflect not only their own desires but also their expectations about what others will do. The decision-makers are always making choices that are interdependent. Yet, most public policies are a combination of rational planning, incrementalism, competition among groups, elite preferences, public choice, political processes and institutional influences. But immigration policy has hardly, if ever, been an example of rational planning. The time has come for immigration policy making to be based on pre-eminently such a model. This is because unlike the game theory model, where there are no independently 'best' choices to be made, in rationalism there are indubitably are. Immigration today at the beginning of the twenty-first century is crying out for such a policy analysis.

A rational policy will show that in the long term, in order to avoid social waste and economic dis-equilibrium, the developed world will have, in the next 20 years, to elaborate rights of entry, stay, leave, and return for migrants in a new global order, rather than set out to restrict or deny entry for its own sake, which has traditionally been a feature of nation-state centrism. It is not yet sufficiently well understood in the developed world that there is a high cost entailed in maintaining present immigration restrictions. Wherever possible, therefore, immigration should be legalized. This is not least because illegal immigrants, while generating a significant amount of capital, do not pay into the system, so millions in tax revenue is lost. Immigration restrictions, such as border controls, welfare costs, maintenance of detention centers, all create high costs for the tax payer. Instead, the national economy could actually be benefiting from an open system which charges for work permits, student and other visas and gains significant tax revenue from its immigrant population. There is, therefore, a case for saying that the developed world should begin by freeing up border controls, and then consider how and where to restrict immigration. This is because the current arbitrary restrictions on immigration are not a reasoned response to global migration. An open entry policy would strip away the arbitrariness and lead to a deeper and more enlightened debate on migration. This may seem to be radical, but it is only so in terms of past policies. It is actually common sense if one understands that the globalized world offers us fewer and fewer alternatives in a world situation that is more and more fluid. The developed world should consider a policy of gradualism. It could extend intermigration privileges to select nations. If boundaries were opened up in this way, other nations could find that they could not stand still because they would be at a disadvantage. This could give rise to a new geo-politics, which would still be grounded in political realism.

Such an approach would be entirely consistent with the requirements of 'common utility' and 'justice' upon which, not just the liberal state, but the entire international system is based. What is interesting about this approach, however, is that it is consistent with the developed world's own interests. This makes it practically necessary, as I shall explain below. It is more than 100 years ago now that Livermore observed, that:

> The people of an independent nation may, if they please, surround their territory with an impassable wall, and totally exclude all intercourse with other nations. But if *a desire to promote their own interests induces them to cultivate an intercourse with other people*, they must necessarily adopt such principles, as a sense of *common utility* and *justice* will inspire …[3] (emphasis added).

My argument here is that the developed world needs to recognize that there is a market for immigration. Provided it recognizes that fact, it may then move to regulate that market in a way that promotes its own interests, cultivates an intercourse with the less developed world, and is cost effective. Immigration control should be implemented in a way which is best both for domestic industry and for migrant workers. It should protect tangible domestic interests but at the same time safeguard basic human rights standards for all potential entrants to the State. The fact is that migration is a market like any other.

Migration is a matter of supply and demand. Rich countries want labour; poor countries have the workers. The key lies in bringing the state in on the market. The state should be a ready participant in this supply and demand. It should not be an impassive and uninterested observer on the sidelines. Worse, it should not regulate migration through half-way, ill-thought out, and irrational measures. The problem is that of an unregulated labour market in immigration. It should regulate fully. Where workers are in short supply, it should unhesitatingly legalize the right to work.

MODERN WRITERS

In previous chapters, we have looked at the writings of classical publicists to make out a case for free movement rights. It is salutary to note that in our current troubled and embattled times, some of the leading and most highly respected writers of the day, have already put forward a case for relaxing immigration restrictions that is even more seemingly radical. These now regularly appear in the major broadsheets of Britain, which have recently seen a spate of bold and provocative articles extolling the virtues of freer immigration. All draw comparisons with the United States immigration policy. All recognize immigration as being not only desirable but necessary to the economies of Western Europe. All recognize the link, in the long-term, between domestic policy and a wider social and diplomatic policy. One writer, Timothy Garton-Ash calls for a policy of 'Californication' in Europe. He argues:

> Look at the demographic map of the world, and you will see one continent above all else that needs either a massive baby boom or large-scale immigration to sustain its aging population. That continent is Europe.

In his opinion, 'What Europe needs is more Californication', a reference to the fact that 'Roughly one in every four of today's Californians was born outside the US. And they come from everywhere'. Yet, as he points out, 'What one might call the great mixing is a product of the last 40 years'. Ever since the *1924 Immigration Act*, there had been quotas imposed in America which ensured the preponderance of white European immigrants. It was only in 1965, when that Act was finally revoked, that new Americans from Asia, Africa and Latin America came in their millions, justifying the phrase, 'God's Crucible' which the Russian-Jewish playright, Israel Zangwill, gave to the great melting pot. The results were dramatic.

Today 80 million Americans trace their ancestry to a country outside Europe whereas in 1960 it was only 16 million Americans who did so. Today 30 million Americans were born outside America whereas 40 years ago the figure was a mere 9 million. What this has done is not only make America a dynamic, self-confident, and prosperous nation, but also to provide the 'ultimate answer to the problem of racial difference' in a world obsessed by racial, ethnic, and religious differences. The process of 'Californication' tells us that if people were consistently to pay no regard at all to race and ethnicity, in deciding who to marry and who to have children with, 'you would eventually reach the point where the premises not just of racial stereo-typing but also of affirmative action and "ethnic" quotas would be undermined' and one would become simply 'human' in a census answer to the question 'ethnic group?'. Timothy Garton Ash considers that there are lessons to be learnt from this process because '[t]his experiment in becoming simply human is currently most advanced in the relatively prosperous, liberal democratic immigrant societies of the Anglosphere: Australia, Canada, the United States and Britain' but 'the process is recent, tense and contested' not least because in Europe '[m]uch of our immigration is likely to come from the Muslim world'.[4]

Other writers declare that Britain is the most strategically placed country in Western Europe to use immigration for wider political, economic and social ends. It actually has an edge over other European countries when it comes to immigration. The lure of London leaves other cities trailing behind. Mary Ann Sieghart, an editor of *The Times*, has observed that:

> London now attracts more international migrants than either New York or Los Angeles – nearly three times as many as New York in proportion to its population. What an incredible statistic.

As to the fear that they may be a drain on the economy, she notes that:

> [T]he vast proportion of immigrants to Britain (most of whom end up in London) are well educated, white and wealthy. According to a Home Office Report, 67 per cent are from high-income countries, compared with 30 per cent of migrants to Germany and 24 per cent of those to France. More of them have degrees than do the native Brits they come to join.

Of course, there are bound to be immigrants also 'from more impoverished countries' such as 'the Somali office cleaner, the Nigerian security guard, the Filipina maid, the Slovakian au pair' but '[a]ll this makes for an incredibly vibrant and cosmopolitan city.' London, she writes, 'is young, it is bustling, it is energetic' and '[t]here is nothing bland or staid about London anymore'. Yet, it is all down to these new migrants. 'The new workers are by definition enterprising and resourceful – otherwise they would not have had the wit to upsticks and move to a foreign country. They create new networks of friendships among their own nationality and also with others from different countries who have adopted London as their new home'. Small wonder then, she writes, that '[i]t's a huge compliment to our city that so many foreigners want to move there'.[5] Another writer, Steve Pope, wrote an article with the heading, 'They are vilified by politicians and the media but the truth about immigrants is simple: we need them'.[6] Referring to 'so-called illegal working' he observes that, 'from construction to catering to clothing manufacture, Britain is making a great deal of money out of it'. In fact, '[t]he Kosovans, Albanians, Bulgarians and Kurds have become to the British construction industry what the Irish were in the 1950s and 1960s'. However, the people who have best understood the importance of immigrant labour, whether legal or illegal, are the Americans. Pope quotes Dr. Stephen Moore of the Republican-founded Cato Institute think-tank, who said that immigrants are '"the lubricant to our (US) economy". The principle, explains Moore, is simple: while the US gives $20bn in direct aid to developing nations, it gets back $30bn from their cheap labour on American soil'. For Pope '[t]he issue of immigration' is 'a sad example of British hypocrisy'. This is because:

> Law firms and other organizations make millions dealing with asylum applications, business, big and small, gets labour cheap, and the rest of us get to travel in clean tube trains or get that loft conversion at an affordable price because of immigrant labour.

The result is that '[w]hile much of the country is happy to despise the new immigrants as a curse on the nation, every one from the government to big business is happy to profit from them'.

British immigration policy is, in fact, now beginning to change in response to these socio-economic developments. Another writer, Anatole Kaletsky has now stated that '[f]or the first time in 40 years, Britain has a Government explicitly and publicly committed to increasing the population through controlled, but numerically significant immigration'. He recognizes that already the profile of British society is beginning to resemble that of America, in that:

> [i]mmigrants (defined as all British residents who were not born in this country) comprize 8 per cent of the UK population and 10 per cent of the people of working age. This is only slightly smaller than the 11 per cent of the US population that was born abroad.

As he explains, 'London, where immigrants now make up 26 per cent of the population, is just as cosmopolitan as New York, whose immigrant population is 28 per cent'. Kaletsky sets out a number of clear benefits that a policy of increased immigration will bring.

Immigration has 'macro-economic, financial and diplomatic benefits' for the British economy and society. First, immigration will help to ensure population growth, which is necessary for competition, which in turn, is necessary for attracting more capital to Britain. Second, immigration can avoid tax increases, as is clear from the Chancellor of the Exchequer's Budget in December 2002, where he forecasts that the Governments long-term revenue and spending plans depend on an increase in the labour force by immigration of 0.5 per cent every year, without which tax would have to be increased. Immigrants invariably contribute more in taxes than take out in public spending. Kaletsky notes that Home Office studies themselves show that 'immigrants on average have somewhat higher earnings and qualifications than native-born British workers'. Third, there are financial advantages. If in Britain, permanent immigration is accepted as a central tenet of economic life, then Britain will attract foreign capital because the domestic market will grow. Yet '[E]ven more importantly, immigration will help reassure British savers that their pensions and insurance will be paid despite the ageing of the British population'. Fourth, there are 'political and diplomatic benefits for Britain in accepting its destination as a country of immigration'. Those coming from other countries, such as Eastern Europe, 'who are encouraged to work in Britain will see this country ... as their natural EU ally and patron' rather than a country such as Germany which is at present less open Eastern Europeans. In this way, 'London will gain even greater stature as the business hub for Eastern and Central Europe'.

For all these reasons, Kaletsky records, Britain has been right to have its Foreign Secretary announce, just before the settlement of the final terms of the enlargement of the European Union into Eastern Europe in mid-December 2002, that Britain, unlike most members of the EU, will give full rights of employment and residence to Poles, Hungarians, and citizens of other accession countries as soon as they join the European Union in May 2004. Britain will be ready to admit 74 million new EU citizens as genuine citizens of Europe. Kaletsky considers this to have been 'one of the most economically intelligent and socially far-reaching decisions to have come out of the present government'.[7]

However, none of this should be in the least surprising. The link between increased immigration and the changes to the structure of post-industrial western economies was well recognized at the highest levels more than a decade ago in 1993. It seemed to me even then that the case for a 'rational' immigration policy was clear-cut even then so that, 'Manpower needs and economic effects are essential criteria for consideration alongside matters of social absorption' given that:

> ... according to *Social Trends*, the Government's annual statistical survey, with the ageing of the larger generation born after the Second World War, deaths would exceed births around the year 2030, whereupon the population will begin to decline in Britain unless immigration acts as a balancing factor. The International Labour Organization (ILO) has also found that although the industrialized economies of the Western world would be reluctant to welcome new migrants, skilled labour is going to be needed in the future if sustained economic growth is to be maintained.[8]

What is happening now was, therefore, clearly envisoned in the early 1990s. It is likely to become truer still as we approach 2030 and beyond.

THE COST OF CONTROLS

Immigration control brings with it heavy financial, economic and human costs that are hardly recognized in public debates in the developed world.[9] More than 30 years ago, Roger Nett sagaciously argued that '[r]esponsible nations might deliberately strive for a relatively quick assimilation of the underprivileged as against the high cost of maintaining present restrictions' and that this was just 'common sense in a world situation with fewer alternatives', not least because '[I]f some nations were to begin opening their boundaries, it would probably put others at a political disadvantage so that they could not stand still' whereby '[a] new geopolitics could begin on that basis, one with sufficient latitude for political realism'.[10]

A 'political realism' is badly needed in international migration policy. Migration flows affect both the developed and the developing countries. But for the developed countries of the affluent North, they are both increasingly impossible to restrict and extremely costly to police. First, take the cost of controlling freedom of movement. It is estimated that the 15 countries that make up the Inter-Governmental Consultations on Asylum, Refugee and Migration Policies in Europe, North America and Australia (IGC) spend, in order to process 450,000 to 500,000 asylum-seekers, some $10 billion per annum. In 2002, the Netherlands spent 120.7 million euros deporting 14,590 people by plane. The UK spends an estimated £73 million annually just on detaining people. The EU spends $17 billion per year on immigration controls, according to the OECD. Compare this to the fact that in 2002, the UNHCR spent $1 billion caring for 20 million people.[11] Or, consider the stark contrast in the fact that the UNHCR's budget for humanitarian assistance in 2002 was just $710 million.[12]

In fact, the relationship between forced labour and deregulated markets is clear and undeniable, as shown by a recent report written by independent academics. This report, *Forced Labour and Migration to the UK*, was jointly commissioned in January 2004 by the International Labour Organization (ILO) in Geneva and the Trades Union Congress in London. The ILO is the UN body which promotes workers rights in 177 countries. Britain is one of ten countries with a permanent seat on its governing body. The report was ready by August 2004 but its publication was suppressed until after the General Election in the spring of 2005 as a result of pressure from the British government because of the unpalatable conclusions it draws about forced labour and the exploitation of migrant workers. The British government had paid £20,000 towards the research costs of the report. The report, which focuses on industries of building, farming contract cleaning and residential care, catalogues the coercive techniques used by private employers to force migrants to work for low wages and in poor conditions, from physical and sexual violence to debt bondage and blackmail. The report makes uncomfortable reading for the Labour Government because it gives examples of State employers paying wages well below the minimum legal wage, following deductions to the agencies. Its findings are that many migrants are forced to work through violence and intimidation; many are forced into debt bondage, after taking loans to fund travel to the UK at exorbitant rates; many are working in dangerous conditions and for excessive hours; and nurses brought to Britain to work in the National Health Service (NHS) and in private care homes complained of exploitative deductions from their wages. Some of the report's most disturbing conclusions are, in fact, in relation to migrants working the State sector, particularly the National Health Service. It gives the example of one, Conrado, a qualified nurse brought from Asia to Britain by an agency to work in a hospital. He and others had to pay £700 to agencies, followed by a month's deposit and rent for accommodation. When they started in the NHS, their monthly pay of £805 was cut to £198 or £46 a week, after deductions were made at source by the NHS trust and handed to the agency.[13] There is clearly, therefore, empirical evidence showing that it is the unregulated market for labour which is a major area of immigration abuse.

Bad regulation, or inappropriate regulation, also leads to human costs. Little is documented about the human cost of bad immigration controls. The Report of the *Medical Foundation for the Care of Victims of Torture* in October 2004 found that in 12 out of 14 investigated cases of ill-treatment of immigrants by officials in Britain, there was 'gratuitous or excessive force used'. The cases comprised, 12 men, and two women, all were black, and at least four of these had already been tortured in their country of origin. The Medical Foundation said that:

> The cases reveal worrying incidences of harm, which in turn suggest certain practices of abuse, with four patterns emerging: (i) the use of inappropriate and unsafe methods of force which carry higher than acceptable injury risk; (ii) the use of force even after termination of the removal attempt, often out of sight inside escort vehicles; (iii) continued use of force even after the detainee had been restrained; and (iv) the misuse of handcuffing, which would appear to be deliberate in some cases, raising concern that there may be a systematic problem of use, rather than a number of isolated incidents.[14]

There are more disturbing findings:

> Midwives say infants are being removed from their mothers, because of a policy that means families, whose asylum claims are unsuccessful, and who do not voluntarily leave the UK within two weeks, of the Secretary of State's decision that they are able to, are denied support. Under this policy, social workers are being forced to remove children from their families on the basis that they do not have the resources to look after them.[15]

There is also a more widespread social cost. *The Commission for Racial Equality (CRE)* has reported a four-fold increase in racist attacks often against asylum-seekers, ethnic minorities have been targeted in operations over possession of immigration papers, and social cohesion has been damaged, in a policy that punishes solidarity and compassion.[16]

The financial cost of asylum adjudication and accommodation of asylum seekers is estimated at 8 billion US dollars a year.[17] Another estimate, in respect of 13 of the major industrialized states, suggests that the cost of administering asylum procedures and providing social welfare benefits increased from 500 million US dollars in 1983 to 7 billion US dollars in 1991.[18] In the United Kingdom, the influx of refugees had more than doubled the legal aid bill for immigration work and the government set out to control the cost in 2003. Immigration had become one of the two fastest growing areas of legal aid work in Britain. In 2000–2001, the legal aid bill for immigration work stood at £81.3m. By 2002–2003 it had risen to £174.2m. This was unsurprising given that immigration appeals had more than trebled from 19,395 in 2000 to 64,125 in 2002. The average cost for each case had also nearly doubled since 2000–2001.[19] No doubt, the fact that there is increasing pressure on governments to process applications speedily leads to increased costs. In the UK, 75 per cent of new applications are determined within six months.[20] However, 20 per cent of all appeals are then successful.[21] Those that have come to the end of the line and are awaiting removal from the United Kingdom also entail high costs. In 2005, Edward Leigh, the chairman of the Commons Public Accounts Committee in Britain, complained that:

> The Immigration and Nationality Directorate has a target to effect as many removals per month as there are new unfounded cases. Despite a massive increase in expenditure on immigration enforcement to £300 million a year, IND has not yet come close to meeting this target.

A report published in July 2005 by the National Audit Office, *Returning Failed Asylum Applicants*, confirmed that it costs £600 million a year to deal with removals, including £300 million on supporting those waiting to leave the country. It costs an estimated £11,000 to remove each failed asylum-seeker.[22] That is a staggering cost which could well be avoided under in a more imaginative and rational immigration policy.

The plain fact is that strict immigration control is particularly difficult for contemporary liberal society. For the first time in history, the world's leading industrialized democracies have become the targets for immigration and 3 per cent of the world's population are defined as international migrants.[23] In *The Age of Migration*, Castles and Miller have argued that:

> Never before have so many people left their countries of origin due to economic deprivation, persecution or ecological catastrophe. Never before have so many migrants and asylum-seekers sought entry – and not only to the rich countries of the North.[24]

According to the authors, migration cannot be analyzed as an isolated phenomenon but as an aspect of global change and development. In the UK alone, 85,865 applications for asylum were received in 2002 of which, 8,100 or 10 per cent of applicants were granted asylum.[25] It is clear, however, that despite this increase, any response in relation to controlling such flows has to be measured and restrained. Indeed, James Hollifield, has argued in *Immigrants, Markets and States*,[26] that the spread of liberal ideas such as free markets and individual rights limits the ability of individual democracies to control immigration. One could add that free movement of capital will also necessitate a more restrained response. But there are even more practical restraints.

The leading Columbia University economist, Jagdish Bhagwati has argued that:

> Paradoxically, the ability to control migration has shrunk as the desire to do so has increased. The reality is that borders are beyond control and little can be done to really cut down immigration.

Populist politicians find it easy to pander to people's prejudices[27] and promise strict controls. The reality is different. In the 2005 election campaign, the British Conservative Party leader, Michael Howard, declared that 'We'll put in place 24-hour security at ports to prevent illegal immigration. We will set up a dedicated border control police with the sole job of securing our borders'.

Yet, only three days later, his Shadow Lord Chancellor, Oliver Letwin, admitted that the Conservatives' promise of a 'round-the-clock watch on borders would be mounted at only 35 of Britain's 650 ports and airports'.[28] When the Conservative Party proposed plans that Britain withdraw from the Geneva Convention on Refugees altogether, the UN's body for refugees, the UNHCR said that this would actually increase the number of asylum seekers, and Anne Dawson-Shepherd, the UNHCR's London representative pointed out that withdrawal would trigger further and more uncontrolled asylum flows.[29] Indeed, in July 2005, a highly critical report by the *National Audit Office* in Britain exposed the chaos of the asylum system, with a catalogue of failings including financial mismanagement and near-shambolic record keeping. The report stated that the *Immigration and Nationality Directorate* in the UK was struggling to meet the Government's latest target that by the end of the year the number of monthly removals should exceed applicants rejected. The number of failed applicants removed from the country had already fallen in the last year. But what the Report now estimated was that, as of May 2004, the number of failed asylum applicants who had remained in the country was between 155,000 and 283,000. However, even the lower figure was likely to be an underestimate because it was based on a government database that excluded cases from before the database was introduced in 2000.[30]

Accordingly, in the view of Professor Bhagwati, governments must alter policies geared to limiting migration to 'coping and working with it to seek benefits for all'. This is because it is clear that migration flows 'cannot be effectively constrained and must be creatively accommodated'.[31] He has gone onto endorse this view in his recent classic, *In Defense of Globalization*, where he has prophesized that:

> [S]ome nations will grasp [the] reality and creatively work with migrants and migration. Others will lag behind, still seeking restrictive measures to control and cut the level of migration. The future belongs to the former.[32]

Closing borders is not an option. As the *Human Development Report 2004* pointed out, 'No country has advanced by closing its borders. International migration brings skills, labour and ideas, enriching people's lives'.[33] Indeed, there is a case to be made for legalizing much of today's migration flows. This is because the:

> pressure will remain for migrants to leave the world's ill-governed countries and head for the ones where demand for cheap labour flourishes. If the rich world does not allow immigrants in legally, they will continue to come through the back door.[34]

A recent Government report in Great Britain, on the asylum policies of five European countries – Britain, Germany, the Netherlands, Sweden and Italy – between 1990 and 2000, concluded that 'get tough' asylum policies only lead to more illegal immigration and people trafficking whilst forcing genuine refugees to go underground. The Home Office Report[35] stated that:

> There is strong circumstantial circumstantial evidence, though little authoritative research, that restrictionism ... led to growing trafficking and illegal entry of bona fide asylum-seekers and economic migrants.[36]

The Report concluded that 'indirect measures' such as the withdrawal of state benefits, administrative detention, and reception facilities had little impact on immigration flows. This led Dr. Heaven Crawley of the Institute of Public Policy Research to say that:

> The number of asylum-seekers in Europe is correlated far more strongly and clearly with conflict, political unrest and human rights abuse than with asylum policies designed to keep people out.[37]

Yet, it does not seem that governments with harsh immigration controls are much interested about human rights abuses abroad. Recently, in a report dated 8th February 2004, Amnesty International, launched a scathing attack on the asylum-decision-making process, accusing the British Home Office of a 'staggering' lack of knowledge about human rights abuses. It said that asylum rejection letters when analysed, displayed a 'startling' ignorance of the situations in many countries; many decisions were 'unreasoned'; and 'many cases simply aren't taken seriously'. Amnesty International further pointed out that, even according to the government's own figures, four out of ten applications from some countries are wrongly refused. The internationally reputed organization highlighted a number of specific cases. For example, a Syrian was rejected because the Home Office denied that an opposition group existed in that country. Similarly an Algerian woman who claimed to have been raped and tortured with soapy rags stuffed into her mouth was told that these crimes were not evidence of persecution. The UK director of Amnesty International, Kate Allen, was uncompromizing in her criticism, stating:

> Getting an asylum decision wrong is not like a clerical error on a tax bill. Wrongly refusing someone's claim could mean returning them to face torture or execution. These are life or death decisions and the Home Office is getting one in five wrong.[38]

All of this highlights the perils of irrational planning and policy-making. What it suggests is that there is no point in passing rafts of legislation if the ability of civil servants who apply that legislation is in question. As the *Prospect* magazine recently said:

> There is no point in changing the tyres on a racing car if the engine is leaking oil or about to blow a gasket. The engine in this case is the Immigration and Nationality Directorate (IND), a branch of the home office with headquarters at Lunar House in Croydon.

It is said that a recent IND letter of refusal concerned a Zimbabwean who had applied for asylum on the grounds that he was a member of the opposition MDC party and had been persecuted by Mugabe's Zanu-PF, was not believed by the IND who took the view that 'It is considered that you would be well aware that the Zanu-PF indiscriminately rape, torture and murder people perceived to oppose their actions and beliefs' and that 'therefore, it is not accepted that you would have been foolhardy enough to sing, distribute T-shirts, tell people that the MDC could change the country and campaign for the party'.[39] This Kafkaesque reasoning was all the more remarkable given that the British government did not at the time have a policy of returning asylum-seekers to Zimbabwe. The problem arises from the need to hit targets. Each year, Lunar House is expected to process some 180,000 applications for asylum, visa, and citizenship. The result is that cases are subject to a pooling system so that although they are called 'case-workers', the decision-makers at Lunar House do not follow an assigned case through to its end in the logical way and anyone telephoning in to check the progress of a case is likely to get a different person everytime, with vital documents such as passports getting lost, and moral inevitably being low.[40]

In February 2005, a report commissioned by the Mayor of London, where more asylum-seekers live than anywhere else outside the capital, found that 'the UK asylum system is a labyrinth, increasingly complex and difficult to navigate, in which the chances of success can depend crucially on legal advice'.[41] The report considered the position of asylum-seekers both *before* a Home Office decision was taken and *after* it was taken by the Home Office. Before the decision was taken, it found asylum-seekers to have little understanding of the asylum process, the provision of legal advice or the progress of their own application. It found that there was no coordinated system for identifying or referring to good quality legal representation. It found the quality of asylum advice to vary enormously, and poor quality advice remained a major problem. After the decision was taken by the Home Office, the report found that the quality of advice and representation was extremely variable. Most startling was its conclusion that in a number of cases, legal advisers simply failed to pursue appeals in meritorious cases because of the legal aid reforms denying public funding, the differing interpretations of the Legal Services Commission's (LSC's) merits test enabling lawyers to justifiably take up cases on public funding, and poor legal advice.

A UNHCR Report, published in March 2005,[42] confirmed the low standard of asylum decision-making. In early 2004, the Home Office invited the UNHCR to assist in the improvement of the overall quality of first instance decision making through auditing and providing recommendations. The UNHCR took as its benchmark the provisions of the *Handbook on Procedures and Criteria for Determining Refugee Status* (i.e. the UNHCR Handbook) and this states that applications for asylum should:

> be examined within the framework of specially established procedures by qualified personnel having the necessary knowledge and experience, and an understanding of an applicant's particular difficulties and needs.

In its report, whilst the UNHCR found efforts to be underway to reach the standards of decision-making by the United Nations, it also concluded that a number of asylum applications[43] had been subjected to flawed procedures such as unsustainable reasoning, misapplications of the law, failure to refer to country of origin information, misapplications of country of origin information, and failure to consider obvious European Convention on Human Rights issues. Given that a large proportion of these claims would consequently end up coming before the Immigration Appellate Authority, the UNHCR considered this to be inconsistent with the requirements of the Handbook and a waste of public resources.

In Britain, the Refugee Council has now, in association with other leading refugee organizations,[44] produced a report *'Refugees: Renewing the Vision'*,[45] setting out a new approach to the asylum system. The focus of the report is on ensuring that protection is granted to those whose safety is at risk if returned to their country of origin, and involves setting up a more independent decision-making process, that is less adversarial and more objective an investigative.[46] What is especially valuable about the report is that it sets out global causes of refugee movement. It stresses the importance of finding viable solutions for the world's refugees. One solution it proposes is the need for more 'joined-up' government approaches, ranging from promoting human rights and gender equality, to building social cohesion, to supporting efforts to improve regional stability and security in areas of conflict.[47] This suggests that rash and ill-thought out government decisions and policies can add to the problem of 'irregular migration' so that 'inter-country movements ... take place in defiance of national laws or regulations'.[48] No doubt in response to increased State regulation today:

> Irregular migration, including trafficking in migrants, has emerged as a major international challenge. It now represents between one-third or more of the yearly legal inflow in the United States and half in Europe. At the global level some US $7 billion is channeled every year into human trafficking.[49]

Given these sobering facts, immigration laws should not be enacted rashly on the crest of populist nativist emotions.[50] Another government report in Great Britain, which has not been fully published, has confirmed that the £1.1 billion Home Office Organization, the National Asylum Support Service (NASS), which was set up in 2000 to disperse asylum seekers around the country on grounds that they would be more easily integrated into society, is 'a shambles and unable to get on top of the job'. The Organization, which prevented the 92,000 asylum seekers from settling wherever they wanted to in the country, was criticized for having confused business practices and procedures and for failing to deal with basic errors in processing applicants.[51] It is, therefore, not good enough to say that immigration control is justifiable simply because that is what the majority in a society wants because if a democractic system is founded on justice, then 'Whether what the majority wants should prevail depends on how oppressive it is to those who do not want it'.[52] Today, in an era of globalization and a world of the haves and have-nots, for migration flows to be 'creatively accommodated' it needs to be unreservedly affirmed that freedom of migration is a human phenomenon that, 'continues to be important for promoting mutual understanding and co-operation among peoples'.[53] Globalization is not new. It has been occurring for hundreds of years. What is new is the scale and degree at which it is now occurring. For the first time, there is a community of interests that is unprecedented. Indeed, Harvard University's Deborah Anker has even demonstrated that international migration has an impact on the observance of international human rights in other countries.[54] And, it is well known that during the Cold War, it was accepted that:

> any policy towards aliens is vitally and intricately interwoven with contemporaneous policies in regard to the conduct of foreign relations, the war power, and the maintenance of a republican form of government.[55]

The maintenance of a sustainable international legal order would be difficult to achieve in a world community if control was predicated on racial and cultural motifs. Foreignness in a national context must be respected and not reviled, otherwise to be foreign will imply fair game. This is nowhere better understood than in the context of post-September 11th hardening of immigration controls in the United States. In 2002 there was a 'remarkable reversal of America's traditional generosity towards the world's displaced' and the United States severely restricted the entry of refugees into its territory by allowing only 30,000 refugees to enter, thus making this the lowest intake of refugees in 25 years. This is remarkable when it is remembered that the USA admits more immigrants every year than the rest of the world combined. It admits 1 million legal immigrants every year and pursues a policy of weak enforcement of laws against illegal immigration, which is driven largely by industry groups concerned with lowering their labour costs. Yet, in 2002 even those that were admitted were made to undergo severe security checks and delays. All males between the ages of 15 and 45 had to undergo complicated security clearance, called Security Advisory Opinion, which resulted in huge delays. In fact, some 31,000 refugees who had already been cleared to enter the US by the procedures of the INS were prevented in 2002 from entering because they had not completed the new checks. This subjected refugees to double-victimization. As the *Economist* complained, these refugees are 'driven from their homes by civil strife, persecution and torture' and they 'cannot find asylum in America until their innocence is validated'.[56]

Of course, freedom of movement is not without consequences. Transnational migration is one of the most intractable policy issues of our time. As Spellman has explained the reason for this is that:

> in a world where capital and information flow instantaneously across international borders, the movement of people, while anything but instantaneous, is nonetheless at unprecedented levels in terms of volume and diversity.[57]

Consequently, the control of illegal immigration in the European Union, has been announced as a top priority, under the Italian EU Presidency of Silvio Berlusconi, on the very day he took over the presidency on 1st July 2003.[58]

Mass sporadic migration today is the result of a wide range of global insecurity-inducing circumstances. Writing in 1995, Arthur Helton explained that many of the world's estimated 125 million international migrants, are forced to move on account of a variety of artificial disasters, including war, persecution, poverty, economic insecurity, population growth, environmental degradation, or other grave failures of governance.[59] The picture indeed is grim. Recently, Mary Coussey, the independent race monitor for the British Immigration Service, produced her first report, after watching the asylum-decision-making process at Croydon. She found that many cases 'presented a horrific catalogue of lives blighted by war, repression, persecution, violence and sometimes torture'. She found that 'significant numbers had a family history of forced expulsion from their homes and had lost parents and relatives'. But rather remarkably, contrary to the popular misconception about immigration control being lax, she found most asylum cases to be genuine, and concluded that:

> I saw no cases in the sample in which the decision to grant asylum or humanitarian protection seemed over-generous. Most seemed beyond doubt. I saw few decisions which seemed harsh.[60]

Thus whether because of war, or population growth, or environmental disasters, insecurity is creating a pressure to seek a better life elsewhere. The admission of aliens by a state has clear domestic implications.[61] It can impact upon a country's absorptive capacity.[62] But if free societies live by the principle of freedom of movement, they must profess it for all. Indeed, in 1904 a young Winston Churchill remonstrated in *The Times*, that the impending passage of the Aliens Act 1905, would abandon, 'the tolerant and generous practice of free entry and asylum to which this country has long adhered and from which it has so greatly gained'. This was not least because of the 'loathsome system of police interference' which immigration controls entailed.[63] Thus, for a free liberal society, any restriction on this right must be based on narrow and objectively justifiable criteria which must also be rationally assessable.

COMMON UTILITY

The positive long-term effects of freer migration, is now sustained by social scientific research, which contradicts popular fears of a country's absorptive capacity, of the moral danger posed by an influx of immigrants, and of a serious displacement of indigenous labor.[64] The developed world needs workers. It has been estimated that the European Union would have to import 16 million migrants each year just to keep its working age population stable until 2050.[65] Added to this is the spectre of declining populations in the West. In Germany, Italy and Spain there are only 1.3 babies born to each mother, but that figure drops well below replacement rate in France and the UK.[66] Furthermore, there is large-scale emigration from the UK. As the *Spectator* magazine characteristically said in November 2004:

[W]e are forever being drawn to the spectre of foreigners coming to take our jobs, steal our women and cause south-east England to be concreted over with little houses. Yet, how often does the anti-immigrant lobby draw attention to the other side of the ledger: emigration? In the past year, the Office of National Statistics announced last week a record 191,000 Britons left the country either to take up jobs abroad or to retire there. With the number of immigrants falling and the number of emigrants rising, it may well be that Britain will soon be experiencing a new outflow of its population: a situation which existed as recently as 1993.[67]

In the United Kingdom migrant workers make a valuable contribution. In 1999–2000, the net fiscal contribution made by migrants, including asylum seekers, was £2.5bn.[68] More recent research by the Institute of Public Policy Research (IPPR) found that immigrants even contribute more to the national economy than the native-born. The IPPR research showed that the total revenue from immigrants grew in real terms from £333.8 billion in 1999–00 to £341.2 billion in 2003–2004. This 22 per cent increase compared to a 6 per cent increase for the UK-born. The gap between the two contribution rates had been increasing in recent years as newer immigrants were filling vacancies in the higher-ends of the economy and paying more taxes. The research evaluated the net fiscal contribution of immigrants and found that in 2003–2004 for every £3100 that the UK-born contributed to the exchequer, immigrants contributed £3112. This was up from £3105 for every £3100 in 1999–2000. It found that immigrants made up 8.7 per cent of the population but accounted for 10.2 per cent of all income tax collected (2003–2004). It further found that immigrants earned about 15 per cent more in average weekly income than UK-born. Most importantly, it found that each immigrant generated £37,203 in government revenue on average in 2003–2004, compared to £36,861 per non-immigrant; similarly each immigrant accounted for £37,277 of government expenditure on average, compared to £37,753 per non-immigrant.[69] As Nick Pearce, the IPPR director said:

> Our research shows that immigrants make an important fiscal contribution to the UK and pay more than their share. They are not a drain on the UK's resources.[70]

Indeed, 90 per cent of UK employers want to take on refugees to meet skills shortages.[71] Within the United Kingdom, in Scotland, the population is expected to fall below 5 million people in five years. In a country where only 2 per cent of Scotland's population, namely, around 100,000 people, are from the ethnic minorities (compared to 9 per cent in England and 29 per cent in London), the First Minster of Scotland, challenged the UK government's new immigration policy by pressing the Home Secretary to offer potential newcomers a home in Scotland. When the British Home Secretary announced plans in early 2005 to curb economic immigration by low-skilled workers from outside the EU, the Scottish executive feared that the proposed measures would undermine an initiative to bring 8,000 immigrants to Scotland annually. Mr McConnell said the projected fall in population was the 'single biggest challenge facing Scotland'. The Scottish executive had already established a relocation advisory service in Glasgow, which was helping to promote visa permits in Scotland. In the summer of 2005 a new system was planned of allowing overseas graduates in Scottish Universities two extra years to stay in Scotland as a prelude to a longer work permit than in England and Wales. Mr. McConnell said that 'we are prepared to take a lead, and the political argument, and promote Scotland on that basis' and he further declared that 'although people are nervous about immigration [they] need to realize it's in their economic and social interest for this to happen'.[72] This was no fear-mongering because by the year 2027, the proportion of Scotland's people of working age is projected to fall by 8 per cent.[73]

Immigrants bring much needed skills to the host country. In Britain, in a largest ever skills audit of refugees undertaken in the UK, a recently published research paper, by the Immigration and Statistics Service of the Home Office, and supported by a cross-governmental steering group, itself found that refugees generally had a high degree of literacy and skills. In a paper, *Skills Audit of Refugees*[74] the research found that the distribution of economic activity of respondents before leaving their country of origin is similar to that of all UK residents.[75] Almost half of those persons surveyed had received ten years or more of education, and over 40 per cent held qualifications before they arrived in the UK. About a third of the respondents could read, write, speak, and understand spoken English as well as their main language; and three-quarters of the respondents could read and write either fluently or fairly well in their main language. There were, however, regional variations. Zimbabweans tended to be highly educated, with almost 90 per cent having received at least ten years of education, and over 90 per cent holding qualifications before coming to the UK, and 98 per cent considering their skills to be either fluent or fairly good in each of the four English language skills, namely, understanding, speaking, reading and writing. By contrast, just over a quarter of the Iraqis had received ten years or more of education and the same proportion held qualifications before arriving in the UK. Of these respondents only 65 per cent were able to read and write in their main language either fluently or fairly well, and 12 per cent considered their skills to be either fluent or fairly good in each of the four English language skills. These regional variations are, however, only to be expected. What is important about these findings is that over 40 per cent of the refugees, from the three countries surveyed, had qualifications before they arrived in the UK. This is important because contrary to popular opinion, Britain like the rest of the developed world, has labour shortages, not just in low-wage, unskilled jobs that have traditionally required foreign labour. They are not just jobs that the domestic workforce wants to shy away from. For example, in London it is said that 'The capital's building trade is now almost entirely dependent on foreign, particularly Eastern European, labour'.[76] Labour shortages include skilled jobs.

A CASE-STUDY: THE UK HEALTH INDUSTRY

The promotion of the free movement of labour within the European Union (EU), which we discussed in the last chapter, has been a keen objective of the EU. In fact, the EU has even encouraged migration into certain regimes and sectors.[77] Yet, the liberalization of labour markets and the mutual recognition of qualifications alone are not sufficient to stimulate labour mobility between countries. Thus, in one of the most labour-starved industries, the Health and Social Services industry, the movement of nurses and physicians between countries still remains at a relatively low level, partly because of linguistic and cultural barriers.[78] However, with the enlargement of the EU to 25 members in April 2004, with ten new countries from Central and Eastern Europe, the context is now changing. Well qualified workers, like nurses and doctors, are likely to be offered inducements in order to migrate so that they can avail themselves of the advantages of both higher salaries and better working conditions.[79] The United Kingdom and the Netherlands have been in discussion with Poland and Hungary about recruitment opportunities[80] for health professionals. Norway, which is not a member of the EU has already been recruiting nurses from Poland.[81] What this suggests is that the opportunities for inward labour migration must continue to be taken on a national basis by individual sovereign countries.

The Health Industry in the UK provides an interesting example in this respect. It also very helpfully illustrates the various points we have made above in this chapter. The Health industry can serve as a case-study, not just because of its sheer importance, but because of the number of foreign health professionals that come into the UK and register to work here. The data on inflows into receiving countries is more reliable, as Stilwell has shown, because most countries tend to underestimate the numbers leaving their countries.[82] Registration data, of course, has its own inherent limitations, as Buchan has pointed out,[83] one of which is that whilst registration indicates an intent to work, it does not necessarily indicate a person's actual employment status. Nevertheless, as Bach has shown, such data has been consistent over time and it is 'a valuable source of trend data', notwithstanding such limitations.[84]

The plight of the Health Industry is emblematic of widespread labour shortages in the West. It tells us about the shortage, not just of highly skilled personnel in the developed world, but also the shortage of much less skilled workers; not just about the use of workers by the West, from the under-developed world, but also about the use of such workers from the developed world; and not just about what are likely to be the future problems facing Britain, but those facing other western countries as well. In short, it makes out a case for a modern and forward-looking migration policy and one which can be utilized to address general domestic concerns of well-being and overall prosperity. Indeed, the lessons are not just confined to immigrants but to refugees as well. It even helps to graphically illustrate how refugees can be used to meet labour shortages.[85] Thus, the London Assembly's Health Committee recently reported on the acute shortage of doctors in London. More than 330 vacant GP posts cannot be filled. This represents a shortfall of 7 per cent compared with a national shortfall of 3 per cent.[86] In some areas 80 per cent of General Practitioner's surgeries are closed to new patients. Unusually, the Health Committee recommended that the answer lay in recruiting refugee doctors and doctors from Commonwealth countries who are unaccredited in Britain.[87] According to a recent report by the Royal

College of Surgeons, the national Health Service (NHS) will need to increase the number of consultant surgeons by more than 50 per cent by 2010 to avert the present shortage of 2,760, up from 1,454 in 2001.[88] The greatest shortages are in the fields of otorhinolaryngology, plastic surgery, neurosurgery and paediatric surgery where the numbers of staff need to double by 2010.[89] In fact, another recent report by *Save the Children*, has found that recruiting doctors and nurses from Ghana has saved the National Health Service £65 million in training costs between 1999 and 2005, which helps save the NHS, but impoverishes the Health Service in Ghana where one in ten children dies before the age of five years compared with one in 150 in the UK.[90]

In looking at the needs of the Health Service, the international context is important. In the 1950s and 1960s, many western European countries expanded their welfare states rapidly. This was accompanied by the recruitment of overseas health workers. As Mejia[91] has pointed out, a World Health Organization (WHO), study[92] of the flows and stocks of physicians and nurses in 40 countries concluded: that already by 1972, about 6 per cent of the world's physicians (140,000) were located in countries where they were not nationals; that 86 per cent of all migrant doctors were working in just five countries, namely, in Australia, Canada, the Federal Republic of Germany, the UK and the US; and that the stock of nurses was lower, but the main recipient countries were the same as for doctors, except for Australia. The establishment of accurate data on stocks and flows of health workers remains a major challenge that continues to inhibit effective migration management. The most common difficulties arise from the variety of disparate sources used by various countries, ranging from work permits and population registers, to record migrants and the absence of data linked to occupation. All of this makes it difficult to analyze health worker migration.[93] Yet, the fact remains that the UK has historically been a key destination country for health professionals. More than 25 per cent of health professional in the UK are non-UK born and current recruitment patterns will augment this trend.

With respect to source countries, at the height of the expansion of health services in the West, in the 1970s, India was the largest source country for doctors in absolute numbers,[94] and Indian doctors still continue today to make up an important proportion of the stock in Canada, the UK and the US.[95] It is, however, the Philippines that is particularly noteworthy today. The Philippines today stands out with an estimated 7 million Filipinos (amounting to a remarkable 10 per cent of the country's population), that live or work abroad. The Philippines is the largest source of nurses working overseas. The Philippines government encourages employment abroad. This policy has been incorporated into the *Medium Term Philippines Development Plan (2001–2004)* whereby overseas employment is viewed as a key source of economic growth.[96] Indeed, the Philippine secretary for Labour and employment is known to have commented that:

> It is an industry. It is not politically correct to say you are exporting people, but it is part of globalization, and I like to think that countries like ours, rich in human resources, have that to contribute to the rest of the world.[97]

In fact, during the mid-1970s there were almost as many doctors working in the USA alone from the Philippines, as there were in the Philippines itself, with a total of 10,410 Philippines-trained doctors who were employed in the US and 13,480 physicians working in the Philippines.[98] In the UK today, it is estimated that there are well over 20,000 Filipino nurses working within the NHS and independent health sectors.[99] Yet, despite this enormous contribution being made by Filipino health care workers, the drive for the recruitment of more workers from other countries goes unabated. Sri Lanka is now being targeted for recruitment of nurses, not just by Europe and the USA, but also by less likely countries such as Malaysia and Singapore. From a stock of approximately 22,000 nurses, it is estimated that about 115–200 are recruited by these countries annually.[100] Another key source country for nurses and auxiliary medical staff is South Africa: the flow of nurses from this country has increased eightfold since 1991, and more than 50 per cent leave for the UK.[101] It is, of course, true that what all of this risks, is the depletion of vital human resources from the countries of economic emigration. The Philippines, while exporting the highest number of nurses overseas, has 30,000 nursing positions unfilled at home.[102]

The continent of Africa faces the clearest challenges from brain drain, and this is highlighted by the inordinately high vacancy rates within the health care sectors in various countries. Thus, according to the World Health Organization (WHO) the shortage of doctors, percentage-wise for four African countries are: 42 per cent in Ghana; 36.3 per cent in Malawi; 26 per cent in Namibia; and 7.6 per cent in Lesotho. The vacancy rates for nurses amount to 25.5 per cent in Ghana; 18.4 per cent in Malawi; 2.9 per cent in Namibia; and 48.6 per cent in Lesotho 48.6 per cent.[103] However, the dimension that these figures overlook is the extent to which sub-saharan countries themselves are significant importers of migrant labour both from other African countries and from further afield. The example of Cuban doctors working in Ghana[104] (which as we saw at the outset is itself losing its own doctors to the UK) only serves to highlight the fact that many doctors do undertake employment in other countries even if there is available employment for them at home. In the same way, the example of some 18,000 Zimbabwean nurses working abroad serves to make the same point.[105] In Britain, the NHS has made a commitment that it will not target developing countries for recruitment, unless those countries have an explicit government-to-government agreement with the UK to support recruitment activities. The difficulty is that such a commitment does not bind private providers for healthcare. In the event, therefore, recruitment via the private sector effectively circumvents any restrictions on the employment of foreign labour.[106]

The fact is that migrant labour is indispensable to, and an integral part of, the health industry in most countries now. The plight of the UK health industry best epitomizes the case for deregulation of strict immigration controls that this chapter sets out to make. Health and Social Services is one of the largest employment groups in Britain. It accounts for a massive 10.5 per cent of total employment in the UK. Its importance is no less staggering for the well-being of society because it is inextricably linked with Health and Social care. The two sectors interact in crucial ways. Labour shortages affect the provision of care facilities directly. Thus, reductions in the availability of appropriate social care have been linked to the recent increases in the number of older people being admitted to hospital in an emergency. Such are the manpower shortages here that the Health and Social Work sector accounted for the highest share of all vacancies, and of 'Hard to Fill Vacancies', of all the industries that were recently outlined in the *National Employers Skills Survey 2003 (NESS)*.[107] This is important because *NESS* was the largest survey of its kind ever commissioned. It involved 72,100 interviews with a representative sample of employers in England. As such, it allowed analysis at a level of detail not possible in earlier surveys. In particular, it provided robust estimates of skills deficiencies and workforce development for each of the 47 local learning and Skills Councils (LSCs) and for 27 industries. With all this, it found that there were disproportionately more vacancies in this industry, so that although Health and Social work accounted for only 10.5 per cent of all employment, it accounted for 13.3 per cent of all vacancies, and 16.7 per cent of all Hard to Fill Vacancies. Health and Social Work also accounted for more than its proportional share of Skill Shortage Vacancies,[108] with 12.76 per cent of all Skill Shortage Vacancies reported by employers.

In absolute numbers, the *NESS* estimated that of 679,072 total vacancies in 2003, there were 89,703 vacancies in the Health and Social Work sector. Of these, 45,313 vacancies were classified as 'Hard to Fill', and of these, 17,261 are Skill Shortage Vacancies. Within the *Health and Social Work Sector*, in 2003, vacancies accounted for 3.9 per cent of all employment in the Health and Social work industry.[109] More than half of these vacancies (58 per cent) were classified as 'Hard to Fill' and of these, 38 per cent were classified as skill-shortage vacancies. Of these 89,703 vacancies, the largest number fell within the Personal Services Category (42 per cent), and just under one quarter fell within the Associate Professional Category. The occupations with the most severe shortages were Associate Professionals, Skilled Trades, Personal Services and Sales.[110] This data is supported by the Department of Health, whose own statistics in 2004, which are specific to the NHS, confirmed the vacancies in the NHS to be so widespread as to affect both the highly skilled and the relatively unskilled positions. Thus, there was a 4.3 per cent job vacancy for the total medical and dental staff; a 4.4 per cent job vacancy for Consultants; a 4.1 per cent job vacancy for other doctors and dentists; a 3.0 per cent job vacancy for General Practitioners; a 2.6 per cent job vacancy for qualified nursing, midwifery and health visiting staff; and a 1.3 per cent job vacancy for Non-medical staff.[111] If these figures are added up, they show a vacancy rate of nearly 20 per cent as whole in the NHS in 2004.

Yet, what is even more alarming is the realization that this figure could be an under-representation of the problem. This is because some studies estimate even larger labour and skills shortages in the NHS in the United Kingdom. For example a 2003 survey carried out by the *Federation of the Royal Colleges of Physicians* between October 2003 and June 2004, suggested that approximately 33 per cent of consultant physician posts were vacant in the UK.[112] That is a shocking statistic. Yet, even this may be an understatement. This is because the two indicators of continuing staff shortages are vacancy rates and the extent of the use of temporary staff. However, the first only records posts that have been vacant for three months or more. It accordingly, under-reports the total number of vacancies at any given time.[113] The figures provided should, therefore, be treated with caution as they are likely to underestimate the extent of the problem of staff shortages in the UK health industry. What is not a matter of doubt by any stretch of imagination, however, is the impact of labour shortages in the health and social work industry of these statistics. In 82 per cent of the cases, there was the reporting of an increased workload for other staff. In 42 per cent of the cases, employers noted that skill shortage vacancies in the health and social work industry resulted in difficulties meeting customer service aims. In 39 per cent of the cases, there was a reported difficulty in meeting quality standards. In turn, 46 per cent of employers mentioned that skill shortage vacancies also resulted in increased operating costs. In short, there was an increase in workload for existing staff and an increase in operating costs. This is not the way for a modern health industry to function.

Yet, the reasons for this shortfall in workers is not hard to see. There has, for some years now, been an increasing acceptance that England is not producing enough doctors to either sustain the current workforce or meet the growing demand. A number of factors account for this, as explained by Curson,[114] including: the acceptance of a doctor to patient ratio that is much lower than other countries; the assumption that growth rates are unlikely to be sustained; the assumption that even if more doctors were trained, there would not be the resources to employ them, and the investment would be wasted; and finally, the belief that, in order to sustain income from private practice, some surgical specialties have colluded to keep consultant posts and those eligible for them low. But there are other reasons also that account for the low levels of health workers in Britain. The emigration of workers in the health and social work industry has for many years now resulted in a reduction in the available labour force. It is true that the data on the emigration of UK health workers is not very accurate. The reasons have already been set out above and they are to do with the inherent limitations of the registration system itself. Thus, the data from the NMC of UK nurse emigration would not account for a Filipino nurse who migrates to the US from the UK, because such data does not distinguish between UK and non-UK trained nurses, because it ignores the possibility of a secondary or tertiary migration.[115] Yet, the fact is that there has been a rising number of UK nurses and doctors seeking to work abroad. This is now an increasing trend. An increasing pattern of UK registered nurses migrating to Australia is now well established so that whereas in 1994–1995, more than 1,100 were recorded as emigrating, some five years later in 2001–2002, that figure nearly doubled to over 1,900. Only a couple of years later in 2004, the UK lost just under 10,000 physicians to the US, Canada and Australia, with it being the top provider of physicians to both Canada and Australia.

So, what are the options? Clearly, a country like Britain must do what other countries are doing, namely, embark upon a policy of recruitment from overseas itself. Already, as a result of domestic under production and emigration, the recruitment of labour from overseas has played a prominent role in filling the demand for health and social work. In the UK, migrant workers make up a very significant proportion of those working in Health and Social Care with the proportion of non-UK born health professionals already being 25 per cent of all health care professionals; 31 per cent of all doctors; and 13 per cent all nurses.[116] In fact, the recent recruitment patterns involve even higher numbers of non-UK born professionals. Thus, over the last decade, 50 per cent of the expansion of the NHS was undertaken on the backs of foreign workers, so that 8,000 of the additional 16,000 staff had qualified abroad.[117] Indeed, in 2002 over 50 per cent of all fully registered doctors were trained overseas,[118] and in the year to March 2003, 43 per cent of all entrants to the nurses register were from overseas.[119] These are quite staggering figures leaving little doubt that without the foreign workers the health service would simply collapse.

The future, if anything, will be even more dependent on healthcare workers from abroad. It is no good saying we should train more because training more workers at home does not stop them leaving for more lucrative posts and sunnier climes abroad. Employers and Home Office projections both suggest that the workforce in the health and social work industry will grow significantly in the coming years. In the Health and Social work industry, 36 per cent of employers have anticipated that their workforce would increase in the next 12 months.[120] However, it is the long term picture that is more challenging. Projections commissioned by the Home Office for the future of the health care industry suggest that over the next 20 years the size of the health care workforce will need to increase by a massive 300,000. Up to a third more nurses and two-thirds more doctors will be needed. The demand for GPs alone is projected to be double that of 2000, increasing from 26,000 to more than 55,000. This demand for healthcare workers over the next 20 years is being driven by a number of well-known factors. First, the rise in primary health care is attributable to an ageing overall population and longer life expectancies. Second, even if the underlying levels of health remain constant, the projected increase in the likelihood of people seeking healthcare in 2020, is attributable to higher levels of income, awareness, and public engagement around health issues. Third, (and as a countervailing force) the initiatives to improve public health (such as the stop smoking and anti-obesity campaigns) may result in a reduction of major preventable diseases, which could decrease the demand for healthcare workers. If there is a drop in the availability of future health care professionals that would give rise to major concerns. Such a drop, however, seems inevitable because a number of factors, such as part-time working and an early retirement age, will work to reduce the effective supply of medical professionals over the next years. Part-time working is likely to become fashionable for a variety of reasons such as, an increased proportion of women in the medical workforce, the practice of part-time working by those who want to undertake part time training, the changing expectations among doctors about working-life, and the gradually increasing acceptance of part-timers. In addition, the adherence to the *European Working Time Directive* means that Junior Doctors' hours are being reduced to 48 hours by 2009. This will impact on the retirement age, not least in the way that many doctors today are hoping to retire earlier.

Already, British policy-makers have realized that they must make more imaginative and constructive use of immigration policy to help solve the problems of the health industry. In order to meet the projected demand, the NHS Plan includes commitments for 15,000 more General Practitioners and consultants; 30,000 more therapists and scientists; 35,000 more nurses, midwives and health visitors. This would not be possible without relaxing strict immigration controls for the entry of economic migrants. Thus, it is important to note that international recruitment plays significant role in the NHS recruitment strategy. As part of the above commitment, fully-trained specialists are being recruited from other countries. Immigration rules have been relaxed to allow the direct recruitment of General Practitioners from overseas, and Pre-Registration House Officer post numbers allow for up to an additional 12 per cent of doctors to come from overseas. In addition to the increased student numbers and international recruitment mentioned above, Curson[121] notes that the NHS plans to meet this additional staff commitment by undertaking such measures as expanding training numbers; modernizing medical careers recruitment and retention initiatives (such as pay increases); and by Job Redesign. Yet, despite these increases, the projected needs for the future outlined above, still anticipate shortages. In fact, assuming that the NHS meets all of its training and recruitment targets over this period, there remain anticipated shortages of 10,000 nurses and 25,000 doctors in 2020.

OUTSOURCING AND OFF-SHORING AS AN ALTERNATIVE TO IMMIGRATION

The outsourcing and off-shoring of jobs is ostensibly one alternative to using migrant labour for key industries in the developed world. In the industry that we have considered above, it seems that outsourcing could potentially alleviate the problem of labour shortages in the Health and Social Work industry over the next few years. In addition, outsourcing has such potential that it is not just confined to medical emergency call centres and other traditional IT functions, but can also be extended to the provision of medical transcription services and radiology. Medical transcription[122] involves doctors verbally recording patient notes, transferring them digitally overseas and having overseas workers transcribe and log them. Radiology off-shoring[123] involves transmitting x-rays overseas digitally to be diagnosed by an overseas doctor. Outsourcing in this way can happen 24 hours a day and so it enables hospitals to meet time pressures at lower costs. Clearly there is potential here because the Department of Health lists 7.5 per cent of radiology posts as vacant (as of March 2004), which indicates a need for alternative servicing strategies in this area. However, in order to accurately estimate what percentage of UK Health and Social Work activities could be moved overseas, there is a need to look at the daily tasks of the workforce. While it is unlikely that entire positions will be moved overseas, the examples given above indicate that large portions of administrative work could be outsourced, reducing the demand for labour in the future. This will mean fewer workers in developed countries.

Off-shoring is the reverse side of inward labour migration. Inward migration occurs when employers from developed countries seek workers from abroad. Off-shoring, by contrast, occurs when employers at home seek employees in developing countries by relocating. The point is that employers may well be economically neutral as between either of these options. What they are not economically neutral about is the cost of labour. Employers will seriously consider relocating abroad once it becomes difficult for them to find workers at the going rate at home, for then there will be a clear incentive for them to do so. Herein lies the importance of off-shoring as an economic activity. Once the demand for labour in the developed countries begins to consistently outstrip the supply of native-born workers, employers will draw in migrant workers whatever the system of control. Off-shoring is important for employers because, by reducing the demand for native-born workers, it serves to solve the problem of labour shortages at home.

Already, it is said that, '[T]he availability of cheaper, skilled labour means that 3.3 million jobs will move overseas from the U.S. over the next 12 years'.[124] These are not just low-grade jobs, but high-level jobs as well, which is why, 'For the first time in history, the professional classes in Britain and America find themselves in direct competition with the professional classes of another nation'. It seems that no major economic activity is left untouched by the implications. In Britain:

> the [London] *Evening Standard* came across some leaked consultancy documents suggesting that at least 30,000 executive positions in Britain's finance and insurance industries are likely to be transferred to India over the next five years.

In 2003, National Rail Inquiries announced it was move to Bangalore in India.

> Two days later, the HSBC bank announced that it was cutting 4,000 customer service jobs in Britain and shifting them to Asia. BT, British Airways, Lloyds TSB, Prudential, Standard Chartered, Norwich Union, Bupa, Reuters, Abbey National and Powergen have already begun to move their call centres to India. The British workers at the end of the line are approaching the end of the line.

It is not difficult to see why. In India:

> [t]he wages of workers in the service and technology industries are roughly one tenth of the workers in the same sectors over here. Standards of education are high, and almost all educated Indians speak English.[125]

For economists, the traditional approach has been to divide economic activities between the 'tradable' and the 'non-tradable'. Tradable goods include manufactured goods, which can be traded world-wide, are subject to competition, and can relocate relative to factor costs. Non-tradable goods include services (particularly public services) are not subject to the same factors. This means that if the consumers cannot go to a service, the service must be brought to the consumer. These non-tradable services have traditionally included such services as education and health care and they comprise 'immoveable' jobs because the dustbins of Munich cannot be emptied in Istanbul. The impact of modern technology may now, however, change this because of the way in which it is able to 'unbundle' a commodity. Manufacturing was the first to see this because different parts of a commodity could be made in different countries, with the result that global supply networks became possible. Services slowly followed suit, so that the processing of the same IT problem may take place collaboratively in California, Bangalore, Manila, and Prague, with the result it becomes impossible to know to what national authority the value added and tax liability should be attributed. In this way, the unbundling of a commodity has allowed more and more of the traditionally untradable service activities to be outsourced, such as most forms of data-processing, statistical services, accountancy/business services, insurance, airline ticketing, managing medical records, library cataloguing, architectural drawing/design work, management consultancy, and the logistics management systems for most activities.

In this way, many formerly non-tradables have begun to behave in the manner of tradeables so that there are now far fewer 'immovable' jobs. A number of examples are worth considering. In the Retail and Wholesale trade, we know that off-shore shopping centres have long been around in the form of duty-free shops, ships in the Baltic, special shopping zones (such as in countries like Bahrain, Singapore, Hong Kong, and Panama). The problem is that all of these require the high-cost mobility of the consumer, and although the internet is now beginning to transform this, delivery of the commodity is still a problem. In Education services, there is already evidence, championed by internationally competitive universities, of tertiary education becoming increasingly tradeable (even where governments have frequently remained ambivalent between sustaining a publicly-funded service, like a University, for the local population and giving a locally-based industry its commercial head to reach a global market). A number of universities in the developed world have responded with aggressive overseas recruitment and the creation of overseas campuses, with the US universities being well ahead in this respect. In addition, distance learning (as with the Open University in Britain), is providing an educational option that does not require the mobility of either the educational consumer or provider. In parallel with these developments British public schools have also been recruiting their students from as far afield as China and Thailand. What is interesting about these developments is that, although at present they appear to amount to no more than a simple export of a supply point for a British product, in future one can begin to envisage the development of global educational networks (with inputs from diverse sources rather than one way exports), in much the same way as has already happened with the manufacturing industry. Something similar is happening in medical care. Here also there is the same tension between providing a publicly-funded service for the local population and a commercially oriented service for global markets. Yet, despite this tension, the 'unbundling' of medical services may accelerate off-shoring, through medical centers in India, Singapore, Qatar and Dubai, which have succeeded in separating surgery from convalescence and diagnosis from treatment (including distance diagnosis and treatment via the web). In the same way, even low-skilled services, could see an explosion in off-shoring, where it has at present barely started. An event like the Doha GATS trade round (Mode 4) could have obliged the advanced powers to open service/construction tendering to global competition. This is what happened in the 1980s in Middle Eastern construction contracts, where companies were flying in construction teams to do the work and then removing them. In this way, the workers remain employed by their company as do present-day multinational staff, and do not become legal migrants. There is no reason why this could not be possible in a variety of low-skilled activities such as cleaning services, low-skilled hospital and transport services, agricultural work and so on.

In any event, some consumers of such services may choose to off-shore their service demands because the ageing of the population is likely to increase the demand for both labour-intensive services and for medical services. Instead of moving doctors, nurses and carers to the developed world to care for the aged, governments may choose, given the immense financial savings involved, to facilitate the movement of the aged in the reverse direction. This is already happening in part for the better off. However, in Mexico there is a township of some 180,000 dwellings, priced deliberately within the reach of the American working class household, and covered by both medical services and US medical insurance, which caters for ordinary American clientele. The Japanese government, sometime ago also tried to develop three 'silver cities' for the aged in Australia, Mexico and Spain (using Filipino staff), but were unsuccessful.[126] Thus, the potential for off-shoring is enormous and barely tapped. The future, however, is likely to see this potential fully exploited. When this occurs, two things may happen, both of which will still leave developed countries with a shortage of labour. First, the pivotal pressure for workers – especially those who are low-skilled – to migrate from under-developed countries to developed countries, may ease off. This is because those workers will now be able to find work outside the developed countries through off-shoring and out-sourcing, leaving the developed countries with a shortfall in labour. Second, the demand for labour may still go up because outsourcing lowers unit costs at home, and this can result in increasing overall domestic demand, as firms and workers have greater profits/wages arising from the production cost savings from outsourcing. This greater demand generated from this source can result in drawing in additional workers to fulfil entirely unrelated roles. Whichever way one looks at it, therefore, labour demand will not be mitigated by off-shoring and out-sourcing. Supply, as is well known, often creates its own demand. These phenomena are likely to increase over the coming half-century as globalization begins to develop global supply networks, collaborative relationships and partnerships which remove the necessity for workers to move from developing to developed countries.

CONCLUSION

This chapter has shown that the overly simplistic categorization of migrants into legal and illegal does not do justice to the complexity of migration issues. Most illegal immigrants who enter the developed world in order to work and send back remittances at home can easily be legalized by opening more categories of work related immigration. What is important is that the right to work should be legalized. There is a ready framework to follow here in the form of an international model. It lies in the ICESCR which provides for the right to work as a 'right of everyone'.[127] It is in this way that the state can regulate migration. This means that restrictive measures taken by governments must conform to strict tests. This is because the impulse to communitarianism remains strong even today as is evidenced by the resistance to the attempts to strengthen the European Union at the end of 1992, with its expansion to 15 members in 1995. While it is the case that the EU's powers have advanced with the Maastricht Treaty:

> the refusal of Norway to join the EU and the continuing reluctance of the United Kingdom to accept the EU's social standard or move towards greater integration underscored the continuing vitality of the state, even within Europe.[128]

This demonstrates that the idea of the traditional, ethnically homogenous nation-state, is still actively pursued by developed nations of the world. The rejection of European Union's Constitution by France on 29th May and by the Netherlands on 31st June 2005, the two founders of the European project, has only helped to exacerbate this tendency. The lengthy text had consolidated all previous treaties and added new powers for Brussels. But the 'rejection of the constitution signals that the dream of deeper political integration and, in the 1957 Treaty of Rome's famous phrase, "ever closer union" is over' so that the EU will now have to 'move in the direction of being a looser, less federalist and more decentralized club' whereby 'the club must pass more powers back to its members'.[129] Nevertheless, the restriction on the right to enter and work must 'bear a reasonable relationship to a legitimate government interest' and the exclusion provisions of present-day immigration laws must '*meet the test of a reasonable relationship to a legitimate state interest*' which can be considered to be those 'falling under the broad interests of public health and safety, public morals, fiscal integrity, and national security'.[130] In short, in the future immigration entry – provided that it is subject to conditions – should be the norm rather than the exception.

NOTES

1 Santos, ibid., at p.228, at para 7.4.3.
2 Nigel Harris, *The New Untouchables* (I.B. Taurus, London, 1995).
3 S. Livermore, 'Dissertations on Questions Which Arise From the Contrariety of the Positive Laws of Different States and Nations', 27–8 (1828).
4 Timothy Garton Ash, 'God's Crucible', *The Guardian*, 14th August 2003, at p.23.

5   Mary Ann Sieghart, 'There is nothing bland or staid about London any more. It is young, it is bustling, it is energetic', *The Times*, 20th August 2003, at T2 p.3.

6   Steve Pope, 'They are vilified by politicians and the media but the truth about immigrants is simple: we need them', *The Guardian*, 28th October 2003, see G2 at p.7.

7   See Anatole Kaletsky, 'Why Britain needs more people like me', *The Times*, 12th December 2002, at p.22.

8   Satvinder S. Juss, *Immigration, Nationality and Citizenship* (London, 1993), at p.5.

9   See 'World Migration: The Costs and Benefits of International Migration' (July 2005) at http://www.iom.int/iomwebsite/Publication/ServletSearch Publication?event=detail&id=4171.

10 '[r]esponsible nations might deliberately strive for a relatively quick assimilation of the underprivileged as against the high cost of maintaining present restrictions. What seems radical in terms of past policies may come to seem more like common sense in a world situation with fewer alternatives. A policy of gradualism extending intermigration privileges between select nations would be one type of beginning. If some nations were to begin opening their boundaries, it would probably put others at a political disadvantage so that they could not stand still. A new geopolitics could begin on that basis, one with sufficient latitude for political realism.'
      See Nett, 'The Civil Right We Are Not Ready For: The Right of Free Movement of People on the Face of the Earth', 84 *Ethics* 212, 227 (1971).
      Another writer has posed the same question in relation to the domestic need for citizenship laws, asking: 'What is accomplished by having a citizenship concept at all? Why, in other words, should the law affirmatively classify all earthlings as citizens or non-citizens and create rights, duties, and disabilities that hinge on that distinction?' and concluding that 'domestic considerations do not convincingly illustrate a need for citizenship, but that the international repercussions furnish compelling rationales for nationality': see, Stephen H. Legomsky, 'Why Citizenship?', *Va Jnl. of Int'L Law* (Vol. 35, No.1, Fall 1994, pp.279–300), at p.285 and p.300.

11 Lisa Schuster, 'The Origins of Fortress Europe', at www.compass.ox.ac.uk.

12 'A Strange sort of Sanctuary', *The Economist*, 15th March 2003, at pp.45–6.

13 The Report was written by Bridget Anderson at Oxford University and Ben Rogaly at Sussex University. *The Guardian* newspaper obtained a copy of the draft report marked 'confidential' and 'not for further distribution' at the beginning of 2005: see Hsia-Hung Pai, 'Damning report on migrants delayed as government fears poll backlash', *The Guardian*, 3rd February 2005, at p.1.

14 Report of the Medical Foundation for the Care of Victims of Torture in October 2004 (quoted in Lisa Schuster, 'The Origins of Fortress Europe', at www.compass.ox.ac.uk) at p.6. It is noteworthy that documented racist behaviour and 'control and restraint' used inappropriately was also found by a BBC Asylum Report in March 2004.

15 *Loc. cit.*

16 *Loc. cit.*

17 See Charles B. Keely and Sharon Stanton Russell, 'Responses of Industrial Countries to Asylum Seekers', 47 *J. Int'l Aff.* 399, 402 (1994).

18 See UNHCR, *The State of the World's Refugees: In Search of Solutions*, 199 (1999).

19 Claire Dyer, 'Curbs proposed on aid in asylum cases', *The Guardian*, 6th June 2003, at p.9. As a result of this escalating cost, the Lord Chancellor's Department published two Consultation Papers on 5th June 2003 aimed at containing the costs in

Immigration and Criminal legal aid work. Asylum seekers' access to legal aid was to be capped under these proposals.

20   See Libby Brooks, '5 Tough Questions About Asylum', *The Guardian* (G2) (1st May 2003), pp.1–9, at p.3.

21   See Libby Brooks, *op. cit.* at p.9.

22   Richard Ford, 'Asylum Chaos as 250,000 people avoid deportation', *The Times*, 19th July 2005.

23   See Libby Brooks, '5 Tough Questions About Asylum', *The Guardian* (G2) (1st May 2003), pp.1–9, at p.8.

24   Stephen Castles and Mark Miller, *The Age of Migration* (Palgrave/St. Martins Press, 2nd edn, 1998).

25   Libby Brooks, at p.2.

26   James Hollifield, *Immigrants, Markets and States* (Harvard University Press, 1992).

27   In the 2005 British general election, it was a reported that 'a survey by *The Independent* reveals Tory candidates from the south coast to the Scottish Highlands are playing the immigration card to win over undecided voters dissatisfied with Labour' and that 'Conservative candidates in marginal seats across Britain are raising fears about the impact of immigration and asylum on council tax, schools, and hospitals to swing the populist vote behind the Tories', see, Colin Brown, Nigel Morris and Marie Woolf, 'Tory candidates in marginal seats stir up storm by playing race card', *The Independent*, 22nd April 2005, at p.2. See also Editorial, 'It is time for the Tories to stop playing the race card', ibid. at p.30. Letters to the editor in the same edition of the newspaper from churchmen, declared, 'We challenge the people of this country to look beyond the political rhetoric emanating from our politicians and the media. Our experience is that genuine asylum seekers make a positive contribution to the life of our church and we ask that this opportunity be replicated in our society. Jesus Christ was an asylum seeker and found refuge in Egypt. As Christians we believe that all our asylum seekers should be treated as human beings': see The Reverends J. Clark and C. Prentis, and D. Young, J. Gibson, and J. Flounders, 'Asylum-seekers escape oppression, only to face gross injustice', ibid., at p.32.

28   See Alan Travis, 'Tory immigration claims unravel', *The Guardian*, 13th April 2005 at p.26.

29   Patrick Wintour, Alan Travis, and Nicholas Watt, 'UN says Tory plans will boost flow of asylum seekers', *The Guardian*, 20th April 2005, at p.1.

30   Richard Ford, 'Asylum Chaos as 250,000 people avoid deportation', *The Times*, 19th July 2005.

31   Jagdish Baghwati, 'Borders Beyond Control', *Foreign Affairs*, Vol. 82, No. 1, January/ February 2003, at p.99.

32   Jagdish Bhagwati, *In Defense of Globalization* (2004), at p.218.

33   Human Development Report 2004, *Cultural liberty in today's diverse world* (published for the United Nations Development Programme, OUP, 2004), at p.12.

34   'A Strange Sort of Sanctuary', *The Economist*, 15th March 2003, at p.47.

35   'An Assessment of the impact of asylum policies in Europe, 1990–2000', Home Office research study 259.

36   Quoted from Richard Ford, 'Asylum controls may make things worse', *The Times*, 24th June 2003 at p.10.

37   See Tony Travis, 'Tough asylum laws "boost trafficking"', *The Guardian*, 24th June 2003 at p.6.

38   See Ben Russell, 'Asylum rejections show "staggering lack of knowledge"', *The Independent*, 9th February 2004, at p.7. The rare Amnesty International report said

that 14,000 asylum appeals were granted in the full year for which figures are available, an average of one in five of the 64,405 appeals heard. Up to nearly four out of 10 applications are wrongly refused. The latest figures, covering the period between July and September last year, show 39 per cent of initial asylum applications from Somalis and 29 per cent of applications from Zimbabwe were later granted on appeal. Figures for 2002, the latest full year available, show the Home Office received 84,130 applications for asylum and eventually granted asylum or exceptional leave to stay in Britain to 43 per cent of them.

39   See 'Britain's Front Line', *Prospect Magazine*, Issue 109, 17th April 2005 at www. prospectmagazine.co.uk/articledetails.php?id=6833.

40   Ibid.

41   See www.london.gov.uk/mayor/refugees/docs/labyrinthreport.pdf.

42   See www.unhcr.org.uk/press/press releases2005/pr11March05.htm.

43   The UNCR, which had placed a team of staff within the Home Office in Croydon, conducted a review of 267 first instance decision-making systems from March– April 2004, which accounted for approximately 2 per cent of all decisions made.

44   Refugee Council in association with Amnesty International UK, Immigration Advisory Service, Immigration Law Practitioners Association, Joint Council for the Welfare of immigrants, Justice, Medical Foundation for the Care of Victims of Torture, Oxfam GB, Refugee Action, Refugee Legal Centre and the Scottish Refugee Council.

45   'Refugees: Renewing the Vision', An NGO working paper on improving the asylum system, June 2004, available at http://www.refugeecouncil.org.uk/ downloads/policybriefings/renewing vision.pdf.

46   Refugee Council press release: http://www.refugeecouncil.org.uk/news/ july2004/relea174.htm, 27th July 2004.

47   *Supra.*, at note 33.

48   See Bimal Ghosh, *Huddled Masses and Uncertain Shores: Insights into Irregular Migration* (Martinus Nijthoff, 1998), Preface.

49   Bimal Ghosh, see back cover of Bimal Ghosh, *Huddled Masses and Uncertain Shores: Insights into Irregular Migration*. The description comes from the Foreword by James N. Purcell, Director General, *International Organization for Migration*.

50   Immigration controls enacted in the last century in Canada, Australia, New Zealand and South Africa were largely influenced by racial considerations: see, S. Juss, at p.51. It is arguable that current policy initiatives in the European Union are also attributable to cultural and racial concerns rather than objective evidence of damage and necessitating such controls: see the discussion at pp.41–6 of this article.

51   See Richard Ford, 'Asylum service is branded a shambles', *The Times*, 16th July 2003, at p.2.

52   Dummett, at p.13.

53   Jagerskiold, 'The Freedom of Movement', in *The International Bill of Rights*, 166.

54   For example, Deborah Anker of the Harvard Law School has argued that the presence of refugee groups in the US has had a positive impact on human rights observance in US policy making in relation to countries such as El Salvador and Haiti: see, Hathaway and Neve, 'Making International Refugee Law Relevant Again', at p.148.

55   *Harrisiades vs. Shaughnessy*, 342 U.S. 580, 588–9 (1952).

56   Joel R. Charney, 'Uncharacteristically Ungenerous', *The World in 2003*, Dudley Fishburn and Stephen Green (eds), *The Economist*, London, 2002 at p.32.

57 Spellman, at p.8. He in turn refers to Ronal Skeldon, *Migration and Development: A Global Perspective* (Harlow, Essex, 1997) at p.ix.

58 See Stephen Castle, 'Immigration will be a priority for Italians', *The Independent*, 1st July 2003, at p.9. The Italian EU Presidency gave immediate backing to a set of European Commission proposals that would co-ordinate the activities of immigration officers from EU nations operating in the Mediterranean in countries like Italy, Spain and Greece, with a view to restricting illegal immigration through a proposed European agency to 'co-ordinate the work of the centers of control of external land and sea borders, in particular in the Mediterranean'.

59 Arthur C. Helton, 'The Role of International Law in the 21st Century: Forced International Migration: A Need for New Approaches by the International Community', 18 *Fordham Int'l L.J.* 1623 (May 1995).

60 Alan Travis, 'Clothes Test for Asylum Seekers', *The Guardian*, 9th July 2003 at p.6.

61 I have elsewhere argued that, 'immigration control should be taken seriously because it tells us not only about a country's attitude to those without, but also to those within it'. See, S. Juss, at p.1.

62 Although even as long ago as the passage of the Aliens Act 1905 – arguably the first piece of modern immigration legislation – the link between immigration and alleged social evils was unproven: see P. Shah, *Refugees, Race and the Concept of Asylum* (London, Cavendish Publishing, 2000), at pp.31–34.

63 Quoted in R. Winder, *Bloody Foreigners* (London, Little Brown, 2004), at p.198.

64 See especially James P. Smith and Barry Edmonston, *The New Americans: Economic, Demographic and Fiscal Effects of Immigration* (National Academy Press, Washington DC, 1997) and also Julian L. Simon, *The Economic Consequences of Immigration'* (Blackwell Press, 1989). Studies in Europe also point to the beneficial effects of immigration. The United Kingdom's annual statistical survey, Social Trends, has shown that with the aging of the largest generation born after the Second World War, deaths could exceed births around the year 2030, whereupon the population will begin to decline in Britain unless immigration acts as a balancing factor (see, S. Juss, at p.5). In Germany, the Institute of Economic Research in Rhineland-Westphalia has calculated that since 1988, 100,000 new jobs have been created in the economy by firms employing cheap migrant labor. Without the tax and social contributions of these workers, estimated at DM29 billion in 1991, German nationals would have had to pay 40 per cent more tax for the same level of service provision. Other surveys in Belgium and Sweden have also demonstrated that immigrants are necessary to maintain the welfare state and the workforce (see, S. Juss, at p.119).

65 See 'Go for it', *The Economist*, 6th May 2000, at p.19.

66 See Hamish McRae, 'New hope for the old lands', reviewing Mark Leonard's book, *Why Europe will Run the 21st Century*, in *The Independent*, 25th February 2005, at p.27.

67 'Outsource those jobs', Editorial, *The Spectator* (Vol. 296; no. 9197), 13th November 2004, at p.7.

68 See Libby Brooks, at p.3.

69 'Paying their way: the fiscal contribution of immigrants in the UK' by Dhananjayan Sriskandarajah, Laurence Cooley and Howard Reed (dated 27th April 2005), is free to download from www.ippr.org/publicationsandreports.

70 Ibid.

71 See Libby Brooks, at p.8.

72 See Peter Hetherington, 'Scotland offers to take rejected migrants', *The Guardian*, 13th April 2005 at p.2.

73   See Peter Guardian, 'Border Terrier', in *Society Guardian*, in *The Guardian*, 13th April 2004, at pp.8–9.

74   Home Office online Report 37/04, Rachel Kirk, available at: http://asylumpolicy. info/skillsaudit.pdf. The respondents were asked to provide information on a broad spectrum of skills, including literacy (in their own main language) English language ability, educational background (including qualifications gained), work related skills and qualifications, and work history. Some 2,000 completed questionnaires were received. The findings were focused on three main countries and did not claim to be representative of the refugee population in the UK.

75   *Supra*, at note 35.

76   See Camilla Cavendish, 'The people we can see only when they die', *The Times*, 9th July 2003, at p.20, where it is also stated that 'almost a quarter of staff working in British restaurants were born overseas' and that 'More than two-thirds of independently-owned local shops belong to people from ethnic minorities'.

77   See *European Foundation*: 'Migration and industrial relations', 2003. www.eiro. eurofounf.eu.int/2003/03/study/TN031053.html.

78   C. Jinks *et al.*, 'Mobile Medics? The mobility of doctors in the European Economic Area', in *Health Policy*, 2000, Vol. 54, No. 1, pp.45–64.

79   J. Irwin, 'Migration patterns of nurses in the EU', in *Eurohealth* (2001, Vol. 7, No. 4, pp.13–15).

80   J. O'Dowd, 'How will the UK cope with an influx of EU nurses?', *Nursing Times* (2003, Vol. 99, No. 21, pp.10–11), at p.10.

81   J. Buchan, 'Here to stay? International Nurses in the UK' (London, *Royal College of Nursing*, 2003), at p.23.

82   'Data on inflows into receiving countries are considered more reliable than data on outflows, not least because there is widespread belief that many countries, through error or omission, underestimate the extent of outflows, as has been shown in the case of South Africa': see Stilwell *et al.* (2003), 'Developing evidence-based ethical policies on the migration of health workers: conceptual and practical challenges', *Human Resources for Health, BioMed Central*, 28 October cited in Dr. Stephen Bach (2003), 'International migration of health workers: labour and social issues' (ILO, Geneva, July), at p.3 http://www-ilo-mirror.cornell. edu/public/english/dialogue/sector/papers/health/wp209.pdf.

83   ' ... registration data record the number of nurses or doctors registered to practice in a particular recepient country. This does not eliminate all difficulties ... The major limitation ... is that registration data indicate the intent to work rather than actual employment status': J. Buchan, *International recruitment of nurses: United Kingdom case study?* (London, Royal College of Nursing, 2002), at p.10.

84   'Because registration data have usually been compiled on a consistent basis over time, however, they provide a valuable source of trend data, despite these caveats'. See, Stephen Bach (2003), 'International migration of health workers: labour and social issues' (ILO, Geneva, July, Working Paper 209), at p.3 http://www-ilo-mirror.cornell.edu/public/english/dialogue/sector/papers/health/wp209. pdf.

85   British Medical Association (2004) 'Number of refugee doctors on BMA database hits 1000', 25 November, accessed from www.bma.org.uk. Also see the, *Employability Forum (2004)*, 'Integrating refugee skills into the workforce – a strategy of refugee nurses', Conference report, 19 July.

86   For example, see Ruth Nutt and James Buchan, *Trends in London's NHS Workforce: An Updated Analysis of Ket Data* (King's Fund Working Paper; March 2005), at www.king'sfund.org.uk/pdf/workforcetrends.pdf.

87   Gabriel Rozenberg, 'Shortage of GPs "at critical level"', *The Times*, 20th June 2003 at p.11.

88   *Developing a Modern Surgical Workforce*, published on 15th February 2005, by the Royal College of Surgeons.

89   Nigel Hawkes, 'NHS faces a shortfall of surgeons', *The Times*, 16th February 2005.

90   Nigel Hawkes, 'NHS strips africa of its doctors', *The Times*, 22nd February 2005.

91   See Mejia *et al.*, 'Physician and nurse registration: Analysis and policy implications' (Geneva, *World Health Organization*, 1979), cited in Bach, S. (2003), 'International migration of health workers: labour and social issues' (ILO, Geneva, July) at p.3 http://www-ilo-mirror.cornell.edu/public/english/dialogue/sector/papers/health/wp209.pdf.

92   World Health Organization, 'International migration, health and human rights', *Health & human rights publication series*, Issue No. 4, December 2003.

93   E. Hoffman and S. Lawrence, *Statistics on international labour migration: a review of sources and methodological issues* (Geneva, ILO, 1996). Also see, OECD: *Trends in International Migration:* Annual Report, 2002 edition (Paris, 2003a), at p.19.

94   See Mejia *et al.*, 'Physician and nurse registration: Analysis and policy implications' (Geneva, *World Health Organization*, 1979), at p.277. Also see, 'Success with internationally recruited nurses', *Royal College of Nursing* (London, 2005).

95   B. Khadria, 'Skilled labour migration from developing countries: a study of India', *International Migration Papers*, No. 49 (Geneva, ILO, 2002). Also see, *BBC News* (2003) 'How Asian doctors saved the NHS', 26 November 2003.

96   S. Go, 'Recent trends in migration movements and policies: The movement of Filipino professionals and managers', in *OECD: Migration and the Labour Market in Africa* (Paris, 2003), at p.350.

97   Cited in D. Diamond, *One Nation, Overseas*, at www.wired.com/wired/active/10.06/philippines-pr.html.

98   R. Goldfarb *et al.*, 'Can remittances compensate for manpower outflows: The case of Philippine physicians', in *Journal of Developmental Economics* (No., 15, 1984), cited in Bach, S (2003). 'International migration of health workers: labour and social issues' (ILO, Geneva, July), p.4 at http://www-ilo-mirror.cornell.edu/public/english/dialogue/sector/papers/health/wp209.pdf.

99   FilNurse Association 2004: http://www.filnurse.com/forum/viewforum.php?f=13&sid=ccfac3917fcbc2567a41e6d9883cb249.

100 K. Thompson, 'Analysis of health worker migration for selected Asian countries, the UK, US and Canada' (Geneva, International Labour Organization, Sectorial Activities Department, unpublished, 2003), at p.5.

101 *The Economist*, 17 May 2003: 33.

102 OECD, ibid., (2003a) at p.75.

103 World Health Organization, Regional Office for Africa, 2001, cited in Stephen Bach, (2003), 'International migration of health workers: labour and social issues' (ILO, Geneva, July, Working Paper 209), at p.5 http://www-ilo-mirror.cornell.edu/public/english/dialogue/sector/papers/health/wp209.pdf.

104 O. Adams and C. Kinnon, 'A public health perspective', in S. Zavelli and C. Kinnon (eds), *International trade in health services: A development perspective* (United Nations/WHO, 1998).

105 Mangwade, cited in T. Prang *et al.*, 'Brain Drain and health professionals', in *British Medical Journal* (2002, Vol. 324, pp.499–500).

106 Stilwell *et al.* (2003), 'Developing evidence-based ethical policies on the migration of health workers: conceptual and practical challenges', *Human Resources for Health, BioMed Central*, October 2003.

107   The *National Employers Skills Survey 2003* (NESS) was commissioned by the Learning and Skills Council (LSC), in partnership with the Sector Skills Development Agency (SSDA) and the Department for Education and Skills (DfES). It provides detailed information about the extent, causes, and implications of England's recruitment problems and skill gaps. It also measures employers' training activities. see http://www.lsc.gov.uk/National/Documents/subjectlisting/Research/LSCcommissionedresearch.

108   'Hard to Fill Vacancies' which were skill related where at least one of the following causes was cited by the respondent: low number of applicants with the required skills, lack of work experience the company demands or lack of qualifications the company demands.

109   See The *National Employers Skills Survey 2003: Key Facts* at http://www.lsc.gov.uk/National/Documents/subjectlisting/Research/LSCcommissionedresearch.

110   *Loc. cit.*

111   See *Department of Health Workforce Vacancy Survey 2004* at http://www.dh.gov.uk/PublicationsAndStatistics/StatisticalWorkAreas/StatisticalWork.

112   D. Andolo, 'Third of Consultant physician posts "unfilled"', *The Guardian*, 8th December 2004.

113   See 'Fragile future? A review of the UK nursing labour market in 2003', NMC Data 2003 at http://www.rcn.org.uk/publications/pdf/labour_market_review_2003.pdf.

114   Curson J., 'Physician workforce planning: what have we learned? Lessons for planning medical school capacity and IMG policies', Paper presented at the 7th International Medical Workforce Conference; 2003 Sep 11–14; Oxford, UK. Available at: www.healthworkforce.health.nsw.gov.au/amwac/amwac/imwcnew.html.

115   See the NMC Data 2003: 'Fragile future? A review of the UK nursing labour market in 2003', at: http://www.rcn.org.uk/publications/pdf/labour_market_review_2003.pdf.

116   See Stephen Glover, Ceri Gott, Anais Loizillon, Jonathan Portes, Richard Price, Sarah Spencer, Vasanthi Srinivasan and Carole Willis, 'Migration: An economic and Social Analysis', Home Office *RDS Occasional Paper* No 67, (2001), at: http://www.homeoffice.gov.uk/rds/pdfs/occ67-migration.pdf.

117   Ibid.

118   See generally, Department of Health, *International Recruitment of Consultants and General Practitioners for the NHS in England* (London, 2002a).

119   See 'Fragile future? A review of the UK nursing labour market in 2003', NMC Data 2003 at http://www.rcn.org.uk/publications/pdf/labour_market_review_2003.pdf.

120   See The *National Employers Skills Survey 2003: Key Facts* at: http://www.lsc.gov.uk/National/Documents/subjectlisting/Research/LSCcommissionedresearch.

121   Curson, J., 'Physician workforce planning: what have we learned? Lessons for planning medical school capacity and IMG policies', Paper presented at the 7th International Medical Workforce Conference; 2003 Sep 11–14; Oxford, UK. Available at: www.healthworkforce.health.nsw.gov.au/amwac/amwac/imwcnew.html.

122   More information on the Medical Transcription process can be found at: http://www.thuriam.com/.

123   More information about Radiology off-shoring can be found at: http://www.outsource2india.com/services/radiology.asp.

124   *Time Magazine*, 4th August 2003.

125   George Monbiot, 'The flight to India: the jobs Britain stole from the Asian sub-continent 200 years ago are now being returned', *The Guardian*, 21st October 2003.
126   Information supplied by Professor Nigel Harris, with the Author.
127   Article 6 reads:

> The States Parties to the present Covenant recognize the right to work, which includes the right of everyone to the opportunity to gain his living by work which he freely chooses or accepts, and will take appropriate steps to safeguard this right.
>
> The steps to be taken by a State Party to the present Covenant to achieve the full realization of this right shall include technical and vocational guidance and training programmes, policies and techniques to achieve steady economic, social and cultural development and full and productive employment under conditions safeguarding fundamental political and economic freedoms to the individual.

128   Hurst Hannum, *op.cit.*, at 497.
129   *The Economist*, 'The Europe that died' (June 4th–10th 2005; vol. 375; No. 8429), pp.11–12 at p.11.
130   'Where the restriction does not involve a suspect classification or impinge on fundamental rights, a restriction on entry would have to bear a reasonable relationship to a legitimate government interest. Present immigration law contains various exclusion provisions which would need to meet the test of a reasonable relationship to a legitimate state interest. We may consider these as falling under the broad interests of public health and safety, public morals, fiscal integrity, and national security, though these categories overlap to a degree'. See, Note, 'Immigrants, Aliens, and the Constitution', 49 *Notre Dame Law Review* [1974], 1075, 1082.

4 The Failed States Phenomenon

INTRODUCTION

In a speech in London in early 2005, 'Not Every Country in the World can be Democracy', Professor John Gray of the London School of Economics, drew attention to the state of the world today, where there are an increasing number of broken, fragmented and corroded states.[1] In much of Africa, Asia and the Balkans, he commented, there is nothing resembling a functioning modern state. Instead, there are failed or semi-failed states. Yet, this is not a new phenomenon. It has been known to the international community for a good many years now. A failed or collapsed state is not simply a state that is institutionally destabilized. This destabilization need not be by civil strife or guerrilla warfare. It can arise in other ways also. The World Bank in 1997[2] highlighted three distinguishing features of a collapsed state. These are: (1) 'states that have lost (or failed to establish) legitimacy in the eyes of most of the population … and are therefore unable to exercise authority'; (2) 'states that have been run into the ground by leaders and officials who are corrupt, negligent, incompetent, or all three'; (3) 'states that have fragmented into Civil War, and in which no party is capable of re-establishing central authority'.[3] State collapse, however, is a process. When does one determine that a state is in full collapse?

It seems to me that one can have a country with internal dissension, such as in Kosovo, where the state has 'fragmented into civil war' but where one party still has central authority, and yet be said to be in a state of collapse. One can even have a state without civil war, such as in Afghanistan or Pakistan, where the central authority does not have sovereign control over outlying areas which are a law unto themselves. In both of these situations one can realistically talk of a failed state phenomenon where the violation of human rights may be at the behest of either state elements or non-state elements. The World Bank definition is unduly limiting in this respect. It is more accurate to say that a failed state is one that has experienced a 'fundamental loss of institutional capability'.[4] It is a *de facto* and not a *de jure* situation. It has nothing to do with the government's intention to offer protection to its population, however well meaning that may be. It has everything to do with the government's inability or incapability to do so. In the light of this wider definition, in this chapter, I want to consider the problem of protection facing the international community in what may be described as 'failed state situations'.

I want to address the problem of protection in this context quite simply because much of this world is likely to remain in a collapsed and corroded state for the foreseeable future. It will remain so no matter how interventionist the major powers become in the internal affairs of weaker nations. These collapsed states threaten rich societies which cannot be insulated from this new form of war. The response of rich societies is to monitor travel and to stringently control the movement of people into their territories. Yet, this is contrary to the basic tenets of a global market which the rich countries want to support today. Herein lies the paradox. The developed world passionately espouses the movement of free trade and capital across the globe. But it wants to severely restrict the free movement of labour which helps to alleviate the hardships in many failed states. To that extent, the developed world is failing to affirm its own commitment to free liberal societies governed by openness, democracy and human rights. This is a very odd form of globalization. It is a state of affairs that is very different from that pertaining in the nineteenth century, as we saw in Chapter 1 when we discussed the work of W.M. Spellman. That was a period of comparable globalization. In the nineteenth century, barriers to immigration hardly existed. But today, globalists have unwittingly pitched themselves against localists. It is hardly surprising that rich societies stand poised against poor societies and poor societies against the rich.

THE FAILED STATES PHENOMENON

Failed State situations have become the focus of increased UN activity over the last decade, but the problem of individual human rights violations at the hands of both state and non-state agents of persecution, is nowhere near being resolved by such increased activity. The result has been to heighten the plight of refugees world-wide. In fact, as I shall argue, the UN has failed dismally to prevent gross human rights abuses in the impending decline of collapsed states. In the 1990s, the UN Security Council did take on a broad range of internal conflicts, ranging from inter-communal strife, to democratic crisis, to internal struggles over the control of national resources, which are germane to any future UN involvement in failed state situations. These were very different from previous inter-state disputes that the Security Council had been involved in. They were intra-state disputes focusing on states undergoing a process of collapse. Intricate mandates more ambitious than the modalities of conventional peace-keeping were called for in these international efforts to mitigate and resolve these conflicts amongst collapsed States.[5] This 'new generation' of peace-keeping operations were not distinguished by their large-scale military deployment (as had been in the case in Sinai, the Congo, and Cyprus of earlier years) but by the diversity of their civilian and police components.[6] Civilian functions are well recognized. First, there is the civil administration component, as evidenced by such operations in Namibia,

Cambodia, the former Yugoslavia, East Timor, and Kosovo. Second, there is humanitarian assistance, as evidenced by the UN mission in Afghanistan which was deployed alongside a coalition peacekeeping operation, namely, the International Security Assistance Force (ISAF). Third, there are a whole gamut of such activities as human rights monitoring and training, police and judicial support, training, and reform, and even a leadership role in economic revival and development.[7] All three functions played a vital role in addressing the condition of collapsed states, but none have truly succeeded in addressing gross human rights violations and the rise in the number of the world's refugees. In 1989–1990, Martii Ahtisaari, who later became President of Finland, initiated very successfully civilian leadership of large-scale UN peace-keeping operations. In other circumstances, these ambitious objectives were more difficult for the Security Council to attain. Peace-keepers lost lives in large numbers in Rwanda, Somalia and the former Yugoslavia when military activities mandated by the Council met with heavy resistance from belligerent elements in those countries. The UN Security Council was unable to induce compliance. In the result, it was left with two choices: either to enforce its decisions where they had failed to generate consent, or to beat a hasty retreat. In the former Yugoslavia,[8] in Somalia,[9] and in Haiti[10] it chose to enforce its decisions. In casualty-ridden Somalia, and in genocidal Rwanda it chose to beat a hasty retreat.[11] Thus, such an approach has failed and there is no evidence that the opening years of the twenty-first century will be more effective in assisting victims of non-state agents of persecution in these broken states.

Collapsed states have become a major feature of the world political landscape in the last few years, and particularly during the last decade and the beginning years of this century. Civil War, clan and tribal based power struggles, and political disintegration have occurred in Afghanistan, Cambodia, Liberia, Somalia, Sierra Leone, and now in Iraq. Other countries, such as Sudan, Zimbabwe and the Democratic Republic of Congo, presently look on the brink of a collapse that is imminent. De-colonization, the end of the cold war, regional instability, have all helped to induce chaos and dysfunction in a number of countries in the 1980s and 1990s. A large number of states are presently unable to offer protection to their own citizens.[12] Thus, failed states, in the well-expressed words of William Zartman, reflect a condition that is 'deeper … than mere rebellion, coup, or riot'. A collapsed state 'refers to a situation where the structure, authority legitimate power, law, and political order have fallen apart and must be reconstituted in some form, old or new'.[13]

A good example is seen in Afghanistan and Iraq, the two countries of increasing international focus in the new millennium. Both are countries which are deemed to have viable sovereign governments in charge. Both are undergoing massive human rights violations. Both have fleeing populations from within their borders. Both have their citizens regularly denied refugee status in Western countries today. Yet, the report of the UK's *Commons Foreign Affairs Select Committee* on 29th July 2004, warned that both Afghanistan and Iraq could collapse in the immediate future, unless Nato countries help:

> There is a real danger that if these resources are not provided soon then Afghanistan
> – a fragile state in one of the most sensitive and volatile regions of the world – could
> implode, with terrible consequences.

This prediction came 24 hours after *Medecins Sans Frontiers* announced that it
was to end its operations in the country after 23 years because of the deterioration in security. The continued power of the Afghan warlords was considered
by the Members of Parliament (MPs) as being part of the problem, and Sir
John Stanley, a member of the Committee and a former Conservative defence
minister, went onto warn that, 'Afghanistan is on a knife-edge'. The MPs visited Afghanistan, Iraq and Pakistan, meeting with both Presidents Hamid
Karzai and Pervez Musharraf of Afghanistan and Pakistan respectively, before
compiling their report. In a 174-page Report, entitled *Foreign Policy Aspects of
the War Against Terrorism*, the cross-party committee of MPs also warned that
Iraq too could become a failed state that will create regional instability, declaring that 'Iraq has become a "battleground" for al-Qaida, with appalling
consequences for the Iraqi people'.[14]

Failed states are not confined to one particular part of the world. There is
no semblance of a modern state in much of Sudan or Yemen, in Kosovo or
Bosnia Herzogovina, or in Pakistan, or even in swathes of Russia. Instead,
political and religious organizations, commanded by clan led or tribal based
leaders lay control over zones of anarchy through irregular armies fighting
internecine battles with a medieval ferocity. No world authority, as is vividly
demonstrated by the example of Iraq, is able to enforce stability and peace.[15]
In this chapter, I will first consider the changing role of the United Nations in
the context of an ever more turbulent and unstable world and conclude that
the international community will be unable to impose democracy, human
rights and the rule of law in these broken states, so as to provide protection
for victims of human rights abuses. I will then consider the *1951 Refugee Convention*. I will observe that international refugee law is predicated on a system
of properly constituted sovereign states that are in the *de jure* position of offering protection to their citizens. Where States are malfunctioning and
corroded, but in existence nonetheless, the basis for the principle of surrogate
international protection in international refugee law, may prevent the grant
of refugee status in another country. Thirdly, I will consider the application
of the *European Human Rights Law* under article 3, which provides protection
for individuals from 'inhuman and degrading treatment'.

CAN THE INTERNATIONAL COMMUNITY IMPOSE DEMOCRACY, HUMAN RIGHTS AND THE RULE OF LAW IN FAILED STATE SITUATIONS?

The Regional Bodies

In the section above, I have argued that I want to address the problem of protection here quite simply because much of this world is likely to remain in a

collapsed and corroded state for the foreseeable future, no matter how inter-ventionist the major powers become in the internal affairs of weaker nations. I will now attempt to make good that argument by arguing that, despite the recent neo-conservative trend of increased intervention by the US-UK led coalitions in conflict ridden regions of the world, there is little evidence of the emergence of democratic and human rights respecting states in those regions. The problem of protection for the victims of failed state situations will accordingly remain. Regional bodies offer a better chance of providing a coherent and concerted approach to conflict resolution, as the example of the OSCE and NATO well demonstrates in Kosovo, but they must have adequate resources and capacity made available to them.

When the political crises in the Western Hemisphere, arising from failed states first arose, the UN Security Council initially left it up to the *Organization of American States* (OAS) to deal with the problems in Central America and of Haiti.[16] Once it became clear that the OAS was unable to achieve a negotiated settlement the Security Council took over the initiative, but not without first leaving the OAS some leeway to develop its own strategies.[17] In the same way, *The Organization of African Unity* (OAU) was also given the chance of dealing with the problems in Africa. It often set out to take a lead role in doing so. Sadly, it met with little success. No major settlements were reached by it. It was unable to challenge the sovereignty of belligerent African states in the most effective ways. It had an able Secretariat, in the person of the well regarded Salim Salim. Its weakness lay in the fact that its member states simply could not agree on what political strategies to adopt for conflict resolution in a continent littered with collapsed states.[18] It lacked resources and political support from member states. It was an under-resourced and divided regional body. It, therefore, felt that the UN was unfairly dumping off responsibility for some of the worst conflicts of the decade onto an already weakened body. The OAU thus resented the United Nations. The OAU now has a successor organization, the *African Union.*

The *African Union* (AU) undertook its first regional peace-keeping mission in Sudan. Today, the AU is the only force actively engaged on the ground in the province of Darfur, in Sudan, where a process of 'arabization' is taking place through ethnic cleansing of African tribes by Arab militias.[19] It had only started off back in May 2004 as an observer mission of 300 monitors to oversea the humanitarian cease-fire between the rebels in Darfur and the Sudanese government. It then massively expanded to a 3,500 force of monitors, peace-keepers and civilian police. Its projected increase by September 2005, was hoped to be 12,000 AU personnel. Yet, notwithstanding the slogan of both the African and Western governments alike, of 'African solutions of African problems'[20] the AU clearly does not have the resources for procuring and transporting troops around an area that is as vast as France. Western governments themselves have been keen to avoid multi-national obligations. The AU itself has not had a clear mandate to enforce the peace. As such, they could not protect the civilians and disarm the militias. In essence, they are guests of the Sudanese government, who would rather have an AU force there than an American or European one. At the end of 2004, the AU's mandate was increased, but they were still unable to protect the burgeoning number of forced migrants known as 'internally displaced persons' that ethnic cleansing was creating. This is because the Sudanese government objected to their having a peace enforcement role. Thus, when in July 2005, the government and the rebels agreed a cease-fire, rape and violation of civilian rights still continued. The AU presence has prevented more widespread atrocities but its effectiveness remains hugely dependent on Western donor support and only a much bigger force will prevent the displacement of peoples from their homes. Time will tell whether this new body of the *African Union* will rise up successfully to further challenges in the twenty-first century. The view of many experts is that the future hope of Africa does indeed lie in the hands of such sub-regional organizations as ECOWAS, SADC, and IGAD when it comes to the security and stability of the African continent. It is not hard to see why. Such bodies have the potential of being more cohesive and effective. They often have the added advantage of working through the leadership of a regional hegemon such as Nigeria within ECOWAS.[21]

Other regional actors had met with some success, such as in the case of the former Yugoslavia the paradigm example of a collapsed state in Eastern Europe in the 1990s. The United Nations and the Security Council both dealt with a range of regional participants here. These comprised European Community monitors, European Union civil administrators in Mostar, OSCE negotiators, and NATO enforcement units. Jointly with the European Community, negotiations with various contending parties in the conflict in the former Yugoslavia were led by the United Nations, with Security Council support, and this happened most notably during the Vance-Owen deliberations. Regional organizations also set out to keep or promote peace in Georgia[22] and in West Africa,[23] where UN missions mandated by the Council monitored their activities. Peacekeeping forces often faced an uphill struggle. Their role was often questioned. For example, in Georgia, many Western powers did not see the Commonwealth of Independent States (CIS) as particularly impartial or as a respectable regional organization. Yet, peace-keeping continued. Sovereign states were made to account wherever possible.

Today regional organizations have a particularly valuable role to play. Already by the end of the 1990s and the beginning of the twenty-first century, it was clear that the UN Security Council faced fractious disunity from within and unmanageable conflicts to contend with from without. Regional organizations were theoretically aptly situated to replace the United Nations. The majority of regional bodies, however, were unable to do so because they had limited resources and capacity. Only NATO was as well endowed as the United Nations. There were institutional shortcomings as well. If international security was to be founded on regional organizations, who would arbitrate the differences between them and how would they do so? Ultimately, one had to turn back to the UN Charter for standard-setting and to the authority of the Security Council however imperfect it was. Yet, there had been a shift in the nature and scope of Security Council decisions. Many such decisions had established precedents. In the end, evolving interpretations of the Charter had deeply affected understanding of sovereignty at the international level.

The Changing Role of the United Nations

In one sense the possibility of intervention in failed state scenarios is greater today then ever before because of a new culture of co-operation and conciliation that is traceable back to the 1990s amongst the permanent members. That period resulted in a seismic shift in the Council's ability to undertake the task of international conflict resolution and to challenge the conception that states are sovereign in what they do. This augured well for the plight of failed states whose internal condition could impact adversely on regional stability. State sovereignty was challenged in a number of ways. There were expansive new re-definitions. The UN redefined what constitutes a threat to peace. Thus, when a democratically elected regime in Haiti was toppled in a coup the UN deemed that to be a threat to peace. More significantly for failed states, the UN also re-defined humanitarian catastrophes adding new ranges. The mass exodus of displaced and refugee persons would be increasingly viewed as a humanitarian catastrophe. And, the UN re-defined its approach to terrorism. Both domestic and international struggles acquired a new significance after September 11th 2001. More and more issues, some hitherto unfashionable, were raised. Some were successful, others were not. Yet, what is remarkable is the way in which Security Council's agenda had opened up to non-traditional issues. When in 1989, the United Kingdom urged discussion of international narco-trafficking and environmental issues as potential threats to peace, the Council refused to oblige;[24] but on 10th January 2000, the Council engaged in a debate about the implications of the AIDS pandemic in Africa for stability and peace on that region in the twenty-first century.[25] But what has shattered them now is the Iraq War. This has destroyed all further international consensus on UN intervention. That augurs badly for failed states where intervention may well be needed.

The parlous state of the world in the last decade, and of the broken states within it, led the UN Security Council to attempt to dismantle the absolute foundations of state sovereignty by taking steps to intervene in the internal affairs of recognized sovereign states. This forever changed the way in which the relationship between state and citizen is being perceived in the world today. One question is whether the UN can intervene to restore stability and respect for human rights in countries where the state apparatus is failing to provide protection to citizens. What we do know is that since the 1990s the UN Security Council has engaged itself in ways whereby both the interpretation of what comprises 'threats to peace', and the interpretation of Chapter VII of the Charter,[26] have been expansively developed. This has been possible because these altered constructions have involved no Charter amendments or clear breaks with earlier amendments. We know that the changing conceptions of sovereignty began in the post-Cold war era. The question is whether the international community can make a concerted effort now to deal with the problem of failed states.

The post-Cold-war era itself began when relations among the Permanent Five (P-5) members of the UN Security Council thawed East-West tensions within the Council in the mid-1980s. An early example was the noticeably amicable manner in which the position of the UN Secretary-General was discussed when the first term of Javier Perez de Cuellar was drawing to a close in 1986. He was appointed to a second term and in 1987 he called for 'a meeting of minds at the highest political level' and publicly challenged the UN Security Council to deal with the catastrophic Iran-Iraq war.[27] Here was the UN Security Council intervening in ways that were significant in the long-term. By mid-1987, Security Council proposals for a cease-fire, monitored by a small UN observer mission, were making serious headway. Such action galvanized other Council members.

Once the Permanent Five learnt to work together, the other Council members, who enjoyed no veto power, found their roles seriously diminished. They, therefore, became quite adroit in playing off one permanent member against the other and thereby acquired significant political clout as time went on. There was the developing influence of the Non-aligned Movement within the Council whose voice and apparent influence had grown in the previous decade. Growing co-operation amongst the Permanent five now led to their increased marginalization. The UN Secretariat began to privately consult with some or all of the P-5 before putting recommendations to the whole Council There was clear collusion between the UN Secretariat and the P-5. Open Council meetings which had been the principal forum Council decision-making in previous decades were now replaced by 'informal consultations'.[28] In this spirit of widespread co-operation, the UN Security Council was able to deal with many more international conflicts than it had tackled in earlier decades. Cold war hostilities amongst the P-5 had hijacked previous initiatives. Vetoes, both actual and threatened by the permanent members, had plagued the Security Council. But the fruits of this unprecedented co-operation meant that by 1990, the use of the veto had plummeted.

What has been important, when we look back to the 1990s, is that the Council has been able to address, in this way, a range of internal conflicts that it simply would not have been able to face up to during the Cold War. This was because in those days antagonists played out their animosities all too frequently through regional proxy conflicts that rendered the Council effete. But that changed noticeably in the last decade of the twentieth century. The creation of International Criminal Tribunals for the former Yugoslavia in 1993[29] and Rwanda in 1994[30] came on the heels of a new and highly innovative normative framework that arose through Council's decisions in the 1990s. International relations were changed forever. Radical legal developments had taken shape. In 1998 a diplomatic conference in Rome,[31] acceded to growing international pressure, and adopted a statute for a universal international criminal court. Yet, it is important for us to also recognize that the post-Cold war honeymoon in the Security Council was short-lived. By the end of the 1990s, there were serious disagreements. By the beginning of the twenty-first century, the War in Iraq had destroyed all consensus. Disquiet among the P-5 on the legitimation of the use of force and a rising tendency among some major UN members to unilateralism raised concerns about the plight of state sovereignty. First there was concern in 1998 and 1999 over the conflicting objectives and approaches among the P-5 to Kosovo. Then there were, by 2002, the heightened differences over Iraq and the promotion of global security leading eventually to the attack in Iraq in 2003. The UN did not support that War and any further incursions into foreign territories, even in order to restore peace and prevent the displacement of peoples, is likely to be met with UN disapproval as is vividly demonstrated by its reluctance over the conflict in Darfur in Sudan.

In Sudan in 2004, ten years after the Rwandan genocide, government sponsored attacks by Arab militias on African villagers in the Darfur province displaced 2 million people and a death toll of between 180,000 to 300,000 people.[32] Yet, notwithstanding the scale and nature of the killings, the UN Commission of Inquiry in a report published on 25th January, exonerated the Sudanese government of embarking on a deliberate policy of genocide, concluding that the key element of 'intent' of wanting to destroy the targeted group was missing.[33] Indeed, between 2003 and 2004, while the siuation in Darfur was deteriorating the UN remained preoccupied with the settlement of the Naivasha Agreement, designed to bring the North-South war to an end.[34] It seemed that Colin Powell's declaration that States should meet their obligations by 'calling on the competent organs of the United Nations or by taking actions they consider appropriate'[35] did not mobilize sufficient UN action. On 25th May 2004, the Security Council's President called for the Sudanese government to disarm the Janjaweed militias, but when the *Security Council Resolution 1547* was passed, establishing a UN mission to be deployed in Southern Sudanm, there was barely a mention of the atrocities in Darfur. The *Resolution* only imposed a ban on the sale of arms to 'non-government entities and individuals' in Darfur and not a blanket arms embargo on Sudan. The government could therefore supply the Janjaweed with arms as it had hitherto done. When the humanitarian situation in Darfur took a turn for the worst, the Security Council passed *Resolution 1564* two months later, stating it had 'grave concern' over the lack of effective governmental action in Sudan, and calling for it 'to end the culture of impunity in Darfur'.[36] It also called for an expansion of the African Union monitoring force and the establishment of a Commission of Inquiry into the atrocities in Darfur. The UN *Resolution*, passed by 11-0 votes in favour, also threatened sanctions, 'such as actions to affect Sudan's petroleum sector' or action against 'the Government of Sudan or individual members of the Government of Sudan',[37] but saw Algeria, China, Pakistan, and Russia abstaining. The result was that months after receiving clear and damning evidence of massive government sponsored human rights violations in Darfur, all that the UN could do was to plead with the Sudanese government that it comply with its requests, seek the support of an inexperienced and under-resourced African Union force, and call for an investigation of facts which were already well known. The UN therefore has been singularly ineffective in preventing genocidal atrocities in the world. Where these atrocities have undergone a cessation, it has almost always been on their own account or on account of a resistance from within. The UN does not have a proud record of curbing human rights violations.[38]

But, what if a situation presents a threat to wider international peace and stability? Can the UN be more effective there? This, we must examine below.

The Enforcement of Chapter VII Provisions

In a detailed and thorough analysis of UN Security Council activity in the post-Cold War era, David Malone – who once served as Canada's Ambassador and Deputy Permanent Representative to the United Nations and chaired the UN Special Committee on Peacekeeping Operations – has argued that Council decisions in the 1990s have 'eroded the foundations of absolute conceptions of state sovereignty'.[39] However, useful as that account is, I take the view that the UN was only able to intervene as boldly as it did in the 1990s because there was no effective exercise of sovereignty by national governments in the first place, and that the subsequent experience of the UN in those instances, only shows that it cannot impose its own sovereignty on other countries. The implicit recognition that some states were on the verge of collapse led the Security Council in the 1990s to adopt Chapter VII decisions to an unprecedented extent. In itself, the enforcement of Chapter VII provisions and of UN Charter provisions were not new, as examples from the early years of the United Nations show, when Council decisions were enforced in Korea as well as in the Congo. It was, however, the frequency of resort which was unique in the last years of the twentieth century. Yet, these actions do not necessarily bode well for intervention in failed state situations. It is one thing to intervene because the country in question is unstable and is unable to provide protection to its citizens. It is quite another thing to enforce stability and provide protection for the citizens of that country, having once intervened. This is clear today from the examples of Iraq and Afghanistan. Even in the 1990s, the UN was incapable of launching and managing enforcement operations as the catastrophic events in the former Yugoslavia and in Somalia showed. Peace-keeping was one thing; peace-enforcement was quite another. They were as different in nature as chalk and cheese. Peace-keeping required consent and impartiality. Peace-enforcement required international personnel to face up to and take on disparate belligerent groups, who were loathe to recognize a neutrally conceived Security Council mandate. That is the problem that the UN Security Council will continue to face today whenever it intervenes in failed state situations. In fact, there is no evidence that UN action has achieved better protection for individuals against non-state agents of persecution in failed states. An analysis of UN action in the 1990s, despite its complex machinations and attempts to enlist broad-based support, makes this only too clear.

In the 1990s, the UN, to its great credit, made many concerted efforts to rein in recalcitrant and wayward regimes. It undertook many a nuanced approach. It was in 1994 that the UN Secretary-General, Boutros Boutros-Ghali, realized that the United Nations should not seek to conduct large-scale enforcement activities. The Security Council then began to entrust the 'coalitions of the willing', for the enforcement of its decisions. Such enforcement action took place, most notably, in Haiti (with Operation Uphold Democracy) in 1994, in Bosnia (with first the IFOR and then the SFOR) in 1995, in the Central African Republic (with the MISAB) in 1997, in East Timor (with the INTERFET) in 1999, and most recently in Afghanistan (with ISAF) in 2002.[40] Yet, there is no evidence that warring factions – sometimes known as non-state agents of persecution – were any less able to harass individual civilians in those countries, and there is no evidence that there was an improvement in human rights protections, such as would obviate the need for sanctuary abroad for refugees. Regional bodies also became involved in enforcement activities. This occurred in Liberia and Sierra Leone, where the UN Security Council supported the enforcement activities by a regional body like ECOMOG, the military arm of the West-African economic cooperation arrangement ECOWAS. The enforcement technique of a naval blockade was used both in the Persian Gulf and the Gulf of Aqaba against Iraq. It was used both in the Adriatic Sea and on the Danube against various belligerent parties in the former Yugoslavia. It was used also against Haiti. In this way, the international community was able to control the access of prohibited goods to regions of conflict. Yet, once again, this did not assist individual citizens facing gross human rights violations in those states. This was a dramatic encroachment on technical notions of state sovereignty by the UN Security Council and the 'coalition of the willing'. Only against Rhodesia had the UN Security Council acted like this once before and that was a very long time ago. Indeed, the mandated use of such blockades at this level was unique.

Yet, it is important to recognize that this occurred only with varying degrees of success.[41] Under Chapter VII mandatory economic sanctions were used even more commonly than military enforcement decisions by the Council.[42] But there was a limit to how far this could go. Sanctions could hurt individual civilians who were already subject to human rights violations. By the end of the 1990s, this gave way to targeted sanctions, which were an even more sustained and focused assaults on state sovereignty. Targeted sanctions came into vogue for two reasons. First, there was the realization of the humanitarian costs of comprehensive trade and economic sanctions against countries such as Haiti and Iraq. Second, it was clear that some governing regimes in countries subject to trade and economic sanctions (such as in Iraq under Saddam Hussein) were actually managing to enrich themselves through the control of black markets in prohibited goods. Targeted sanctions took various forms. In respect of Libya, there was a ban on air flights to and from that country. In this way, the Security Council set out to procure Libyan cooperation over the resolution of a number of terrorist aircraft bombings that it was investigating. In respect of Sudan, there was the use of diplomatic sanctions, with the reduction in the level of diplomatic representation, and after an assassination attempt against Egyptian President Hosni Mubarak, in Addis Ababa, there was a further reduction in the level of diplomatic representation mandated by the Council.[43] In respect of the Taliban in Afghanistan, both financial and airline flight sanctions were used on November 14, 1999, when it was realized that the Taliban were affording protection to the alleged terrorist Osama bin Laden[44] (leading eventually to an outright military attack by the US and British forces in 2001). Targeted financial sanctions remain difficult.[45] They are not easy to orchestrate or to implement. More innovative methods are needed.[46] This is despite a record of proven success in their use by the Security Council.[47] Pressure can then be brought to bear more effectively on recalcitrant countries.[48] Thus, whether it is Libya, Sudan, Angola or Afghanistan, there is no evidence that such concerted and innovative methods of UN intervention made any long-term difference to the security concerns of individuals at the hands of non-state agents of persecution. In the case of Sudan and Afghanistan, their position is arguably worse today. In fact, such action against renegade or recalcitrant nations has not even produced a more ordered international system.

Conclusion: A Greater Commitment to Peace-Keeping?

I have argued above that peace-keeping is one thing and peace-enforcement is another. Peace-enforcement is not likely to work. Regime change is even less likely. Active UN involvement is needed in failed state situations, but it is needed in the form of peace-keeping and with far greater resources, training and equipment with an overall commitment from the affluent countries of the North, including seeing a greater representation from the poorer countries themselves. In conclusion, I would like to make this point in relation to the example of Africa. Africa has the largest number of failed states on any continent in the world today. Yet, the UN Security Council has been least successful in Africa. It has a catalogue of failures on that Continent. In February 1999, the failing UN peacekeeping operation was withdrawn from Angola.[49] Guinea-Bissau, a small territory with severe problems had only a half-hearted response from the UN Security Council.[50] Eastern Congo became a battleground for warring neighboring countries, all pouring into the cauldron, with some troop withdrawals only taking place after negotiations in mid-2002. A chasm opened up in the sub-regional organization of Southern Africa, SADC, and its two most powerful members, Zimbabwe and South Africa, fell out with each other. Sierra Leone had a UN peacekeeping operation there, running in tandem with the deployment of UK troops, but at the start of its operations 500 UN members were taken hostage by rebel forces, and the situation did not stabilize until 2002. Ethiopia and Eritrea were mired in a petty but costly war over the disputed border between the two countries, the war was only ended when after 2000, the United Nations, deployed a large and effective peacekeeping force along the border, and after OAU mediation. The truth is that Africa needs active UN involvement. This is borne out by the fact that despite attempts from some of the P-5 countries, such as the United States, the United Kingdom, and France, to encourage the creation of a regional peacekeeping force by providing equipment and training to a number of African armed forces, demand for the services of the UN has remained high. This has placed the UN in some difficulty as it does not have the resources to match this demand.

The affluent countries of the North are not on the whole keen to participate in peace-keeping operations in Africa and when, for example, the UN peace-keeping operation moved into the Congo, there was no Western involvement of any significance at all. Plainly, major moral, ethical and policy issues are raised by this lack of involvement by the West.[51] Conflict prevention, peace implementation, and postwar reconstruction in war-torn parts of the world, such as Africa, are only possible if more assistance and support are forthcoming from those countries that are best able to provide it, namely, the affluent countries of the developed North. This does not let Africa off the hook. The African Union and sub-regional organizations will work best when they are fully supported by African leaders. In this way, regional bodies can, with support of the richer countries, make a real difference in strife-torn areas, ending the plight of individual victims of human right abuses. A recent example has occurred over Zimbabwe, long regarded as posing a most intractable problem, not least for Britain which faced accusations of neo-imperialist designs from its belligerent leader. In August 2005, the African Union appointed the former Mozambican president, Joaquim Chissano, to mediate in the Zimbabwe crisis, to persuade Robert Mugabe to negotiate with his political opponents, in particular Mr. Tsvangirai, the leader of the Movement for Democratic Reform. The Foreign Office in London applauded the AU initiative stating:

> We welcome the fact that a number of African leaders are now working constructively to pressure Mr. Mugabe to end the crisis in Zimbabwe through internal dialogue and changes in policies.

Mr Mugabe himself was understood to be seriously interested in such talks – which was remarkable given his well-publicized tirades against the West – since he was now keen to end his international isolation which was costing him dear. A one billion dollar loan had been offered by Mr. Mbeki's South African government to help Mr. Mugabe pay for urgent fuel, electricity and food imports – but only on condition that the Zimbabwean government began talks with the Opposition.[52] Thus, here was a good example of how action on improved governance can take place if it is actively supported by the leaders of the African countries. This is provided that the West also gives its full support. Moreover, in both economic and social areas, the New Economic Program for African Development now provides such a model to be followed by the countries of Africa.

Nevertheless, some reform of the UN Security Council is also clearly warranted.[53] Its involvement in international affairs in the last decade of the twentieth century and the beginning of the twenty-first, made it a serious player on the international scene, and one that many countries wanted to have a role in influencing. Its decisions were becoming genuinely important. More and more countries wanted to sit on the UN Security Council. The permanent members were increasingly resented because of the P-5 tendency to impose decisions on the remainder of the Council, and not least because of their possession of the veto, which was deeply ironical given that the veto had only been used on 12 occasions since January 1990, compared to on 193 occasions between 1946–1989. Given the obvious under-representation of the developing countries in existing seat distribution arrangements, the least controversial reform is their accommodation on the Council through a small increase in the Council's non-permanent seats.[54] Yet, apart from the move towards transparency in the Council's *modus operandi*, progress on reform has so far been only slow. In the result, pressure on the victims of failed state situations, to migrate to other countries, and there seek international surrogate protection, will remain. At present, they can only do so as refugees since the only treaty obligations on third countries to grant refugee status arises from the *Geneva Convention on the Status of Refugees 1951*. It is to this that we must now turn.

FAILED STATES AND THE CHALLENGE TO REFUGEE LAW

The Basis for Surrogate Protection in Refugee Law

The problem of 'protection' for the citizens of dysfunctional states has already been highlighted in the valuable work of Jennifer Moore, who has pointed out that the sort of 'enforcement of state obligations' that we have seen the UN and other international bodies above engage in, 'is not always feasible … in an internal conflict or a failed state situation where the state is compromised or dysfunctional', and not least because, 'as a tactical matter it becomes difficult, if not impossible for the international community to hold accountable the state in which the violation occurred …' Clearly, therefore:

> [i]n instances where victims of human rights abuses flee the repressive jurisdiction, the most feasible form of relief … is likely to involve surrogate protection from an alternate state in which the victim has sought refuge.[55]

Further significant work has also been undertaken by Tara Magner in this respect who has drawn attention to how 'state collapse in a handful of countries has raised questions about the status of asylum-seekers from nations with dysfunctional and disintegrated governments'.[56] She, however, focuses essentially on persecution by non-state agents in failed state situations, whereas the problem of protection remains equally for victims of state persecution in a situation of state collapse.

The *Geneva Convention on the Status of Refugees 1951* describes a 'refugee' in international law as any person who:

> as a result of events occurring before 1 January 1951, and owing to well-founded fear of being persecuted for reasons of race, religion, nationality, membership of a particular social group or political opinion, *is outside the country of his nationality and is unable or unwilling to avail himself of the protection of that country*; or not having a nationality and being outside the country of his former habitual residence as a result of such events, is unable or, owing to such fear, is unwilling to return to it.[57]

The requirement that a person laying claim to refugee status be 'outside the country of his nationality' and be 'unable or unwilling to avail himself of the protection of that country' is at the root of modern refugee law. It emphasizes the basic principle of international refugee law that an individual is only offered international surrogate protection where his or her own state is unable to do so. The emphasis in the Refugee Convention to the existence of 'the country of his nationality' is accordingly an essential pre-requisite to the triggering of international protection. By implication, technically speaking, the *Refugee Convention 1951* does not cover applicants from failed states with disintegrated governments. Similarly, the refugee definition technically excludes the persecution of individuals by warring tribes and ethnic groups in dysfunctional states because these cannot, strictly speaking, be designated as state agents, as there is no viable state to begin with. If this is right, then the 1951 Refugee Convention suffers from serious limitations because large parts of the world today are littered with collapsed states.

Modern refugee law does not strictly help people fleeing from failed states. The extent of a state's duty under International Law to afford protection to someone escaping the savage conditions of a failed state is not unequivocally settled in international law.[58] There is no internationally mandated minimum role that governments must play to protect the basic needs of their citizens, and so failed states are not breaching an international standard if they fail to protect their citizens. By the same token, there is no universally accepted standard of living that must be met by failed states.[59] On the other hand, Professor James Hathaway has drawn attention to the emergence of new human rights standards, whereby:

> the international community has recognized that there are certain basic rights, including both freedoms from interference and entitlements to resources, which all states are bound to respect as a minimum condition of legitimacy.[60]

This would imply that a state that fails to meet this basic standard is not legitimate. When that happens, international protection becomes available. At that stage, the *1951 Refugee Convention* is operative and can be utilized to provide protection.[61]

Yet, the ambit of the Refugee Convention is still limited. There has long been a dispute amongst the advanced nations of the world as to whether protection under the 1951 Convention is available to victims of unofficial abuse, known as 'non-state agents of persecution'. In the European context, this has only now been resolved when, as of 1st January 2005, when Germany's new immigration law came into force, Germany fell in line with the rest of Europe in:

> explicitly recognizing that victims of persecution by entities other than a recognized state apparatus, as well as victims of gender-specific persecution, fall within the protection scope of the 1951 UN Refugee Convention.[62]

So, this means those who are the victims of non-state agents of persecution in the context of a Civil War are just as much protected by the Refugee Convention as those who are the victims of state agents of persecution in an authoritarian but stable state. Yet, in both cases, there is a functioning state. What is the position, when there is no viable state? It seems that once that state has descended into chaos and dysfunction, there is an argument for saying that it cannot be regarded as a state, in relation to which surrogate protection must be afforded by a signatory state. By the same token, if the persecution by non-state agents takes place in the context of a state, which is at peace, the Refugee Convention does not apply because this state, as a functioning state, is able to provide such protection. Whether an applicant from a failed state is helped or hindered in his application for refugee status because his or her own state is in a state of collapse is a question that cannot be definitively answered.

The basic difficulty is that the Refugee Convention does not in its definition explicitly examine failed state situations, with the result that some states seek to exploit this omission by restricting domestic asylum laws, with a view to considering only applicants from functioning and stable societies. If this approach were to be universally applied, persecution by non-state actors in failed states would never qualify as persecution for the purposes of the Refugee Convention definition.[63] Yet, there is little guidance from original texts. The *Handbook on Procedures and Criteria for determining Refugee Status under the 1951 Convention*, produced by the United Nations High Commissioner for Refugees (UNHCR handbook) does not address the specific situation of persecution of refugees in a failed state. Its focus is more generally on the failure of a properly constituted state to protect its citizens from persecution by non-state actors.[64] However, what about persecution by a 'state' that is not properly constituted? Is this persecution by a functioning state? Is Eriteria, for example, a failed or functioning state? This is a country where government consists of former fighters who have taken control.[65] There is a major crackdown on civil society with arbitrary arrests and detentions.[66] National Assembly members are at risk.[67] Independent journalists are at risk.[68] Even ordinary citizens are at risk.[69] Indeed, returning refugees have not been spared.[70] Importantly, the *Amnesty International Report (2002)* – covering events from January to December 2002 – refers to 'the prisoners of conscience', who were people 'detained for leading post-war calls for democratization and human rights reforms'.[71] To adopt the language of the World Bank, this is a state which arguably has not undergone a 'fundamental loss of institutional capability'. Yet, it is 'unwilling' (as distinct from being 'unable') to protect the majority of its citizens.

This brings us to the question of how the Refugee Convention is failing at the moment to specifically examine failed state situations. This failure can have serious consequences for two reasons.

Being Unable or, Owing to Such Fear, is Unwilling to Avail Himself of the Protection of that Country

The first serious consequence of the *Refugee Convention* failing to specifically deal with failed state situations arises from the phrase 'unable' in the refugee definition. Under that definition, a refugee is:

> any person who ... owing to a well founded fear of being persecuted for reasons of race, religion, nationality, membership of a particular social group or political opinion, is outside the country of his nationality and is *unable* or, owing to such fear, is unwilling to avail himself of the protection of that country[72]

is obviously critical to the obligation upon the failed states to provide surrogate protection. However, it only applies where the applicant's own 'state' is unable to provide such protection. Strictly speaking, where a state has failed or where it has collapsed to the point where it is dysfunctional, a refugee is not in a position to say that he is unable to seek protection from it. This controversy is heightened by the fact that there is considerable debate about whether persecution must, under the 1951 Refugee Convention, be a State act or whether non-state actors can also engage in it, so as to trigger the protections under the 1951 Convention.[73] This is a fundamental question. A state that has failed is, strictly speaking, not capable of persecution of its citizens. In fact, it is capable neither of offering its citizens rudimentary protection nor of persecuting them.[74] The state is simply not in existence. This distinction has real practical relevance. Some developed states do take this argument to its logical conclusion. They do take the position that if persecution must be aided and abetted by the state, then a failed state can no longer perpetrate such persecution. A very good example in this respect is Afghanistan.

Following the fall of the Taliban regime, in June 2001, a political process was initiated under the *2001 Bonn Agreement*, an accord signed by representatives of the militia forces who fought with the US-led coalition against the Taliban, representatives of the former King of Afghanistan, Zahir Shah, and representatives of various exiled Afghan groups. The agreement brought President Karzai to power as the first interim leader of Afghanistan. Two national Loya Jirgas (grand councils) were held in 2002 and 2003, and a constitution approved, but both processes were marked by widespread threats and political repression by warlord factions. 'Warlordism' was principally responsible for undermining the Bonn Agreement in Afghanistan. As the *Human Rights Watch World Report* in January 2003[75] early stated, 'the loya jirga selection process in June was marred by manipulations and abuses by Afghan warlords, who interfered with decision-making of more legitimate representatives'. Indeed:

> many of the delegates selected to the loya jirga were little more than puppets of the local commanders, and the delegates who were legitimate representatives of afghan society were in many cases afraid to speak or vote freely during the loyal jirga.

By 2002, there were 'a wave of attacks on Pashtun civilians in the north of the country, seemingly because they shared the same ethnicity as the Taliban leadership'.[76] In April 2003, an *Amnesty International* Mission to Afghanistan, 'pointed in particular to serious problems of sustainability of returns, highlighting continuing denial of economic, social and cultural rights as well as a grave lack of security'[77] which was shortly confirmed by another very well known Amnesty Report.[78] By 2004, independent observers were able to say that that 'warlordism' still prevails and that in a recent poll:

> Afghans named security as their top concern, and they identified the warlords – whom Karzai has now rebuffed – as the greatest threat. Hence Afghans are most vulnerable to intimidation and bribery from the very forces now allied against the president.[79]

In January 2005, Human Rights Watch (HRW)[80] was able to conclude that:

> many of the Bonn Agreement's most important provisions have been forgotten or ignored. Militia forces occupying Kabul were never withdrawn from the city, no significant disarmament of militia forces nation-wide has taken place ... and many militia leaders have retained their autonomous leadership over what are essentially private armies.[81]

So Afghanistan remains plagued by 'warlordism', the presence of US forces does not help because:

> [g]enerally, the United States does not comply with legal standards applicable to their operations in Afghanistan, including the Geneva Conventions and other applicable international human rights law.[82]

In short, Afghanistan remains a failed state and is likely to do so for many years to come yet.

A typical refugee from Afghanistan today may be a person of Pashtun ethnicity. Pashtuns comprise the largest ethnic group, being some 38 per cent of Afghan society. Such a refugee's claim may be that because the majority of the Taliban consisted of Pashtun fighters, he will be subjected to harassment and persecution from the forces of the Northern Alliance which is largely dominated by Uzbeks. He may argue that he cannot turn to the police for protection because they largely consist of the former Mujahideen, who fought against the Taliban. He may also argue that Pashtuns are at risk because they are not confined to any particular safe area, but rather are dispersed all around Afghanistan.[83] An Immigration Judge hearing his appeal against refusal may well take the view that his account of persecution suffered at the hands of other ethnic groups is 'entirely credible' and that 'all the evidence is consistent with the background material'[84] and end up concluding that, 'there is no effective protection within most areas of Afghanistan. People have been killed, particularly Pashtoons'.[85] He may find that 'in a country that has become brutalized' that 'it is very likely' that some people having 'existing or previous rivalries, grudges and vendettas may seek to bring about revenge upon the Pashtoons for their involvement with the Taliban' and that this may involve 'a degree of violence and brutality' that is 'quite severe'. Yet, he may reject the appeal on the grounds that 'the international Conventions were not designed to protect individuals from inadequacies within their systems of law and order'.[86] This is despite the fear stemming from 'warlordism' in Afghanistan today.

Agents of Persecution who are 'Normally Related to Action by the Authorities of a Country'

The second serious consequence of the *Refugee Convention* failing to specifically deal with failed state situations arises from the fact that, in the absence a definition in the *Convention* itself, the UNHCR handbook defines agents of persecution as 'normally related to action by the authorities of a country'.[87] The handbook maintains that persecution:

> may also emanate from sections of the population that do not respect the standards established by the laws of the country concerned ... Where serious discriminatory or other offensive acts are committed by the local population, they can be considered as persecution if they are knowingly tolerated by the authorities, or if the authorities refuse, or prove unable, to offer effective protection.[88]

However, the example of a country like Afghanistan above raises the question of authority in a failed state. Who are the 'authorities'? Are the authorities here the 'state authorities'? What if there is no state authority in a dysfunctional state? Given the expressed reference to 'unable', who is the authority that should be able or 'unable' to provide such protection? These questions must be answered before it can be said that state authorities 'prove unable to ... offer effective protection' and before it can be said that this is 'persecution by the state'.[89] Yet, it may not always be possible to do so. If it is not, then receiving states may well decide not to offer surrogate protection.

Yemen is an example of a state where it is difficult to say who the authorities are in the country. Many instances of persecutory attacks emanate in Yemen from land disputes. A number of immigration judges in Britain have allowed asylum appeals from the Yemen with the recognition, for example, 'that incidents of failures to abide by accepted standards of human rights are endemic and have been so since the civil war'.[90] Yemen is a tribal society and the government has little sway over the tribes. In fact, the *Yemen Times* has reported that 'The traditional status of tribes with their heavily armed individuals pose quite a threat to the democratization process' and that '[t]he State treasury is being bled by paying out regular allowances to tribal leaders and dispensing with huge handouts to solve tribal conflicts'.[91] Highly regarded human rights NGOs such as the *US State Department Report of 2002* confirm this.[92] The *ICG Middle East Report*,[93] has pointed out that, '[u]nrest in Yemen in both urban and rural areas has taken the form of tribal clashes, kidnapping, military-tribal confrontations'. Neither the areas of central government control nor the outlying provinces are spared, and there is an important question about whose authority prevails in the country. Thus:

> [t]he government's lack of control over areas of the country, and particularly its scarcely populated governorates of al-Jawf, Marib, and Shabwa and parts of the Sanaa governorate, magnifies these problems.

Tribal authority reigns unchecked because:

> [f]or roughly half the population of Yemen, tribal affiliation is a vital component of identity. Disputes within tribes, and between tribes and the central government, have been longstanding features of Yemeni politics. Usually, these clashes are referred to as *thar*, a term that translates as 'vendetta' or 'blood revenge', but is more widely employed to describe any armed tribal feud ... tribal fighting can often stretch on for years or even decades destabilizing entire regions of the country. Local

reports indicate that hundreds of Yemenis are injured or killed in tribal clashes every year.

Once again, as a failed state, the problem in the Yemen is increasing and not diminishing. There is no realistic prospect of a person who is threatened being able to seek the protection of the state authorities or being able to seek internal relocation by moving to a safer part of the country because, 'local reports indicate not only that the number of such clashes has risen but that their nature has changed'. Indeed, even the capital city is not immune from such clashes because, 'tribal conflicts … increasingly … are being exported to the cities, including the capital …'.[94] One cannot turn to the Courts for assistance because, '[j]udges are weak, ill-educated and accept bribes' so that their 'verdicts are often not implemented …'. What is most worrying, however, is the fact that the government deliberately keeps 'tribal areas in a state of permanent unrest in order to deflect potential tribal challenges to central authority' and indeed, 'tribal issues also have served as proxies for the lingering North/South divide …'.[95] Thus, the above examples do serve to demonstrate that, if applied strictly, the *1951 Refugee Convention* has clear shortcomings in the protection of individuals from some of the most perilous parts of the world. The question that arises is, therefore, whether other human rights instruments have been any better. Unfortunately, regional conventions have also failed to provide a coherent approach.

Widening the Definition

The *OAU Convention 1969* and *The Cartagena Declaration 1984* do take a liberal view of agency of persecution so as to extend the definition of refugees to embrace victims and other groups.[96] Under the *OAU Convention*, protection is afforded to a person:

> who, owing to external aggression, occupation, foreign domination or events seriously disturbing public order in either part or the whole of his country of origin or nationality, is compelled to leave his place of habitual residence in order to seek refuge in another place outside his country of origin or nationality.[97]

Under the *Cartagena Declaration*, refugees are:

> persons who have fled their country because their lives, safety or freedom have been threatened by generalized violence, foreign aggression, internal conflicts, massive violation of human rights or other circumstances which have seriously disturbed public order.[98]

In Europe, however, it is the *European Convention of Human Rights and Fundamental Freedoms*,[99] which is increasingly the principal instrument that is used to provide protection for those fleeing violation of fundamental human rights in far-off lands.

Technically, it is well placed as a European regional instrument to provide ready relief to refugees from failed states who seek sanctuary in European states. It does so, most notably, through Article 3, which states that, 'no one shall be subjected to torture or to inhuman or degrading treatment or punishment'. The *European Court of Human Rights* has already held that the protection offered by Article 3 is broader than the non-refoulement protections of Article 33 of the Refugee Convention, with the result that, a deportation of an asylum seeker to a failed state, where he risked being tortured and subjected to inhuman and degrading treatment, would violate Article 3 of the 1950 Convention.[100] However, the notion that that convention covers all non-state actors is deeply contested by European countries. An instrument of increasing importance, however, is the *Convention Against Torture and other Cruel, Inhuman or Degrading Treatment or Punishment*.[101] Although the *Torture Convention* does say that 'no state party shall expel, return ('refouler') or extradite a person to another state where there are substantial grounds for believing that he would be in danger of being subjected to torture',[102] most governments have interpreted the Torture Convention to apply only where there is state sponsored or state-condoned acts. The 'act' defined as 'torture' in the Torture Convention, are limited to acts 'inflicted by or at the instigation of or with the consent or acquiescence of a public official or other person acting in an official capacity'.[103] Once again, this does not help in respect of people fleeing from failed states.

An asylum seeker from a failed state may not be able to point to a person 'acting in an official capacity'. How often could it be said, for example, that a persecutory act committed by a member of the Taliban was undertaken in an 'official capacity'? Or, take the example of Liberia, which has seen harrowing human rights violations, particularly over its state-backed policy of the violation of children's rights during much of the 1990s. It is difficult to know who is responsible for which particular act. The British Government's own report for 2003 from the Country Information and Policy Unit (CIPU) from the IND records that:

> [a]ll groups in the civil conflict have abducted or otherwise compelled large numbers of children to serve as soldiers, sex slaves, or in other service capacities. Mistreatment of these children by all sides was common, girls were sexually abused[104]

and even the capital city was unsafe.[105] Many could not return because their homes were insecure.[106] Voluntary return was impracticable.[107] Here also, by 2004 the situation had yet to improve, as confirmed by the *Amnesty International Report 2004*.[108] The ill-treatment of children has been characterized as a 'crime against humanity' affecting 'tens of thousands of girls and boys'.[109] The peace agreement has not helped because 'civilians have continued to be raped, beaten, used as forced labour and driven from their homes …'.[110] Which of these acts, one may well ask are under the 'acquiescence of a public official or other person acting in an official capacity' so as to be covered by the Torture Convention?

From 'Generalized Societal Violence' to 'Individualized Risk': Proving the Link between Violence and Persecution under the Refugee Convention

Neither of the four instruments mentioned above are, accordingly, entirely helpful in the adjudication of asylum claims under the *Refugee Convention 1951*. The *OAU* and *Cartegena* instruments are of course, expansive enough to assist in the facilitating of claims under the Refugee Convention, but it has long been settled that generalized societal violence does not on its own amount to persecution under the 1951 Convention. This can be hugely problematic in respect of a country like the *Democratic Republic of Congo* (DRC) which, like Afghanistan, has seen a recent peace process leading to an agreement. Yet, no western journalist or NGO easily ventures into this heart of darkness where, as the *Amnesty International Report (2003)* has found, there is routine persecution of 'human rights defenders' of 'journalists' and of 'students'[111] and where:

> the population continued to suffer enormous hardships, with widespread hunger and frequent human rights abuses by government forces, armed opposition factions and foreign troops. Abuses included killings of unarmed civilians, torture, including rape, and repression of political dissent.[112]

One of the most insightful accounts given is by *Human Rights Watch* in *Congo: War is International, Not Local* (New York, July 8, 2003)[113] which refers to the recent peace agreement but concludes that:

> The war in Congo has been mis-described as a local ethnic rivalry when in fact it represents an ongoing struggle for power at the national and international levels

after stating that:

> [a]greements between governments don't do much when the government armies are just passing their guns on to local militias. The crisis on Congo won't be resolved without addressing all levels of this conflict.[114]

Yet, in the UK a recent appeal tribunal 'country guidance' decision has found that failed asylum-seekers *per se* do not face a real risk of serious harm upon return to the DRC.[115]

The notion that violence in the form of civil unrest, guerrilla warfare, or other destabilising and violent occurrences does not on its own amount to persecution has led different courts in different jurisdictions to take differing positions. Three different gradations of judicial reasoning may be examined, ranging from the illiberal to the liberal. At its most illiberal, there is the general position that the requirement of 'a well-founded fear of persecution' in the Refugee Convention means that an applicant for refugee status must be able to point to a link between themselves and the persecution and that the persecution must be 'for a Convention reason'. This is demonstrated in the 1992 Canadian case of *Rizkallah*.[116] At an intermediate level, there is the view that the entire context of the violence should be taken into account by the Court in order to determine the motivations or purposes behind the acts of persecution. This is demonstrated in the 1998–1999 Australian cases of *Abdalla* and *Abdi* respectively.[117] It is also reflected in the 1998 British case of *Adan*,[118] where the House of Lords said that in cases of clan-related group violence, it was necessary to show a risk of selective harm for a convention reason. At a liberal level, there is the non-comparative approach in civil war situations which merely requires an applicant for refugee status to establish a link with a serious harm and a refugee ground, without the need to demonstrate that he/she is more at risk than anyone else in the country. This is demonstrated in the 1996 United States case of *Reh*.[119]

Taking the most illiberal position first, it was the Canadian case of *Rizkallah* which first determined that:

> refugee claimants must establish a link between themselves and persecution for a convention reason. In other words, they must be targeted for persecution in someway, either personally or collectively.[120]

This can present a problem with the kind of wanton carnage where all are targeted but none are specifically. This leads to the preposterous result of a great many victims of crimes being found but none who can be said to have been 'persecuted' under the terms of the 1951 Convention. It would avoid the kind of decision taken by the British Home Office recently where it was determined that the Secretary of State 'is of the opinion that your problems allegedly stem from the fact that there was a general civil war situation in Sierra Leone and not specifically on account of a Convention reason'.[121] In any practical and realistic sense, the failure of international protection here is indefensible. Take the example of Algeria in the 1990s. There one did not even have to be noteworthy of any political activities or of racial or religious affiliations in order to be at risk of being killed. Thus, in 2001, the *Amnesty International Report of December 2001* stated that:

> The conflict which has ravaged the country since 1992 continued; the level of violence and killings remained high. Hundreds of civilians, including women and children, were killed in targeted and indiscriminate attacks by armed groups which define themselves as 'Islamic groups'.[122]

The general position therefore is that put by the Canadian Court in *Rizkallah* that:

> It is essential for a decision maker to look beyond the existence of the state of war and to determine whether the war is directed to objectives such as securing power, property, and access to resources, or whether in reality it is directed against persons or groups because of race, religion or group membership.[123]

This may, however, be problematic. Can this distinction really be so clearly made? It is submitted that it cannot because very often securing power is only achievable by a targeted persecution on grounds of race, religion or social group. A failed state may be unable to protect its subjects from persecution. The individual may be seeking protection precisely because he comes from a situation of state collapse. Yet, such a person must still show persecution on a convention ground.[124] This may not be possible as the persecutory acts may be quite indiscriminate. Take the example of Zimbabwe, where the use of indiscriminate violence reached new heights by 2005. Yet, already in 2002 its existence was well documented. Thus, the *US State Department report of 2002* stated that 'Government supporters continued to beat and torture suspected opposition members ...'. However, the so-called opposition members were anyone and everyone because:

> [p]ersons perceived as supporting the opposition, including judges, teachers, civil servants, health workers, and labourers in the manufacturing sector, were singled out for assault or intimidation by ruling party supporters.[125]

At times it seemed that the 'victims were primarily targeted for their perceived or real affiliation with the political opposition'.[126] The *Human Rights Watch Report 2003* is replete with references to the fact that the indiscriminate violence is predicated on a perception – however misguided and erroneous – of certain areas being strongholds of supporters of the main opposition party, the *Movement for Democratic Reform* (MDC). However, the violence is not just directed at such perceived supporters. It is noted, for example, that:

> [I]n areas seen to be MDC strongholds, civilians with no links to the opposition party or to activist organizations have also been assaulted, sometimes with the aim of obtaining information.[127]

Such a situation clearly brings into sharp relief the limits of the *1951 Refugee Convention*, with its focus on persecution, for a Convention reason. The position is rendered all the more worrying given that Zimbabwe is at the forefront of countries producing refugees today.

Yet, in such a situation, surrogate international protection will only be available subject to strict criteria. Where courts go beyond a situation of Civil War and consider state failure, they still do require persecution. The Courts have, however, in a series of cases attempted to redress the shortcomings of the *Refugee Convention*, by taking the entire context of the violence into account. In *Abdi*, the court said that 'it is not enough to dismiss an application simply on the basis that there is a war without looking at the motivations or purposes involved'.[128] In other words, persecution can be even more prevalent in the case of war conditions. Courts must therefore investigate the causes of civil strife. In another case, *Abdalla*,[129] the court said that:

> it is not correct to proceed on the basis that because fear arises within a recurring pattern of communal violence in a civil war context, therefore, it cannot amount to 'persecution' for a convention reason.[130]

Although therefore, it is possible for a convention persecution to be perpetrated in the context of civil war, nevertheless, it must still be a convention persecution to bring relief. This can be problematic as the example of Zimbabwe above well demonstrates. Here the escalating violence by the State, resulting in mid-2005, in 'the terrible scenes left behind in towns and villages destroyed by Mugabe's Operation Murambatsviva, or Drive Out Rubbish, a violent programme that can be likened to pol Pot's',[131] cannot be said to be persecution based on 'political opinion' grounds. The violence has a logic all of its own. 'More than 100 failed asylum-seekers' just had to be allowed to stay in Britain, even where they did not satisfy the strict requirements of the Refugee Convention and:

> [i]mmigration officers were ordered … to halt deportations to Zimbabwe despite Tony Blair's insistence that there would be no official suspension of forced removals.[132]

In the end, therefore, common sense prevailed where the Refugee Convention did not.

Thus, the requirement of individualized persecution can present problems to those asylum-seekers who are genuinely at risk of harm. This is clear from the 1998 case of *Adan*,[133] where the House of Lords held that in cases of clan, or clan related, or civil war related conflicts, the issue was not whether an individual or groups was a combatant or a non-combatant, but whether he, she, or the group is exposed to the risk of selective harm for a convention reason.[134] The court said that:

> killing and torture which were incidental to a clan and some sub-clan based civil war did not give rise to a well-founded fear of being persecuted within the convention definition because in such a case the asylum seeker was at no greater risk of such ill treatment by reason of his clan or sub-clan membership than others at risk of war.

This is troubling because it applies the requirement of differential risk over and above the basic targeting of an individual or social group. The House of Lords in *Adan*, characterized the situation in Somalia as a civil war or a clan-based war. It did not describe it as a failed state scenario. In short, the House declared that because the whole clan was equally at risk, clan based persecution of the applicant did not amount to convention persecution. Such a decision places a high threshold on applicants from failed state situations. Somalia is certainly a country where entire clans and sub-clans have been targeted with no functioning government to provide state protection.[135] Instead, their lordships regarded and categorized the Somalian situation as one of 'indiscriminate violence or oppression manifested toward all clans'.[136] This is seen in Lord Lloyd's phrase that there must be 'selective harassment' over and above 'differential risk'.

Whilst it is certainly true that Somalia is a text-book case of a clan-based society,[137] the categorization that this was not Convention persecution but clan-based persecution, in *Adan* is excessively legalistic and rigid. The plain fact is that clan members are at risk of persecution in Somalia. As the *US State Department Report (2003)* makes clear, '[d]uring the civil war the minority groups were amongst the most vulnerable and victimized groups in the country' and ends by saying that 'This was and still is the case in parts of central and southern Somalia'.[138] This opinion was earlier confirmed in 2002 by the *Joint British, Danish and Dutch Fact-Finding Mission to Nairobi*[139] which also noted that the position in Mogadishu is unsafe because 'Armed clashes and banditry have continued in Mogadishu'[140] and that even the majority 'Hawiye clans ... remain at odds with each other'.[141] The British Government Home Office's *CIPU Report* confirms this analysis when it refers to the fact that 'rival Hawiye factions' control much of the area.[142] In particular, it confirms that:

> fighting between rival clans and factions continues in many parts of the country. There are continued reports of killings and reprisal killings of clan opponents, expulsions of members of other clans, cases of kidnapping as well as detention, and torture and ill-treatment of prisoners. Women and minorities are particularly vulnerable to abuses.[143]

Moreover, the British Government's *Home Office Operational Guidance on Somalia*[144] states that whilst each case must be assessed on its own merits:

> ... we accept that based on the available country information bona-fide member of the Bajuni and Benadiri minority groups are likely to be able to establish the need for international protection.

In the circumstances, it would not be surprising if a different court took a different view. A different approach has, however, been taken by the USA in *Reh*, also involving an asylum seeker from Somalia.[145] In this case, the BIA ruled that the applicant had been persecuted on account of his membership of a social group as a member of the *Darood* clan and the *Marehan* sub-clan. The distinguishing feature of this approach is that the BIA adopted a 'noncomparative' approach to determining status in civil war situations, which focuses not on whether the asylum seeker is more at risk than anyone else in the country, but on whether the applicant has established a link with a serious harm and a refugee ground.[146] This means that, whereas the refugee must show a nexus requirement by demonstrating that there is a risk of harm based on membership of the particular clan, he need not show a differential risk. This approach by the US Court contrasts sharply with the United Kingdom approach in *Adan*. The merits of this approach is that where a large percentage of the population, such as in Somalia, faces real risks based on convention grounds, the non-comparative approach allows such a group to have its members individually considered by the court, which would consider the circumstances of each applicant. The above shows that an asylum seeker from a failed state may have his case adjudicated differently depending on which country assesses his claim. This is because persecution by nonstate actors is not considered acceptable by Germany, Austria, France and The Netherlands.

The decision in *Reh*, that an applicant for refugee status succeeds where that applicant has established a link with a serious harm and a refugee ground has, however, been limited in the European context by being pinned down to a requirement to show human rights abuses that are State sponsored. In 1996, a joint position on harmonized approach to interpretation of the refugee definition was adopted, which suggested that 'persecution' should be understood narrowly as Human Rights abuses that are state sponsored or state tolerated.[147] This joint position is non-binding. It may have had the advantage of being less strict then the requirement of having to demonstrate 'persecution' for *Convention* reasons in the *1951 Refugee Convention*. It, nevertheless, still required State implication in the persecution. Yet, it has now been tempered by the language of the *1999 Tampere Conclusions*,[148] under which the efforts at harmonization have resulted in tighter restrictions being placed on asylum seekers into Western Europe, in as much as harmonisation and the Tampere Conclusions adopt the lowest common denominators.

Conclusion: Correlating Individualized Risk with Failed State Situations

The shortcomings of the *1951 Refugee Convention* can be met if the Courts adopted the language of the World Bank and began to distinguish between failed and non-failed states. They should not simply continue to refer to civil war, civil unrests, and other generalized violence. Where these states are symptomatic of a failed state situation, they should say so (as the ECtHR did in Ahmed v. Austin below) and where the Courts are dealing with claimants from failed states they should show a willingness to make a finding of individualized risk in circumstances of generalized violence.[149] Yet, since courts base their judgements on standards laid down in the Refugee Convention, they often do not use terms like 'failed state' or 'collapsed state' when deciding cases from such countries, preferring instead to analyse the situation in a nation at the time of the alleged persecution and to make a determination based on Convention standards. They do not give particularized attention to the fact that a claimant is from a failed state and may because of that be at a higher risk of individualized ill-treatment.[150] There are two reasons for this. First, often a failed state may reconstitute itself and become a functioning government capable of providing protection (as it seems has sometimes appeared likely with the re-emerging power of the Taliban in Afghanistan in recent years). Secondly, to give specific and particularized attention to a claimant from a failed state may privilege such an asylum seeker over one who comes from a functioning state. That would lead to discrimination against claimants from functioning states. The result would be to disadvantage them. Neither of these arguments, it seems to me, are compelling. Refugee law exists to provide protection where a person's own state is 'unable' to do so. That is the basis of international surrogate protection. Neither the provenance of the risk nor the question of whether a state is functioning or not, should be relevant to that question.

ARTICLE 3

The 'Soering Principle'

Article 3 of the *European Convention of Human Rights 1950*, seeks to resurrect the importance of fundamental human rights violations by stating that '*no one shall be subjected to torture or inhuman or degrading treatment or punishment*'. This is an absolute right and one which signatory states cannot derogate from. Where there are substantial grounds shown for believing that expulsion will lead to a person facing a real risk of being subjected to treatment contrary to Article 3 in the receiving country, the contracting state shall not expel that person from its territory (whether by extradition, deportation or any other form of removal and for whatever reasons). Article 3 is a pivotal human rights provision in the 25 countries of the European Union today and is therefore worth considering here. It has also become increasingly important *vis-à-vis* international refugee law ever since the tightening of borders and transit opportunities under the 1999 Tampere Conclusions, because these have adopted the lowest common denominators, with the result that nowadays the only solution to the restrictions on asylum seekers from failed states under a harmonized European Policy, is the use of international and regional instruments such as Article 3.

The '*Soering* principle' arises from the decision of the European Court of Human Rights (ECtHR) in *Soering v United Kingdom* (1989) 11 EHRR 439.[151] This principle has been repeatedly re-stated in a whole series of subsequent Strasbourg cases.[152] In a number of these case, the Strasbourg Court has stated the Soering principle in almost identical terms[153] as follows:

> [T]he expulsion of an alien by a contracting state may give rise to an issue under article 3, and hence engage the responsibility of that state under the Convention, where substantial grounds have been shown for believing that the person in question, if expelled, would face a real risk of being subjected to treatment contrary to article 3 in the receiving country. In these circumstances, article 3 implies the obligation not to expel the person in question to that country.

Critical to an understanding of Soering is paragraph 91 of the court's judgment.[154] This is worth setting out in full (with the sentences below being numbered and italicized for convenience):

> (1) In sum, *the decision* by a contracting state to extradite a fugitive *may give rise to an issue under article 3*, and hence engage the responsibility of that state under the Convention, *where substantial grounds have been shown* for believing *that the person concerned, if extradited, faces a real risk of being subjected to torture or to inhuman or degrading treatment* or punishment in the requesting country.

> (2) The *establishment of such responsibility inevitably involves an assessment of conditions in the requesting country* against the standards of article 3 of the Convention.

(3) Nonetheless, there is *no question of adjudicating on or establishing the responsibility of the receiving country*, whether under general international law, under the Convention or otherwise.

(4) In so far as any liability under the Convention is or may be incurred, *it is liability incurred by the extraditing* contracting state by reason of its having taken action *which has as a direct consequence* the *exposure of an individual to proscribed ill-treatment*.

What is most significant about the recital of paragraph 91 above is that the third sentence of that paragraph appears to clearly imply that there is no need for the person concerned to establish that the feared risk is of harm such as would place the receiving country itself in actual or notional breach of Article 3, as this makes it plain that there is *no question of adjudicating on or establishing the responsibility of the receiving country*, under any law. In 2004, the British House of Lords held that Article 3 operates to constrain the actions of a contracting state within its own borders, such being described as '*domestic cases*'.[155] The '*Soering principle*' by contrast may be described as a '*foreign case*' because it is the act of expulsion, which is committed in the contracting state's own territory, that itself constitutes proscribed ill-treatment. The ordinary principle in these 'foreign cases' is that the proscribed form of treatment must emanate from intentionally inflicted acts on the part of the public authorities, to which risk the victim is being subjected in the receiving country, following expulsion, if he is to be able to successfully rely on Article 3.

The notion above, arising from the third sentence of paragraph 91 that there is no need for the person concerned to establish that the feared risk is of harm such as would place the receiving country itself in actual or notional breach of Article 3, appears to have been followed by the Strasbourg Court in *Ahmed v. Austria*. Here the court ruled that sending home a Somali asylum seeker would violate Article 3 of the European Convention because there was a high degree of likelihood that he would be subjected to torture and degrading treatment.[156] The European Court of Human Rights (hereafter ECtHR) specifically rejected Austria's argument that Ahmed's persecutors were not state agents and therefore, no relief should be granted under Article 3. It made an expressed reference to the fact that Somalia was a failed state when it said that the Austrian Government's position was untenable given the current lack of state authority on Somalia. The question, however, is whether such an enlightened approach can be taken in relation to countries other than Somalia. Tara Magner, who has undertaken a study of international protection in respect of the failed state situation has argued that 'Germany and certain other states place high barriers to refugees from failed states, but their policies are coming into question, most directly by the decision in *Ahmed*'.[157] Whatever may have been the situation in 2001 when she made that remark, it is clear that this is not the case today. *Ahmed* has not heralded in a new era.

The year after *Ahmed v. Austria*, the Strasbourg Court took a different view. In *HLR v France* 26 EHRR 29, the application in fact failed even though the case was put on the basis of the twin ideas of the risk of harm and the lack of reasonable protection.[158] This was a deportation case from France where, however, the source of the alleged risk to the applicant in Colombia was not the public authorities but rather drug traffickers who allegedly threatened reprisals. The ECtHR for the first time in 1997 expressly recognized that Article 3 could apply to non-state agents of persecution, but that it had to be shown that the receiving state could not avert the risk to the victim. As it explained:

> Owing to the absolute character of the right guaranteed, the court does not rule out the possibility that article 3 of the Convention may also apply where the danger emanates from persons or groups of *persons who are not public officials*. However, it must be shown that the risk is real and that *the authorities of the receiving state are not able to obviate the risk by providing appropriate protection* (emphases added).[159]

This has been followed through in other cases.[160] HLR was put simply in terms of the court *'not rul[ing] out the possibility'*[161] of the Soering principle applying in non-state agent cases. However, the court just three days later stated in its well-known judgment in the AIDS case, *D v United Kingdom (1997)*[162] that:

> It is true that this principle [the Soering principle] has so far been applied by the court in contexts in which the risk to the individual of being subjected to any of the proscribed forms of treatment emanates *from intentionally inflicted acts of the public authorities* in the receiving country *or from those of non-state bodies* in that country *when the authorities there are unable to afford him appropriate protection*.[163]

This suggests that the Soering principle can indeed apply in cases where the risk arises from the actions of non-state agents on the same principles as it can to persecution by state agents. In referring to that passage in *D* the court adverted to *Ahmed v Austria (1996)*[164] where it had noted that Somalia (the country to which Austria had proposed expelling the applicant):

> was *still in a state of civil war* and fighting was going on between a *number of clans vying with each other for control of the country*. There was no indication that the dangers to which the applicant would have been exposed in 1992 had ceased to exist *or that any public authority would be able to protect him*.

However, the question that is still left outstanding is whether this means that an applicant succeeds in demonstrating a breach of Article 3 if he can establish only a real risk of harm on return to his own country. This question has now been definitively answered by the British House of Lords in a leading case in 2005.

The House of Lords Decision in Bagdanavicius

In 2005, the House of Lords in *Bagdanavicius*[165] considered the case of a husband and wife aged respectively 29 and 31, nationals of Lithuania, with a 3-year-old son, who feared ill-treatment because the husband was of Roma ethnic origin, but the wife was not. They argued that they would be subjected to persistent harassment and violence in particular at the hands of the wife's brother and various of his associates, all stemming from the brother's objection to his sister having married a Roma. The husband and wife left Lithuania with their son and arrived in the UK on 7 December 2002, whereupon they immediately claimed asylum under the Refugee Convention, and also in addition asserted that the UK would be in breach of its obligations under Article 3 of the *European Convention of Human Rights 1950*,[166] if they were returned to Lithuania. However, their applications for leave to enter the UK were refused by the Secretary of State who also certified their claims as *'clearly unfounded'*.

The issue that the House considered was whether an applicant, in order to avoid expulsion on Article 3 grounds, had to establish only that in the receiving country he would be at real risk of suffering serious harm from non-state agents; or whether additionally, he must go further and establish also that the receiving country does not provide for those within its territory a reasonable level of protection against such harm. The husband and wife argued that they must establish only a real risk of harm on return, but the UK government argued that they must also establish that the receiving country would fail to discharge the positive obligation inherent in Article 3 to provide a reasonable level of protection.[167] It is to be noted that this argument is closely aligned to the decision in *Reh* where it was held that an applicant need only establish a link with a serious harm and a refugee ground to succeed.

It was argued on behalf of the husband and wife that the third sentence of paragraph 91 in *Soering*, which which states that *'there is no question of adjudicating on or establishing the responsibility of the receiving country'* in Article 3 cases, was designed to mean that there was no need for the person concerned to establish that the feared risk is of harm such as would place the receiving country itself in actual or notional breach of Article 3.[168] However, Lord Brown, giving the judgment of the House, declared that 'the argument is a hopeless one' because:

> [a]ll that the third sentence of paragraph 91 is saying is that the court need not and should not reach any decision as to whether the receiving country (a sovereign state which in any event is not represented before the court) actually is or notionally would be in breach of article 3.

Accordingly, in the words of Lord Brown, '[a]ll that need be decided is whether there are "*substantial grounds … for believing*" that there would be "*a real risk*" of this'.[169] Lord Brown explained this by saying that 'the risk referred to in the first sentence of paragraph 9,[170] is of *'being subjected to torture or to inhuman or degrading treatment or punishment'* ("*proscribed ill-treatment*" as that is conveniently summarized in the fourth sentence);[171] the later formulation speaks of "*a real risk of being subjected to treatment contrary to article 3*"'. In His Lordship's judgment:

> [a]ll these expressions in terms refer to harm which, if it eventuates, would involve a violation (actual or notional) of article 3. The position surely is plain. There is no

warrant whatever for reading *Soering* or any of the other cases as barring expulsion where the real risk is not of "proscribed *ill-treatment*" but is merely of harm, however serious.[172]

What this suggests is that on this basis, even serious harm, will not attract the protection of Article 3 unless it can be designated 'proscribed ill-treatment'. However, this is a reading of Article 3 as if it were 'persecution' under Article IA of the Refugee Convention, where the Courts often make the distinction between severe ill-treatment and persecution, and where the latter alone brings an applicant within the ambit of the Refugee Convention.[173] It is not a reading of Article 3 in the sense of 'serious harm' which it clearly should be. It will also have the effect of creating a very high threshold to be satisfied for applicants from failed states.

Yet, Lord Brown, giving the House's judgment, held that the failure of the state to provide protection was a pre-requisite to a successful claim under Article 3. In his view:

> non-state agents do not subject people to torture or the other proscribed forms of ill-treatment, however violently they treat them: what, however, would transform such violent treatment into article 3 ill-treatment would be the state's failure to provide reasonable protection against it.[174]

This is troubling, however, bearing in mind that we are not thinking about international surrogate protection here under the Refugee Convention, but about the violation of the absolute right to be free from inhuman and degrading treatment under the European Human Rights Convention. He did not consider there to be in existence Strasbourg jurisprudence in non-state agent cases to be to the contrary. Whilst there was the case of *Ahmed v Austria*,[175] Lord Brown considered this to be the only such case where the court has in fact concluded (as by then Austria too had concluded) that:

> the applicant's deportation to Somalia *would breach article 3* of the Convention *for as long as he faces a serious risk of being subjected there to torture or inhuman or degrading treatment*.[176]

But in Lord Brown's judgment, '[a]s, however, had already been pointed out at p.291, para 44 (see para 10 above), there existed in Somalia both danger and a complete absence of state protection'.[177] Is the principle in *Ahmed*, however, that Article 3 crystalizes where there is 'a serious risk of being subjected to torture or inhuman or degrading treatment' only to apply where there is a 'complete absence of state protection'? It is by no means clear that *Ahmed* was intended to be read only in that way. The reference to 'faces a serious risk of being subjected to torture' is certainly amenable to being read in the way that such risk alone is enough to qualify an applicant for article 3 protection without the need to have to adjudicate on state protection as well. Moreover, if *Ahmed* is a recognition of the possibility of a failed state situation it is a very limited and narrow recognition. The examples of failed states that we have discussed above are not all states where there is 'a complete absence of state protection'. So, why should the risk of serious harm from non-state agents alone not suffice in these cases to bring an applicant within the protection of Article 3? It is well known that human rights protection does have to be 'real and effective', under European human rights law. It does not mean that such protection can be artificial and illusory. Yet, Lord Brown's sole requirement that, *'What the state is expected to do is take reasonable measures to make the necessary protection available'*[178] surely cannot rule out the possibility that the protection afforded by the state is illusory. Many of the States we have discussed here – from Afghanistan to the Kosovo – would purport to 'take reasonable measures' to make 'the necessary protection available', but that is a very different thing from saying that such protection would be available.

Let me return here to the example of Afghanistan to make this point. In 2005, the British Government in its *Immigration, and Nationality Department* (IND) own *Afghanistan Bulletin 1/2005*,[179] refers in its report, under the heading 'Influence of Warlords and Commanders', to the first report of the independent expert of the *Commission on Human Rights*, dated 21 September 2004, which stated that:

> Most human rights violations occur at the hands of warlords, local commanders, drug traffickers and other actors who wield power of force and who exercise varying degrees of authority in the different provinces and districts … despite the Government's best intentions, it cannot with the 10,000–15,000 troops of the fledgling Afghanistan National Army (ANA) effectively oppose the estimated 100,000 armed and battle-tested forces loyal to the warlords and local commanders.[180]

It is plainly pointless in this situation to look to a system of state protection. Not only is the violation of human rights being perpetrated by non-state agents, such as the Warlords, but it is quite clear that the Afghan government, if taken to task, cannot oppose the forces of the battle-tested forces of the warlords. It is artificial and false in such a case to say that all that a country like Afghanistan need do 'is take reasonable measures to make the necessary protection available'. If nothing else, this violates the cardinal principle of European Convention law that all human rights protections must be 'real and effective' and not 'artificial and illusory'.

Lord Brown's categorization would not work in a country like Afghanistan where ironically failed asylum-seekers are technically removable. Concerns about continuing insecurity in Afghanistan are well-founded today and it is quite clear that there is no viable protection available there because[181] respectable human rights reports documentation confirms that:

> … the Afghan police services and the National Security Directorate (NSD), are unable to exercise control over the warlords, local commanders, drug cultivation and trafficking, common criminality and human rights abuses, resulting in a situation where gross violations of fundamental human rights are commonplace.[182]

Moreover, it is well known that[183] that when refugees return:

> ... whether to their original homes or to new settlement areas, they face an array of problems and, as highly vulnerable populations, they are often the victims of serious human rights violations. Returning refugees and resettled IDPs are commonly subjected to acts of violence, including killing, arbitrary arrest and detention; illegal occupation and confiscation of their land by warlords, commanders and others ... There are thousands of reported cases of returnees being subjected to these violations in many communities.[184]

This suggests that even a majority ethnic group like the Pashtuns ought not to be returned at present to Afghanistan because of reasons of sheer lawlessness and lack of protection. A reading of Article 3 in terms of reasonable risk of serious harm is far more workable than an added requirement that there be evidence of 'reasonable measures' taken by the state to dispel such human rights violations. The plain fact is that Afghanistan is an example of a failed state that is likely to be in a failed situation for a long time to come. Parts of Afghanistan are already disintegrating. Today, '[t]he government does not control most provinces, which are ruled by powerful warlords',[185] and there is increased insecurity.[186] A *NATO News Report* of 25th June 2005 stated that 'The United Nation's top envoy for Afghanistan has said that violence is threatening security in the run-up to September's elections'[187] and the *BBC News UK Edition*, drawing upon this information, confirms that 'The situation is especially worrying in the southern provinces ... and in Pashtun regions bordering with Pakistan'.[188] The *Amnesty International Report* of 25th May 2005 has actually stated that 'Lawlessness and insecurity increased, hampering efforts towards peace and stability'.[189] Indeed, a sign of Taliban emboldenment and the deteriorating security situation is seen in the kidnapping and hanging, of Agha Jan, a tribal leader and vital ally of Afghanistan's President, Hamid Karzai, in July 2005 as the September elections approached.[190] Thus, in a provision like Article 3 which focuses on the prevention of inhuman and degrading treatment, the existence of the risk of serious harm from non-state agents alone should be enough. The irony is that Lord Brown had at the outset accepted 'that a real risk of injury may remain despite the state's provision of a reasonable level of protection against it'.[191]

Conclusion

Article 3 is an absolute right. It cannot be negotiated away. Whereas great strides have been made in the application of article 3 rights to asylum-seekers in the field of refugee law,[192] recent jurisprudence culminating in the case of *Bagdanavicius* has curtailed its logical application to all cases where it is accepted that there is 'serious risk' of human rights violations, by requiring a state to simply show that there are 'reasonable measures' in place 'to make the necessary protection available'. Practitioners of human rights law know only too well that there is a world of difference between making protection available and taking reasonable steps to make it available. Article 3 may not be quite the panacea for the shortcomings of the Refugee Convention. As Lord Brown summarized:

> It is, of course, plainly established that, in cases under the Refugee Convention where the well-founded fear of persecution emanates from non-state agents, the asylum seeker must establish not merely the risk of severe ill-treatment but also that his home state was unwilling or unable to provide a reasonable level of protection from it — see *Horvath v Secretary of State for the Home Department* [2001] 1 AC 489. As, however, Mr Nicol was at pains to emphasize, that is a different Convention from the ECHR, providing in certain respects narrower, though in others wider, protection than the ECHR, the one founded on the principle of surrogacy, the other on more general humanitarian considerations, one (the ECHR) subject to the rulings of a supranational court, the other (the Refugee Convention) not. Moreover, not all those party to the Refugee Convention recognize even the concept of persecution by non-state agents.[193]

Yet, as the Court heard in argument before it, in cases where violence in the receiving country is threatened by non-state agents, expulsion is barred irrespective of whether or not the receiving state itself would thereby be in breach of Article 3 (or, if not itself a contracting state, in what has been called '*notional*' breach of Article 3). In such a case, all that would be required is that the person concerned is at substantial risk of suffering harm to a degree sufficient to engage Article 3. In other words the member state expelling the person can be in breach of Article 3 because of the risk of injury he runs on return even though, were that risk to eventuate, the receiving country itself would not be.[194] This argument was compelling or it can be justified by reference to the different kinds of obligation which Article 3 places on member states. Member states are under an absolute obligation not to take steps which would expose people to the risk of Article 3 ill-treatment, and this is 'a negative obligation'. However, they are also under 'a positive obligation' to take reasonable steps to protect people against serious harm. Yet, Lord Brown rejected this argument on essentially policy grounds, namely, that 'this obligation, however, is not absolute'[195] because of the burdens it will impose on the receiving state, given the ECtHR's judgment in *Osman v United Kingdom* (1998)[196] which held that the *obligation must be interpreted in a way which does not impose an impossible or disproportionate burden on the authorities*. Yet, if the obligation not to expel someone at substantial risk in the receiving country is a negative obligation then it must be an absolute obligation. The House of Lords failure to so hold has thwarted the application of Article 3 to failed state situations. One must hope that it will not be long before the Strasbourg Court revisits this area and gives Article 3 the kind of expansive interpretation that it deserves in the current conditions of the world today.

NOTES

1   See John Gray, 'Not every country in the world can be democracy', from a Speech by the LSE Professor of European Thought, given at the Royal Society of Arts, London, *The Independent*, 25th February 2005, at p.29.

2   World Bank, *1997 World Bank Development Report* 158 (1997) [hereinafter World Development Report].

3   See World Development Report, *Supra*, at p.158.

4   Ibid., World Development Report, at p.158.

5   For a discussion of the evolution of peacekeeping, see Thomas G. Weiss *et al.*, *The United Nations and Changing World Politics*, 21–137 (3rd ed. 2001).

6   See Michael C. Williams, *Civil-Military Relations and Peacekeeping* (Adelphi Papers, No. 321, 1998).

7   See generally Steven R. Ratner, *The New UN Peacekeeping: Building Peace in Lands of Conflict After the Cold War* (1995).

8   There is a plethora of literature regarding the former Yugoslavia and constraints and obstacles encountered in the field. See, e.g., Adam Roberts, *Communal Conflict as a Challenge to International Organization: The Case of Former Yugoslavia*, 21 Rev. of Int'l Stud. 389, 389–410 (1995); *Kosovo: Let's Learn from Bosnia*, ICG Balkans, Rep. No. 66 (Int'l Crisis Group, Brussels, Belg.), May 17, 1999, at http://www.intl-crisis- group.org/projects/balkans/kosovo/reports/A400197_17051999.pdf.

9   See John L. Hirsch and Robert B. Oakley, *Somalia and Operation Restore Hope: Reflections on Peacemaking and Peacekeeping*, 111, 116–17 (1995); see also Mark Bowden, *Black Hawk Down: A Story of Modern War*, 71, 344 (1999) (describing how initially positive Somali perceptions of the UN mission turned sour).

10   See David M. Malone, *Decision-Making in the UN Security Council: The Case of Haiti, 1990–1997* (1998). On Haiti and Somalia, see David Bentley and Robert Oakley, *Peace Operations: A Comparison of Somalia and Haiti*, Strategic F. (Nat'l Def. Univ., Inst. for Nat'l Strategic Studies, Occasional Paper No. 30, 1995), at http://www.ndu.edu/inss/strforum/forum30.html.

11   See Gérard Prunier, *The Rwanda Crisis: History of a Genocide* (1995); Michael N. Barnett, 'The UN Security Council: Indifference and Genocide in Rwanda', 12 *Cultural Anthropology* 551 (1997); J. Matthew Vaccaro, 'The Politics of Genocide: Peacekeeping and Disaster Relief in Rwanda', in *UN Peacekeeping, American Politics, and the Uncivil Wars of the 1990s*, at 367, 367–68 (William J. Durch (ed.), 1996).

12   See World Bank, *1997 World Development Report*, 158 (197) [hereinafter *World Development Report*]. Also see, Tara Magner, 'Does a failed state country of origin result in a failure of international protection? A review of policies toward asylum seekers in leading asylum nations', *Georgetown Immigration Law Journal* (Summer 2001, 15), at page 703.

13   William Zartman, 'Introduction to collapsed states: The Disintegration and Restoration of Legitimate Authority' page 1 (I. William Zartman, (ed.), 1995).

14   See Ewen MacAskill, 'Afghanistan could implode, MPs warn', *The Guardian*, Friday, July 30th 2004, which wrote that 'Afghanistan will fall apart unless Nato countries urgently fulfill promises to send troops, the Commons Foreign Affairs Select Committee warned yesterday': http://www.guardian.co.uk/international/story/0,,1275301,00.html.

15   See Rory Stewart, 'Degrees of Not Knowing', *The London Review of Books* (Vol. 27, No. 7, 31st March 2005), at pp.9–11.

16   See David M. Malone, 'Haiti and the International Community: A Case Study', *Survival*, Summer 1997, at 126, 129.

17   See William G. O'Neill, 'Human Rights Monitoring vs. Political Expediency: The Experience of the OAS/U.N. Mission in Haiti', 8 *Harv. Hum. Rts. J.* 101, 104 (1995).

18   For a firsthand account of this, see Salim Ahmed Salim, 'The OAU Role in Conflict Management', in *Peacemaking and Peacekeeping for the New Century*, 245, 247 (Olara A. Otunnu and Michael W. Doyle (eds), 1996); see also, in the same volume, Ali A. Mazrui, 'The Failed State and Political Collapse in Africa', in *Peacemaking and Peacekeeping for the New Century*, 233, 233–43, *supra*.

19   See 'Thousands die as world defines genocide: The international community's response to the crisis in Sudan may depend on how the Darfur tragedy is classed', *Financial Times*, 6th July 2004.

20   Micheal Clough, 'Whose Responsibility to Protect?', *Human Rights Watch Report 2005*, at p.8.

21   For a detailed discussion of the potential of SADC and ECOWAS respectively in the security field, see *From Cape to Congo: Southern Africa's Evolving Security Challenges* (Mwesiga Baregu and Christopher Landsberg (eds), 2003); *Toward a Pax West Africana: Building Peace in a Troubled Sub-Region* (Adekeye Adebajo and Ismail Rashid (eds)) (2003).

22   The UN Observer Mission in Georgia (UNOMIG) was established by UN *Security Council Resolution 853* in 1993 with the task of observing the operation of the peacekeeping force of the Commonwealth of Independent States (CIS), among others. See S.C. Res. 853, UN SCOR, 48th Sess., 3268th mtg., UN Doc. S/RES/853 (1993).

23   The UN Observer Mission in Liberia (UNOMIL) is a pertinent example of the United Nations' working closely with regional organizations: Established in September 1993 under UN *Security Council Resolution 866*, its mandate was to exercise its good offices to support the efforts of ECOWAS and the Liberian transitional government. See S.C. Res. 866, UN SCOR, 48th Sess., 3281st mtg., UN Doc. S/RES/866 (1993).

24   See Paul Lewis, 'Security Council Bars Drug Fight', *N.Y. Times*, Oct. 11, 1989, at A12.

25   The Council did so under the US presidency of Vice-President Al Gore, See 'UN Security Council Holds Historic Session on AIDS in Africa', *Afr. News Service*, Jan. 11, 2000, LEXIS, Nexis Library, Afr. News Service File. This development struck some observers as ironic given long-standing US skepticism of Security Council debates on 'thematic' issues. To the irritation of some Security Council members, accustomed to – and comfortable with – an increasingly stodgy and defensive US stance in the Council, the new US Permanent Representative to the United Nations, Richard Holbrooke, was seizing with more imagination than some of his predecessors on the opportunities the Council presents for debates of wide public interest. See 'Africa's Moment Under the UN's Gaze', *Economist*, Feb. 5, 2000, at 41; Barbara Crossette, 'Chief American UN Delegate Charts Course for His Month at the Helm', *N.Y. Times*, Dec. 21, 1999, at A20.

26   UN *Charter* art. 39.

27   See John Kifner, 'Iran Reports Breaking Through Iraqi Defensive Line East of Basra', *N.Y. Times*, Jan. 14, 1987, at A6.

28   For an account of the evolving dynamics within the Security Council, see Cameron R. Hume, *The United Nations, Iran, and Iraq: How Peacemaking Changed* (1994); C.S.R. Murthy, 'Change and Continuity in the Functioning of the Security Council Since the End of the Cold War', 32 *Int'l Stud.* 423, 423–8 (1995).

29   See S.C. Res. 827, UN SCOR, 48th Sess., 3217th mtg., UN Doc. S/RES/827 (1993).

30   See S.C. Res. 955, UN SCOR, 49th Sess., 3453d mtg., UN Doc. S/RES/955 (1994).

31   See Alessandra Stanley, 'US Dissents, but Accord Is Reached on War-Crime Court', *N.Y. Times*, July 18, 1998, at A3.

32   See 'Mild Rebukes for Darfur's Killers', *The Economist*, 31st March 2005, which cites the UN Under-Secretary General, Jan Egeland's estimate of the number of dead through hunger and disease alone in the first 18 months to be 180,000. The British Parliament's Report of the *International Development Committee: Darfur, Sudan: The Responsibility to Protect* puts the number of overall dead at 300,000.

33   *International Commission of Inquiry on Darfur: Report to the Secretary General*, 25th January 2005, at p.4, 132.

34   See 'Reckoning in Darfur: Did the World ingnore yet another African genocide? The UN investigates Darfur's horrors', at www.beliefnet.com/story/160_16040_html, at p.3.

35   His speech is cited in Samantha Power, *It's Not Enough to Call it Genocide* (2004 Harvard Univeristy Press), at p.2.

36   *UN Security Council Resolution 1547* passed 18th September 2004.

37   Ibid.

38   In fact, it now apprears that the USA has found in the current Sudanese regime a new ally in its 'war on terror' and is courting visits from General Gosh, a Sudanese government official, believed to be on the list of 51 names recommended to the International Criminal Court, for his complicity in crimes against civilians in Darfur: see, 'Sudan becomes US ally in war on terror', *The Guardian*, 30th April 2005.

39   David M. Malone, 'The Security Council in the Post-Cold War Era: A Study in the creative interpretation of the UN Charter', 35 *N.Y.U.J. Int'l L & Politics* 487 (Winter, 2003).

40   For an excellent reference work covering UN peacekeeping operations from 1947 to the present, see generally Oliver Ramsbotham and Tom Woodhouse, *Encyclopedia of International Peacekeeping Operations* (1999).

41   See UN Dept. of Political Affairs, 'A Brief Overview of Security Council Applied Sanctions' (Mar. 1999) (informal background paper prepared for the Second Interlaken Seminar on Targeting United Nations Financial Sanctions), at http://www.smartsanctions.ch/Papers/I2/2unoverview.pdf.

42   The Security Council had used economic sanctions as an enforcement tool only twice prior to 1990: against Southern Rhodesia in 1966 and against South Africa in 1967. See Office of the Spokesman of the Secretary-General, 'The Use of Sanctions Under Chapter VII', at http:// www.un.org/News/ossg/sanction.htm. For an in-depth discussion of the Council's experience with sanctions regimes since 1990, see David Cortright and George A. Lopez, *The Sanctions Decade: Assessing UN Strategies in the 1990s* (2000); see also their follow up volume, David Cortright and George A. Lopez, *Sanctions and the Search for Security: Challenges to UN Action* (2002).

43   For a recent general discussion of sanctions, see Daniel W. Drezner, *The Sanctions Paradox: Economic Statecraft and International Relations*, 4–6 (1999).

44   See S.C. Res. 1267, U.N. SCOR, 54th Sess., 4051st mtg., UN Doc. S/RES/1267 (1999).

45   Canada carried out research on the need for more effective, less counterproductive sanctions regimes, with particular focus on the Security Council, in 1999:

See J. Tuyet Nguyen, '"Smart Sanctions" Needed, Axworthy Tells UN Body', *Toronto Star*, Apr. 18, 2000, LEXIS, Nexis Library, Toronto Star File.

46 Canada advocated a stern and uncompromising application of the Security Council's mandate to eradicate the power of UNITA in Angola to fund its war activities by the trade in diamonds. As a result, the De Beers corporation closed down its operations in Angola altogether: See 'UN Welcomes De Beers Embargo on Angolan Diamonds', *Agence France-Presse*, Oct. 7, 1999, available at *DIALOG*, File No. 614.

47 This has been highlighted in research carried out by a number of different countries. One such piece of research was published in 1998–1999, the Interlaken process, and was sponsored by the Swiss government: see Claude Bruderlein, *The Security Council at the Crossroads: Towards More Humane and Better Targeted Sanctions*, at 7 & nn. 26–7 (U.C. Berkeley, Inst. Of Gov't Stud., Working Paper No.15, 1999) available at: http://www.igs.berkeley.edu/publications/working-papers/99-15B.pdf. Another research project was undertaken by the German government on the use of arms embargoes and other forms of targeted sanctions in 1999: See generally 'Bonn International Center for Conversion, Design and Implementation of Arms Embargoes and Travel- and Aviation-Related Sanctions: Results of the "Bonn-Berlin Process"', available at: http://www.smartsanctions.de.

48 In the example of Angola above, a Commission of Experts on sanctions in Angola, chaired by Ambassador Anders Möllander (of Sweden), was established, following pressure from the Canadian Ambassador. A ground-breaking report was then published in March 2000 which advocated the 'naming and shaming' of third countries as 'sanction busters': see, *Report of the Panel of Experts on Violations of Security Council Sanctions Against UNITA*, UN SCOR, U.N. Doc. S/2000/203 (2000).

49 See S.C. Res. 1229, UN SCOR, 54th Sess., 3983d mtg., U.N. Doc. S/RES/1229 (1999).

50 Security Council Resolution 1233 of April 6, 1999, weakly emphasizes that 'the primary responsibility for achieving lasting peace in Guinea-Bissau rests with the parties and strongly calls upon them to implement fully all the provisions of the Abuja Agreement and subsequent undertakings'. See S.C. Res. 1233, UN SCOR, 54th Sess., 3991st mtg. P 1, U.N. Doc. S/RES/1233 (1999) (emphasis in original).

51 See *Comprehensive Review of the Whole Question of Peacekeeping Operations in All Their Aspects*, UN GAOR, 55th Sess., Provisional Agenda Item 87, at 17–20, U.N. Docs. A/55/305-S/2000/809 (2000).

52 Basildon Peta, 'Africans hope Mugabe's best man will make him negotiate', *The Independent*, 11th August 2005 at p.25.

53 For a review of the options that have been bandied regarding the reform of the Security Council, see *Report of the Thirty-First United Nations of the Next Decade Conference, The United Nations and the Twenty-First Century: The Imperative for Change*, 32–33 (1996).

54 For an eclectic discussion of reform and issues facing the United Nations today, see generally *Multilateral Diplomacy and the United Nations Today* (James P. Muldoon *et al.* (eds), 1999).

55 See Jennifer Moore, 'From nation state to failed state: International Protection from Human Rights abuses by non-state agents', 31 *Columbia Human Rights Law Review*, 81, at pages 96–7 (1999).

56 Tara Magner, 'Does a Failed State Country of Origin result in a failure of Inter-

national Protection? A Review of Polices Toward Asylum-Seekers in Leading Asylum Nations', 15 *Geo. Immigr. L.J.* 703 (Summer 2001), at p.11.

57   Refugee Convention art 1A(2) and High Commissioner's Statute art 6(ii).

58   See James C. Hathaway, *The Law of Refugee Status* (1991), at p.105.

59   Ibid.

60   Ibid., at p.106.

61   See *Refugee Convention*, July 20, 1951, Article 1(A) (2) 19 U.S.T. at 6259, 189 U.N.T.S. at 150.

62   'New German immigration law includes advances in refugee protection, says UNHCR', *UNHCR News Stories* (12th July 2004), available at http://www.unhcr. ch/cgi-bun/texis/vtx/news/=rwwBmeou2sewwxwwwwnwwwwwwwwhFqn N0bItFqnDni5zFqnN0bIAFqnN)bIDzmxwwwwwww1FqnN0bI/opendoc.htm. The UNHCR's Representative in Germany, Stefan Berglund, emphasized that the adoption of the law is also of particular significance to European and international refugee protection, commenting that the fact that Germany finally recognizes that victims of non-state and gender-specific persecution fall within the protection scope of the 1951 Convention is 'a very welcome development' (at note 40 above).

63   Such a strict approach is rejected by the leading commentators on refugee law. See Goodwin-Gill, at page 42; Hathaway, at page 128, and Atle Grahl-Madsen, *The Status of Refugee in International Law* (1966), at p.191.

64   See UN High Commissioner for Refugees, *Handbook on procedures and criteria for determining refugee status under the 1951 Convention* and the 1967 protocol relating to the status of refugees (1979).

65   See *US State Department Report (2002)* dated 31st March 2003, which states that, 'Citizens have not ... had the right to change their government in multiparty elections. Authority within the Government was held very narrowly among a small group of former fighters'.

66   See the *Human Rights Watch Press Release* (dated 17th September 2003) which demands that '[t]he Eriterian government should release political prisoners and allow for freedom of the press. *Human Rights Watch* said on the second anniversary of a major crackdown against civil society. Eriteria's practice of arbitrary arrests and detentions continues to this day' (see Headnote).

67   See *US State Department Report (2002)*, dated 31st March 2003 which states that 'Certainly, someone who has perceived ties with dissidents is greatly at risk' because, 'the government has arrested scores ... either because of their ties to the dissidents or their perceived political views'.

68   Which observes in relation to journalists, that '[a]lthough the Government stated that the arrests were not related to opposition views, it offered no evidence against them and did not charge them formally'.

69   The *US State Department Report (2002)*, dated 31st March 2003, notes that 'other persons were arrested arbitrarily and remained in custody without charge at year's end'.

70   The *US State Department Report (2002)*, dated 31st March 2003 refers to the fact that, 'Arbitrary arrests and prolonged detention without trial has not been limited to politicians and journalists. In late 2002, the government detained 250 refugees who attempted to flee Eriteria after being involuntarily repatriated from Malta. The refugees have been held incommunicado ever since'.

71   *Amnesty International Report 2002* which observes that 'scores of supporters of these reforms who had been arrested in late 2001 remained in secret incommunicado detention without trial throughout 2002'.

72 See *Refugee Convention*, 19 UST at 6261, 189 U.N.T.S, at 152.
73 See Goodwin-Gill, at page 42. Also see Moore, at pages 94–5.
74 See Zartman, *op. cit.*
75 *Human Rights Watch*, 'World Report 2003: Afghanistan' (January 2003) at http://
    www.hrw.org/. This report also importantly referred to a number of additional
    problems. In fact, this eminent and well-respected human rights organization
    had real concerns about the viability of return of failed asylum-seekers, holding
    that, 'Most returnees faced a grim reality in their former towns and villages – no
    shelter, food, roads, schools, health clinics, effective security, law enforcement or
    employment opportunities'. Even where they relocated to the 'urban areas such
    as Kabul, Jalalabad, and Mazar-e-Sharif' there was also risk to their lives as 'many
    refugees continued to fear persecution at the hands of local commanders in sev-
    eral areas of Afghanistan, such as former government officials, journalists,
    political opponents, and critics of the current authorities'. The result is that 'The
    Afghan authorities, UNHCR, other UN and humanitarian agencies, and donors
    were seriously ill-equipped to cope with the scale and speed of the repatriation'.
    Indeed, 'returnees also faced serious ongoing security problems throughout
    Afghanistan'.
76 See under the heading 'Resurgent Warlordism'.
77 See http://web.amnesty.org/library/print/ENGASA110122003.
78 See *'Afghanistan: Out of Sight, Out Of Mind: The Fate of the Afghan Returnees'*
    http://web.amnesty.org/library/print/ENGASA110142003. It states that 'the
    resurgence of forces allied to the Taliban, have resulted in a situation of general-
    ized instability in up to two-thirds of the country'. It states that 'Urban areas,
    including Kabul, cannot be considered sufficiently secure or stable to satisfy re-
    quirements of return in safety and dignity'. It records that 'On 7 June four ISAF
    soldiers and one Afghan civilian were killed and a large number of people were
    injured when a car bomb exploded near a bus transporting ISAF soldiers to the
    Kabul airport'. More importantly, it concludes that 'there are no clear indications
    of when and how the Afghan National Army (ANA) will be able to operate ef-
    fectively in areas currently under the control of factional militias'.
79 See Barnett R. Rubin, 'The "warlords" threat', *International Herald Tribune* (IHT),
    Wednesday, 4th August 2004.
80 *Human Rights Watch*, 'World Report 2005: Afghanistan' (13th January 2005), at
    http://www.hrw.org/.
81 Ibid., at p.2 of 4.
82 Ibid., at p.4 of 4.
83 These are the facts of *Abdul Wali Mohammad Khail* (App. No. HX/41369/02;
    promulgated on 16th October 2002).
84 Ibid., at para 31.
85 Ibid., at para 19.
86 Ibid., at para 34.
87 At para 65 which is headed, 'Agents of Persecution' and reads as follows:

> Persecution is normally related to action by the authorities of a country. It
> may also emanate from sections of the population that do not respect the
> standards established by the laws of the country concerned. A case in point
> may be religious intolerance amounting to persecution, in a country otherwise
> secular, but where sizeable fractions of the population do not respect religious
> beliefs of their neighbours. Where serious discriminatory or other offensive
> acts are committed by the local population, they can be considered as persecu-

tion if they are knowingly tolerated by the authorities, or if the authorities refuse, or prove unable, to offer effective protection.

88 See para 65.
89 See para 65.
90 See judgment in *Mahmood Mohd. Basheer BUX* (HX/04526/01) at para 13. For another case see judgment in *Saeed Mohd Sedeq EBRAHIM* (HX/64206/2000) at para 49.
91 See the *Yemen Times* (1998, vol. III).
92 *US State Department Report 2002* which states that 'Tribal violence resulted in a number of killings and other abuses and the Government's ability to control tribal elements remained limited'.
93 *ICG Middle East Report*, No.8, 8th January 2000.
94 The causes of tribal clashes, as the Report states, range 'from insults' 'to a marital row' to 'material disputes' including those 'related to land or water'.
95 Ibid.
96 See Joan Fitzpatrick, 'Temporary Protection of Refugees: Elements of Formalized Regime', 94 *AM. J. INTL'L. L.* 279, 293 (2000); see also *OAU Convention* governing the specific aspects of refugee problems in Africa, September 10, 1969, 1001 U. N.T.S. 45; *Cartagena Declaration on Refugees*, November 19–22, 1984, reprinted in UN High Commissioner for Refugees, *Collection of International Instruments and other legal texts concerning refugees and displaced persons*, Vol. 2; *Regional Instruments* 206 (1995).
97 *OAU Convention*, 1001 U.N.T.S. at 57.
98 *Cartagena Declaration*, supra, at Article III (3).
99 See *Convention for the Protection of Human Rights and Fundamental Freedoms*, November 4, 1950, 213 U.N.T.S. 222, Europe.T.S. 5.
100 See *Ahmed v. Austria*, 24 Eur. H.R. Rep. (Ser.B) at 278, 279–80 (1996).
101 *Convention against torture and other cruel, inhuman or degrading treatment or punishment*, December 10, 1984, 1465 U.N.T.S. 85 (1984).
102 See para 114.
103 At paras 113–14.
104 *CIPU Report* at para 6.40.
105 See *US State Department Report (2003)* which states that, '[t]here were thousands of children on the street of Monrovia; however it is difficult to tell who were street children, ex-combatants, or IDPs', at para 6.41.
106 Ibid., at para 6.51 which states that, '[t]he UNHCR is attempting to assist those who have returned, and to evaluate their needs. However, many remain in camps within safe areas, as they cannot return to their homes, which are in areas that remain insecure …'.
107 Ibid., at para 6.52. which states that, 'While the improved security situation within Liberia would appear to be a factor , there may be other reasons for these spontaneous returns. Many have returned from Sierra Leone, where there have recently been violent clashes between refugees and the host communities'.
108 *Amnesty International Report 2004*, which confirms that '[a]s the armed conflict worsened, government forces and armed opposition groups were responsible for widespread abuses against civilians, including killings, torture, rape and other forms of sexual violence …'.
109 Ibid.
110 Ibid.
111 *Amnesty International Report 2003*, at para ibid.

112   Ibid.
113   *Human Rights Watch* in 'Congo: War is International, Not Local' (New York, July 8, 2003).
114   Ibid.
115   In the case of [2004] UKIAT 0007 (DRC), (promulgated on 28-01-04), the Immigration Appeal Tribunal (IAT), (as it then was) held that there was no a real risk of serious harm upon return to the DRC. However, it came to this decision by referring to an earlier IAT case at para 98, namely, [2003] UKIAT 00058 (DRC). However, what that case decided was that membership of an organization *per se* (such as an opposition group) was not enough but had to be allied with the belief that the claimant was conspiring with rebels and that the UDPS members (as an opposition group) were either prominent high level party officials and activists or members of any level who took part in political demonstrations which are generally illegal and broken up by the authorities. The IAT referred to a report by Dr. Kennes that those at real risk on return were those identified as of adverse interest prior to departure. They also referred to the UNHCR description of the 'military or political profile or background' category. However, that did not draw a distinction between high level and low level individuals. Nevertheless, the Tribunal was of the view that those at risk must have brought themselves to the adverse notice of the authorities. In other words, they must have acquired a certain profile in the eyes of the authorities before the departure.
116   *Rizkallah v. Canada* (Minister of Employment and Immigration), 33A.C.W.S.3d 940 (1992).
117   See *Abdalla v. Immigration and Multicultural Affairs*, 51 A.L.B.11 (1998) (Federal Court of Australia). See also *Minister for Immigration and Multicultural Affairs v. Abdi*, 162 A.L.R 105 (1999) (Federal Court of Australia).
118   *Adan v. Secretary of State for the Home Department*, 2 W.L.R 702 (1998) H.L.
119   *In Reh*, Interim Decision 3276, 1996 W.L 291910 (B.I.A. 1996).
120   *Rizkallah v. Canada (Minister of Employment and Immigration)*, 33A.C.W.S.3d 940 (1992), where a Lebanese claimant failed in his refugee claim because he was not targeted as a Christian but as a victim of generalized violence.
121   *Denis Baah v. SSHD* (Home Office Ref: B1093483; decided 30th November 2001) App. No. IA/02638/2005; Heard before an Immigration Judge in Walsall on 27th July 2005.
122   *Amnesty International Report, December 2001.*
123   See Rizkallah, *op.cit.*
124   See *Minister for Immigration and Multicultural Affairs v. Abdi*, 162 A.L.R 105 (1999) (Federal Court of Australia).
125   *US State Department Report of 2002.*
126   *Amnesty International Report 2003* which recorded that 'The authorities also organized, coordinated and encouraged militias and "War Veterans" to carry out threats, assaults abductions, torture and killings against real or perceived opposition supporters and human rights defenders'. It has been observed that '[m]ore than 1,000 cases of torture and ill-treatment were reported during 2002'.
127   *Human Rights Watch Report 2003.*
128   Abdi, *op.cit.*
129   *Abdalla v. Immigration and Multicultural Affairs*, 51 A.L.B.11 (1998) (Federal Court of Australia).
130   Ibid.
131   See Kate Hoey MP, 'Silent Diplomacy can't stop Mugabe's mission to destroy homes and lives', *The Times*, 16th June 2005.

132   Richard Ford, Phillip Webster and Daniel McGrory, 'Britain agrees to second chance for Mugabe refugees', *The Times*, 28th June 2005.

133   *Adan v. Secretary of State for the Home Department*, 2 W.L.R 702 (1998) H.L.

134   At page 702.

135   See *Adan, op.cit.* at page 702 and Abdi at page 105.

136   See Lord Lloyd in *Adan* at page 714.

137   *US State Department Report (2003)* which states that 'clan and factional militias' operate so effectively in Somalia, that 'more than 60 per cent of the budget was allocated to maintaining a militia and police force'.

138   See the heading, 'Present situation of minority groups in Somalia', Ibid.

139   *Joint British, Danish and Dutch Fact-Finding Mission to Nairobi, (17–24 September 2000)*, at para 4.2.

140   Ibid., at para 3.3.5.

141   Ibid., at para 3.3.3.

142   CIPU report at para paragraph 5.12, 5.13 – 5.14 and at para 6.87–8.

143   Paragraph 6.13 of the *CIPU Report*.

144   Disclosed by the Home Office in a letter dated 25th July 2003 to Paul Morris of the South Manchester Law Centre.

145   *In Reh*, Interim Decision 3276, 1996 W.L 291910 (B.I.A. 1996).

146   See Von Sternberg, 'The plight of the noncombatant in civil war and the new criteria for refugee status', 9 *Int'l J. of Refugee L.* 169, 178 (1977).

147   See Joint Position 96/196/JHA, defined by the council on the basis of Article K.3 of the Treaty of the European Union on the harmonized application of the definition of the term 'refugee' in Article 1 of the Geneva Convention of 28 July 1951 relating to the status of refugees, 1996 AOJ (L63/2).

148   *The Tampere Conclusions* were the result of October 1999 meeting in Tampere, Finland of the Prime Ministers and Presidents of the fifteen member states of the European Union. The purpose of the meeting was to further develop a common asylum policy for the European Union. The commitment to do so was made by European Union Member States in the Treaty of Amsterdam, which entered into force on 1 May 1999 and set a five year time line for harmonization of policies.

149   See *Keita v. INS*, 175S.3d 1024 (8th cir.1999). Also see in Reh, *Interim Decision* 3276, 1996 WL 291910 (B.I.A. 1996).

150   See *Keita, op.cit.*

151   *Soering v United Kingdom* (1989) 11 EHRR 439.

152   *Cruz Varas v Sweden* (1991) 14 EHRR 1, 33–34, para 69, *Vilvarajah v United Kingdom* (1991) 14 EHRR 248, 286–7, para 103, *Chahal v United Kingdom* (1996) 23 EHRR 413, 453, para 80, *Ahmed v Austria*, 24 EHRR 278, 290, para 39, *HLR v France* 26 EHRR 29, 49, para 34, *Tomic v United Kingdom* Application No 17837/03 (unreported) 14 October 2003, *Ammari v Sweden* (unreported) 22 October 2002 and *Nasimi v Sweden* Application No 38865/02 (unreported) 16 March 2004.

153   It is in the last five of the above cases that it has done so in almost identical terms.

154   *Soering v. UK* (1989) 11 EHRR 439, 468–9.

155   See Lord Bingham of Cornhill in *R (Ullah) v Special Adjudicator* [2004] 2 AC 323, 340–341 paras 7 and 9.

156   *Ahmed v. Austria*, 24 Eur. H.R. Rep. (ser. B) at 278, 289 (1996).

157   Tara Magner, 'Does a Failed State Country of Origin result in a failure of International Protection? A Review of Polices Toward Asylum-Seekers in Leading Asylum Nations', 15 *Geo. Immigr. L.J. 703* (Summer 2001) at p.11.

158   As the Court recounted:

In the present case the source of the risk on which the applicant relies is not the public authorities. According to the applicant, it consists in *the threat of reprisals by drug traffickers*, who may seek revenge because of certain statements that he made to the French police, *coupled with the fact that the Colombian state is, he claims, incapable of protecting him from attacks by such persons*.

See *HLR v France* (1997) 26 EHRR 29, 50, para 39.
159   *HLR v France* (1997) 26 EHRR 29, 50, para 40.
160   For example, in *Ammani v Sweden* the EctHR used almost identical language where the alleged risk of ill-treatment was 'not only by the Algerian authorities but also by the Islamic armed organization GIA': see, *Ammani v Sweden* Application No 60959/00 (unreported) 22 October 2002.
161   See 26 EHRR 29, 50, para 40.
162   *D v United Kingdom (1997) 24 EHRR 423, 447, at para 49.*
163   D, however, was a very exceptional case – just how exceptional has recently been made clear by the decision of the House of Lords in *N (FC) v Secretary of State for the Home Department* [2005] UKHL 31.
164   This was footnoted to that passage in D was a reference to *Ahmed v Austria* (1996) 24 EHRR 278, 291, para 44.
165   *R. v. Secretary of State for the Home Department, ex parte Bagdanavicius* (per Lord Nicholls of Birkenhead, Lord Hope of Craighead, Lord Walker of Gestingthorpe, Baroness Hale of Richmond, and Lord Brown of Eaton-under-Heywood (judgment 26th May 2005), at [2003] EWCA Civ 1605].
166   Article 3 of the European Convention on Human Rights (the ECHR) enshrines one of the fundamental values of democratic societies and the protection it provides is absolute. It states that:

No one shall be subjected to torture or to inhuman or degrading treatment or punishment.

167   The UK Government had argued that: 'the sufficiency of state protection is an integral part of the "real risk" test: the reality of risk is assessed by reference to the sufficiency of such protection. Where a reasonable level of protection is provided, the threshold for the engagement of article 3 will not be met'. It rather seems as if this essentially fallback submission was the main basis of the Court of Appeal's decision in the Secretary of State's favour – see [2004] 1 WLR 1207, 1230–1231, para 55(7)–(16).
168   At para 21.
169   At para 22. Lord Brown said that this is the effect of sentences 2 and 3 is to my mind clear: for good measure they are run together as a single sentence in paragraph 69 of the court's subsequent judgment in *Cruz Varas v Sweden* 14 EHRR 1, 34.
170   Which states that the decision to extradite may engage the responsibility of the State in question 'where substantial grounds have been shown for believing that the person concerned, if extradited, faces a real risk of being subjected to torture or to inhuman … treatment'.
171   Which states that 'any liability under the Convention … is liability … incurred … by reason of … action which has as a direct consequence the exposure of an individual to proscribed ill-treatment'.
172   At para 23.
173   The reasoning Lord Brown gave for this was as follows: 'The plain fact is that the argument throughout has been bedeviled by a failure to grasp the distinction

in non-state agent cases between on the one hand the risk of serious harm and on the other hand the risk of treatment contrary to Article 3. In cases where the risk *"emanates from intentionally inflicted acts of the public authorities in the receiving country"* (the language of para 49 of *D v United Kingdom* 24 EHRR 423, 447) one can use those terms interchangeably: the intentionally inflicted acts would without more constitute the proscribed treatment. Where, however, the risk emanates from non-state bodies, that is not so: any harm inflicted by non-state agents will not constitute Article 3 ill-treatment unless in addition the state has failed to provide reasonable protection. If someone is beaten up and seriously injured by a criminal gang, the member state will not be in breach of Article 3 unless it has failed in its positive duty to provide reasonable protection against such criminal acts. This provides the answer to Mr Nicol's reliance on the UK's obligation under article 3 being a negative obligation and thus absolute. The argument begs the vital question as to what particular risk engages the obligation. Is it the risk merely of harm or is it the risk of proscribed treatment? In my judgment it is the latter' (see para 24).

174   At para 24.
175   *Ahmed v Austria* 24 EHRR 278.
176   Ibid., at p.292, para 47.
177   At para 25.
178   Adopting the view of Sedley L.J. in *McPherson v Secretary of State for the Home Department* [2002] INLR 139, 147, para 22, where the court said that the protection does not have to be sufficient to *'obviate'* the risk as this *'cannot be right'*.
179   See http://www.ind.homeoffice.gov.uk/ind/en/home/0/country_information/bulletins/afgh, at para 3.14 of the UK IND Report.
180   Ibid., This is a reference to para 14 at p.4 of the *Commission on Human Rights Report*.
181   Ibid., This is at para 3.15of the UK IND report.
182   Ibid., at para 14 of p.12 of the Commission on Human Rights report.
183   Ibid., see heading, *Refugees and Internally Displaced People (IDPs)* at para 3.20 of the UK IND Report.
184   Ibid., at para 14 at p.22.
185   Danish Immigration Service, 'The political conditions, the security and human rights situation in Afghanistan: Report on fact-finding mission to Kabul, Afghanistan' (2nd December 2004). See under para 3.1 'The general security situation', at p.6 of 47, at http://www.udist.dk/, e-mail:dok@udlst.dk.
186   Danish Immigration Service, 'The political conditions, the security and human rights situation in Afghanistan: Report on fact-finding mission to Kabul, Afghanistan' (2nd December 2004). See, para 1.1 under 'Recent political and security related development', at p.3 of 47 at http://www.udist.dk/, e-mail:dok@udlst.dk.
187   See *NATO News* at p.1 at pp.1–3; at http://www.natonews.com.
188   See *BBC News, UK Edition*, at p.1 see, http://news.bbc.co.uk/1/hi/world/south_asia/4622167.stm.
189   See *Amnesty International Report* (25 May 2005) at http://web.amnesty.org/report2005/afg-summary-eng, at page 1.
190   Justin Huggler, 'Karzai ally lynched as Taliban violence rocks Afghanistan', *The Independent*, 18th July 2005 at p.23.
191   At para 12.
192   See, *Rv. Secretary of State for the Home Department, ex parte Razgar* [2004] UKHL 27 at http://www.publications.parliament.uk/pa/ld200304/ldjudgmnt/jd040617/razgar-1.htm.

193 At para 29.
194 At para 18.
195 At para 19.
196 *Osman v United Kingdom* (1998), 29 EHRR 245, 305, para 116 which was an article 2 case.

5 Tackling Forced Displacement

INTRODUCTION

The law on forced migration continues to be divorced from general international law. Yet, at a time when it is possible for the international community to intervene in the internal affairs of ostensibly sovereign states to prevent human rights abuses, enforce democracy, and to fight international terrorism, it is surely right that the fluid distinction between refugees and other groups of forced populations is also recognized, because all these actions create displaced populations. In the last chapter, we have seen how the actions of 'non-state agents' in a State often go unredressed by the *1951 Refugee Convention* and by general and specific provisions of human rights law. In this chapter, we will see how the *1951 Refugee Convention* also fails to catch the emerging categories of 'environmental refugees' and 'internally displaced persons' (IDPs). The international community had much rather subject these wider categories of displaced populations, on the whole, to a policy of 'containment', which can be described as comprising a variety of deterrent, exclusionary and diversionary measures, designed to avoid having to take international responsibility for displaced populations.[1] However, 'forced displacement' presents a problem that is far bigger and complex than that of Convention refugees. Indeed, the term 'refugee' does not apply happily to so-called 'environmental refugees'. These are people who have crossed borders. As a result, they cannot be IDPs. Yet, they are not environmental refugees in the strict sense either under the *1951 Refugee Convention*. Nor are they pure environmental refugees as often an environmental disaster has complex political or man-made factors behind it. Powerful nations often make the distinction between refugees who are properly so-called and those who are fleeing environmental disasters because they want to avoid having to deal with the problem of forced migrations. In doing so, they create an even greater instability in the international system. This attitude of the international community is not only dangerous. It is inconsistent and illogical in the light of its own recent history. In this chapter, I want to argue that the focus of the international community today should be on 'forced displacement' and that the continued adherence to the rigid classification between IDPs and refugees is making less and less sense, because it over-looks a practical inter-connectedness and unity between these two groups. I shall then deal with those who may be referred to as seeking, ecological sanctuary, namely, the 'environmental refugees' because if the position of IDPs is precarious, that of 'environmental refugees' is even more so, since they are technically neither refugees nor IDPs, having crossed borders into another state.

DISPLACED POPULATIONS AND INTERNATIONAL RESPONSIBILITY

The neglect of forced displacement by the Northern States is inconsistent and illogical in the light of its own policies because the displacement of populations has long been seen as both capable and worthy of evoking international action. The international community has been seen as having a duty to respond to such calamities. From the early years of the twentieth century – nearly 100 years now – help has been forthcoming under the Red Cross system (comprising the ICRC and the Federation of World Red Cross and Red Crescent Societies) and then later the UN High Commissioner for Refugees. When the United Nations was set up in 1947, and when it began considering situations of conflict and crises, the UN Security Council was well placed to focus on the humanitarian plight of civilian victims of conflicts. Indeed, early in its history, the UN Security Council had to consider the position of Palestinian refugees that arose from the Arab-Israeli dispute following Israel's war in 1947–1948, culminating in the mass exodus of the population of Palestine, necessitating the setting up of a specific UN agency, UNRWA, to deal with the Palestinian refugees.[2] Thus, from the time of its inception, the UN Security Council had concerned itself with refugees.[3] Nevertheless, it is accepted that one of the most creative and imaginative areas of the UN Security Council decision-making, by the closing years of the twentieth-century, has still been in the field of the protection of refugees. In fact, in the 1990s as never before, the Security Council invoked the plight of refugees and their implied destabilizing effect on neighboring states as grounds for its own involvement in conflict. In the former Yugoslavia,[4] and again, in Somalia[5] early Council resolutions had the effect of involving the Security Council in the conflicts in those countries. This action emanated from a new view that refugee flows could actually be a primary cause of regional conflict and not merely an incidental effect of it. It was a view that had acquired widespread currency. Thus, it was strongly believed that in the 1991–1994 Haitian democratic crisis, the threat to international peace and security was posed, not by the prospect of military warfare, but from the outflow of Haitian boat-people, which threatened to swamp the surrounding Caribbean countries, once their preferred destination to the shores of Florida was blocked by the US coast guard. Indeed, in the event a number of Caribbean countries and dependencies did have to deal with the inflow of Haitians.

The international community acted through the United Nations for a number of reasons. First, bilateral assistance in war-torn areas of the world had often been ineffectual. Second, a number of specialized UN agencies had the requisite skills and experience to deal with conflict-ridden areas. Third, the United Nations could deploy peace missions with a specific mandate to achieve humanitarian objectives. The international community often acted because of pressure at home from their electorates watching images of a horror-stricken humanity on their television screens. There were few vital national interests at stake. Yet, their governments could afford to delegate action on their behalf to the United Nations because the costs and risks of so doing could be minimized when they acted in this way. So it was, that in the last decade of the twentieth century the international community began to speculate whether they had the right to involve themselves in the affairs of sovereign nations in order to save the lives of their citizens, including an international duty to do so.[6] As the horrors of civilian casualties worldwide began to unfold, especially with wanton carnages in countries like Sierra Leone and the Congo in Africa, the imperative to intervene to save lives increased. This was less easily done than said. In Kosovo, for example, the successful NATO- dominated military deployment of KFOR was followed by the far less successful United Nations attempt to administer peace in Kosovo.

INTERNALLY DISPLACED POPULATIONS

Refugees and Forced Displacement

It is in this context that it can be said that it is wrong to focus on refugees but not on other forms of human displacement. The two are inter-connected and go hand-in-hand. Western powers have attempted, however, to distinguish the two for reasons that are entirely to do with their perceived self-interest. This manifests itself in three ways. First, with the end of the cold war, most northern countries were concerned to curb refugee flows. There was no longer a critical advantage in accepting refugees as there had been under the cold war. Western governments today are less interested to accept large numbers of refugees. Instead, they are focussed on the need to promote protection and assistance for those displaced *within* their own communities. This is a policy of 'containment'. Indeed, containment would appear to be the hallmark of contemporary refugee policy since, according to the late Joan Fitzpatrick:

> large numbers of persons with unadjudicated but potentially valid, claims to political cal asylum have been funneled either into off-shore temporary refuges or into temporary protection schemes in European states.[7]

What this is, however, is a very different form of 'containment' because although the internally displaced have not as yet crossed internal borders, the policy is to ensure that they do not do so through the guise of providing them with protection and assistance within their own borders.

Yet, the policy is not without practical and moral risks. For example, the *United States State Department Country Report* for Sierra Leone for 2003 suggests that:

[s]ince April 2001, approximately 220,000 registered internally displaced persons (IDPs) have been resettled; many more were unregistered and returned to their homes without assistance

but that 'NGOs estimate that approximately 10,000 to 20,000 unregistered IDPs remained in urban areas'.[8] Returned refugees have added to the population of IDPs so that '[a]pproximately 32,000 refugees were repatriated during the year [2003]'.[9] Paradoxically, therefore, while the number of refugees in the world has been decreasing, the number of IDPs has been increasing correspondingly. Second, there was a realization that peace and reconstruction in war-torn societies could not take place without the effective integration of displaced persons. It was impossible to talk about reconstruction and development without taking into account the return and the integration of refugees and internally displaced persons. Yet, the *United States State Department Country Report* for Sierra Leone for 2003 casts doubts on the policy of integration over grant of refugee status when it states that:

[t]he large influx of IDPs and refugees and the lack of resources caused tension with local residents ... There were numerous reports that refugees and IDPs returned to find their homes occupied.[10]

Third, internal displacement was seen as a possible threat to internal instability, which could spill over across borders and upset external and regional stability. Thus, the same *United States State Department Country Report* for Sierra Leone for 2003 states that:

[a]n estimated 40,000 persons remained in refugee camps in Guinea and Liberia; smaller numbers remained in Cote d'Ivoire, the Gambia, Ghana, and other countries and were expected to integrate locally in those countries[11]

although prospects of this integration, as we have noted above, were not entirely sanguine.[12] The international community had to support national efforts at reconstruction. In fact, the UN Security Council has drawn connections between situations of humanitarian disaster and international peace and security.

The UN was established to protect and safeguard all human beings on earth 'from the scourge of war'[13] with the calamity affected IDPs and refugees equally. Wars here can surely mean domestic wars as well as international wars. As the cold war ended, the super powers which had previously been engaged in proxy wars in Angola, Mozambique, El Salvador or Afghanistan, began to focus on the humanitarian dimension of conflict as the geopolitical struggles began to subside. By 2000, there were almost 20 million 'persons of concern' to the UNHCR, but IDPs did not have their own treaty and so their welfare was heavily dependent on the compassion of the international community. The general view is that new possibilities opened up for crossing borders and reaching the internally displaced since there was no fear of super power retaliation. There arose a greater acceptance of the idea that events taking place within a country are the legitimate concern of the international community.

In the 1990s, the UN began to involve itself in such conflicts, as when the Iraqi Government attacked the Kurds after the first Gulf War (1991), during the Rwanda genocide (1994) and the war in the former Zaire (1996).[14] The view emerged that governments should be held accountable for their failure to meet their obligations under the UN Charter and international human rights agreements. The international community intervened in Iraq, Somalia, Bosnia and Rwanda where the Security Council demanded access and even used force to deliver relief to displaced persons. Various UN General Assembly resolutions from 1992 onwards have conferred a selective limited mandate to undertake humanitarian assistance and provide protection to IDPs.[15]

I do not, therefore, think that the failure or reluctance of the UN to intervene can be justified on the basis that there were specific treaties in relation to refugees, but not IDPs, because even before the 1990s the UNHCR had already managed to assist 'several million' IDPs over the years.[16] It did so through 'extra-statutory'[17] means when the situation so warranted it. The attempt to craft a formal international mandate for IDPs only in 1992 was unjustifiably long over-due. This is clear when one looks at the fact that when this process was initiated back in 1990, by *UN Economic and Social Council* (hereafter ECOSOC) under UN Charter, Article 62 (2) of which mandates it to 'make recommendations [to the UN General Assembly] for the purpose of promoting respect for, and observance of, human rights and fundamental freedoms for all', it did so by requesting the UN Secretary General in terms that it could have done a long time ago, namely, to:

> initiate the United Nations system-wide review to assess the experience and capacity of various organizations in the coordination of assistance to all refugees, *displaced persons* and returnees and, on the basis of such review, to recommend ways of maximizing cooperation and coordination among various organizations of United Nations system in order to ensure an effective response to the problems of refugees, displaced persons and returnees.[18]

The ECOSOC itself did not make a distinction between between IDPs and refugees, but chose to address the problem of forced migration gnerally.[19] The jurisdiction of the ECOSOC is set down under Article 62 of the UN Charter, which outlines four major functions, including 'making recommendations for the purpose of promoting respect for, observance of human rights and fundamental freedoms for all'[20] and to 'prepare draft Conventions for submissions to the General Assembly, with respect to matters falling within its competence'.[21] A specific IDPs mandate could have been proposed in the 1980s or even earlier. After all, when IDPs were first counted in 1982 by the US Committee for Refugees, there were 1.2 million in 11 countries. By 1997, 25 million were found in more than 40 countries. These are mostly created by civil wars resulting from the end of the cold war.[22] It is often said that there are problems of theory and principle with such intervention. International Refugee Law and International Humanitarian Law were originally only crafted for inter-state conflicts and focused on trans-border population movements. However, the practical evidence on the ground shows this is not strictly true. What, I believe has happened is that the political imperatives of affording refugee status from the Soviet Bloc countries have gone and the cold war tactics have shifted away from admission of refugees to their non-admission and rejection. Today the developed world is making a moral case for the accommodation of the world's oppressed and persecuted in other ways. Refugees are denied admission and being sent back. Even when they come from oppressive regimes it is being said that they have the option of 'internal relocation' available to them. Where they are being admitted, they are offered short term 'humanitarian leave'. If actually admitted as refugees, they are expected to return as soon as the situation at home improves. In short, repatriation has become the preferred methodology. The result is to increase the size and suffering of the global IDP population, and it is not something that international law can properly ignore. This is because such a policy is likely to increase the size of the world's refugee population and present its own threat to global peace.

The Guiding Principles on Internal Displacement

In 1992 the UN General Assembly distinguished IDPs as a specific class for the first time.[23] This acknowledged the previous efforts the High Commissioner had made in responding to requests from the Secretary General or other UN Organizations to meet the plight of IDPs. This late focus on IDPs as a specific category demonstrates the fact that until the early 1990s, the focus of the UN was firmly on refugees alone.[24] Yet, the main distinctive feature of IDPs is simply that they have not yet crossed an external border. In other respects they are no different from refugees. This is clear from how in 1992, ECOSOC described IDPs (as distinct from refugees) as:

> Persons who have been forced to flee their homes, as a result of armed conflict, internal strife, systematic violation of human rights or natural or man-made disasters.[25]

From this definition, we can say that IDPs have three characteristics, only the last of which is different from that of refugees. First, they are subject to involuntary or forced movement. Second, their displacement stems from conflict, internal strife, systematic human rights violations and natural or man-made disasters. The reference to 'in particular' means, that although the focus is on conflict situations, generalized violence, or violations of human rights, it is not confined just to these situations but could extend to wider causes of IDPs. Third, IDPs are confined to their own country. It is in this respect that refugees are different because they are not confined to their own countries.

A later resolution in 1993 was adopted, which allowed UNHCR's Executive Committee to 'extend on a case by case basis and under specific circumstances, protection and assistance to the internally displaced'.[26] Later, two UN General Assembly Resolutions addressed 'human rights and mass exoduses of peoples'[27] and 'strengthening the coordination of humanitarian emergency assistance of the UN'.[28] These two resolutions marked a significant landmark on the road towards specific IDPs mandate. It was not, however, until the establishment of the permanent office and appointment of the IDPs representative, in July 2002, that the protection of IDPs finally came into its own right. In 1995, the UN Representative, Deng, described his terms of reference of his office as follows:

> To cooperate and coordinate with the Department of Humanitarian Affairs of the Secretariat, the office of the (UNHCR), and the (ICRC), and call upon these agencies and other intergovernmental and non-governmental organizations to continue to cooperate with … facilitate (its) tasks.[29]

A revised definition was put forward in 1998, by the Representative of the UN Secretary General for IDPs who was appointed in 1992, and he defined IDPs as follows:

> Persons or groups of persons who have been forced or obliged to flee or leave their homes of habitual residence, in particular, as a result of or in order to avoid the effects of armed conflict, situations of generalized violence, violation of human rights or natural or human-made disasters, and who have not crossed an internationally recognized state border.[30]

This IDPs representative's definition is similar to the ECOSOC. It still has much in common with a number of refugee definitions (such as in the OAU definition) with the exception of the fact that they have not yet crossed an external border. State parties and other agencies are gradually adopting this definition. Nevertheless, this revised definition aims to remedy two important deficiencies in the earlier ECOSOC definition. First, it has done away with the temporal and quantitative aspects of the working definition which are capable of creating complications. For instance, in Iraq, there was nothing 'sudden or unexpected' about the displacement of the Kurds which took place over a considerable period in the late 1970s, 1980s and the early 1990s. Also, in Colombia, internally displaced people often flee in 'small' rather than in 'large numbers'.[31] Second, this latter definition has also broadened the notion of coerced flight to encompass not just those 'forced to flee' but those 'forced to leave' as well, the latter being those who have not fled from their homes but who have been expelled or forcibly moved.[32]

It is still the case, however, that specific international treaties apply only to refugees. There is no treaty that is specific to IDPs. The result is that refugees alone are entitled to international protection. The IDPs are not so entitled. The basis of this distinction lies in the fact that refugees are forcibly displaced *across borders* whereas the internally displaced are only forcibly displaced within their own communities. This is meant to appear tidy and uncomplicated. Accordingly, the condition of IDPs falls within the 'internal affairs'[33] of a sovereign state, and so the international community is reluctant to intervene on their behalf. Technically the UNHCR does not have a mandate here. Yet, the UNHCR is aware that the plight of IDPs can be even more serious than refugees. It has stated that '[IDPs] often face a far more insecure future'.[34] But they are also insecure in international protection because of their chimerical nature since, in the words of Perluss and Hartman, 'unlike a refugee, a person fleeing from internal armed conflict does not seek to dis-establish his ... nationality or religion of his country on a temporary or permanent basis' which means that their 'need for relief, and therefore temporary refuge, lasts only until the government can [guarantee] ... *de facto* protection'.[35] There is also a practical difference in protection arising from the fact that different agencies deal with refugees and IDPs. In the case of IDPs, it is the International Committee of the Red Cross (ICRC) that does the most useful work and not the UNHCR. The focus of the ICRC is to find protection for IDPs within their own countries, whereas the focus of the UNHCR is protection in a foreign state for refugees. There is an international treaty in respect of one, but not the other. Therefore, it is now increasingly being asked whether there should not be an international legal instrument for people uprooted in their own countries, and whether some international institutional arrangements should not help them and, as a result, international responsibility is beginning to emerge for IDPs.

The Rising Tide of IDPs

The emergence of this international responsibility for the plight of IDPs is traceable to the events in the former Yugoslavia which had the dramatic effect of changing what was hitherto an 'internal matter' into an international one. In 1992 the United Nations General Assembly declared that, '[T]he number of refugees and displaced persons are of concern to the High Commissioner', because requests for 'assistance and protection, has continued to increase' while at the same time:

> their protection continues to be seriously jeopardized in many situations as a result of ... threats to their physical security, dignity and well being, and lack of respect to their physical security, dignity and well being, and lack of respect for fundamental freedoms and human rights.[36]

By 1999, the world situation was such that millions were uprooted from their homes by war – '1.2 million in Angola, 850,000 in Kosovo, 750,000 in Ethiopia and Eritrea, 550,000 in East Timor, 200,000 in Chechnya and countless more in other conflicts around the world'.[37] By the end of 2001, the UNHCR had reported some 5 million IDPs.[38] It is estimated that there are in the world today 25 million IDPs caused by civil war, ethnic violence, internal strife, and mass human right violations. Women and children form the largest category. Africa has 10 million, Asia has 5 million, Europe has 4 million, and the Americas have 2 million.

Today IDPs abound in states that are not necessarily classified as failed states. Whether it is officially recognized or not, they pose a potentially serious threat to regional peace and security, to say nothing of the violations of human rights. Thus, a report in early 2005 by the Norwegian Refugee Council[39] confirmed that conflict and religious persecution have led to a large number of people being internally displaced in Bangladesh. In the south-eastern Chittgong Hill Tracts, tribal requests for religious autonomy in 1971 sparked off a 25-year armed conflict which displaced tens of thousands of people (estimates range between 60,000 and 500,000). As well as building up a massive military presence in the Chittagong Hill Tracts, the government countered requests for autonomy by forcibly settling Muslim Bengali popula-tions from elsewhere in Bangladesh on land traditionally belonging to tribal groups, thus evicting them without compensation. The majority of the dis-placed have not been able to return to their former villages, including many refugees who returned from India upon the signing of the peace agreement. During the past few years, Bengali settlers, allegedly supported by the army which is still heavily present in the region, have been involved in attacks against the tribal population. In addition, tensions between the tribal groups have led to further displacement on several occasions. The second main rea-son for displacement in Bangladesh has been persecution of religious minorities the election of the right-wing Bangladesh National Party (BNP) in October 2001. The elections triggered a wave of violence under which Is-lamic fundamentalists groups forced upto 200,000 Hindus and other minority groups to flee the country. The Hindu population of Bangladesh has steadily diminished since the partitioning of Indian in 1947; repressive policies have forced many people to leave after having been deprived of land; forests and other property. Violence against minorities has continued and in general, gone unpunished. Although several episodes of displacement during 2004 have been reported by a local NGO, there is no overview of the extent of the problem as information about people displaced by conflict in Bangladesh is virtually non-existent.[40]

The Norwegian Refugee Council has also produced a report in 2005 on Guinea's forgotten internal displacement crisis. For 15 years the instability and armed conflict in Liberia, Sierra Leone and, more recently, in Cote d'Ivoire have spilled over into Guinea, causing death, physical injury, material destruc-tion and large-scale displacement of civilians. Guinea has not fully recovered form the impact, especially of a series of armed incursions in 2000/2001. While refugees across international frontiers are being catered for in Guinea, pro-grammes to help internally displaced people (IDPs) and Guineans returning from neighbouring countries are insufficient and seriously under-funded. Unless better provision is made for these groups, then tensions among long-suffering host communities, could escalate into renewed conflict and undermine hopes for peace in the region. At the height of the conflict, there were up to 360,000 IDPs in Guinea. A census conducted in February 2002 found that some 82,000 people were still internally displaced at the time, mostly in Guinea *forestiere abd Haute* location, but since then no systematic assessment and evaluation of the living conditions and location of IDPs has been done. However, a number of surveys and rapid assessments carried out throughout 2004 indicate how vulnerable IDPs, returnees and host communi-ties are. Four years after the rebel attacks, the living conditions of the IDPs and returning Guineans who fled persecution in neighbouring countries are deteriorating. Clearly, they have not been able to integrate into the places of their accommodation and their presence has put a heavy burden on the absorptive capacity of host communities sharing their meagre resources and land with others. This threatens the already precarious social infrastructure and services in the area of displacement. Most of the displaced are not able to return to their homes because of a lack of infrastructure, public services and support for the reconstruction of houses in the areas devastated by the 2000/2001 attacks.[41]

Both these examples demonstrate the lack of visibility of the plight of IDPs, despite the fact that their suffering has been ongoing for many decades. Yet, while the international community is aware of the flight of refugees from Bangladesh and Guinea, the condition of IDPs in these countries is barely known. Much better prioritization of the plight of IDPs is needed and it would seem that only a multi-agency approach that co-ordinates the activities of such agencies as the UNHCR and the ICRC, can most effectively work in the complex situations of forced migrations such as these.

The UNHCR and the ICRC

The United Nations deals with victims of war, civil strife, and conflict through two agencies. First, there is the *International Committee of the Red Cross* (ICRC) established in 1863. Second, there is United Nations High Commissioner for Refugees (UNHCR) in 1950.[42] The two agencies are distinct. The UNHCR is a public international organization of which governments have direct influence.[43] By contrast, the ICRC is a unique private international organization. It is neither an intergovernmental organization nor a UN organ. Nevertheless, governments have conferred upon it an international mandate.[44] This, therefore, distinguishes it from other NGOs. Both agencies pursue humanitarian goals. They are similar in this respect. The UNHCR is mandated to protect refugees once they have fled across borders into third states.[45] The ICRC's original mandate was to protect victims of international armed conflicts,[46] and it does not matter whether or not they have crossed an international frontier. In 1977, this mandate was extended through an Additional protocol II, Relating to Protection of Victims of Non-International Armed Conflicts.[47] The Preamble to the Additional Protocol II acknowledged that:

> [T]he only provision applicable to non-international armed conflicts before the adoption of the [Additional Protocol 2] was article 3 common to all four Geneva conventions ... This Article proved to be inadequate in view of the fact that about 80 per cent of the victims of armed conflicts since 1945 have been victims of non-international conflicts ...

The UNHCR and ICRC both decide their refugee mandate through 'protection'. But, this is a term of art. As Odhiambo-Abuya states of 'protection' in his excellent account of the competing and complementary jurisdictions of the UNHCR and the ICRC, this is 'a term repeatedly used but not formally defined in the working and statutory languages of these agencies'.[48] Protection can mean different things in different contexts. What is protection in Africa may not be protection in Europe. Different communities are protected in different ways. Much depends upon their location. Two elements of 'protection' nevertheless, need to be identified. The first is set out by the ICRC which considers that:

> ... 'to protect' implies preserving victims of conflicts who are in the hands of an adverse authority from the dangers, sufferings, and abuses of power to which they may be exposed, defending them and giving them support.[49]

Second, under the refugee treaties, the additional protocols,[50] and the 1949 Geneva Conventions, the term called 'protection' refers to the use of legal and administrative procedures in order to protect the lives of human beings from 'military operations'[51] and natural causes. 'Protection' means at a very minimum the maintenance of a lifestyle that is as close as possible to a level that is normal. The ICRC has a flexible mandate that allows it to offer protection and assistance to both IDPs and cross border refugees. The UNHCR's mandate is more restricted. It is confined to cross border refugees only. In reality, it has given protection to 'several millions' of IDPs. Even so, the UNHCR cannot act on its own initiative to protect IDPs. Its 'good offices' role is a passive one. It requires action from other UN agencies. However, once that request is made, the UNHCR assistance is more permanent in terms of repeated assistance and offering 'durable solutions'. One such may be resettlement. By contrast, the ICRC offers only temporary emergency relief and assistance.[52] Yet, there is an overlap. Both provide material assistance, food, water, and medical aid to refugees and IDPs. Both are involved in the legal protection of displaced persons. Both offer placing facilities for family reunification purposes. Both issue protected refugees' travel and identification documents while they are in third states. Both pay special attention to the needs of unaccompanied minors. Most importantly, however, International Humanitarian Law and International Refugee Law come together in the *Guiding Principles*, which contain the current international statement of principles to be applied as basic standards for the protection and assistance of IDPs.

There is surely a case for saying that the roles of the two agencies of the UNHCR and the IDPs should today be conflated because the distinction between refugees and IDPs is not a practical one. Indeed, the UNHCR has, despite its mandate, assisted several millions of IDPs over the years.[53] It has done so in the following ways. First, it has used its 'good offices' powers to bring IDPs within its area of concern by acting in a 'flexible' and 'extra-statutory' way.[54] Second, various General Assembly Resolutions have conferred upon the UNHCR a selective limited mandate to undertake humanitarian assistance and provide protection to IDPs. This is important because previously the closest that the UNHCR had come towards addressing the plight of IDPs was within its general mandate of voluntary repatriation, rehabilitation and resettlement of refugees.[55] However, what really enlarged the extension of the UNHCR's mandate is General Assembly Resolution 1388 (XIV) of 20 November 1959.[56] It was this which authorized the High Commissioner to use its 'good offices' to transmit humanitarian aid to Chinese refugees in Hong Kong. They did not fall within the UN competence technically because they had the protection of the Republic of China. This precedent was followed again in 1961 when people from Angola fled to the Democratic Republic of Congo in large numbers making it impossible to assess their claims properly.[57] Further, when the question of voluntary repatriation of refugees occurred in southern Sudan in 1972, ECOSOC called upon the High Commissioner's 'good offices' and that of other agencies to extend rehabilitation measures both to refugees returning from abroad and to 'persons displaced within their country'.[58] There is, therefore, clear evidence going back almost to the beginnings of the human rights movement in the 1950s of the ability and willingness of the international community to involve itself in the plight of the IDPs.

The internally displaced are the most difficult forced migratory group to locate because access is so difficult. As the UNHCR has itself recognized, '[T]hey may be trapped in an ongoing internal conflict, without a place of safety to stay' and it may likely be that '[T]he domestic government, which may view the uprooted people as enemies of the state, gains ultimate control over their fate'. Yet, despite this:

> [T]here are no specific international instruments covering the internally displaced, and general agreements such as the Geneva Conventions are often difficult to apply.

The result is that '[U]ntil now, donors have been reluctant to intervene in internal conflicts and help this group.[59] International organizations invariably find it difficult to reach the internally displaced because often continued ongoing fighting puts them beyond the reach of such organizations. Governments or non-state agents also deliberately prevent contact with them. This is why a multi-faceted and all encompassing approach is necessary. Different manifestations of internal displacement also often mean that their identification is difficult in other ways. IDPs do not group together in easily accessible camps or settlements. They prefer dispersal to avoid identification. They often mingle in local communities. One reason is that in civil wars countries divided along racial, religious, ethnic or linguistic lines often see displaced populations as the 'enemy' within. They are not treated as citizens of the same country.[60] As mentioned above, the problem of IDPs only reached the international stage in the 1990s after the fall of the Berlin wall and the end of the cold war. It was then that the prospect of international wars was replaced by internal conflicts where non-state actors were pitched against the government in the form of militia and rebels. Today, the United Nations has pointed out how, 'civil wars have become a central cause of emergency situation'.[61]

Today, the number of people who are forced to seek sanctuary within the borders of a state is actually larger than the numbers who seek international surrogate protection. These *Internally Displaced Persons* (IDPs) are directly related not just to conditions of hunger, malnutrition, and bad governance, but are also more directly related to the expulsion and return of refugees by foreign states. Two forces in particular have contributed to the increase in IDPs.

First, internal conflict at home, and second, the refusal of sanctuary abroad, with the result that IDPs have now become the 'fastest growing group of uprooted persons in the world'. [62] Yet, because IDPs do not have their own treaty their welfare is dependent on external *ad hoc* humanitarian aid and there are often obstacles to be encountered in getting humanitarian aid through. State or rebel forces refuse to allow humanitarian aid to pass through their territories. States try to block humanitarian aid under the principle of state sovereignty,[63] and characterize the conflict as 'an internal matter'.

Three problems remain at present. First, there is the question of protection of IDPs. Most agencies provide food, medicine, and shelter. They pay less attention to the physical security and human rights of the displaced. This is clear from Darfur in Sudan. There has been scant protection of the weak there. No binding legal framework for IDPs is yet in place. Several war situations require special skills to protect IDPs. Access in civil war situations needs to be negotiated. Safe areas need to be created to relocations and evacuations. The *Guiding Principles on Internal Displacement* do not do that. Second, there is no consensus over which international organizations and NGOs should become involved in protection and what steps they should take. The ICRC has been most active compared to the UNHCR. Human rights organizations themselves are considering novel methods of being more effective. The traditional human rights rules of monitoring and reporting have not always being effective, as recent experiences in Iraq, Somalia, Rwanda, Bosnia, Kosovo, and East Timor all demonstrate. Third, the international system set up after second-world-war to protect persons outside their countries of origins is incomplete. There is still no effective or predictable international system to respond to the needs of those forcibly displaced within their own countries. Fourth, those who continue to question whether the internally displaced should be identified as a special category at all on the grounds that sending out this group will lead to discrimination against others have been saying that situations, and not categories of people, should be addressed. This overlooks the fact that IDPs have special needs, whether or not they are in camps.[64]

The Effectiveness of the Guiding Principles

So, what exactly have the *Guiding Principles* achieved? Richard Plender has noted that[65] the UN set out to 'define possible solutions' that the international community could undertake. In this way, the process of developing a normative and institutional framework to protect IDPs was started with the appointment of the IDP representative in July 1992[66] and the adoption by the UN in April 1998 of the *Guiding Principles on Internal Displacement*. Yet, how effective is this normative and institutional framework? The definition of IDPs took many years to create. A number of questions loomed large. For example, who were the internally displaced? How are they different from refugees? Who was responsible for this? What was the international legal framework for them? To what extent could international organizations take on responsibilities for them? How could they best be resolved?

The *Guiding Principles on Internal Displacement* set out to do two things. First, they seek to 'address the specific needs of [IDPs] worldwide'. Second, they set out to:

'identify the rights and guarantees' of persons subject to 'forced displacement', and to ensuring their protection and assistance during displacement ... Return, resettlement and integration.[67]

The Guiding Principles are based on the basic international norms derived from Human Rights Law, Humanitarian Law, and Refugee Law. They are intended to provide guidance for IDP representative, states, all other authorities, groups and persons, IGOs and NGOs.[68] In order to further these two objectives, the the *Guiding Principles* are based on a number of conceptual ideas. First, that unlike refugees internally displaced persons have not left the country of which they are citizens and therefore have the guarantees of international humanitarian law applicable to them. Second, that internally displaced persons have had a specific experience and therefore have specific needs, in much the same way as children and the wounded have specific needs, under international humanitarian law. Third, that international law should be restated in more detail wherever necessary to address the needs of the internally displaced persons for their specific protection.[69] Three further complications arise from the fact that different sets of laws apply in different situations. First, where there is no internal armed conflict or disaster, but only a situation of tensions and disturbances, human rights law alone is applicable. Second, where there is a situation of non-international armed conflict, the principles of humanitarian law and human rights guarantees are applicable. Third, where there is a situation of inter-state armed conflict, then the provisions of international humanitarian law apply together with human rights guarantees. Although in practice it may be difficult to determine which of the myriad sets of laws apply in each of these different situations, it is clear that the *Guiding Principles* will cover all three situations. The task at hand is to identify the specific guarantees which have to be observed and to differentiate between them where necessary.[70] In contemporary international law a general norm may well exist, the implementation of which depends on the articulation of a specific norm. It is these general norms which are specified in the *Guiding Principles* with a view to the special situation of displacement. Thus, one principle which is found across the range of international human rights instruments is Principle 12 which states that, 'every human being has the right to liberty and security of person'. So as to address the special situation of displacement, however, it further stipulates that 'in order to give effect to this right for internally displaced persons, they shall not be interned or confined to a camp ...'.[71]

It is in this way that the *Guiding Principles* have set out to progressively develop certain general principles of human rights law and to fill in the gaps of existing treaties and conventions. The prohibition of return to situations of imminent danger is one important example. The prohibition of inhuman treatment is located in a general norm of contemporary international law from where it has been recognized by international monitoring bodies. No person may be returned to a country where he or she will face torture, death or inhuman and degrading treatment. The prohibition, however, is confined in international case-law to the situation of refugees who are threatened with a return across international borders. Accordingly, what is needed is a specific articulation of the prohibition of inhuman return, with respect to internally displaced persons, to dangerous areas within their own country. Principle 15 does exactly that when it stipulates that the right of internally displaced persons 'to be protected against forcible return to or resettlement in any place where their life, safety, liberty and/or health would be at risk'. It is true that this principle is not, as yet, stated in an authoritative international law instrument. Yet, its articulation here is in keeping with the spirit of existing international law and consistent with its underlying principles.[72] It is in this way that the *Guiding Principles* succeed in clarifying some of the nebulous areas of international law by giving them particularized articulation in the context of the protection of internally displaced populations.

Notwithstanding, the *Guiding Principles* some legal problems remain. Unlike the refugee definition, the IDP definition does not confer legal status on the internally displaced. Unlike refugees, who are entitled to surrogate international protection, because they have left the safety of their own borders, IDPs are not entitled to international substitute legal protection. What, then, does this definition do? What it does is to identify those who are displaced and who amongst them needs special assistance and protection. It is unclear, however, when the status of IDPs ends. It is well known that for refugees their status ends when they return to their countries or find another durable solution at the hands of the UNHCR. For IDPs, there is no cessation clause. There is no international organization that can make that determination. As Roberta Cohen asks, 'does internal displacement end when the displaced return home? What if their homes are occupied by others? Does it end when they integrate into other areas? What if they continue to want to return home, as many Greek Cypriots or Bosnians do, despite their integration elsewhere? Does it end when the situation causing the displacement has seized to exist? In the absence of guidelines, calculations are made on a case-by-case basis and are arbitrary'.[73]

However, these *Guiding Principles* are at best non-legally binding guidelines. This is clear from Principle 2 (2) which states that:

> these principles shall not be interpreted at restricting, modifying or impairing the provisions of any international human rights or international humanitarian law instrument or rights of any international humanitarian law instrument or rights granted to persons under domestic law.

What this means is that to achieve legal efficacy, the Guiding Principles must be incorporated into domestic law. Within the framework of municipal legal framework, they will have direct effect. At the moment, they neither restore rights nor impose duties in domestic law. It is through incorporation that the *Guiding Principles* have had a far-reaching effect. In a short period of time, they have been variously adopted, published, and applied. Many global institutions such as:

The CHR, ECOSOC Commission and UN (GA) have adopted resolutions taking note of the principles and of the IDP representative's intention to use them in dialogues of governments, intergovernmental bodies and NGOs'.[74]

Indeed, the organization of African states has hailed the Guiding Principles as 'the most comprehensive re-statement of norms applicable to the internally displaced' which, 'will provide authoritative guidance to the commission on how the law should be interpreted and applied during all stages of displacement'.[75] In Europe also, the Organization for Security and Cooperation of Europe has expressed support for and begun to disseminate the *Guiding Principles* to its field staff.[76] The African Union has also formally expressed its support for the principles and several AU sponsored seminars have emphasized their importance of Africa.[77] Some states have gone further. Angola and Burundi have accepted the authoritative nature of the Guiding Principles by incorporating them into their domestic laws and policies. NGOs have undertaken to widely disseminate the principles. They have organized workshops and meetings to discuss how best to implement them.[78] The Guiding Principles have been given some international standing through the work of NGOs such as ICRC, UNHCR, World Food Programme, United Nations Children's Fund, Norwegian Refugee Council, US Committee for Refugees and International Organization for Migration.

In short, what we can say is that what the IDPs definition in the *Guiding Principles* has done is to ensure that both national and international action must be taken. This is because they affirm the doctrine of sovereignty as responsibility. The primary responsibility for displaced persons rest with their own governments. This is clear from the way in which the crisis in Darfur in Sudan has been tackled with international pressure being imposed on the Sudanese Government to resolve their own problem in Darfur. The *Guiding Principles* assert that governments must allow rapid and unimpeded access by humanitarian organizations to IDPs. The *Guiding Principles* have set down the rights of internally displaced. They have set down the obligations of governments and insurgent groups towards these populations. They are placed on humanitarian and human rights. Most importantly, they have been universally welcomed. It is significant that they have been unanimously acknowledged by UN bodies and by several regional organizations. The UN Secretary General has urged the Security Council to encourage member states to observe the *Guiding Principles* in situations of mass displacement. Indeed, a number of governments have begun using the *Guiding Principles* as the basis of their laws. Furthermore, international organizations and NGOs are finding them valuable in monitoring and advocating human rights principles and they have changed the notion of sovereignty by turning it into responsibility.

Failing International Protection: The Problem of Access

The principle obstacle to the protection of the internally displaced today, however, is the lack of access afforded to the international agencies by the host governments. A basic principle of the UN is to promote and encourage 'respect for human rights and fundamental freedoms'.[79] This is, of course, subject to the limitation that the UN and its member states are prevented from 'intervening in matters, which are essentially within the domestic jurisdiction of any state'.[80] This principle can only be overturned if there is a breach or threatening breach to international peace and security.[81] However, states that wish to block humanitarian assistance generally abuse this principle and often external political intervention is concealed as humanitarian assistance. That leaves IDPs exposed. As the late Joan Fitzpatrick in 2002 said, '[T]he internally displaced also have a compelling need for international human rights protection'. Unfortunately, the:

> UNHCR's role in protecting IDPs still remains a daunting barrier to assuring their safety and fundamental rights. IDPs remain under the formal protection of their own state, even though officials of their state may have deliberately caused their displacement.

Yet, the case for international surrogate protection of the sort accorded to refugees, and the case for UNHCR jurisdiction for IDPs, is surely compelling in view of her statement that:

> [W]here the state has violated human rights treaties or customary law in its treatment of IDPs, it is subject to international scrutiny and cannot invoke its sovereignty as a shield.[82]

This situation must be addressed and it can only be properly addressed by the UN. In recent years, UN has acted to prevent the gross violation of human rights. The UN Security Council has invoked Chapter VII to characterize certain violations as threats to international peace and security, as we saw in the last chapter. This began to occur in the later years of the twentieth Century. The first Gulf War saw in its immediate aftermath the Kurds trying to establish their own state in 1991. This attempt was repressed ruthlessly by the Iraqi Government. There was massive displacement and flow of Kurds towards the Turkish border. The UN Security Council passed Resolution 688.[83] It condemned the repression and insisted that the Iraqi Government should 'allow immediate access'[84] to all international humanitarian aid to the Kurds. Second, during the 1994 genocide and civil war in Rwanda, French forces were authorized under Resolution 929[85] to 'implement a temporary operation under national command and control aimed at contributing ... to the security and protection of displaced persons, refugees and civilians in Rwanda'.[86] Third, in 1996 following the civil war in the former Zaire[87] and the subsequent mass internal displacement, the Security Council authorized under Resolution 1078[88] the formation of a military force to create 'safe-havens guarded as temporary sanctuaries'[89] to facilitate the delivery of international humanitarian aid such as food, water, and medicine. The UN in this case acted in a proactive fashion. In all these cases it did so to safeguard the welfare of displaced persons which, if left unredressed, could have had wider implications for peace and security. In Sudan, the UN has acted belatedly. Sudan presents the best current example of a group of people who have attracted UN intervention. Humanitarian agencies estimate that 1.2 million people have become internally displaced within the Darfur region of Sudan, and another 200,000 live as refugees in neighbouring Chad because of government sponsored Janjaweed militia attacks on the African population by Arab tribes that started as long ago as 1997. Yet, it was only in July 2004 that the Security Council adopted[90] a resolution paving the way for action against Sudan in 30 days if it did not make progress on pledges to disarm the militias accused of indiscriminate murders, rapes and other attacks against civilians in the Darfur – a move that was immediately welcomed by Secretary-General Kofi Annan. With China and Pakistan abstaining, and the other 13 members approving the text, the Council agreed to impose an arms embargo against the Janjaweed militias and all other non-governmental forces in Darfur, which has been described as the site of the world's worst humanitarian crisis. The resolution states that the Council might take measures against Sudan if it does not show progress on achieving the commitments, which it outlined in a joint communiqué with the UN on 3rd July 2004. The major commitment were the Sudanese government's pledges to disarm the Janjaweed and restore security to Darfur. Yet, more than a year later in 2005, these pledges had still not be fulfilled, and with no impending threat of action by the international community over them.

ENVIRONMENTALLY DISPLACED PERSONS

'*Environmental refugees*' are said to be those persons who have been displaced through natural and man-made disasters and environmental degradation.[91] I would say that a more accurate description is '*Environmentally Displaced Persons*' (EDPs) since the displacement may be either internal or external. If it is internal, such persons are categorized as 'internally displaced persons' (IDPs). If it is external, they are *de facto* refugees (although not under the *1951 Refugee Convention* as they do not ostensibly fit into any of its classes). Either way, they are migrating because they are seeking ecological sanctuary. Such a group may fall into three broad divisions. First, a reversible environmental change, caused by such calamities as drought, flooding, or industrial pollution, may result in a temporary displacement of people. Second, a long-term or irreversible environmental change, such as through desertification or rising levels, may result in a permanent displacement of people. Third, a resource-based environmental degradation which destroys the means of sustenance of a community, for example where there is salination of the soil or deforestation, may force people to seek a better life elsewhere. The phrase that is in vogue, however, is 'environmental refugees', and not '*Environmen-*

tally Displaced Persons'. The term 'environmental refugees' was coined by El-Hinnawi in a seminal UN publication in 1985.[92] The phrase provides a good illustration of the difficulties caused by the maintenance of a rigid distinction between displaced populations generally and refugees specifically. This is not least because, although there are 10 million environmental refugees[93] today, this is likely to go up dramatically through global warming alone. Thus, Dr. Norman Myers, a Visiting Fellow at Oxford University, has suggested that sea level rise and agricultural distribution caused by climate changes may displace 150 million refugees, which equates to 1.5 per cent of the 2050s predicted global population of 10 billion. This compares to the estimated 10 million environmental refugees or 0.2 per cent of the current global population. In his words, '[T]he consequences of large numbers of environmental refugees would be among the most significant of all upheavals entailed by global warming'.[94] For the moment, however, most environmental refugees result from a combination of factors. Natural disasters, long-term environmental degradation, development, industrial accidents, and remnants of war, all play their part. Three of the biggest causes of population displacement are natural disasters, industrial accidents, and war. These may be considered in turn.

First, let us consider 'natural disasters'. Throughout history, natural disasters have played a major role in causing migration. Unlike Wars, however, natural disasters tend to displace persons temporarily rather than permanently. Nevertheless, the year 1998 was the first time when, ever since records were kept, more people were displaced through 'natural disasters' then were displaced through wars and other conflicts worldwide.[95] Some 144 million people per annum are affected by natural disasters, such as volcanic eruptions, droughts, earthquakes, and all other types of disaster generated by an unstable natural environment. Such is the impact of natural disasters on people that the 1990s were declared the International Decade for Natural Disaster Reduction by the United Nations. In recent years natural disasters have increased significantly as has been pointed out by the Geo Science Division of the Munich Reinsurance Group.[96] Recent global temperature anomalies such as El Nino and La Nina had contributed to this.[97] Ever since records began 150 years ago, 1998 was also the hottest year ever.[98]

Natural disasters disproportionally affect the poorer parts of the world namely, Africa, Asia, and South America. More than any other county on the list of countries warranting humanitarian intervention, it is Bangladesh, China, Philippines, Vietnam, Ethiopia, Iran, and India that are far more frequently affected. The list of countries warranting humanitarian intervention is maintained by the United Nations Office for the Coordination of Humanitarian Affairs.[99] Developing countries account for 96 per cent of all deaths occurring from natural disasters.[100] These figures are significant because by the year 2025, it is estimated that 80 per cent of the world's population will live in developing countries.[101] The income level of a particular country often is directly related to the impact of the natural disaster. For example, when a comparison of the effects of earthquakes was undertaken by El-Hannawi, he compared the earthquakes in Tokyo in Japan with similar earthquakes in

Managua, Nicaragua. Whereas Tokyo had strict building codes in place as well as earthquake training, Managua found people living in mud brick houses on hill sides, with the result that the effects of the earthquakes were largely mitigated in Japan.[102]

Second, let us consider 'industrial accidents'. Industrial accidents also create environmental refugees. In 1984, in Bhopal, India, a chemical accident killed over 10,000 people and displaced 200,000 people. A nuclear accident at Three Mile Island in the United States displaced 10,000 people. In Seveso, Italy, an explosion at a chemical factory caused chemical products similar to the defoliants used in Vietnam to be released into the atmosphere. The most famous example of an industrial accident is the nuclear accident at Chernobyl. The Soviet Government evacuated thousands of people following the accident.[103] Some 100,000 people were displaced. A 30-mile zone around Chernobyl remains uninhabited. Radiation contamination has a life of 25,000 years. The area will be effectively contaminated forever as a result of this.[104] A feature of displacement caused by industrial accidents is that the majority of people will seek refuge within the borders of their own country where the accident occurred. The residents around Chernobyl were internally displaced persons. They were not caught by the refugee convention.

Third, let us consider the impact of war. War also causes environmental refugees. Indeed, the destruction of the environment is a central weapon of the war. This is most clear where the dispute is over the possession of land and its natural resources. During the Vietnam War, there was a deliberate destruction of the environment as a military tactic employed by the United States.[105] Military operations set out to empty the countryside and force the population to relocate in the cities. There was a massive campaign of deforestation, which resulted in the use of millions of tonnes of herbicides as a bombardment of agriculture zones.[106] Other wars have not been dissimilar. For example, in El Salvador, in the early 1980s, the government used the method of the destruction of the ecosystem in order to eradicate guerilla bases in the forest.[107] When the civil war ended, thousands of displaced persons found it impossible to return home because the reserves of water in some regions have disappeared as a result of erosion of soil caused by the policy of deforestation.[108] Following the first Gulf War in 1991, oil fires and spillages were started in Kuwait as a deliberate policy of ecocide.[109] Earlier, when a sea borne allied invasion of Kuwait city took place, there was an attempt to frustrate this when Saddam Hussein opened up the pipelines to the oil terminals in the Gulf, thereby releasing millions of gallons of crude oil into the sea. The desalination plants that fed water to the greenhouses were also destroyed by the Iraqi troops.[110] Depleted uranium was also used for the first time as a weapon in 1991. Today, the uranium dust still blows across the desert presenting a semi-permanent hazard in a dry climate.[111] On 3 April 1991, the United Nations Security Council passed Resolution 687 affirming that Iraq was liable under international law for any direct loss or damage, 'including environmental damage'.[112]

The use of environmental destruction as a war policy is now fully acknowledged internationally. Thus, the Rome Statute of the International Criminal

Court, which entered into force on 1 July 2002, lists as a war crime, 'intention-ally launching an attack in the knowledge that such attack will cause ... long-term and severe damage to the natural environment'.[113] This widely recognizes the fact that environmental destruction can also result when there is a conflict over the control of important natural resources. A good example here is how the lack of waterbed has definitely contributed to the violence in Gaza. The World Bank has stated that 90 per cent of the water in the region is used for Israel's profit. Palestinians use only 10 per cent. When one person in three in the world today suffers from shortages of water, the problem is likely to become more and more acute.[114] Very often, lacking natural resources caus-ing people to move from a fertile source to a less fertile land.[115]

Are Environmentally Displaced Persons a Legal Category?

The problem for international law is how to provide protection for such en-vironmentally displaced persons. What we have observed above may help us to construct a legal category for environmentally displaced persons. This is not easy. Whilst it is accepted that environmental problems – from natural hazards to pollution by chemical toxins or radioactive waste – can cause hu-man displacement, it is less readily accepted that such forced migrants fall inside the categories protected by instruments of international refugee law. This is because neither the terms of the text, nor the intent of the drafters, or the terms of much current practice of Western states, provide a ready basis for inclusion of this new class of refugee. The fact is refugee law does not generally cover such a population flow. As is well known, the international refugee regime was originally intended to deal with refugees from commu-nism following the Second World War. The concept of a 'well-founded fear of persecution' in the current refugee definition was defined in narrow political terms, so as deliberately to limit refugee status to those outside their country of origin. When one considers the root causes of flight in many developing nations, however, it is clear that a focus on a narrow political interpretation of 'persecution' excludes the bulk of the world's refugees today thereby mak-ing such a definition wholly inappropriate for a global application. Thus, the definition can exclude those suffering economic and social persecution. It can exclude those suffering from the effects of war. It can exclude the victims of natural disasters in countries where the state offers no protection. It can ac-cordingly all too easily exclude the migration of people attributed to climate change. In short, it excludes most of the world's humanitarian refugees.

Yet, unsatisfactory as this situation may be, on one view there are strong arguments of principle against expanding the refugee definition beyond cases of governmental oppression. This view argues that there are three objections to any extension to the refugee category. First, that government oppression is rarely a specific cause of environmental refugees. Second, since the majority of environmentally displaced persons are not fleeing state persecution, they are not cross border refugees, but are internally displaced. As internally dis-placed persons, they do not meet the definition of requirements of Article 1 of the refugee convention. Third, the number of environmentally displaced persons is enormous so that they could never be all fully accommodated in an expansive definition of Article 1. Any expectation would have to be limited. The difficulties of extending protection to environmentally displaced persons are accordingly manifold. Although in 1998, Francis Deng proposed on behalf of the UN, a definition for internally displaced persons, by referring to displaced persons as those escaping, 'violations of human rights or natural or human-made disasters, and who have not crossed an internationally recognized state border',[116] this is not authoritative. It does not make it a legally binding obligation. There are no international conventions that mention displaced persons. There is no definition that is fully recognized by international law for internally displaced persons. It is true that since 1975, displaced persons have been included in the mandate of the UNHCR, but this does not include environmentally displaced persons.[117] The UNHCR defines displaced persons as any person or group who, if they had reached the international border would be refugees. Environmentally displaced persons do not fit into this category. Displaced persons are not a separate category under international law. It is not a known juridical concept.

It is, however, arguable that there are compelling reasons why environmentally displaced persons should not be excluded from international protection. Whether or not environmentally displaced persons are a known juridical concept, the categories of the Refugee Convention should be expanded to meet the emerging requirements of environmental and other refugees, because one should not lose sight of the inter-connectedness of all humanitarian refugees and that this being so, we should seek to find the answer in the existing *Refugee Convention* of 1951 as it exists. Refugee law is a specific illustration of the application of human rights law on the international plane. This being so, it is possible to argue that the definition of a refugee remains rooted in the expanding canvass of human rights law. Thus, provided that it could be said that the suffering of environmentally displaced persons amounted to a first order violation of human rights, then those who are forcibly displaced across international boundaries for 'environmental' reasons should be eligible for international assistance and protection. This is because the state has a duty to protect its citizens from harm. Ecological disasters and environmental change are not just 'acts of God'. They are either commonly the result of human actions or are causative of an individual's vulnerability to them. A state that cannot meet its obligations to protect its citizens' basic needs is either negligent or indifferent to its citizens' suffering. In the circumstances, the grounds for international assistance lie in this breach of the contract with the state.[118]

The *Ditchley Conference Report* in 1994, took the view that the term 'environmental refugee' should only be applied to people forced to move in circumstances where serious environmental disaster was compounded by crass human political failure. This was because the most catastrophic forms of environmentally-generated migration, which were accompanied by an immediate element of compulsion, also involved the intervention of a human agency. It was noted that the most serious crises of this kind arise when environmental degradation, concentrated populations, and poverty combine with civil strife, leaving only a small margin for disaster. Therefore, the overall consensus seemed to be that the concept of refugee should be reserved for people whose migration is forced by political or man-made factors.

For this reason, the use of the term 'environmental refugee' would not only dilute the refugee concept but would do nothing to clarify questions of institutional responsibility in relation to prevention and response. If refugee protections are extended to people who do not fear the persecution on account of one of the five grounds set out in the 1950 convention, the result will be that it will devalue the current protection for refugees.[119] Thus, the answer to the problem of 'environmental refugees' lay in the current Refugee Convention because where movement is forced by a combination of environmental and political factors, existing refugee instruments and institutions should suffice. In the other cases, a flexible policy framework was likely to continue to prove most appropriate.[120]

In fact, a number of people have criticized the term 'environmental refugees' as being meaningless and confusing.[121] If the term has come into vogue, it is at the behest of national governments who want to use it to deny applicants refugee status.[122] Accordingly, it has been said that it has been invented, 'at least in part to depoliticize the causes of displacement, so neighboring states could derogate their obligation to provide asylum'.[123] Although 'environmental refugees' may not be a juridical concept, and although the law may not favour the expansion of the legal definition, environmental literature, as opposed to asylum literature, does advance an argument for the expansion of the concept of protection for environmental refugees. Norman Myers has said, as an ecologist, that the rising number of environmental refugees is related to environmental problems of deforestation, desertification, and climate change, which these migrations highlight.[124] He has argued that if the international community wishes to prevent large numbers of refugees or migrants, it must prevent the environmental causes of those migrations. The 1994 UN Symposium on 'desertification and migration' at Almeira, or 'Almeira Declaration' stated that:

> The number of migrants in the world, already at very high levels, nonetheless continues to increase by about three million each year. Approximately half of these originate in Africa. These increases are largely of rural origin and related to land degradation. It is estimated that over 135 million people may be at risk of being displaced as a consequence of severe desertification.[125]

The fact is that environmental change cannot be a single cause of migration. Academic writing on the subject widely recognizes this and asserts that environmental change, as a cause of migration, cannot be meaningfully separated from political, economical and social changes.[126] Those who emphasize these divisions do so as a guise to prevent the extension of refugee protections under the *1951 Refugee Convention* to people who are fleeing ostensibly as a result of economic and social change. In this way, the implication of using the term 'environmental refugee' is that political, economic and environmental causes of migration can be clearly and properly separated. Yet, in practice this is often not the case. More often, it is the role of human agency which either causes the disaster itself or is instrumental in causing populations to be more vulnerable to disasters.[127] In the circumstances, the use of the term 'environmental' can imply a false separation between overlapping and interrelated categories. Thus, the State may have a role in directly or indirectly undermining the coping strategies of the people and thus making them more vulnerable. Or, the state may prevent the recovery of the people by a failure to provide insurance and relief. This happened in the Dust Bowl disasters in the United States in the nineteenth and early twentieth centuries.[128]

A more recent instructive example is the 7.6 magnitude earthquake on 8th October 2005 which, across northern Pakistan, Kashmir and parts of Afghanistan, left towns and villages destroyed, tens of thousands dead and injured, and hundreds of thousands left without power, water or shelter as winter set in. It was the strongest earthquake to hit the region in a century, being followed by twenty powerful after-shocks. The EU pledged £2.5 million, China pledged £4 million, and America pledged an initial $100,000.[129] Interestingly, 'the earthquake ... brought unprecedented cooperation' between long-time rivals India and Pakistan, because 'Pakistan ... accepted India's offer to fly 25 tonnes of food, tents and medicine to Islamabad' and 'New Delhi, meanwhile, has allowed Pakistani army helicopters to fly near the line of control ... to drop essential items'.[130] Yet, just as human agency was responsible for alleviating the hardship of this natural disaster, it was also responsible for exacerbating it. Even as it dawned that the death toll had been under-estimated, with the small city of *Balakot* destroyed and half of its population dead, the relief effort was inadequate at both the national and international level. Nationally, it was said that:

> [T]he absence of a proper infra-structure, a dearth of reserve funds to deal with unexpected tragedies, and a total lack of preparedness despite annual disasters on a lesser scale, have cost innumerable lives.

Internationally, it was said that:

> [A] few miles north of the disaster zone, there is a large fleet of helicopters belonging to the western armies occupying parts of Afghanistan. Why could the US, German and British commanders not dispatch these to save lives? Is the War so fierce that they are needed every day? Three days after the earthquake, the US released eight helicopters from 'war duty' to help transport food and water to isolated villages. Too little, too late.[131]

Yet, even more poignant than this was the fact that even though 'Indian soldiers had crossed the line of control to help a dozen Pakistani border guards trapped in a bunker' by the fourth day it was clear that they were not to be allowed to cross into disputed territory to offer help. One of the worst affected was the Pakistani town of *Bagh*, the geographical position of which was such that it was inaccessible and so bereft of aid, even though from the Indian side of the border, '... you can almost reach out and touch them'. This was because it was barely 4 kilometers from the Indian border town of *Uri*, where aid was beginning to arrive in trucks and military transporters, 'but none of this desperately needed aid can be pushed on over the border' even though 'as a human being you want to help those fighting for their lives within sight of you, but it is impossible'.[132] This is a remarkable illustration of how crass human failings can make a natural disaster so much worse. It is an even more dramatic example of the pivotal role of international politics in human suffering worldwide. As the death toll approached 80,000 people telephone lines between the two sides of Kashmir were restored for the first time in over 15 years to enable Kashmiris to call their relatives across the ceasefire line.[133] However, an even more serious failing was the lack of aid from the international community as a whole. Within days the UN Secretary-General, Kofi Annan, had warned on 20th October of a 'second massive wave of death' unless the relief effort for earthquake survivors was stepped up. Jan Egeland, the UN's senior relief co-ordinator drew a comparison with the Tsunami Disaster a year earlier on 26th December 2004 which killed 200,000 people and declared that 'We have never had this kind of logistical nightmare ever. We thought the tsunami was the worst we could get. This is worse' and warned that 'The world is not doing enough'. He called for an operation on the scale of the 1940s Berlin airlift to get aid into affected areas and evacuate tens of thousands of stranded victims before the winter set in.[134] Yet, despite the fact that unlike the Tsunami Disaster aid was proving difficult to get through here, this was not done. In fact, it was reported that '[W]orld governments have been miserly in pledging funds' because by mid-October only $86 m (£48.6m) had been offered out of the $312m (£176.2) the UN had requested. When it is remembered that 92 countries pledged financial help following the 2004 Tsunami Disaster, only 20 countries had heeded the call for help in Pakistan.[135] Such is international politics.

A State can contribute to an environmental disaster in other ways. A State can interfere through war with people's strategies for coping with environmental unpredictability. It is not insignificant that drought induced famine most commonly occurs in those countries afflicted by wars.[136] Thus, Clay *et al.*[137] have noted the correlation between famine areas and specific government policies on the cause of the 1987–1988 Ethiopian famine. The correlation is startlingly revealing. For example, in one part of Tigray and in Eritrea, there was a famine because these were areas outside government control and under military attack; in another part Tigray and in Wollo, there was famine because these were areas of forced resettlement; in the areas of northern Bale, Hararghe and Shoa, there was famine because of the government's enforced villagization programme; and in Wolega, Illubabor and other administrative regions, there was famine because the forcibly resettled were themselves unsettled and local production was disrupted, causing widespread destabilization and instability. In fact, when migrants' make decisions to flee their reasons for doing so are commonly much more complex than a simple 'environmental' push of the effects of climate change, as studies sometimes wrongly imply. When migrants' make decisions to flee the decision to migrate is usually only one decision amongst a variety of survival strategies pursued by families, either simultaneously or consecutively. These other survival strategies include equally momentous acts such the selling of assets, giving up wage-labour, eating bush foods or undertaking short distance migration. Indeed, it is often only after other survival strategies have been tried and have failed that long-distance migration is then contemplated. In the 1987–1988 drought in Ethiopia, coping strategies other than migration were undermined by state restrictions on travel, declining opportunities for both rural and urban wage-labour, and the grossly disadvantageous terms of trade arising from the escalating increase in grain prices. Indeed, such were the livelihood changes that occurred that aid itself imposed pressure on peasants to migrate.[138]

There appears, however, to be one practical reason for excluding the responsibility of the international community over environmentally displaced persons. A study by Richard Black suggests that migration causes environmental degradation and that this has important implications for the host country, the aid agencies, and the international community alike.[139] First, refugees have to rely on natural resources in order to sustain themselves in the early period for the arrival of aid. The requirements for fuel, cooking and heating will continue even after the arrival of aid. In this situation, the sustainability of natural resources will be difficult in the long term.[140] Second, it is not only refugees who rely upon the surrounding area for natural resources, but also the host population as well. Where natural resources are finite and unsustainable, there will arise a tension between the host community and the refugee population. Where heavy burdens are imposed on natural resources, the host community can use this as an excuse to stop asylum seekers from entering their country. This happened when Tanzania closed its borders to around 70,000 Rwandan refugees fleeing violence in Burundi in 1995.[141] Third, of particular international concern is the maintenance of biodiversity. Many conservation agreements have been put in place to protect diverse forests and wetlands. The arrival of migrants suddenly can disrupt environmentally fragile areas. A conflict emerges between the longer term global concerns of protection of endangered species or lands and the immediate living needs of a newly arrived population. Thus, both Turkey and Honduras have closed their borders in the past to asylum seekers and have cited environmental damage as their justification.[142] Having said this, it must be noted that there is at the moment a lack of evidence of significantly negative consequences from environmental displacement.[143] Yet, these concerns appear to be overplayed. A more recent study by David Keane, has concluded that:

> preventable environmental damage is rarely the sole factor in large scale migration. Similarly, large-scale migrations are rarely the sole factor in environmental damage. There is a certain appeal in citing refugees as a reason for protecting the environment and in citing the environment as a reason for protecting refugees. However, it has little practical benefit for either.[144]

Even if there is evidence of environmental degradation consequent upon the arrival of a large number of displaced persons, however, this is not a reason for refusing recognition to a group of refugees where that recognition is plainly warranted.

Can Environmentally Displaced Persons Comprise a Legal Category?

It is well known that a person 'does not become a refugee because of recognition, but is recognized because he is a refugee' and this being so, 'recognition of his refugee status does not therefore make him a refugee, but declares him to be one'.[145] What this means is that regardless of whether or not international law at present recognizes environmentally displaced persons as a legal category of refugees, their plight will need to be addressed simply because of the dramatic projected increase in their number in the future. In fact, there is evidence to suggest that the major causes of human conflict in the future are increasingly going to be to do with the environment. This means not only that international law risks becoming redundant in the field of refugee law if it does not address this phenomenon soon. It also means that the distinction between what is political, economical and social is well nigh impossible in the circumstances. One writer, Homer-Dixon traces the main causes of international and domestic political conflicts directly to the environment. He states the following three things.[146] First, that environmental scarcity leads to simple scarcity conflicts between states. Second, that environmental scarcity causes large population movements, which in turn leads to group-identity conflicts. Third, that environmental scarcity causes economic deprivation and disrupts social institutions, leading to 'deprivation conflict'.[147] Even when refugees are protected in camps, there is large scale devastation of the environment. Damage to the environment begins in the refugee camps because:

> areas in the immediate vicinity of refugee camps are stripped of vegetation cover because wood is needed for cooking and shelter. This alters soil and water balances and leads to erosion, soil depletion and decreased productivity.[148]

So the link with refugees as popularly understood is unmistakable in this respect.

In any event, the fact remains that the UNHCR has long assisted, by its mandate, groups of displaced persons known to be far wider, than those narrowly defined by the mandate in the *Refugee Convention 1951*. In this way, the UNHCR's protection has extended to groups known as the 'internally displaced', 'war displaced' and even 'other need groups' by 1992.[149] The difference lies here in the matter of obligation. What I have argued here is that it is going to be both necessary and inevitable for States to assume responsibility as a matter of both practice and principle given the increasing importance of environmentally displaced persons, whereas what the UNHCR has done is to expand the class of beneficiaries without any corresponding broadening of states' legal obligations.[150] My argument here has been that widespread peace and security problems will arise in the future if only the so-called 'Convention Refugees' continue to receive protection in the international system which goes beyond the assistance given to disaster victims. It is, of course, accepted that from the point of view of the refugee-hosting states, they want to be able to strictly define and limit their legal obligations. This is because the designation of 'refugees' for a group subjects a refugee-hosting state to an injunction against returning (i.e. refouling) that group to a state where an individual with a 'well-founded fear' may be persecuted. These principles sit at the cornerstone of refugee protection. On the other hand, those with humanitarian needs have far less legally defined rights and claims in respect of a states' responsibilities to them. Given this scenario, the fear has been expressed that however important the plight of those fleeing from environmental problems may be, any attempt to conjoin the notion of disaster victim and refugee under the appellation 'environmental refugee', will raise the danger that core aspects of refugee protection will be undermined and the lowest common denominator adopted.[151] I do not accept that. There is no evidence of this. The reception of refugees by host-countries has always had more to do with domestic and foreign policy considerations (or the geo-political considerations since the end of the Cold War) than with the numbers *per se*. A number of countries have been passing ever more restrictive refugee legislation since the advent of the new millennium even where refugee numbers have been falling. Accordingly, it is fair bet to say that principle should not be sacrificed in this way over the pressure of new migrants for whom a host State may have to be legally responsible.

NOTES

1   The paradigmatic example of containment is the US and Cuban governments' *Migration Accord*, which seeks to contain populations fleeing from Cuba and create channels for orderly migration of Cubans by limiting all irregular migration flows. See *The US-Cuba Joint Communique on Migration*, 5 US Dep't St. Dispatch 603 (Sept. 12, 1994). A similar strategy has been used to control the migration of people from Indochina. See Stem A. Bronee, 'The History of Comprehensive Plan of Action', 5 *Int'l Refugee L.* 534 (1993).

2   See *Assistance to Palestine Refugees*, G.A. Res. 302 (IV), U.N. GAOR, 4th Sess., UN Doc. A/RES/302 (IV) (1949).

3   See Weiss, *supra*, note 9, at 188.

4   See Letter Dated 24 September 1991 from the Permanent Representative of Yugoslavia to the United Nations Addressed to the President of the Security Council, U.N. S.C., 46th Sess., U.N. Doc. S/23069 (1991); S.C. Res. 713, U.N. SCOR, 46th Sess., 3009th mtg., U.N. Doc. S/RES/713 (1991) (declaring that the 'heavy loss of human life and material damage' were 'a threat to international peace and security,' largely due to the spillover of refugees on neighboring countries).

5   See Letter Dated 20 January 1992 from the Charge D'Affaires A.I. of the Permanent Mission of Somalia to the United Nations Addressed to the President of the Security Council, U.N. S.C., 46th Sess, U.N. Doc. S/23445 (1992); S.C. Res. 733, U.N. SCOR, 47th Sess., 3039th mtg., U.N. Doc. S/RES/733 (1992) (discussing similar concerns regarding the spillover of refugees on the safety and security of bordering countries).

6   See generally *Hard Choices: Moral Dilemmas in Humanitarian Intervention* (Jonathan Moore (ed.), 1998) (debating whether there is a moral duty to intervene in another state's affairs in order to protect human rights).

7   Joan Fitzpatrick, 'Flight from Asylum: Trends Toward Temporary 'Refuge' and

Local Responses to Force Migrations', 35 *Va. J. Int'l L.* 13, 65. For a detailed discussion of containment see Andrew Shacknove, 'From Asylum to Containment', 5 *Int'l J. Ref. L.* 516 (1993).

8   Quoted in the report of *Country information & Policy Unit, Immigration & Nationality Directorate, Home Office, United Kingdom* (April 2004), at para 6.53.

9   Ibid., at para 6.54.

10   *Loc. cit.*

11   *Loc. cit.*

12   For example, although the government of Sierra Leone itself had 'continued to provide temporary protection to an increasing number of Liberians who had fled the conflict in their home country' as the same *United States State Department Country Report* for Sierra Leone for 2003 makes clear (see ibid., at para 6.56) 'in 2003 and early 2004, there were violent clashes between Liberian refugees and host communities in Sierra Leone' (see ibid., at para 6.57).

13   See preambles to *UN Charter and Universal Declaration of Human Rights*, GA res.217 (III), UNGAOR, 3D Sess., Supp. No. 13, UNDOC.A/810 (1948) (Hereafter UDHR).

14   See generally UN Charter Chapter V11.

15   It has been said that such resolutions are evidence of customary international law on a particular subject matter. See David J. Harris, *Cases and Materials in International Law* (4ᵗʰ Edition, London, 1991), at 63.

16   See UNHCR, 'Protecting Refugees: Questions and Answers' available at the UNHCR website at http://www.unhcr.org.

17   See also Elizabeth E. Ruddick, 'The Continuing Constraint of Sovereignty: International Law, International Protection, and the Internally Displaced' (1997) (77) (2) *Boston Univ.L.R.*429 who observes that the UNHCR has 'acted pursuant with flexible, extra-statutory "good offices" powers to bring IDPs in this area of concern' despite the fact that it has no formal IDP mandate (at 431).

18   See Note by Secretary General, 'Internally Displaced Persons', UNDOC. GA/48/579 (9 November 1993).

19   ECOSOC is one of the principal organizations established by the UN under Article 7 (1) UN Charter.

20   See Article 62(2) of the UN Charter.

21   See Article 62(3) of the UN Charter.

22   See Roberta Cohen, Co-Director of the Brookings Institution Project on Internal Displacement: http://www.brookings.edu. See 'Exodus Within Borders: The Global Crisis Of Displacement' (May 31, 2001).

23   GA Resolution 47/57/105 of 1992.

24   See *UNHCR Statistical Year Book*.

25   Francis Deng, 'The International Protection of the Internally Displaced' (1995) Special Issue, *International Journal of Refugee Law* 74 at 76. See also UN Charter Article 62 (2) mandating ECOSOC to 'make recommendations for the purpose of promoting respect for, and observance of, human rights and fundamental freedoms for all'. This definition was first used in the Secretary-General's 1992 analytical report on internally displaced persons: See UN Doc. E/CN.4/1992/23 (1992) (para 17).

26   UNGA RES.48/135 (20 December 1993).

27   A/46/721.

28   46/182.

29   See Francis Deng, 'The International Protection of the Internally Displaced' (1995), *Special Issue International Journal of Refugee Law* 74 at 75.

30 See the *Guiding Principles on Internal Displacement* (1992) at Principle 2. UN Doc. E/CN.4/1998/53/ Add.2, para 2.
31 See R. Cohen and F.M. Deng, *Masses in Flight: The Global Crisis of Internal Displacement*, 16– 9 (1998).
32 Such instances have taken place in Myanmar, Iraq, Ethiopia and the erstwhile Yugoslavia. See R. Cohen and F.M. Deng, *Masses in Flight: The Global Crisis of Internal Displacement*, 16–19 (1998).
33 See *UN Charter*, Article 2(7).
34 See UNHCR, 'UNCHR and Internally Displaced: Questions and Answers' available at the website of the UNHCR at http://www.unhcr.ch.
35 See Deborah Perluss and Joan S. Hartman, 'Temporary Refuge: Emergence of a Customary Norm' (1986), 26 *Virginia J. of Int'l L.* 551, at 597–8.
36 See preamble to UNGA and Doc. A/RES/47/105, adopted at the 89th plenary meeting, 16 December 1982.
37 See website of the United Nations at http://www.un.org.
38 See UNHCR, *Statistical Year Book: Refugees, Asylum Seekers and Other Persons of Concern – Trends in Displacement, Protection and Solutions* (2002) (Hereafter UNHCR Statistical Year Book at 22).
39 See Global IBP Project (Norwegian Refugee Council) 21st January 2005 at http://www.ein.org.uk/members/country/full.shtml?x=181470.
40 The human rights situation in Bangladesh is grim and under-reported. In December 2004, a well-respected human rights organization in Bangladesh, found that there were 90 publicly reported custodial deaths due to torture in Bangladesh during the year. The Asian legal Resource Centre (ALRC) was of the view that these deaths comprised only a handful of the total number of cases of severe torture, including torture resulting in death, occurring in Bangladesh each year. The Government of Bangladesh has ratified the Convention against Torture and other Cruel, Inhuman or Degrading Punishment, but it has taken virtually no steps to implement the Convention. Torture is not a crime in Bangladesh. The government has passed no enabling legislation. There are no legal provisions enacted for the compensation and rehabilitation of victims. There is no provision of any medical facilities for treatment of physical and psychological injuries caused by torture. Worse, the government still has no plans to take any action in relation to torture: see, the report of the United Nations High Commissioner for Human Rights (UNHCR), 7th February 2005 at http://www.ein.org.uk/members/country/full.shtml?x=182606.
41 See *Global IDP Project* (Norwegian Refugee Council) 17th February 2005 at http://www.ein.org.uk/members/country/full.shtml?x=182650.
42 See Article 1 of the *Statutes of the International Committee of the Red Cross* underscoring that ICRC is a 'humanitarian organization'. Article 1 of the office of the United Nations High Commissioner for refugees, adopted by *General Assembly Resolution 428* (V) of 14 December 1950 also states that the UNHCR's mandate is 'to provide international protection … to refugees … and [seek] permanent solutions for this problem … by assisting governments and, private organizations to facilitate the (IR) voluntary repatriation … of assimilation within new national communities'.
43 See Article 1 of the *UNHCR Statute* which states that, '[UNHCR], acting under the authority of the General Assembly, shall assume [its] function [S] … under the auspices of the [UN] …'.
44 See ICRC, *International Humanitarian Law: Answers to your Questions* (Geneva: ICRC Public Productions) at 2 declaring the ICRC's 'mandate was handed down by the international community'.

45 See UNHCR Statute, Articles 1 and 6.

46 See the four Geneva Conventions of 12 August 1949.

47 8 June 1977, U.N.T.S. 1125 (entered into before 7 December 1978).

48 E. Odhiambo-Abuya, 'Refugees and Internally Displaced Persons: Examining Overlapping Instituional Mandates of the ICRC and the UN High Commissioner for Refugees', 7 *Sing. J. Int'l & Comp. L.* 236 at p.244.

49 ICRC 'The ICRC, the League, and the Report on the Re-Appraisal of the Role of the Red Cross', March–April 1978 to January-March 1979) *Int'l Rev. of the Red Cross* 1.

50 *Protocol Additional to the Geneva conventions of 12 August 1949*, and relating to the protection of victims of the national armed conflicts 8 June 1977, 1125 U.N.T.S (entered into before 7 December 1978) (hereafter Additional Protocol I) and *Additional Protocol II*.

51 See *Additional Protocol 1*, at Article 51.

52 See Vitit Muntarbhorn, 'Protection and Assistance for Refugees in Armed Conflicts and Internal Disturbances' (1988) 265 *Int'l Rev. of the Red Cross* 351 which states that, 'Red Cross protection – cum – assistance is more transitory by nature, since it is conceived in terms of emergency relief, usually in the form of material assistance and immediate physical relief' at p.365.

53 See UNHCR, *Protecting Refugees: Questions and Answers*, available at UNHCR website at http://www.unhcr.org.

54 See also Elizabeth E. Ruddick, 'The Continuing Constraint of Sovereignty: International Law, International Protection, and the Internally Displaced' (1997) (77) (2) *Boston Univ.L.R.*429 at p.468.

55 This is normally referred to as 'durable solutions' to the plight of refugees: See UNHCR Statute Articles 8 (C) and Article 9.

56 UNGA RES 1388 (XIV) adopted at the 841st plenary meeting 20 November 1959.

57 See UNGA RES.1673 (XVI) adopted at the 1081st plenary meeting (18 December 1961).

58 UN DOC. EC/1994/SEB/CRP.2 (4 May 1994).

59 See UNHCR, 'UNCHR and Internally Displaced: Questions and Answers' available at the website of the UNHCR at http://www.unhcr.ch.

60 See Roberta Cohen, Co-Director of the Brookings Institution Project on Internal Displacement: http://www.brookings.edu. See 'Exodus Within Borders: The Global Crisis Of Displacement' (May 31, 2001).

61 See the website of the United Nations at http://www.un.org.

62 See UNHCR, 'UNCHR and Internally Displaced: Questions and Answers' available at the website of the UNHCR at http://www.unhcr.ch.

63 See UN Charter Article 2 (7). International Humanitarian Law recognizes this principle through Protocol II article 3. *Starke's International Law* also argues that this concept 'signifies that within this territorial domain jurisdiction is exercised by the State over persons and property to the exclusion of other states' (at p.144).

64 See UNHCR, 'UNCHR and Internally Displaced: Questions and Answers' available at the website of the UNHCR at http://www.unhcr.ch.

65 Richard Plender, 'The Legal Basis of International Jurisdiction to Act with regard to the Internally Displaced' (1994) 6 (3) *International Journal of Refugee Law*, 345 at 351.

66 UN DOC.E/CN/4/1998/53/Add.2 of 11 February 1998. Since 1995, there has been a growing body of literature in the area of IDPs. For a general overview and evolution of the IDP representative's office and the principles, see, Simon

Bagshaw, 'Internally Displaced Persons at the 54th Session of the United Nations Commission on Human Rights' (1998) 10 (3) *International Journal of Refugee Law* 548.

67 See principle 2.

68 See preamble paragraph 3 (A-D) inclusive.

69 See Walter Kalin, 'The Guiding Principles on Internal Displacement – Introduction', 10 *International Journal of Refugee Law* 557, 559–60 (1998).

70 A good example in this respect is Principle 7. This carefully distinguishes the different forms of displacement, such as in the emergency stages of armed conflicts and disasters, where on any realistic view, only very minimal guarantees can be observed by authorities, and other situations which allow for procedural safeguards to be observed. Principle 10 is yet another example because it delineates in paragraph 1, the right to life in general, and then stipulates in paragraph 2 what guarantees may be relevant to situations of armed conflict only.

71 In the same way, Principle 17 first states the general right to respect for the family and only then emphasizes the particular features of this right as being of special importance to internally displaced persons. In this way, careful and particularized treatment is given to the right of internally displaced families to remain together when relocated or interned in camps.

72 Principle 6 is another such example, referring to 'the right to be protected against being arbitrarily displaced'. This right is not yet expressly enumerated by any existing international law document. It is, however, a general norm of contemporary international humanitarian law, which prohibits displacement in a number of specific and limited situations. It is also a general norm of contemporary human rights which, in a more general sense, guarantees not only the freedom of movement but also the right to choose one's own residence. From this can be deduced a general right to remain. International law documents also preserve a specific right not to be displaced for indigenous populations. From this it can be deduced that international law implicitly contains a right not to be arbitrarily displaced. See, Walter Kalin, 'The Guiding Principles on Internal Displacement – Introduction', 10 *International Journal of Refugee Law* 557, 561 (1998).

73 See Roberta Cohen, Co-Director of the Brookings Institution Project on Internal Displacement: http://www.brookings.edu. See 'Exodus Within Borders: The Global Crisis Of Displacement' (May 31, 2001).

74 See Kalin.

75 Kalin, at 647.

76 See Roberta Cohen, Simon Bagshaw, and Vladamir Shlolnikov, *Background Memorandum of the Regional Workshop on Internal Displacement in the South Caucasus*, WC Tblisi, Georgia (May 10–12 2000) 3.

77 See Cohen, Bagshaw, and Shlolnikov, *supra* at 3.

78 See Bagshaw, *supra* at 550–51.

79 See UN Charter Article 1 (3).

80 See Article 2 (7) of the UN Charter, which states that, 'nothing contained in this charter shall authorize the United Nations to intervene in matters, which are essentially within the domestic jurisdiction of any state …'.

81 Ibid.

82 See Joan Fitzpatrick, (ed.), *Human Rights Protection For Refugees, Asylum Seekers, and the Internally Displaced Persons: A Guide to International Mechanisms and Procedures* (New York, Transnational Publishers, 2002), at 5.

83 UNSC Res. 688 (1991) adopted at the 2982 Security Council meeting.

84 Ibid., Para 3.

85   UN DOC S/RES/(1994) (adopted at its 3392 second meeting, on 22 June 1994) on 'establishment of a temporary multinational operation for humanitarian purposes in Rwanda until the deployment of the expanded U.N. Mission for Rwanda'. See also U.N.DOC S/RES/925 (1994) paragraph 4, which affirmed that the [United Nations Assistance Mission to Rwanda] will:

> Contribute to the security and protection of displaced persons, refugees and civilians at risk [via] establishment and maintenance ... _____ humanitarian areas. Provide security and support for the distrubution of relief supplies and humanitarian relief operations.

86   Ibid., Para 2.
87   Now the Democratic Republic of Congo (DRC).
88   UN DOC S/RES/1078 (1996) (adopted at 3710th meeting on 9 November 1996) on 'The Situation in the Great Lakes Region'.
89   Ibid., introductory paragraph.
90   See http://www.un.org/apps/news/story.asp?NewsID=11507&Cr=sudan&Cr1=UN News Centre, 30th July 2004.
91   El-Hinnawi E. 'Environmental refugees', United Nations Environmental Programme, Kenya, 1985; Jacobson, J., 'Environmental refugees: a yardstick of habitability', *Worldwatch Institute*, Washington DC, 1988; Tickell, C., 'Climate change could cause world refugee crisis', *British Overseas Development*, 7:16, 1989.
92   See Essam El-Hannawi, U.N. Envtl. Program, *Environmental Refugees* 4 (1985).
93   Jodi Jacobsons, 'Environmental Refugees: A Yardstick of Habitability'; 6 (World Watch Institute, World Watch Paper No. 86, 1998). However, Norman Myers places the figure at 25 million. See Norman Myers, *Environmentally Induced Displacements: The State of the Art, Environmentally-Induced Population Displacements*, and *Environmental Impacts Resulting from Mass Migration* 72 (1996).
94   Norman Myers, 'Environmental Refugees in a Globally Warmed World', *BioScience* (Vol. 43, December 1993), at p.11.
95   See Int'l Fed'n of the Red Cross and the Red Crescent Societies, *World Disasters Report* 20 (1999) [Herein after World Disasters Report 1999].
96   Munich Reinsurance Group, *Topic 2000: Natural Catastrophes – The Current Position* 62 (1999).
97   See *World Disasters Report 1999* at 85–100.
98   See *Press Release*, World Meteorological Organization. 'According to the World Meteorological Organization, extreme weather events might increase' (July 2, 2003) available at http://www.wmo.ch/web/press/press695.doc. Also see *Global Situation Report, hottest year*, at http://www.gsreport.com/articles/art000009.html.
99   UN Office for the Coordination of Humanitarian Affairs (UCHA) available at http://www.reliefweb.int.
100 *World Disasters Report 1999* at Page 88.
101 Ibid.
102 See Essam El-Hannawi, *U.N. Envtl. Program, Environmental Refugees* 4 (1985). The term 'environmental refugees' was coined by El-Hannawi in this seminal UN publication. Its origin, however, was an International Institute for the Environment and Development (IIED) briefing document in November of the previous year. See Gaim Kibreab, Environmental Causes and Impact of Refugee Movements: A Critique of the Current Debate, 21 *Disasters* 20–38 (1977).
103 See Robert E. Ebel, *Chernobyl and its aftermath* IX (1994).

104   Ibid.
105   See Richard H. Wagner, 'Indo-China: The War Against an Environment and Man', pp.360–364 (1971).
106   Ibid., at p.364.
107   James K. Glassman, 'Counter-Insurgency, Ecocide and the Production of Refugees', *Refuge*, June 1992 at 28.
108   Ibid.
109   Adam Roberts, 'Destruction of the Environment during the 1991 Gulf War', *Int'l Rev. of the Red Cross*, 1992, at 538.
110   See Paul Brown, 'Battle Scarred, The Environmental Fallout After The Tanks Have Departed', *The Guardian*, 19ᵗʰ September 2003 available at http://society.guardian.co.uk/societyguardian/story/017,7843,897977,00.html.
111   Ibid.
112   Res. 687 U.N.SCOR, 56–46 sess., 2981 MPG., at 16, U.N.DOC.S/RES/687 (1991).
113   Rome Statute of the International Criminal Court, Article 8 (2) (B) (IV), UN DOCA/CONF.1834/9 (1998), 37ILM999. See Mark A. Drumbel, 'Waging War Against The World', 22 *Fordham Int'l L.J.L.*122,126 (1998).
114   Joseph Yacoub, *Les Minorites Dans Le Monde: Faits Et Analyses* (Minorities in the World: Facts and Analysis) 94 (1998).
115   Thomas S. Homer-Dixon, 'Environmental Scarcities and Violent Conflict: Evidence from Cases', *Int'l Security*, Summer 1994, at 5 and 10.
116   UN Office for the Coordination of Humanitarian Affairs, *Guiding Principles on Internal Displacement*, at 1, UN DOC E/CN.4/1998/53/add.2 (1998). The full definition reads as follows: 'displaced persons are persons or groups of persons who have been forced or obliged to flee or leave their homes or places of habitual residence, in particular as a result of or in order to avoid the effects of armed conflict, situations of generalized violence, violations of human rights or natural or human-made disasters, and who have not crossed an internationally recognized state border'.
117   See *UNHCR Basic Facts*, available at http://www.unhcr.org.
118   Shacknove A. 'Who is a refugee?', *Ethics*, 95, pp.274–84, 1985.
119   See Suzette Brooks Masters, 'Environmentally-Induced Migration: Beyond a Culture of Reaction', 14 *geo.immigr.LJ*855 (2000) at Page 872.
120   See, Sarah Collinson, the *Ditchley Conference Report No D94/10*; the Ditchley Foundation's Conference on 'International Migration and Population Pressures', (September 1994, UK).
121   See McGregor, *supra*, at 159. Where it states that, 'the use of the term "environmental" can imply a false separation between overlapping and interrelated categories'.
122   See Kibreab, *supra*, at 21.
123   See Kibreab, *loc cit*.
124   See Norman, 'Environmental Refugees in a Globally Warmed World', *Bioscience*, December 1993, at 752–61; Norman Myers, 'Tropical Forests: The Main Deforestation Front', 20 *Envt'l. Conservation* 9 (1993).
125   See Intergovernmental Negotiating Committee on Convention to Combat Desertification (INCD) quoted in *Geography and Refugees* above at page 13.
126   Joann McGregor, 'Refugees and Environment', in *Geography and Refugees: Patterns and Processes of Change* 159 (Richard Black and Vaugn Robinson (eds), (1993).
127   Wijkman, A. and Timberlake, L., *Natural Disasters: Acts of God or Acts of Man?*, Earthscan, London, 1984.

128 Warrick R.A., 'Drought in the US Great Plains, shifting social consequences', 1983, in Hewitt, K., *Interpretations of Calamity*.

129 Richard Beeston, 'Villages wiped off the face of the earth', *The Times*, 10ᵗʰ October 2005, at p.10.

130 Randeep Ramesh, 'Aid effort in chaos as victims mob convoys', *The Guardian*, 12ᵗʰ October 2005 at p.18.

131 Tariq Ali, 'Pakistan will not forget,' *The Guardian*, 12ᵗʰ October 2005, at p.33. As the author also commented, '[P]akistan's army has been put into action, but armies are not suited to relief work. They are not trained to save lives, and reports yesterday that aid convoys are being attacked and seized by angry crowds long before they reach their destinations are an indication of the chaos', ibid.

132 Dan McDougall, 'Border stand-off blocking aid', *The Guardian*, 13ᵗʰ October 2005, at p.18 (Quoting an Indian Air Force navigator).

133 Justin Huggler, 'India and Pakistan unite as death toll approaches 80,000', *The Independent*, 20ᵗʰ October 2005, at p.28.

134 Justin Huggler, 'New wave of deaths will hit Pakistan, says Annan', *The Independent*, 21ˢᵗ October 2005, at p.29.

135 See 'An inadequate response', *The Independent* (Editorial and Opinion), 21ˢᵗ October 2005, at p.34.

136 Duffield, M., 'The internationalization of public welfare: conflict and the reform of the Donor/NGO safety net', 1991.

137 Clay, J., Steingraber, S. and Niggli, P., *The Spoils of Famine: Ethiopian Famine Policy and Peasant Agriculture, Cultural Survival Inc* (Cambridge MA, 1988).

138 Pankhurst, A., *Resettlement and Famine in Ethiopia: The Villagers' Experience* (Manchester University Press, UK, 1992).

139 Cited in *Geography and Refugees*, at page 15.

140 Ibid.

141 See US Committee for Refugees, *Country Report: Tanzania* available at http://www.refugees.org/world/countryrpt/africa/1997/tanzania.htm.

142 Elizabeth G. Ferris, *Beyond Borders: Refugees, Migrants and Human Rights in the Post Cold War Era* (1993).

143 See *Geography and Refugees*, above at p.50.

144 David Keane, 'The Environmental Causes and Consequences of Migration: A Search for the Meaning of "environmental refugees"', 16 *Geo.Int'l Envt'l.Rev.* 209.

145 *UNHCR Handbook*: see 'General Principles' at para 28.

146 See Homer-Dixon, above at pp.18, 20, 23.

147 The second and third hypotheses are more compelling.

148 See J. Sorenson, 'An Overview: Refugees and Development', in *African Refugees: Development Aid and Repatriation*, 175 at 181 (H. Adelman and J. Sorenson (eds), 1994).

149 EXCOM 'Note on international protection', *UNHCR Executive Committee*, 43rd Session, October 1992, Document A/AC.96.799.

150 Goodwin-Gill, G., 'Refugees: the expanding mandate of the office of the UNHCR', unpublished, 1988.

151 See Richard Black and Vaughan Robinson (eds), *Geography and Refugees: patterns and processes of change*, Belhaven Press (1993, pp.159–62).

6 Conceptualizing Refugees

INTRODUCTION

The term 'refugee' referred initially to two categories of individuals. First, those recognized as refugees by the pre-1950 legal framework.[1] Secondly, any person who:

> as a result of events occurring before 1 January 1951, and owing to well-founded fear of being persecuted for reasons of race, religion, nationality, membership of a particular social group or political opinion, is outside the country of his nationality and is unable or unwilling to avail himself of the protection of that country; or not having a nationality and being outside the country of his former habitual residence as a result of such events, is unable or, owing to such fear, is unwilling to return to it.[2]

The temporal and geographical limitations were written into the *Refugee Convention* since European states, then recovering from World War II, were reluctant to saddle themselves with uncertain refugee influxes in the post World War II era.[3] Concerns gradually arose, however, over the limited nature of the 1951 Convention. The global persistence of this problem after 1951, particularly stemming from the African wars of independence in the late 1950s and 1960s, eventually necessitated a removal of these limitations.[4] For the *Refugee Convention* to remain relevant and apply as a universal treaty, it had to change its Euro-centric[5] orientation. Consequently, the *1967 Protocol Relating to the Status of Refugees*[6] (hereafter *Refugee Protocol*), was adopted[7] to enable the Refugee Convention to cater to new refugee situations on a universal basis.[8] The *Convention* remained confined, however, to the five protected grounds of race, religion, nationality, political opinion, and membership in a particular social group.

In this chapter, I will first consider the various categories of ill-treatment under the *1951 Refugee Convention* and their impact on modern refugee law. Second, I will consider the arguments of critics regarding the inherent limitations of the *1951 Refugee Convention*. Third, I will undertake a comparison of the *1951 Convention* with the two leading regional regimes that offer a more expansive definition of refugee status, namely, the OAU's *Convention Governing the Specific Aspects of Refugee Problems in Africa* and the *Cartegena Declaration*.

Fourth, I will suggest that there is a case for recognizing a new type of refugee, namely, the humanitarian refugee, under current refugee law norms. Fifth, I will then ask why refugees have been so restrictively interpreted under the *1951 Convention*. Sixth, I will suggest that there is a case for removing the requirements of 'persecution' and 'flagrant breach' of human rights in a modern and forward-looking definition of refugee law. Finally, I will end by arguing that there are obstacles to this because powerful Western countries have a vested interest in keeping the refugee definition narrowly confined in the way that it is.

THE 1951 REFUGEE CONVENTION

The five protected grounds in the *1951 Refugee Convention* of race, religion, nationality, political opinion, and membership in a particular social group are not easy concepts to apply. They require considerable ingenuity of thought and application. Yet, the case law from various jurisdictions shows that the courts have been willing to give them an expansive application.

The first ground was 'race'.[9] It is not 'ethnicity'. Yet, an increasingly common basis for asylum claims in recent years has been ethnicity,[10] although it may also be subsumed under race.[11] In addition, prospective refugees had to be able to choose to characterize their protected characteristics, as among race and nationality or among race and membership of a particular social group. Much would depend on the facts. But it would also depend on the way that the situation in question was perceived by the persecutor and persecuted.[12] The second ground was 'religion' and the general understanding here was that it would be considered persecution if it involved the forced suppression of a prospective refugee's religious identity or religious practice[13] or if it required him to follow a particular faith.[14] The third ground was 'nationality' and like race it was to be interpreted broadly, as the *UNHCR Handbook* makes clear, to include a specific cultural or linguistic minority that would identify itself as such.[15] British jurisprudence confirms that the persecution of Gypsies may be on grounds of race or of nationality.[16] The denial of full rights of citizenship in one's country of nationality (as with the Ahmadiya religious sect in Pakistan) may also amount to persecution on grounds of religion.[17] The fourth ground was 'political opinion' and here persecution had to be on account of the victim's political opinion, and not that of the persecutor[18] as there had to be a nexus between the persecution and the holding of the political opinion. The term 'political opinion' itself was not defined but it covers a broad range of views.[19] Indeed, according to Goodwin-Gill the concept should cover 'any opinion on any matter in which the machinery of State, government, or policy may be engaged'.[20] This meant that one had to take account of how the prospective refugee's actions, words, or beliefs would be viewed in his or her home country before deciding whether it constituted political opinion.[21] Indeed, neutrality could be considered to be a political opinion, and where a person was able to establish that neutrality was a conscious choice and that the persecution resulted from it, he or she would have made out their case.[22]

The difficulty was that many asylum applicants were likely to be reluctant to characterize their views or conduct as political because political activity is discreditable and disparaged in many repressive countries.[23] This is because the governments of such regimes often try to stifle even peaceful forms of legitimate activity and expression designating its participants as 'political opponents'.[24] Yet, political opinions may not be expressed at all.[25] Where expressed, they may be expressed through actions and/or words. Moreover, the potential persecutor's awareness of a person's opinions could lead to him or her having a well-founded fear of persecution.[26] Additionally, applicants may be persecuted for political opinions that they do not in fact hold, but that are attributed to them by their persecutors.[27] This is what is known as a claim based on an 'imputed' belief or characteristic.[28] A claim that is imputed in this way is also possible in relation to the other protected grounds of the refugee definition.[29]

The fifth ground, and currently the most challenging, was 'Membership in a particular social group'. Like 'political opinion' the refugee Convention does not define this ground either, but it is clear that it was intended to cover groups of people, who might not be covered by one of the other four grounds, and yet who were deserving of international refugee protection.[30] Since its inclusion in the *Refugee Convention* over 50 years ago, this ground has given rise to a surprisingly large number of claims, leaving behind a trail of controversy.[31] The *UNHCR Handbook on Procedures and Criteria for Determining Refugee Status* (*UNCHR Handbook*) describes a particular social group as 'persons of similar backgrounds, habits or social status'.[32] The US Board of Immigration Appeals in 1985 defined 'particular social group' as referring to persons who 'share a common immutable characteristic', either 'an innate one such as sex, color, or kinship ties, or in some circumstances … a shared past experience such as former military leadership or land ownership', which the members of the group 'either cannot change, or should not be required to change because it is fundamental to their individual identities or consciences'.[33]

Yet, it was a British case in 1999 which forged new ground when – whilst recognizing that in general 'persecution' may not in itself create a social group – went onto imply that that 'discrimination' may do so and on that basis found that women in Pakistan were a social group. In *Shah and Islam*, Lord Steyn in the House of Lords declared that, where it was possible to say that there was persecution directed toward an individual who is a member of a group of persons all of whom share a common immutable characteristic, persecution as a member of a particular social group would be made out. This reasoning could, therefore, be extended to '[P]akistani women because they are discriminated against and as a group they are unprotected by the State'.[34] Lord Steyn adopted Australian jurisprudence that:

> … the actions of the persecutors may serve to identify or even cause the creation of a particular social group in society. Left-handed men are not a particular social group. But, if they were persecuted because they were left-handed, they would no doubt quickly become recognizable in their society as a particular social group.[35]

Shah and Islam was quickly followed in Britain by the Immigration Appeal Tribunal (as it then was) when it held in a case that the applicant:

> has now been stigmatized – labelled by serious criminal elements for conscientiously fulfilling an important civic duty and she cannot now escape that stigma. In the eyes of the persecutors an immutable characteristic has been branded on her person.[36]

Examples of particular social groups which have proliferated to form the basis of successful asylum claims include members of a particular family;[37] of members of a Somali clan;[38] of homosexuals;[39] of students;[40] and of parents of Burmese student dissidents.[41] Indeed, as the canvas of human rights law expanded beyond the areas of civil and political rights, so has asylum protection also extended its boundaries into hitherto neglected frontiers. At the turn of the beginning of this Millennium, there have already been successful asylum applications based on child abuse before the US courts[42] and of child trafficking before the Canadian courts.[43] Indeed, one US court has even granted refugee status based on the denigration of childhood autism.[44] Bhabha has pointed out how in the last decade US courts have granted asylum to:

> Salvadoran street children fleeing gangs, Indian child laborers escaping from slavery-like status, Chinese children sold into forced marriages, and Honduran child abuse victims. These claims exemplify the expanded substantive universe to which human rights concerns and by association, asylum protection, now apply.

The Criticism of the 1951 Convention

Nevertheless, and despite such vigorous activity by the courts in a number of liberal western jurisdictions, several leading commentators still continue to regard the UN definition as being too restrictive. Woehlcke[45] pointed out that as a post-War instrument, the focus of the UN Refugee Convention was originally the regulation of the European refugee problem after the Second World War, but that it was inapplicable to the bulk of the world's refugees today who were either fleeing poverty and economic hardship as 'economic refugees' or fleeing ecological catastrophe as 'environmental refugees', or both. Indeed, the distinction between 'political' and 'economic' refugees was hard to make because, as Loescher[46] elaborated:

> … in many developing countries which have few resources and weak government structures, economic hardship is generally exacerbated by political violence. Thus it has become increasingly difficult to make hard and fast distinctions between refugees (as defined by the *1951 UN Convention* with its political bias) and economic migrants.

On the other hand, scholars like Nobel[47] argue strongly for the retention of the *1951 Convention*, pointing out that any confusion relating to the status of refugees, is actually harmful to their protection. He attacks commentators like

Woehlcke and Loescher, who wish to extend refugee status to economic and environmental migrants. In his view, such terms as 'economic refugee' and 'environmental refugee' do not exist in international law.[48] Others such as the African writers, Toolo and Bethlehem,[49] note that in the context of a decision to migrate:

> [W]hile such an individual decision may reflect the conditions faced by people in the home country, this would be different from the crisis-driven nature of refugees. Refugees are only in a position to return home when the crisis in their own country has been resolved.

In my view, this is a false distinction caused by the need to show 'persecution' under the Refugee Convention. As Astri Suhrke[50] has only too rightly pointed out, the UN Refugee Convention's central plank of refugee status determination was persecution, which was a governmental act against an individual. This, however, inevitably excluded those fleeing from generalized conditions of violence, insecurity and oppression, and it also excluded the inhabitants of states where violence is externally induced. In fact, Solomon has gone onto to give a number of examples of externally induced unrest, including 'South Africa's destabilization of the Front-Line States (FLS), throughout much of the 1980s through its support of proxy groups – such as Renamo in Mozambique; UNITA in Angola; the Lesotho Liberation Army in Lesotho, and the Mashala Gang in Zambia'.[51] African scholars in particular, such as Chris Dolan of South Africa, have argued that the conventional distinction between illegal immigrants and refugees, that such a caterorization often leads to, does not reflect empirical reality adequately and therefore is bound to produce ineffective policies.[52] Some notable scholars, like Shacknove, continue to argue that the UN Convention is too state-centric and is not sufficiently sympathetic of the human imperatives driving people away from their homes.[53]

Yet, others disagree that the *UN Convention on Refugees* does not remain widely applicable to the world's global migration crisis. Goran Melander[54] notes that the definition provided in the *UN Convention* is as relevant today as it has been in the 1950s when originally adopted. In fact, he argues that the 1951 definition is far more flexible than its critics would have us believe and that this flexibility was evident as early as the 1950s. When in the immediate aftermath of the Soviet suppression of the 1956 Hungarian uprising, the United Nations High Commissioner for Refugees (UNHCR) declared all Hungarians fleeing from their native land as refugees, all Western governments agreed and followed suit. This was at the height of the Cold War and I am not convinced, however, that Western governments would have done the same if it was not a Soviet invasion of a buffer eastern European state, that threatened the stability and security of the West by its actions. It remains true, however, that to its credit the UNHCR interpreted the *1951 Convention* as broadly enabling it to become involved in the early stages of the Yugoslav crisis. Weiner also explains how later over Iraq, the UNHCR was able to set up 'safety zones' within Iraq to provide protection for displaced Kurds under

UN Security Council Resolution 688 of 1991.[55] In so doing, the UN was clearly involving itself in the plight of the 'internally displaced populations' within a sovereign state which, if a narrow interpretation of the refugee definition in the *1951 Convention* is taken, excludes the consideration of internally displaced people from refugee status. A broader interpretation of the *1951 Refugee Convention*, however, would not agree that the UNHCR was overstepping its mark because the record of the organization shows it holds a wider interpretation of the *1951 Convention*'s definition of a refugee. In any case, there is a clear linkage existing between the internally displaced and refugees in general.[56] It is in this context that the question of broadening the parameters of the Refugee Convention is considered. In the words of Solomon:

> The question posed is why the definition of the term 'refugee' is not simply broadened, if it is to be interpreted broadly anyway? Then it would be interpreted even more broadly and be open to wider abuse. The broader the definition, the wider the borders, the more the numbers of refugees will be, and the more chances there are of domestic instability developing.[57]

Solomon concludes that 'any attempt to widen the definition of the term "refugee" should be resisted'.[58] Yet, this overlooks the fact that later treaties have broadened the definition.

THE OAU REFUGEE CONVENTION AND THE CARTEGENA DECLARATION

Later refugee protective treaties, particular regional ones, displayed a realistic appreciation of altered armed conflict patterns.[59] Many of the critics mentioned above favour these regional approaches as amounting to a more inclusive definition of refugees. Two examples may be cited, which both contain a more pragmatic definition of the term 'refugee'. First, the Organization of African Unity's (OAU) *Convention Governing the Specific Aspects of Refugee Problems in Africa*, adopted in Addis Ababa on 10 September 1969[60] (hereafter *OAU Refugee Convention*) recognized internal wars and civil strife as root causes of forced migration. Article 1(2) of the OAU Refugee Convention defined 'refugee' to include:

> every person who, owing to external aggression, occupation, foreign domination or events seriously disturbing public order, in either part or the whole of his country of origin or nationality, is compelled to leave his place of habitual residence in order to seek refuge in another place outside his or origin or nationality.

This is clearly a noticeably wider definition than the *1951 Refugee Convention*. Not only does it include a person who is compelled to leave his place of habitual residence as result simply of 'events seriously disturbing public order', but it does not contain any requirement of 'persecution' or any requirement of 'for reasons of race, religion, nationality, membership of a particular social group or political opinion'. I do not agree with Myron Weiner that there are more similarities than differences between the two conventions. He argues that both definitions view refugees as individuals who lack the protection of their own government. He argues that neither definition applies to displaced persons within a country, irrespective of whether there is persecution or violence, or to individuals fleeing from natural disasters such as floods, droughts, or earthquakes. Finally, he states that neither definition includes individuals who flee from a tyrannical regime, unless they are personally persecuted or their society is torn by life-threatening violence.[61] In short, it would be wrong to counterpose the two conventions, since they are so similar. Furthermore, in the preamble to the *1969 OAU Convention*, it is categorically stated that it is meant to complement and not oppose the *1951 Refugee Convention*.

This may be so, but I believe Weiner fundamentally overstates his case. As Hathaway observes, this 'first regional arrangement' was such that it 'broke new ground by extending protection to all persons compelled to flee across national borders by reason of any man-made disaster'[62] because as Coles has pointed out:

> [t]he second part of the definition would virtually cover all man-made disasters and would embrace that class of persons sometimes called 'displaced persons'.[63]

For Hathaway, the OAU definition actually 'successfully translates the core meaning of refugee status to the reality of the developing world'[64] because as Hyndman had earlier observed in relation to the *1951 Refugee Convention*:

> [t]oday, circumstances have changed and many people who need international protection of the kind provided by the Convention do not fall within its ambit.[65]

In the event, the OAU definition has today succeeded in the developing world in becoming 'the most influential conceptual standard of refugee status apart from the Convention definition itself', because as Hathaway reminds us:

> [i]t has provided the basis for enhanced UNHCR activity in the Africa, was at the root of the proposed convential definition of persons entitled to territorial asylum, and has inspired the liberalization of a variety of regional and national accords on refugee protection'.[66]

It is doubtful if it could have achieved all that if it was merely complementary to the *1951 Refugee Convention*.

Secondly, in 1984 ten Latin American States in the *Cartagena Declaration on Refugees*[67] (hereafter *Cartagena Declaration*) drew upon their 'experience' with mass influx in this region, to address the inadequacy of the *1951 Refugee Convention* definition and adopt a defintion that would embrace the many involuntary migrants escaping from generalized violence and oppression in Central America. They argued, 'it was necessary to enlarge' the definition of the term refugee beyond the *Refugee Convention* and *Protocol* and incorporate internal conflict as a root cause of forced migration. Whilst acknowledging the *OAU Refugee Convention* definition as a suitable 'precedent' the *Cartagena Declaration* defined a 'refugee' more expansively to include:

> persons who had fled their country because their lives, safety or freedom have been *threatened by generalized violence*, foreign aggression, *internal conflicts*, massive violation of human rights ... (emphasis added).[68]

In 1985, the General Assembly of the Organization of American States approved this enlarged definition and resolved 'to urge Member States to extend support and, insofar as possible, to implement the conclusions and recommendations of the Cartegena Declaration on Refugees'.[69] In the words of Hathaway, this definition 'acknowledges the legitimacy of claims grounded in the actions of external powers' and 'offers a qualified acceptance of the notions of group determination and claims in which the basis or rationale for harm is indeterminate'. Nevertheless, the big difference with the OAU definition is that, unlike the OAU Convention's 'deference to individuated perceptions of peril' the *Cartegena Declaration* requires that the claimant 'be demonstrably at risk due to generalized disturbance in her country' and it also 'does not explicitly extend protection to persons who flee serious disturbance of public order that affects only part of their country'.[70] In short, 'the OAS definition of refugee status marks something of a compromise between the Convention standard and the very broad OAU conceptualization'.[71]

A NEW CATEGORY OF REFUGEE?

There is no doubt that the trend has been in the last 50 years in favour of recognizing newer categories of refugee wherever such recognition was properly warranted in the absence of state protection in the face of a violation of basic human rights. Thus, the Council of Europe in the Parliamentary Assembly's Recommendation 773 of 1976 drew attention to the existence of '*de facto* refugees', namely, those persons who, whilst meeting the Refugee Convention's criteria, either have not been formally recognized as Convention refugees, or who are, 'unable or unwilling for ... other valid reasons to return to their countries of origin'.[72] The Council of Europe to that end, enjoined Member governments to 'apply liberally the definition of "refugee" in the Convention' and 'not to expel *de facto* refugees unless they will be admitted by another country where they do not run the risk of persecution'.[73] This Recommendation has only been partially implemented.

What all of this suggests are various attempts to give refugee law a contemporary relevance and application. The forces arraigned against this attempt must not, however, be underestimated. Any attempt to expand the refugee definition is going to be fiercely contested by the refugee receiving countries of the world. Even so, by the mid-1986, a person no less than Professor Goodwin-Gill has been able to argue that the collective developments on both the national and international scale point to a new class of refugee being recognized in customary international law. Once persons are placed in imminent danger because their own governments deny them protection in the face of harmful events to which they become subject, the principle of 'non-refoulment' kicks in, argues Goodwin-Gill, and it matters not whether such persons are Convention refugees or not, because they must be given temporary refuge.[74] As he explains:

> … the essentially moral obligation to assist refugees and to provide them with refuge or safe haven has, over time and in certain contexts, developed into a legal obligation (albeit at a relatively low level of commitment). The principle of non-refoulment must now be understood as applying beyond the narrow confines of articles 1 and 33 of the 1951 Refugee Convention.[75]

Goodwin-Gill develops this to say that 'the existence of danger caused by civil disorder, domestic conflicts, or human rights violations generates a valid presumption of humanitarian need' and that 'this has important consequences for … the entitlement to protection of individuals or specific groups'.[76] This idea is strongly opposed by another expert in the refugee field, namely, Professor Kay Hailbronner, who describes this viewpoint as 'wishful legal thinking' declaring that '[t]here is no evidence at all for a generalized recognition of an individual right of humanitarian refugees not to be returned or repatriated'. Indeed, in his opinion, 'states have generally taken care not to narrow the range of possible responses to mass influxes of aliens …'.[77] Hathaway holds to the view that 'Goodwin-Gill's assertion of a right to protection against "refoulment" overstates the extant scope of customary law in regard to non-Convention refugees' because (as Hailbronner argues):

> developed states have felt free to reject members of the broader class of asylum seekers by imposition of visa requirements, penalties on transportation companies, naval blockades, and the establishment of strictly discretionary mechanisms to cope with those asylum seekers who do reach their territory.[78]

There is, however, very little evidence that developed states, faced with persons who are on their territories in imminent danger, are refouling them back to their home countries to be placed in harm's way. Where that happens, it is universally condemned. States may have elaborate systems in place to forestall or prevent the entry of such persons by either making their initial entry difficult or by returning them to a supposedly safe third country. But that still does not mean that moral obligation to assist refugees has not been strengthened. This is done by the application of human rights norms so as to make provision by way of a legal obligation of a refuge or safe haven to persons who would not have qualified under the strict interpretation of articles 1 and 33 of the *1951 Refugee Convention*. Even if Professors Hathaway and Hailbronner are right in their own very different ways, the position in the mid-1980s is markedly different to what it is today in the mid-2000s some 20 years later. In my view, it is the developing canvas of human rights law – to which the interpretation of refugee law throughout the European Union at the very least is now subject – that materially alters the interpretation of international refugee law. This has been dramatically illustrated in the case of *Shah and Islam* in 1999, when Britain's highest court upheld a claim to asylum status on grounds that claimant was a 'member of particular social group' as a Pakistani, which the lower court summarized as follows:

> She cannot return to her husband. She cannot live anywhere in Pakistan without male protection. She cannot seek assistance from the authorities because in Pakistan society women are not believed or they are treated with contempt by the police. If she returns she will be abused and possibly killed.[79]

Thus, it is clear from the above that in modern times, Western Europe has both generated, and accepted as refugees, those individuals with '*a well-founded fear of being persecuted*' for reasons of '*race*', '*religion*', and '*nationality*',[80] whereas non-European countries (as in the case of Africa) have accepted, and generated, as refugees, entire groups of people fleeing from '*events seriously disturbing public order in either part of or the whole of his country of origin or nationality*',[81] or (as in the case of some Latin American States[82] from '*generalized violence*',[83] which category western countries certainly have not been willing to accept as refugees. Alongside this have been other attempts, such as by the Council of Europe in 1977, to give recognition to '*de facto* refugees' and those non-Convention Refugees who have 'other valid reasons' not to return to their country of origin. The definition of a 'refugee', is thus a term of art and as such it remains an elusive and slippery concept. Different drafters have been adopting different formulations in order to achieve different kinds of purposes.

As early as the seventeenth century, national legislatures had begun to define 'refugees' amid a corpus of emerging drafts of nationality legislation,[84] although the international legal treaties only arose in the twentieth century on refugees. During the inter-war period in the twentieth century, there were a number of differing attempts to define specific groups of 'refugees' and these have been well described by Professor James Hathaway, as consisting of three groups of definitions and approaches. Thus, between 1920–1935, there was the 'juridical' approach comprising a group-based definition, whose membership, according to the international community, would deprive a 'refugee' of governmental protection. Between 1935–1939, there was the 'social' approach, applied predominantly to those fleeing Nazi persecution, and designed to ensure provision of international assistance for the safety of the 'refugee'. Finally, between 1938–1950, there was the 'individulist' approach, which priortized the individualized consideration of each case on the basis of its merits through systematic examination, with due regard to any perceived injustice or fundamental incompatibility of the 'refugee' with his home state, and the concomitant abandonment of a determination procedure based on political and social categories.[85] This suggests that by the time of the drafting of the *1951 Convention* by the international community, there was no axiomatic reason why one particular approach should be favoured over another, since there were at least three different approaches that had been used in the space of a few decades.

Yet, even at the time of the drafting of the *1951 Convention*, there was recognition of the existence of, what may be called 'humanitarian refugees', which is why it is wrong to suggest as Kristen Walker does, that:

there is a plausible argument for placing the needs of persosn persecuted for arbitrary reasons, such as race, religion, political opinion or membership in a particular social group, ahead of claims from persons with more generalized needs.[86]

There were already in existence 'mandate refugees' the best known of which were the Palestinian refugees from the 1947 exodus. Neither particularized violence nor persecution were requirements here. Palestinian refugees were victims of generalized violence and they could not point to a particular persecutor as such. Yet, they fell under the protective mantle of the UNHCR. So as to ensure that other deserving cases were not left out in the cold, the 'good offices' of the UNHCR were also used from 1957 onwards to assist 'refugees who do not come within the competence of the United Nations'. In this way, even those who had not crossed external borders into the territory of another state, such as 'displaced persons' were by 1975 brought under the cloak of the UNHCR's 'good offices' while still failing to qualify as Convention Refugees.[87] Such 'refugees' were apparently both distinct and indistinct from 'asylum-seekers' which was a category of migrant who emerged in Europe in the 1970s as 'a kind of position of suspense' in the figurative language of Jerzy Sztucki, 'subject to the outcome of screening which leads to the recognition as a refugee'.[88] The confluence of all these different migrant groups led to the UNHCR in 1996 to declare that the label 'refugee' could be applied to:

> (i) those recognized as such by states party to the Convention and/or Protocol; (ii) those recognized as such under the OAU Convention and the Cartegena Declaration; (iii) those recognized by UNHCR as 'mandate refugees'; (iv) those granted residence on humanitarian grounds; and (v) those granted temporary protection on a group basis.[89]

One of the perennial questions of modern-day refugee law is whether the *1951 UN Convention* remains applicable to today's global migration crisis. They clearly do not cover much of the world's humanitarian refugees, as distinct from 'political', 'racial', or 'religious refugees'.

This can have crucial implications for refugee protection. For example, a recent British Home office decision, observed that:

> Jamaica is reported to have one of the highest crime and murder rates in the world. In 2001 more than 1,100 murders were recorded in Jamaica. The National Security Minister, Dr. Phillips, has noted that the breakdown of the statistics shows that reprisal and drug/gang related killings constitute the highest percentage of murders in the country.[90]

However, the applicant's claim for asylum was rejected when he alleged to have 'a well-founded fear of persecution in Jamaica from local criminals' on the grounds that this amounted to mistreatment on non-convention grounds and therefore, 'not one that engages the United Kingdom's obligations under the Convention'.[91] As a matter of law, this decision was clearly right for under the applicable law, an asylum-seeker who claims to be in fear of persecution is only entitled to asylum if he can show a well-founded fear of persecution for a Refugee Convention reason and that there would be insufficiency of state protection to meet it.[92]

THE IMPORTANCE OF DEFINING REFUGEES

Nevertheless, the crucial question is not *how* we define refugees, but *why* we define them the way we do. In another words, why do we have a definition of refugees of the type that we do? What is it intended to do, and for whom? Professor Guy S. Goodwin-Gill helpfully reminds us that 'the main purpose of any definition or description of the class of refugees is to facilitate, and to justify, aid and protection'.[93] But to justify for whom, and in whose interests? Emma Haddad, in a perceptive analysis explains that '[t]he refugee "problem" is, first and foremost, one of categorization, of making distinctions'. As she explains, this is important because none of the discussions in the field – among politicians, policy workers or academics – can proceed without an idea of who exactly we are talking about when we use the label "refugee"'.[94] So, labels have become all important. They are indispensable. Without labels, as the argument runs, the refugee cannot be marked out indelibly for special consideration by the international community. She draws upon Roger Zetter who explains that:

> [w]ithin the repertoire of humanitarian concern, refugee now constitutes one of the most powerful labels. From the first procedure of status determination – who is a refugee? – to the structural determinants of life chances which this identity then engenders, labels infuse the world of refugees.[95]

For him, 'labelling matters so fundamentally' and 'a non-labelled way out cannot exist'.[96] Yet, which kind of label is one to use? As Emma Haddad herself notes, 'the actual meaning behind the concept "refugee" is anything but self-evident'[97] and that '[a] look at the literature shows a multitude of definitions, some legal, some sociological and some anthropological'.[98]

What I find interesting is that the UNHCR itself does not appear to have deemed labels to be fundamentally decisive. Its *Handbook of Refugees*, states that 'a person is a refugee … as soon as he fulfills the [refugee] criteria' of the *1951 Convention*, and that:

> [r]ecognition of his refugee status does not … make him a refugee but declares him to be one. He does not become a refugee because of recognition, but is recognized because he is a refugee.[99]

The question should be reformulated as not one of 'labelling' but as one of 'conceptualizing' in much the same way as the *OAU Convention* and the *Cartegena Declaration* sets out to conceptualize refugees. Labelling through language is problematic not least because language itself is inherently limited as a medium of communication. Labelling does not tell us how best to conceptualize refugees. Not everything we see and feel can be reduced to words. Labeling refugees through language is necessarily limiting. In the words of

Zolberg *et al.*, 'language serves to mystify rather than clarify the social processes it depicts' particularly with a concept like that of a 'refugee' where 'standard refugee lexicon is highly normative and thus self-evidently legitimizing'.[100] This is recognized by Zetter who states, that there are 'severe conceptual difficulties in establishing a normative meaning to a label which is as malleable and dynamic as a refugee'.[101]

Refugees are a phenomenon. They should be understood as a phenomenalism. Labelling does not do justice to the inherent complexity of refugee phenomenon. The result, as Michael Dillon observes, is that the refugee, 'while categorizable, nonetheless exceeds categorization'.[102] Even where we establish criteria for the recognition of refugees, we do not escape the problem of categorization because the concept of refugees is inherently complex 'with a broad and variable set of criteria but each criterion itself is relatively complex and open'.[103] Connolly says that the term 'refugee' is 'a cluster concept to which a broad range of criteria apply'[104] because if we swirl around the 'ingredients' of 'persecution', 'international', 'state' and 'forced' in a mixer, we will come up with a 'refugee'. A 'cluster concept', however, has other concepts such as 'state', 'sovereignty' and 'protection' and for the cluster concept to be meaningful, these other concepts too must be clear.[105] With concepts like 'persecution' and 'sovereignty' which, as Zetter, explains are themselves highly contested, this becomes difficult.[106] The definition of a refugee is subject to controversy because it can never be determined outside normative considerations. As Connolly explains, this controversy is not:

> just *about* the concepts of politics but [is] *part of* politics itself ... for to get others to accept my account of any appraisive concept is to implicate them in *judgements* to which I am committed and to encourage political activity congruent with those commitments.[107]

It is for this reason that I say the relevant question is 'Whose refugee?' and not 'Who is a refugee?'. It is because, as Connolly says the word, 'refugee' is an 'essentially contested concept'.[108] In this cauldron, as Emma Haddad observes:

> [t]he problem becomes one of how to define a concept that is labelled differently according to context and discipline. How to name a concept which by definition defies definition, since it is impossible to generalize about the vast array of horrific events that force individuals to become refugees?

It seems to me, however, that this is precisely the reason why we should avoid setting out to define something that is undefinable. What we need is a definition that is both wide enough and narrow enough to cover the humanitarian refugee. The OAU definition with its focus on massive conflicts, human rights violations, external aggression and occupation does this. It enables the vast array of horrific events to which refugees are subject to be taken into account. Yet, as Emma Haddad emphasizes there has to be 'a working definition of the term "refugee"' because, as she explains:

[w]ithout a clear understanding of who, broadly we are talking about, however general we choose to keep this 'who', we cannot expect to further our grasp of how refugee flows occur and how to attempt to solve them ...[109]

However, the foundational document of the human rights movement, the Universal Declaration of Human Rights, only declares that, 'Everyone has the right to seek and to enjoy in other countries asylum from persecution'[110] thereby signifying that the right to claim asylum is not to be restricted to any particular type of person.

It may well of course, be asked why it is necessary to conceptualize refugees at all in that case? Why have a concept of refugee status? Why do so given a state-based international system with the sovereign right to exclude? There are a number of reasons why states may wish to exclude non-citizens. They range from Michael Walzer who even finds restrictions on immigration to be justifiable on the basis that 'restraint of entry' protects the 'politics and culture of a group of people committed to one another and to a shared life'[111] to Kristen Walker who writes that:

it is legitimate for states to impose restrictions on immigration. States owe duties to their citizens – such as protection from violence, an adequate standard of living, the opportunity to participate in community decision-making and so on. States cannot fulfill these functions unless they can control who may enter and become members of the community – if the number of members becomes too great, a state may cease to be able to provide such services to all its citizens.[112]

Whatever, the various reasons, Jacqueline Bhabha, one of the most foremost thinkers in the field of asylum law and policy, explains that 'the institution of asylum' acts as a 'filtering process that is designed to separate eligible from ineligible travelers' and 'is constructed to be a strictly limited humanitarian safety valve, permitting only a fraction of would-be migrants, the discrete class of 'genuine' refugees, to trump immigration restrictions and gain access to the developed world'.[113] This is similar to Roger Zetter's observation when he observed that the label 'refugee' applies to one 'who conforms to institutional requirements' where the purpose of the label is merely to serve as 'linguistic shorthand for policies, programmes and bureaucratic requirements'.[114] This is unsurprising given that, as David Martin notes, the refugee status is a 'scarce resource'[115]. Not everyone can be given it. Bhabha quotes from David Held, who writes that asylum acts as a 'bridge between morality and law',[116] and she explains how the institution of asylum has the effect of:

entrenching a regime of international sovereignty and solidarity within an increasingly harsh and discriminatory state-based system. 'Genuine' refugees are to be sifted out from the mass of 'illegal' migrants who purport to be eligible for international protection but are not, and are increasingly perceived as a danger to the security, cohesion and well-being of destination states. Asylum is the process that keeps migration exclusion morally defensible while protecting the global gate-keeping operation as a whole.[117]

Yet, it is questionable that it is even doing that if it is discriminatory in the protection it affords to individuals and if it leaves large swathes of mankind's suffering multitude untouched by asylum law. As Bhabha herself recognizes, the current 'system produces benefits for a somewhat arbitrarily selected minority of forced migrants'.[118] This is because:

> while thousands of applicants gain refugee status or some form of subsidiary humanitarian protection, tens of thousands live in a limbo of illegality without access to basic civil rights.[119]

REMOVING 'PERSECUTION' AND 'FLAGRANT BREACH'

Given these concerns, refugee law today is an attempt by the international community to reconcile two irreconcilables: humanitarian need on the one hand, and sovereign state control on the other. Thus, in the words of Bhabha:

> [f]rom the outset, the refugee protection regime was intended to be restrictive and partial, a compromise between unfettered state sovereignty over the admission of aliens, and an open door for non-citizen victims of serious human rights violations.[120]

Even as a compromise, it was a partial compromise. The *Refugee Convention* did not cover all forced migrations. As such, it was, and is, less than morally defensible. As Bhabha explains, '[I]t was always clear that only a subset of forced transnational migrant persecutees were intended beneficiaries'.[121] Thus, the priortisation of civil and political rights in the *1951 Convention*, which defines a refugee as a person who:

> owing to a well-founded fear of being persecuted for reasons of race, religion, nationality, membership of a particular social group or political opinion, is outside the country of his nationality and is unable or, owing to such fear, is unwilling to avail himself of the protection of the country.[122]

clearly does not include an emphasis on the woes of clan-based, tribalistic societies subject to generalized violence and economic impoverishment in a collapsed state system, like much of Africa and the Middle East today. As Bhabha explains:

> [t]his definition clearly excludes those forced to flee because of personal vendettas and private feuds, non-discriminatory economic duress, famine, or internal civil turmoil – in short, those whose persecution is not based on some form of egregious systemic discrimination or rights violation.[123]

Indeed, what do we mean by 'persecution' and why should a person facing a flagrant denial of his or her basic human rights have to prove 'persecution' before qualifying for international surrogate protection? How do lawyers, using court-room skills, give a legally verifiable meaning to 'persecution'?

While stipulating a requirement of 'persecution' the Refugee Convention leaves its contours unspecified. The pioneering refugee scholar, James Hathaway, described 'persecution,' as 'the exclusive benchmark for international refugee status',[124] but as Bhabha observes, this is 'not a well-circumscribed legal concept'.[125] The *Refugee Convention* chooses not to define it, preferring to face-lift it from the previous international refugee regime. It is 'a familiar term and a useful western tool', but most importantly, its value lies in the fact that it is 'flexible enough to cover the circumstances of both victims of Nazism, and Soviet and other eastern dissidents fleeing a polarized Cold War'. The important question, however, is whether it would be flexible enough to also fit the circumstances of the rest of the world, less immediately apparent and pressing on Western Europe. Bhabha rightly points out that:

> the advantage of this somewhat elusive standard was less apparent in a changed era, when foreign policy considerations no longer dominated the selection of worthy recipients of refugee protection to the same extent as in the past.[126]

Yet, even before the end of the Cold War – even while victims of race, religion and nationality persisted – there was concern over the test of 'persecution'. In his classic, 'Who is a Refugee' in 1983, Andrew Shacknove, stated that persecution is simply one manifestation of a much larger notion of the absence of state protection of the citizen's basic needs. Other forms of state action or inaction could equally constitute a threat to a person's physical security.[127] This suggests that individual threat could materialize across a range of governmental responses, from how it deals with environmental disasters to how it deals with the allocation of economic resources. It covers the condition of the humanitarian refugee. For Shacknove, the centrality of the state and its policy-making is crucial when determining the causes of refugee flows. Accordingly, Shacknove concludes that refugees are those people:

> whose government fails to protect their basic needs, who have no remaining recourse other than to seek international restitution of those needs, and who are so situated that international assistance is possible.[128]

The reference to people 'who are so situated' is important because the requirement of alienage, namely, that a refugee must have crossed an international border before acquiring the designation 'refugee' is a condition precedent for the application of the Refugee Convention.

On this basis, if one were to take a current example from the present decade, those subject to ethnic cleansing in Darfur, Sudan, in 2005, are not refugees, because they have yet to cross an international border. If one were to take a past example, those subject to ethnic cleansing in the last decade, in Kosovo, in 1995, are refugees because they were able to cross borders. Shacknove, however, rejects this distinction maintaining that what is relevant is the physical access of the international community to the unprotected person and that the actual crossing of an international frontier by the unprotected person *per se*, is irrelevant to his status as a refugee. In my view, this is clearly right given the globalization of rights issues – in much the same way as there has been the globalization of health, development, and resource issues – in the world today. Indeed, an over-concentration on the state-system with fixed borders is increasingly inapposite in a world with a growing number of failing and corroded states with porous borders. As Shacknove explains:

> [w]hether a person travels 10 miles across an international border or the same distance down the road into a neighbouring province may be crucial for determining logistical and diplomatic action [otherwise] conceptually ... refugeehood is unrelated to migration ...[129]

This fits in with Shacknove's fundamental premises. The *Refugee Convention 1951*, he says, is predicated on four assumptions that tie the state to its citizen and it is the severing of that tie which mandates surrogate international protection. These are the bonds of trust, loyalty, protection, and assistance.[130] Neither the requirement of persecution nor of alienage are a *sine qua non* of the severing of the bond between the citizen and his state, though both may be an illustration of that.

Where I think Shacknove's erudite analysis, has limited legal utility is in his description of a refugee as a person 'whose government fails to protect their basic needs', for how is a court of law to determine this? And, may it not suggest a standard so low, which despite being humane, would be unacceptable to refugee receiving countries? A shanty-town dweller may go hungry one day, may be unable to access vital medical treatment periodically, and may be exposed to occasional bouts of sporadic violence, but unless these infractions are flagrant or sustained or gross, it may be difficult to make out a case for international surrogate protection. Shacknove could also be criticized, it seems to me, for overly-focusing on the state-system and the role of the state, in addressing the needs of refugees. His implication is that it is state action that necessarily always causes refugee flows. However, this fails to take due account of environmental catastrophes and other natural and economic disasters generating refugees, where the bond of trust, loyalty, and even assistance, may yet still be unbroken between citizen and state.

It is this which calls into question the requirement of 'persecution' since one of the most fundamental criticisms of the *1951 Refugee Convention* is that it is unclear on what constitutes persecution. Critics assert that emphasis on the individual negates the concept of 'group persecution'. This criticism, however, is unfair. While the UNHCR in its *Handbook on Refugee Status*, makes it clear that there is no universally accepted definition of persecution, this does not mean that there is no internationally acceptable criteria for determining whether a person has a 'well-founded fear of persecution'.[131] In the 1980s, Melander observed that there was a growing tendency to refer to basic human rights as a set of criteria for defining persecution. In other words, that the applicant fears the violation of his or her basic human rights. These human rights violations need not only include civil and political rights, but also economic, social and cultural rights violations. According to Melander, the existing human rights instruments may also be used by the UNHCR as a means of assistance to interpret 'persecution'. For instance, the *Universal Declaration on Human Rights of 1948* and the *International Covenant on Civil and Political Rights of 1976*[132] provide good guidelines, when persecution is involved.

A person who fears arbitrary detention, contrary to Article 9 of the *Universal Declaration*, may be persecuted. The same applies to a person who fears punishment, contrary to Article 19 of the *Universal Declaration*. Melander notes that all substantive articles of the *Declaration* can be used to understand the meaning of 'persecution'. However, this could lead to a very broad understanding of who a refugee is, depending on how expansive the basic rights are. Therefore, it is also stipulated that not every person who has been or will be faced with a human rights violation in his country of origin will be considered to be a refugee. An important prerequisite is that the violation must reach a certain degree of severity in order to be considered as persecution. An arbitrary arrest must be for a certain period of time to fulfill the criterion. Thus, the continued incarceration of Moshood Abiola in a Lagos jail for more than three years would warrant preferential treatment under the refugee regime; the overnight imprisonment of a Nigerian journalist critical of the Abacha regime would not.

European human rights law now requires there to be a 'flagrant denial or gross violation'[133] of a right before an international remedy can be said to be forthcoming against an offending state. What is 'flagrant' and what is 'gross' and whether these are to be determined with scientific precision or are mere terms of art, is an altogether more difficult question, and one which may be an unrealistically high threshold for humanitarian refugees to reach. This is especially so given that in addition, the human rights violation must also be motivated by one or more of the five causes of persecution mentioned in the 1951 Convention: race, religion, nationality, membership of a particular social group, or political opinion.[134] In the British case of *Ullah and Do*,[135] Lord Bingham in the House of Lords explained that:

> The reason why flagrant denial or gross violation is to be taken into account is that it is only in such a case – where the right will be completely denied or nullified in the destination country – that it can be said that removal will breach the treaty obligation of the signatory state however those obligations might be interpreted or whatever might be said by or on behalf of the destination state.[136]

Yet, whereas it may be argued that only a 'flagrant' violation by a contracting State of the *Refugee Convention* may put it in breach of its international obligations, it does not follow that the violation of the putative refugee's rights have to be in 'flagrant denial or gross violation' before he can qualify for refugee status under the *Refugee Convention*. At any rate, this overlooks the plight of humanitarian refugees. Why should the right 'be completely denied or nullified' before one can say there is persecution?

In the early 1990s, Professor James Hathaway trenchantly argued that the definition of 'persecution' should be located and understood in the context of the evolving human rights regime. In his path-breaking, *The Law of Refugee Status*, he argued that the *Refugee Convention* would become 'a mere anachronism'[137] unless the concept of persecution was reconceived and to this end he proposed that it be defined as 'the sustained or systemic violation of basic human rights demonstrative of a failure of state protection'.[138] This formulation has met with widespread approval, from Professor Goodwin-Gill to the European Commission. Yet, it is noteworthy that it is not the same as a 'flagrant denial or gross violation' of human rights, which is an altogether more stricter test. Bhabha observes of Hathaway's formulation that:

> [T]his suggestion proved influential: advocates, judges, even governments, seized on it and it has now become an orthodoxy within refugee jurisprudence.[139]

Hathaway's suggestion, in my view, clearly underscored the point that the *Refugee Convention* suffered from its euro-centric bias and was not universal. Whilst the attempt to give 'persecution' real practical value by placing it in the context of developing human rights law was clearly essential, I do not accept that any violation of basic human rights needs to be 'sustained' for the *Refugee Convention* to apply. Many extreme forms of violations of human rights are one-off violations against individuals. In *Demirkaya*, the Court of Appeal in Britain, whilst accepting Professor Hathaway's analysis that 'persecution is a question of degree' went onto hold that a single instance of ill-treatment can amount to persecution by declaring that:

> [a]t one end of the scale there may be arbitrary deprivation of life, torture and cruel, inhuman and degrading punishment or treatment. In such a case the conduct may be so extreme that one instance is sufficient.[140]

This seems to be difficult to square with the requirement of a 'sustained' breach – although it may satisfy the standard of a 'flagrant denial or gross violation' of human rights!

On the other hand, the requirement of a 'flagrant denial or gross violation' of human rights may itself be difficult to apply. The oft-neglected British case of *Jeyakumaran*[141] is instructive in this respect. The applicant in this case was a Tamil citizen of Sri Lanka who was given leave to enter the UK as a student for 12 months in January 1975. Subsequently, his leave was extended to September 1982, whereupon he left for Sri Lanka. On July 24th 1983, race riots broke out in Colombo. The applicant was beaten up. His family home was looted. He spent a fortnight in a refugee camp. The Tamil minority were being harassed and the army were said to be looking for Tamil youngsters. The applicant travelled to the UK and claimed asylum. The Secretary of State decided that the applicant did not qualify for asylum since (1) the applicant's family had not been singled out for persecution; (2) the applicant's position was no different from other Tamils; (3) neither the applicant nor his family had ever engaged in political activity; and (4) recent violence had been more in the nature of a conflict between factions than persecution of individuals. On an application for judicial review in the High Court, it was held that the Secretary of State's decision to remove the applicant, was an error of law for the following reasons. First, that an applicant may qualify for asylum even though neither he nor his family members had been singled out for persecution. Second, that the violence flowing from a conflict between factions may amount to persecution even though that conflict was not condoned by the authorities. Third, that political activity on the part of an applicant for asylum status was not necessarily a critical factor in determining whether the applicant had refugee status. Finally, that the Secretary of State, in coming to the decision in the manner that he did, had taken irrelevant factors into account and had not taken relevant factors into account. This case throws into doubt many of the core requirements of the *Refugee Convention*, such as the need to show 'persecution', on a Convention ground such as 'political opinion', that did not stem from 'generalized violence', and in which 'state authorities' did not have a part to play. It is also a case that would provide clear protection to those fleeing from human rights violations from Failed States.

Criticism of the requirement of individual persecution as a sole cause of external flight before grant of refugee status, was also made in 1989 in the seminal work, *Escape from Violence: Conflict and the refugee crisis in the developing world* by the highly respected authors, Zolberg, Suhrke and Aguayo.[142] They argued that what made people flee from their countries was generally 'a well-founded fear of violence'[143] and not persecution *per se*, and this was true whether one was looking at the causes of flight of an activist, a target, or a mere victim. Moreover, it was factually wrong to conceive of persecution as something entirely internal to states that precipitated an external exodus. This is because, 'persecution is related to broad historical processes in which complex internal and external forces interact'.[144] Zolberg *et al.* argued that the well-founded fear of violence may by direct or indirect; it may be the result of internal or external conflict; it may even have resulted quite simply from the imposition of intolerable conditions that made existence impossible in the home state. But the crucial feature was the violence it did to the fleeing person in question. 'Violence' was to be conceived broadly. It had an amorphous definition. Where a person's flight was triggered by the risk of harm or an expulsion order, that itself was a form of violence.[145] In this way, refugees could be conceived of as 'a category of unfortunates' whose plight could only be ameliorated by sanctuary in another state, thereby acquiring 'a strong claim to a very special form of assistance, including temporary or permanent asylum in the territory of states of which they are not members'.[146]

WHOSE REFUGEE?

It is trite that the conceptualization of refugees requires both a political choice and an ethical judgment.[147] If one holds to the view, however, that the label of refugee is reserved to a person who can only be protected under the aegis of another state, then one can begin to develop 'an approach to the problem of refugees grounded on the distinctive and urgent needs of the people concerned'.[148] In this way, Zolberg *et al.* were able to incorporate ethical considerations into the definition of refugee status. However, in my view, whereas, the concentration on the 'distinctive and urgent needs of the people concerned' is clearly essential for an ethically sustainable refugee policy, the description of refugees by Zolberg *et al.* as 'a category of unfortunates' is over-broad and also of limited legal utility. It would not, as it stands, be acceptable to the refugee receiving countries of the affluent North. What western governments prefer is a more legally workable definition which allows them to limit the number of people that can have access to the scarce commodity that we call 'refugee' and this means the imposition of a requirement that the human rights violations to be manifest, flagrant or gross. Otherwise, the primary duty of protection should, according to western jurisprudence, still lie with the state of the person's nationality.

This is because there is concern that broadening the refugee definition, in particular by the removal of the requirement to show 'persecution' will have wide-ranging implications beyond the mere admission of more refugees into safe countries. It is argued that there could be adverse impacts on domestic stability. Borders will be thrown open. Prosperous and politically stable polities will see their national boundaries quickly traversed by a flood of people who will swamp in from impoverished and authoritarian states. Since the majority of the world's people do not live in stable liberal democracies, they will be drawn by the attraction of those states that do protect human rights and meet the fundamental needs of their members, but who are unfortunately far fewer in number. According to Myron Weiner, who strongly opposes such an expansion of the refugee definition, by the mid-1990s the existing 1951 Refugee Convention definition already enabled 18.9 million of the world's migrants to be classified as refugees.[149] For Weiner:[150]

> There are, however, several legitimate objections to broadening the definition of refugees. If acts of discrimination short of persecution are the basis of claiming asylum, a large part of the world's population could do so. Asylum on the basis of discrimination could plausibly be claimed, for example, by over a hundred million Indian Muslims whose mosque at Ayodhya was destroyed and who were fearful after many Muslims in Bombay and elsewhere were killed by Hindus. Millions of women around the world could similarly point to discriminatory restrictions imposed by their state or society as justification for seeking asylum. Moreover, a country that does not want its minorities could engage in systematic discrimination and impel countries that embrace a liberal conception of refugees to admit all whose human rights have been violated. The more liberal democratic states and international agencies become in granting asylum to persecuted minorities, the greater the inducement for a nationalist regime to engage in some form of ethnic cleansing.

Weiner illustrates this by reference to the relations between the US and Cuba. The practice of the US for many years had been to automatically grant refugee status to all those who fled from the Communist regime in Havana. Fidel Castro took a perverse advantage of this fact. Opening up the jails and mental asylums in Cuba, he encouraged criminals and psychopaths to enter the US. When these undesirables began to stream across the shores, the US government anxiously clamped down and withdrew its policy of affording refugee status to all Cubans nationals. In this way, Weiner argues that individuals who have been granted refugee status are in a privileged category. The grant of refugee status allows people to move to a safe country for protection and assistance. Weiner argues that it is for governments to decide to whom they must accord the entitlement of refugee status and how generous that entitlement should be. The broader the definition and the greater the entitlements, the more refugees will enter such a country.[151] The cost of supporting these refugees must mainly be carried by the host government.

There are, however, a number of difficulties with this ostensibly attractive argument. First, the US policy to grant asylum status to all and sundry from Cuba was wrong in the first place, because there was no examination of individual merits. Second, that policy of the grant of automatic refugee status to all Cubans was simply an extension of US foreign policy (which policy changed after the fall of the Communist Soviet Union) into its domestic refugee policy to treat as Convention refugees all those who were fleeing from communist regimes. Thirdly, the cynical attempt by Castro to exploit this free-for-all US policy by opening up his jails and mental hospitals to emigration, obviously did not work once US officials began looking at the individual merits of each case and applying the test of serious violations of human rights to those cases. It is moreover, no different from any other cynical attempt by a private individual to claim a public benefit to which he is not entitled and for which he does not qualify. That is why we have exacting procedures in place to sift out the deserving from the undeserving. Finally, applying those tests does not in any way detract from the principle that the refugee status is indeed a privileged category. It only raises the question how that privileged category should be defined.

The *Refugee Convention* is problematic in other ways. It is not clear which reasons for persecution on one of the five posited grounds that comprise the refugee definition, will be acceptable and which reasons will not be. Clearly, the three persecutory grounds of race, and religion and nationality are relatively easy to comprehend and consequently require less by way of interpretative aids. However, the grounds of 'political opinion' and 'membership of a social group' have been far more challenging, requiring certain identifiable parameters to be workable. This has been a major issue in recent years.[152] Moreover, both these grounds are amongst the most over-worked in the refugee definition: 'political opinion' has in the past attracted by far the largest number of asylum applications, while 'membership of a social group' looks set to rival that in the future, as more and more classes of women from different parts of the world, and more and more minority practices, get recognition as 'social groups'. This is nowhere better put than by Bhabha when she asks rhetorically:

> What types of opinion count as political (neutrality? pacifism? opinions imputed by the persecutor but which the persecutee may not hold?)? How should one construe the broad, open-ended, amorphous category of 'particular social group' (is a sense of group belonging essential? do broad demographic characteristics such as gender or age qualify? do characteristics that are chosen rather than innate or immutable qualify?)? As pressure to expand the scope of refugee protection has increased, so the impetus to broaden the scope of these terms has grown.[153]

It is, however, in my view, one thing to say that there has been pressure to expand the scope of refugee protection; quite another to say that such pressure has brought real dividends to the world's most oppressed and imperiled people.

In my view, there is as much reason to believe (if not more) that all such pressure to expand the scope of refugee protection is being resisted by powerful affluent countries of the northern hemisphere – which are setting up diversionary tactics to forestall the arrival of new arrivals – as there is reason to believe that it is providing better and more secure protection to people hitherto rendered invisible to the *Refugee Convention*. A good example is the requirement that the violation of human rights must reach a level of severity such that it is a 'flagrant denial or gross violation'.[154] What is 'flagrant' or 'gross' may not be characterized by the intensity of the act itself but simply by the fact that particular societies come to regard particular actions as unacceptable infringements of human rights. As Bhabha points out there was a time in the 1990s when during an 'expansionist phase of asylum advocacy' it was established that 'forcible sterilization or mandatory veiling might count as persecution'.[155] Yet, neither are arguably 'flagrant' if the approach of the Canadian Refugee Appeals Board in a 1993 case are anything to go by. In that case, it did itself less than credit, when it decided a forced sterilization case from China by declaring that:

> [T]he possibility of coercion in the implementation of the policy is not sufficient to make it one of persecution. I do not feel it is my purpose to tell the Chinese government how to run its economic affairs.[156]

Mercifully, this decision was over-ruled by an appellate court which thundered that, '[B]rutality in furtherance of a legitimate end is still brutality'.[157] There was no requirement that the acts complained of had to be 'flagrant' or 'gross'. It was just assumed that they were.

Yet, if the requirement of 'brutality' alone suffices then there are many societies in the world that are brutalized. From this perspective, it would be arguable that '[D]iscriminatory state policies that result in food insecurity, high incidences of HIV/AIDS infection, water deprivation, oil pollution, land flooding for particular populations or subsections of the population, might all count as persecution, though this approach has yet to be developed' not least because '[I]t highlights the fundamentally problematic distinction between "genuine" and "economic" refugees'[158] as Bhabha explains. As she states, asylum law today needs recognize 'within the protective mantel of asylum new categories of rights bearers – women, children, sex workers, even "terrorists" in a climate of xenophobic exclusion'.[159] Yet, this only serves to underscore the removal of labels in refugee law and the overwhelming importance of human rights protections for the world's wretched and destitute. If the language of refugee law were changed it would be possible to disagree with the statement by Bhabha that 'economic desperation itself cannot be a basis for claiming asylum'.[160] It was after all, not too long ago, and within living memory, that the economically desperate from across the Iron Curtain were given refuge in the West's democracies. But then, they were quintessentially their refugees.

NOTES

1   See *UNHCR Statute* (art 6A(i)) and *Refugee Convention* (art 1A(1)) for a complete list.
2   *Refugee Convention* art 1A(2) and *High Commissioner's Statute* art 6(ii).
3   See Paul Weis, 'The International Status of Refugees and Stateless Persons' (1956) 1 *Journal du droit International* 4 citing a 'Report of the Ad Hoc Committee on Refugees and Stateless Persons', which drew up the *Convention* UN Doc E/1618, p.38, which stated: 'It would be difficult for Governments to sign a blank cheque and to undertake obligations towards future refugees, the origin and number of whom would be unknown' (at 30).
4   There is a great deal of academic writing expressing similar sentiments see, for instance: Atle Grahl-Madsen, 'The Emergent International Law Relating to Refugees: Past-Present-Future', in Institute of Public International Law and International Relations of Thessaloniki, *Refugee Problem on Universal, Regional and National Level* (ed.), Vol. XIII (Thessaloniki, 1987) 169 at 190; Paul Weis, 'The 1967 Protocol Relating to the Status of Refugees and Some Questions of the Law of Treaties' (1967) *British YBIL* 39 at 40; Paul Weis, 'The Office of the United Nations High Commissioner for Refugees', *Revue de Droit International et Compare* 243 at 247.
5   See Goran Melander, 'Further Development of International Refugee Law', in Institute of Public International Law and International Relations of Thessaloniki, *Refugee Problem on Universal, Regional and National Level* (ed.), Vol. XIII (Thessaloniki, 1987) 473 at 484 arguing stating: 'The [Refugee] Convention was considered to be a European agreement, which dealt with a European problem. The African states wanted to draw up an instrument, which took into consideration the fact that in Africa there were new categories of refugees who were compelled to leave their country of origin without being persecuted for reasons mentioned in the 1951 Refugee Convention'.
6   31 January 1967, 606 U.N.T.S. 267 (entered into force 4 Oct 1967).
7   See art 1(2).
8   For a discussion of the current state of the law under the 1950 Convention, see the useful compilation of essays in Susan Kneebone (ed.), *The Refugees Convention 50 Years On* (Ashgate Publishing Limited, Aldershot, 2003).
9   In the well known New Zealand case of *King-Ansell*, it was said of 'race' that 'It is a meaning which is concerned, not with genetic processes, but with shared characteristics of a socio-political nature such as customs, philosophy and thought, history, traditions, nationality, language or residence without any reference to biological considerations': per Woodhouse, J., in *King-Ansell v. Police* [1979] 2NZLR 531, NZCA at p.533, line 50.
10 Indeed, race includes '... all persons of identifiable ethnicity ...': see J. Hathaway, *The Law of Refugee Status* (LexisNexis Canada, 1991), at p.141.
11 Thus, the Federal Court of Canada in one case reprimanded the Refugee Division for taking the view that a Ms Pluharova was not dark skinned enough to qualify under the racial ground, holding: '[I]t is inherently dangerous for the Board members to base a finding on whether people in another country would regard a claimant as of particular ethnicity solely on the basis of the members' observa-

tion of the person concerned ... since Ms Pluharova had black hair and a 'sun tanned' apprearance, the panel's "common sense" was an insufficiently reliable basis for the panel's assessment of such a sensitive matter': per Evan, J., in *Pluharova v. Canada (Minister for Citizenship and Immigration)* (MM-5334-98; 27 August 1999).

12   Thus, persecution on racial grounds can occur even from members of one's own racial group. The Federal Court of Australia in *Perampalam* explained that: '[T]he words "persecuted for reasons of" look to the motives and attitudes of the persecutors (see Ram at 569), and if the LTTE practices extortion, with violence and threats of violence, against Tamils, the government being unable to provide protection, because the LTTE holds, that Tamils must be coerced into supporting it, the terms of the Conventin are satisfied': per Burchett, J., in *Perampalam v. Minister of Immigration and Multicultural Affairs* (1999) 55 ALD. This was also supported by the US Court of appeal in *Maini* when it was said that, '[T]hat a person shares an identity with a persecutor does not, in other words, foreclose a claim of persecution on account of a protected ground ...': per Ferguson, C.J. in *Maini v. Immigration and Naturalization Service* (No. 98-70894) (9ᵗʰ Circuit 2000).

13   As the Federal Court of Australia explained in *Zheng*, '[F]or my part I am prepared to accept that the prohibition legally to practice one's religion could, and probably would, constitute persecution on religious grounds for the purposes of the Convention': per Hill, J., in *Zheng v. Minister for Immigration and Multicultural Affairs* [2000] FCA 50. Although less easy to prove, limitations upon religion (as distinct from a complete ban) may still be persecutory as explained by the Federal Court of Canada in its criticism of the Refugee Division, '... the Refugee Division unduly limited the concept of religious practice, confining it to "praying to God or studying the Bible". The fact is that the right to freedom of religion also includes the freedom to demonstrate one's religion or belief in public or private by teaching, practice, worship and the performance of rites. [Accordingly], it seems that persecution of the practice of religion can take various forms ...': per Denault, J., in *Fosu v. Canada (Minister of Employment and Immigration)* (1990) 90 F.T.R. 182.

14   The US Court of Appeals in *Bastanipour* explained this in relation to the laws on apostasy, stating: '[T]he offence in Moslem religious law is apostasy – abandoning Islam for another religion ... That is what Bastanipour did. He renounced Islam for Christianity ...': *Bastanipour v. Immigration and Naturalization Service* 980 F.2d 1129 (7ᵗʰ Cir. 1990).

15   *UNHCR Handbook*, at paras 74–6.

16   See *Harangova* (8ᵗʰ November 2000, unreported, 00/TH/01325). Also see, *Franczak v. Secretary of State for the Home Department* (CC/10255/00) (High Court).

17   See J. Hathaway, *The Law of Refugee Status* (LexisNexis Canada, 1991), at p.144.

18   See *INS v. Elias-Zacarias*, (1992) 502 U.S. 478, 112 S.Ct. 812, 117 L. ed 2d. 38.

19   The Federal Court of Australia in *Y & Z* explained that, '... an opinion could be thought to be a political opinon if it were such as to indicate that its holder, the claimant for refugee status, held views which were contrary to the interests of the state, including the authorities of the State': per Davies, J., in *Minister for Immigration & Multicultural Affairs v. Y & Ors* [1998] 515 FCA (15 May 1998) and *Minister for Immigration & Multicultural Affairs v. Z & Ors* [1998] 516 (15 May 1998).

20   G. Goodwin-Gill, *The Refugee in International Law* (OUP, 1996), at p.44.

21   Political opinion may include trade union activity (see Munby, J. in the British High Court case of *R v. Immigration Appeal Tribunal, ex parte Walteros-Castenada*

(CO/2383/99, 27th June; unreported) and it may include oppositon to corruption in one's country (see, Hill, J. in the Federal Court of Australia case of *Voitenko v. Minister for Immigration & Multicultural Affairs* [1999] FCA 428).

22   The US Court of Appeals has has explained that 'political neutrality' may include the absence of any political opinion (*Arriaga-Barrientos v. INS*, 937 F.2d 411 (9th Cir. 1991), but it has also talked of 'hazardous neutrality' explaining that, 'We define hazardous neutrality as "show[ing] political neutrality in an environment in which political neutrality is fraught with hazard, from governmental or un-controlled anti-government forces"' (Aldisert CJ in *Rivera-Moreno* citing *Sanghan v. INS*, 103, F.3d 1482, 1488 (9th Cir. 1997)).

23   As the High Court of Australia explained in *Ranawalage*, 'Asylum seekers are more likely to come from troubled countries where political violence is rife than from peaceful and stable societies. Accusations of involvement in violence and other criminal conduct is likely to from part of political discourse. It would be a surprising intention to impute to the drafters of the Convention that only people who were persecuted because theiur 'opinion' consisted of views on abstract questions of legislative policy or political philosophy would be within its protec-tion', see Heeray, J., in *Udaya Saman Perera Ranwalage v. Minister for Immigration & Multicultural Affairs* [1998] 1480 FCA (20 November 1998).

24   In *Klinko*, the Federal Court of appeal in Canada found that, '[T]he opinion ex-pressed by Mr. Klinko took the form of a denunciatio of state official's corruption. This denunciation of infractions committed by state officials led to reprisals against him. I have no doubt that the widespread government corruption raised by the claimant's opinion is a 'matter in which the machinery of state, govern-ment, and policy may be engaged': per L'etourneau, J.A., in *Klinko v. Canada (Minister for Citizenship and Immigration)* (A-321-98; 22 February 2000).

25   In *Desir*, the US Circuit Court explained that, '... to resist extortion is to become an enemy of the government. Moreover, it is not unreasonable to assume that when a single individual has the unfettered power to determine who is an enemy of the government, the individual's enemies are soon classified as the govern-ment's enemies ... Virtually any encounter with a members of the security forces is a political encounter', per Circuit Judge Tang in *Desir v. Ilchert* 840 F.2d 723 (9th Cir. 1998) citing *Haitian Refugee Centre v. Civiletti* 503 F.Supp.442, 498–500 (S.D. Fla. 1980).

26   The Federal Court of Appeal in Canada explained in *Vassiliev* that, '... in this case criminal activity permeates State action. Opposition to criminal acts becomes opposition to State authorities. On these facts it is clear that there is no distinction between the anti-criminal and idealogical/political aspects of the claimant's fear of persecution'. per Mouldoon, J., in *Vassiliev v. Canada (Minister for Citizenship and Immigration)*, IMM-3443–96, 4th July 1997.

27   *UNHCR Handbook*, at para 81. The Supreme Court of Canada in *Ward* explained this as follows: '... the political opinion ascribed to the claimant and for which he or she fears persecution need not necessarily conform to the claimant's true beliefs. The examination of the circumstances should be approached from the perservtive of the persecutor, since that is the persepective that is determinative in incting the persecution': per La Forest, J., in *Canada (Attorney-General) v. Ward* (1993) 2 SCR 689.

28   In *Chan*, the High Court of Australia explained that, '[T]he appellant was exiled ... It is irrelevant that the appellant may not have held the opinions attributed to him. What matters is that the authorities identified him with those opinions and, in consequence, restricted his liberty for a long and indeterminate period':

per McHugh, J., in *Chan v. Canada (Minister of Employment & Immigration)* [1995] 3 S.C.R 593.

29 The Supreme Court of Canada has held that, '[T]he political opinion that lies at the root of the persecution ... need not necessarily be correctly attributed to the claimant. Similar consideration would seem to apply to other bases of persecution', per La Forest, J., in *Canada (Attorney-General) v. Ward* (1993) 2 SCR 689.

30 The High Court of Australia in '*A*' stated that, '[T]he fact that the actions of the persecutors can serve to identify or even create "a particular social group" emphasizes the point that the existence of such a group depends in most, perhaps all, cases on external perceptions of the group. The notion of persecution for reasons of membership of a particular social group implies that the group must be identifiable as a social unit': per McHugh, J., in *Applicant A v. Minister for | Immigration & Ethnic Affairs* (1997) 190 CLR 225.

31 This is why the British Court of Appeal in *Savchenko* early emphasized that persecution itself cannot create a social group because, '[I]f a group can have existence solely based on fear of being subjected to persecution, then any person who can establish that he would be persecuted for a reason other than race, religion, nationality or political opinion could automatically claim to be part of the social group and meet the requirements of Article 1', per McGowan, L.J., in *Savchenko v. Secretary of State for the Home Department* [1996] Imm AR 28.

32 See *UNCHR Handbook* at para 77.

33 See *Matter of Acosta*, 19 I & N Dec. 211 (BIA 1985).

34 *R v. Immigration Appeal Tribunal and another, ex parte Shah* [1999] 2 all ER. 545 (H.L) per Lord Steyn.

35 Citing McHugh J in *Applicant A v. Minister for Immigration & Ethnic Affairs* (1997) 190 CLR 225.

36 *Acero Garces* [1999] INLR 460.

37 *Gebremichael v. INS*, 10 F.3d 28 (1st Cir. 1993).

38 *Matter of H-*, 21 I. & N. Dec. 337 (BIA 1996).

39 *Matter of Toboso-Afonso*, 201. & N. Dec. 819 (BIA 1990).

40 *Matter of Villalta*, 20 I. & N. Dec. 142 (BIA 1990).

41 *Lwin v. INS*, 144 F.3d 505 (7th Cir. 1998).

42 A Court in the US granted asylum to a Mexican child for reasons of persistent child abuse by her father: see, *Aguirre-Cervantes v. Immigration and Naturalization Service*, 273 F.3d 120 (9th Cir. 2001); cited in Bhabha, op. cit at fn 91.

43 A court in Canada granted refugee status to a child subjected to trafficking: see, *Y.C.K. (re)* [1997] C.R.D.D. No. 261, V95-02904 (Nov. 26,1997); cited in Bhabha, op. cit at fn 91.

44 Refugee status has been granted to a ten-year old Pakistani autistic boy on the grounds of disability: see Letter Opinion by Robert Esbrook, A 78 642 704 (Chicago Asylum Office Feb. 21, 2001), WL 78 No.13 INTERREL 604; cited in Bhabha, op. cit at fn 91.

45 M. Woehlcke, *Environmental Refugees*, Aussenpolitik, 43(3), 1992, pp.287–8.

46 G. Loescher, *Refugee Movements and International Security*, Adelphi Papers, 268, Brasseys for the International Institute for Strategic Studies, London, 1992, p.7.

47 P. Nobel, *Protection of Refugees in Europe as seen in 1987*, Report 4, Raoul Wallenberg Institute of Human Rights and Humanitarian Law, Lund, Sweden, 1987, p.28.

48 Ibid., pp.26–7.

49 H. Toolo and L. Bethlehem, *Labour Migration to South Africa*, paper read at the Workshop on Labour Migration to South Africa, National Labour and Economic Development Institute (NALEDI), Johannesburg, 31 August 1994, p.5.

50 Quoted in H. Solomon, in 'Search of Canaan: A Critical Evaluation of the Causes and Effect of Migration within Southern Africa, and Strategies to Cope with them', *Southern African Perspectives*, 24, Centre for Southern African Studies, University of the Western Cape, Bellville, 1993, pp.3–4.

51 H. Solomon, 'Who is an Illegal Immigrant?' (Published in *African Security Review Vol 5 No 6, 1996*) at p.3 (a Senior Researcher, Human Security Project, Institute for Defence Policy, quoting from his earlier research: H. Solomon, 'Change and Continuity in South Africa's Foreign Policy', 1978–1991, unpublished MA dissertation, University of Durban-Westville, 1994, p.169).

52 C. Dolan, *Policy Challenges for the New South Africa, Southern African Migration: Domestic and Regional Policy Implications*, Workshop Proceedings, 14, Centre for Policy Studies, Johannesburg, 1995, pp.53–4.

53 See in this regard, A. Shacknove, *Who is a Refugee?*, Ethics, January 1985, pp.274–84.

54 G. Melander, *The Two Refugee Definitions*, Report 4, Raoul Wallenberg Institute of Human Rights and Humanitarian Law, Lund, Sweden, 1987.

55 Weiner, *op. cit.*, p.156.

56 See Chapter 5 'Tackling Forced Displacement' which deals with IDPs.

57 Solomon, 'Who is an Illegal immigrant?', ibid., at p.4.

58 Solomon, 'Who is an Illegal immigrant?', ibid., at p.5.

59 For a brief description, see, E. Odhiambo-Abuya, 'Refugees and Internally Displaced Persons: Examining Overlapping Institutional Mandates of the ICRC and the UN High Commissioner for Refugees', 7 *Singapore J. Int'l. & Comp. L* 236 at p.242.

60 Adopted by the Assembly of Heads of State and Government at its Sixth Ordinary Session (Addis Ababa, 10 Sept 1969) (entered into force 20 June 1974).

61 Weiner, *op. cit.*, pp.188–9.

62 James Hathaway, *The Law of Refugee Status* (Butterworths, 1991), at p.16.

63 See, G. Coles, 'Background Paper for Asian Working Group on the International Protection and Displaced Persons', p.83 (unpublished, 1980) Quoted in Hathaway, *The Law of Refugee Status* (Butterworths, 1991), p.16 at fn. 81.

64 James Hathaway, *The Law of Refugee Status* (Butterworths, 1991), at p.17.

65 Patricia Hyndman, 'Refugees under International Law with reference to the Concept of Asylum' (1986), 60 *Australian L.J.* 148 at p.150.

66 James Hathaway, *The Law of Refugee Status* (Butterworths, 1991), at p.19.

67 Adopted at a colloquium entitled: 'Coloquio Sobre la Proteccion Internacional de los Refugiados en American Central, Mexico y Panama: Problemas Juridicos y Humanitarios' held at Cartagena, Colombia from 19–22 November 1984. For an excellent comparison between the Cartagena Declaration and OAU Refugee Convention 'refugee' definitions see Eduardo Arboleda 'Refugee Definition in Africa and Latin America' (1991), 3 (2) *Int'l J. of Refugee Law* 185.

68 Art III(3).

69 UNHCR, 'OAS Gneral Assembly: an inter-American initiative on refugees' (1986), 27 *Refugees* 5.

70 James Hathaway, *The Law of Refugee Status* (Butterworths, 1991), at p.20.

71 James Hathaway, *The Law of Refugee Status* (Butterworths, 1991), at p.21.

72 Council of Europe, *Parliamentary Assembly Recommendation 773* (1976).

73 Ibid.

74 See generally, Guy S. Goodwin-Gill, 'Non-Refoulment and the New Asylum Seekers', (1986), 26(4) *Virginia J. Intl. L.* 897.

75 Ibid. at p.898.

76 Ibid., at p.905.
77 K. Hailbronner, 'Non-refoulment and "Humanitarian" Refugees: Customary International Law or Wishful Legal Thinking?', (1986), 26(4) *Virginia J. Intl. L.* 857 at 887.
78 James Hathaway, *The Law of Refugee Status* (Butterworths, 1991), at pp.25–6.
79 *Regina v. Immigration Appeal Tribunal and Another, ex parte Shah* [1999] 2 All E.R. 545 (H.L.)
80 Refugee Convention art 1A(2) and High Commissioner's Statute art 6(ii).
81 For example, see the definition of the *Organization of African Unity Convention Governing the Specific Aspects of Refugee Problems in Africa*, Addis Ababa, 10 September 1969, Art 1.2, p.2, the text of which describes a refugee as a person who: '… owing to external aggression, occupation, foreign domination or events seriously disturbing public order in either part of or the whole of his country of origin or nationality, is compelled to seek refuge in another place outside his country of origin or nationality'.
82 See the *Cartegena Declaration on Refugees*. Adopted at a colloquium entitled: 'Coloquio Sobre la Proteccion Internacional de los Refugiados en American Central, Mexico y Panama: Problemas Juridicos y Humanitarios' held at Cartagena, Colombia from 19–22 November 1984. For an excellent comparison between the *Cartagena Declaration* and *OAU Refugee Convention* 'refugee' definitions see Eduardo Arboleda 'Refugee Definition in Africa and Latin America' (1991) 3 (2) *Int'l J. of Refugee Law* 185.
83 Art III(3).
84 The history of the legislation relating to refugees is well set out by Ate Grahl-Madsen, *The Status of Refugees in International Law* (Leiden, Sijthoff, 1966 and 1972) (Vols 1 and 2).
85 James C. Hathaway, *The Law of Refugee Status* (Toronto, Butterworths, 1991) at pp.2–5.
86 Kristen Walker, 'Defending the 1951 Convention Definition of Refugee', *Geo.Immigr. L.J.* (Vol. 17, pp.583–609), at p.597.
87 See Jerzy Sztucki, '"Who is a Refugee?" The Convention definition: universal or absolute?', in Frances Nicholson and Patrick Twomey (eds) *Refugee Rights and Realities: Evolving international concepts and regimes* (Cambridge, CUP, 1999), at p.64.
88 Jerzy Sztucki, 'Who is a Refugee?', ibid., at p.53.
89 United Nations, Office of the United Nations High Commissioner for Refugees, *The State of the World's Refugees, 1997–8: A Humanitarian Agenda* (Oxford, OUP, 1997), at p.1.
90 *Gregory Malcolm Daley v. Secretary of State for the Home Department* (AA/01502/2005), see Refusal Letter, dated 15th April 2005 at para 15.
91 Ibid. at paras 5, 6 and 8.
92 *Horvath v. Secretary of State for the Home Department* [2001] AC 489.
93 Guy S. Goodwin-Gill, *The Refugee in International Law* (2nd edn., Oxford, Clarendon Press), at p.2.
94 Emma Haddad, 'Who is (not) a Refugee?' (European University Institute, Florence, June 2004) (EUI Working Paper SPS No. 2004/6) at p.1, at www.iue.it.
95 Roger Zetter, 'Labelling Refugees: Forming and Transforming a Bureaucratic Identity', *Jnl of Ref. Std.* (vol. 4, issue 1, 1991), pp.39–62, at p.39.
96 Zetter, 'Labelling Refugees', at p.59.
97 Referring to Zetter's 'Labelling Refugees', at p.40.
98 Emma Haddad, ibid., at p.1.

99 *Handbook on Procedures and Criteria for Determing Refugee Status*, under the 1951 Convention and the 1967 Protocol relating to the Status of Refugees (UNHCR, Geneva, 1979, Re-edited 1992), at para 28.

100 Zolberg *et al.*, *Escape from Violence*, at p.274.

101 Zetter, 'Labelling Refugees', at pp.40, 60.

102 Micheal Dillon, 'The Scandal of the Refugee: Some Reflections on the "Inter" of International Relations and Continental Thought', in David Campbell and Michael Shapiro (eds) *Moral Spaces: Rethinking Ethics and World Politics* (Minneapolis, Univ. of Minnesota Press, 1999), at p.106.

103 William E. Connolly, *The Terms of Political Discourse* (2nd ed., Princeton Univ. Press, 1983), at p.12, 14.

104 William E. Connolly, *The Terms of Political Discourse* (2nd ed., Princeton Univ. Press, 1983), at p.14.

105 William E. Connolly, *The Terms of Political Discourse*, at pp.14–15.

106 Zetter, *Labelling Refugees*, at p.40.

107 William E. Connolly, *The Terms of Political Discourse* (2nd ed., Princeton Univ. Press, 1983), at p.30 (Italics inserted by Connolly).

108 William E. Connolly, ibid., at p.10.

109 Emma Haddad, ibid., at p.21.

110 Article 14(1).

111 Michael Walzer, *Spheres of Justice* (1983) at p.39.

112 See Peter Singer and Renata Singer, *The Ethics of Refugee Policy in Open Border? Closed Societies? The Ethical and Political Issues*: see Mark Gibney (ed.) (1988, p.111) at pp.123–4.

113 See Jacqueline Bhabha, 'Internationalist Gatekeepers?: The Tension Between Asylum Advocacy and Human Rights', *Harv. Hum. Rts. Jnl* (Vol. 15, Spring 2002) 155 at p.161, drawing from Matthew J. Gibney, *The State of Asylum: Democratization, Judicialization and Evolution of Refugee Policy in Europe*, 1–20 (U.N. Refugee Agency Evaluation and Policy Analysis Unit Working Paper No. 50, 2000).

114 Zetter, 'Labelling Refugees' at p.51.

115 D Martin, 'The Refugee Concept: On Definitions, Politics and the Careful Use of a Scarce Resource', in H. Adelman (ed.), *Refugee Policy*, York Lane Press, Toronto, 1991.

116 David Held, 'Laws of States, Laws of Peoples: Three Models of Sovereignty', in *Legal Theory* (forthcoming 2002) (manuscript at 19, on file with Jacqueline Bhabha]. See Bhabha, ibid., at p.161.

117 Bhabha, ibid., at p.161.

118 *Loc. cit.*, where she refers to Deborah E. Anker, 'Determining Asylum Claims in the United States: An Empirical Case Study', 19 *N.Y.U. Rev. L & Soc. Change* 433, 454 (1992); Amnesty International, Most Vulnerable of All: The Treatment of Unaccompanied Children in the UK (1998).

119 *Loc. cit.*, referring to the fact that the European Union (EU) is proposing to harmonize this two tier international protection across member states. See Commission of the European Communities, Proposal for a Council Directive, COM(2001) 510.

120 Bhabha, ibid., at p.166 referring to, Andrew E. Shacknove, *Who is a Refugee?*, 95 Ethics 274, 276 (1985).

121 *Loc. cit.*, referring to David A. Martin, 'The Refugee Concept: On Definitions, Politics and the Careful Use of a Scarce Resource', in *Refugee Policy: Canada and the United States* 30–51 (Howard Adelman (ed.), 1991).

122 Convention Relating to the Status of Refugees, *opened for signature* July 28, 1951, art. 1(A)(2), 189 U.N.T.S. 150. In fact, the Convention narrows the scope of protec-

tion further to those, within the above definition, who have not committed war crimes or crimes against humanity. See *id*. arts. 1(A)–(F) for the full definition.

123 Bhabha, *op. cit*., at p.167.

124 James C. Hathaway, *The Law of Refugee Status* 99 (1991).

125 Bhabha, *op. cit*., at p.168.

126 Bhabha, *op. cit*., at p.168.

127 Andrew Shacknove, 'Who is a Refugee?', *Ethics*, 95 (1985) pp.274–84, p.275.

128 Shacknove, ibid., at p.284.

129 Shacknove, ibid., at p.283.

130 Shacknove, ibid., at p.275.

131 UNHCR, *Handbook on Procedures and Criteria for Determining Refugee Status*, UN-HCR, Geneva, 1979, p.14.

132 C. Humana, *World Human Rights Guide*, Hutchinson, London, 1983, pp.13–23.

133 *Bensaid v. United Kingdom* (2000) 33 EHRR 205.

134 UNHCR, *op. cit*., p.14; Melander, *op. cit*., pp.13–14.

135 *R (Ullah) v. Special Adjudicator and Do v. Secretary of State for the Home Department* [2004] UKHL 26.

136 Adopting the formulation of the Immigration Appeal Tribunal in *Devaseelan v. Secretary of state for the Home Department* [2003] Imm AR 1, para 111, cited by Lord Walker in *R v. Secretary of state for the Home Department ex parte Razgar* [2004] UKHL 27 at para 32.

137 James C. Hathaway, *The Law of Refugee Status* (Canada, Butterworths, 1999), at p.104.

138 James C. Hathaway, *The Law of Refugee Status*, at pp.104–05.

139 Bhabha ibid., at p.168 referring to Guy S. Goodwin-Gill, *The Refugee in International Law* 51–66 (1996); Karen Musalo *et al*., *Refugee Law and Policy: Cases and Materials* 353–456; 549–98 (1997); Commission of the European Communities, Proposal for Council Directive laying down minimum standards for the qualification and status of third country nationals and stateless persons as refugees, COM(2001) 510; T. Alexander Aleinikoff, 'Membership in a Particular Social Group: Analysis and Proposed Conclusions' (2001) (unpublished manuscript, on file with author).

140 *Demirkaya v. Secretary of State for the Home Department* [1999] Imm Ar 498; [1999] INLR 441, CA, per Stuart-Smith LJ at para 18.

141 *R v. Secretary for State for the Home Department, ex parte Jeyakumaran (Selladurai)* [1994] Imm AR 45 (per Taylor J.). The case is also highly relevant to the discussion in the chapter on *Failed States* above.

142 Zolberg, Aristide R., Suhrke, Astri and Aguayo, Segio, *Escape from Violence: Conflict and the refugee crisis in the developing world* (Oxford, OUP., 1989).

143 Zolberg, *et. al*., *Escape from Violence*, at pp.30, 33.

144 Zolberg, *et. al*., *Escape from Violence*, at p.25.

145 Zolberg, *et. al*., *Escape from Violence*, at p.33.

146 Zolberg, *et. al*., *Escape from Violence*, at p.33.

147 Zolberg, *et. al*., *Escape from Violence*, at p.4.

148 Zolberg, *et. al*., *Escape from Violence*, at p.33.

149 M. Weiner, *The Global Migration Crisis: Challenge to States and to Human Rights*, Harper Collins, New York, 1995, p.2.

150 Weiner, *op. cit*., p.189.

151 Weiner, *op. cit*., p.190.

152 See, Karen Musalo, *et al*., *Refugee Law and Policy: Cases and Materials* 353–456; 549–98 (1997).

153 Bhabha, *op. cit*., at p.168.

154   *Bensaid v. United Kingdom* (2000) 33 EHRR 205.
155   Bhabha, *op. cit.* at p.171 referring to Karen Musalo *et al.*, *Refugee Law and Policy: Cases and Materials* (1997) ,at pp.600–601.
156   *Cheung v Canada (Minister of Employment & Immigration)* [1993] 102 D.L.R 4th 214 (Can.)
157   See *Cheung*, 102 D.L.R. at 214. However, a different approach was taken at the appellate level in the *Matter of G*, Interim Decision 3215 (BIA 1993).
158   Bhabha, *op.cit.*, at p.171.
159   Bhabha, *op.cit.*, at p.180.
160   *Loc. cit.*

7   The Burden of Burden-Sharing

INTRODUCTION

It should be clear by now that the international refugee regime, defined by the *United Nations Convention Relating to the Status of Refugees 1951*[1] (*Refugee Convention*) and its *1967 Protocol*[2] (*Protocol*), is becoming conceptually and practically obsolete.[3] One reason for this is that the affluent countries of the North do not want to take on more than their fair share of the world's refugees (as they see it), and would rather have a world system where refugee burdens are shared with other nations – preferably with those in the South – from where the majority of the world's refugees come. For this reason, nation-centered 'burden-sharing'[4] is replacing the historical tradition of asylum, which has provided 'freedom from seizure' to refugees since the time of antiquity.[5] The result is that the international refugee regime has now deviated from its historical roots. There are also changes on the world level which allegedly make it difficult to grant asylum-status to every person who qualifies for it. First, the rise of a post-modern globalized and de-territorialized economy has in itself undermined governments' abilities to deal with such international problems as mass migration.[6] Second, the escalation of religious, racial and ethnic strife in many parts of the world has led to more and more people fleeing from countries that they find uncongenial.[7] As a result, more than at any other time before, the rights of refugees today are embattled and are therefore uncertain and shrinking.[8]

Yet, such a situation only serves in itself to highlight the inadequacies of the current refugee regime in two very important ways. First, the regime[9] does not meaningfully protect basic human rights.[10] As we have already noted, the *Refugee Convention* defines the term 'refugee' vaguely as a person with a 'well-founded fear of being persecuted for reasons of race, religion, nationality, membership of a particular social group or political opinion ...'.[11] The *Convention* protects refugees only through its requirement that '[n]o Contracting State shall expel or return ('refouler') a refugee ... to the frontiers of territories where his life or freedom would be threatened ...'.[12] It does not grant forced migratory populations the positive rights to receive asylum, to receive admission, or to be protected from interdiction at sea, and does not protect them from any non-Convention harm (such as gender-based violence) that does not have a 'persecutory' focus.[13] Second, the current international regime does not address the changed political dynamics of the post-Cold war era which rely on more conciliatory, and less condemnatory, approaches to dispute resolution. This means that because liberal democracies are no longer engaged in an ideological struggle with repressive regimes, they can choose to have a policy of effective and expeditious voluntary repatriation of refugees,[14] rather than one of prompt and permanent admission.[15] States can do so because the Refugee Convention does not prevent them from evading their asylum obligations by devising deterrent devices such as stringent visa requirements, carrier sanctions,[16] distant re-settlement programs, migration agreements and safe third country arrangements.[17]

Yet, if the boundaries of refugee protection should be extended (as we have also argued in the previous chapters), on whom should the burden of providing protection fall? Some writers have no doubt that it should be the Western countries of the North because on a global scale their contribution is far less than that of the poorer nations in the South who have traditionally carried the burden of the bulk of the world's refugees. Santos describes these affluent countries of the North as the 'core' countries. In his view:

> [N]otwithstanding the chauvinistic alarms in the core countries, the majority of these subordinate transnational migrant flows have taken place within the South, and have meant an enormous burden for neighbouring countries whose social conditions are often equally grim. Ought not burden-sharing to be conceived on a global scale? And will this be possible in an interstate system based on state self-centredness?[18]

Other scholars have taken a more nuanced view. While recognizing the apparent insufficiencies of the current regime, James Hathaway has sought to re-conceptualize international refugee law in another way. Hathaway made his proposals first in 1991[19] and expanded his ideas in a 1997 article co-authored with R. Alexander Neve, *Making International Refugee Law Relevant Again: A Proposal for Collectivized and Solution-Oriented Protection*.[20] Later in 1997, Hathaway further elaborated his ideas in a collection of essays entitled *Reconceiving International Refugee Law*.[21] Hathaway explained that the 'essential purpose' of his new book *Reconceiving International Refugee Law* is both to invite critical engagement with the 'building blocks' of the reformulation model by providing readers with the underlying empirical analysis for the model; and second to lay the groundwork for an eventual transition from regionalized protection models to a more honestly global regime – when there is confidence in the viability of such a universal system.[22] However, I have previously argued, in a critique of those proposals in 1998, that Hathaway and Neve's proposals are unacceptable on moral and practical grounds as they will not advance currently embattled refugee rights.[23] I have argued for an alternative paradigm in which the long term reform of refugee law is seen as a specific component of rights within a broader system of immigration rights. This broader system of immigration rights has been neglected for too long and Professor Hathaway's proposals do not take sufficient account of this. Indeed, he has principled grounds for objecting to such a paradigm.[24] In this chapter, however, I want to demonstrate that the proposals of Hathaway and Neve are, if anything, even more unworkable on moral and practical grounds today then they were when they first so eloquently made them in 1997, nearly a decade ago. Indeed, burden-sharing as then conceived by them will lead to ever more increased instability in the world today.

I will begin by first briefly summarizing Hathaway and Neve's proposals to reform international refugee law. Second, I will argue that from the point of view of international law, proposals such as these are in danger of being highly discriminatory and hence immoral in practice. Third, I will argue for an alternative paradigm for reforming refugee law, which integrates refugee law with immigration and migration law in general.

A SUMMARY OF HATHAWAY AND NEVE'S PROPOSALS

Proposals for burden-sharing, such as those by Hathaway and Neve, often try to place reform within a human rights framework,[25] by suggesting that refugee law reform should recognize that, for the sake of human dignity, refugees have the right to leave threatening situations at home.[26] What is interesting, however, is that Hathaway and Neve advocate their proposals on instrumentalist, rather than moral, grounds,[27] for their scheme rests on the conviction that the dominant states of the North will not honour the new system unless they believe that it serves their long-term interests.[28] As a result, they do not set out to challenge the status quo but only to provide a framework in which the North can deploy its resources to provide refugees with better protections in their regions of origin.[29] They therefore support a refugee regime that emphasizes temporary protection and the repatriation of refugees as danger subsides.[30] The difficulty with such an approach is that it does not reject the role of nativism and racism in shaping state refugee policy.[31] Yet, it is surely possible to advocate responsibility-sharing proposals as a practical reform by rejecting the role of racism in refugee policy. In fact, the opposite is likely to be true. Thus, the first and most important factor that Hathaway and Neve propose for assessing protective responsibility among states is 'a careful assessment of implications for physical security'.[32] However, the three subsidiary factors they propose – functional compatibility, cultural harmony and geographic proximity – will undoubtedly bring about precisely this result indirectly and inadvertently.[33] They do not protect human dignity. They will not work on instrumentalist grounds. They will result in increased instability in the international system. In short, they will lead to highly immoral consequences.

THE IMPRACTICALITY AND IMMORALITY OF BURDEN-SHARING

One problem with the Western World's schemes of burden-sharing is that they continue to advocate that the largest share of the world's refugees should be confined to the poorer southern part of the world. This is both immoral and impractical given the increasing inability of the South to cope. Take the example of 'environmental refugees'. A think-tank report by *The New Economics Foundation* in 2003,[34] has argued that the polluting states of the world should be responsible for a greater share of the world's refugees. Global warming is responsible for 20 million environmental refugees a year. Many so-called economic migrants cannot make a living in their home country because of environmental changes caused by the policies of the rich countries. That results in their fleeing from 'environmental persecution'. America through its energy plans is responsible for the largest share of global warming. The UK also is responsible for 3 per cent of the world's global warming through carbon emissions.

Andrew Simms, one of the authors of the Report states that the UK should therefore be responsible for 300,000 displaced persons per year. Rich countries spend £50 billion a year subsidizing fossil fuel industries. Yet, they only spend £300,000 a year helping poor countries manage their emissions and adapt to climate change. This surely gives the lie to any reform policy of resource allocation by the rich countries. It simply is not happening. The rich countries are not ever likely to make a proportionate resource allocation to help poor countries manage the consequence of environmental disaster even where they – the rich countries – are responsible for such disaster. This is why *The New Economics Foundation* Report states that that those countries which are destroying the environment of poorer nations by contributing to global warming and using tropical hardwoods should be prepared to take a fair share of the refugees they have created. This is because '[T]he causes and consequences of climate change – who is responsible and who gets hurt – are now sufficiently understood'. Accordingly, to disregard that knowledge must be classed as 'intentional behaviour' the Report states. The idea of being responsible for environmental refugees is an extension of the 'polluter pays' principle. As the Report explains:

> Is it unreasonable to expect the wealthier members of the international community to pay for their profligate enjoyment of the earth's finite fossil fuel supply? We believe not. Only by creating a new legal responsibility towards environmental refugees will the international community – and especially industrialized countries – accept their obligations.[35]

The Report, however, does not just make a moral case by arguing that fossil fuels, coal, gas and oil, which drive the global economy, allow the wealthier nations to enjoy a lavish life-style, that is not only beyond the reach of the developing world, but impoverishes it. It also makes out a strong practical case for the richer nations accepting a wider and larger number of the world's refugees. It points out that by 2050, some 150 million people may be displaced by the effects of global warming. When whole countries such as Tuvalu in the South pacific are subject to drowning and large areas made too barren for crops, people will simply have nowhere to go. Millions of refugees will then inevitably move across international borders. This will cause global instability.

But its most chilling conclusion is that these refugees will become a fertile breeding ground for bitterness and resentment as well as a recruiting ground for terrorism. This is the most compelling reason why refugees cannot be confined indefinitely to the poorer parts of the world. Accordingly, *The New Economics Foundation* Report concludes that the *Geneva Convention on Refugees* should be expanded to include people fleeing environmental degradation because, 'A well-founded fear of starvation or drowning is a compelling reason to escape'. In fact, environmental refugees already outnumber those fleeing from war, political or religious persecution. They could reach 20 million people a year. An amendment to the Geneva Convention should not be difficult because it already defines a refugee as someone forced to flee because of a well-founded fear of persecution, be it religious, political or 'other'.

A system of burden-sharing through resource-allocation is therefore unworkable even on instrumentalist grounds because it is likely to engender international instability in an already unstable world system. The fact is, as Santos maintains, already large parts of the under-developed world have seen a 'calamitous deterioration of native survival systems' and 'national boundaries are a major political device to maintain inequality across the world system'.[36] Given such a state of affairs, no amount of the deployment of the West's resources will provide refugees from those areas with better protections in their regions of origin. Reform based on resource-allocation alone will make the plight of refugees worse because we are already witnessing today, 'flows of people still more at odds with international and domestic refugees legislation: hundreds of thousands of people fleeing from famine, starvation and natural disasters'.[37] The basic criticism of any proposed reform based on resource-allocation, therefore, is that it fundamentally misunderstands the nature of modern refugee flows because it continues to treat refugees as if they were all fleeing 'persecution' for reasons of 'race, religion, nationality' and the like, who could be afforded protection in some neighbouring country. Where a substantial number of the world's refugees are seeking 'ecological asylum',[38] as environmental refugees, it is facile to think in terms of resource allocation alone. When Hurricane Katrina hit Louisiana in September 2005, '[80 per cent of New Orleans was under-water by the third day' and 'people without cars or gas or money were abandoned for days at the city's Superdome' whilst others were left 'waiting on roofs for five days with no milk for their babies and no road on which to make their escape'. What is interesting about this calamity in the richest country in the World, is that:

[T]he devastation and chaos caused by the hurricane were understood – by FEMA, the government, the police and the military – as a threat not to life and limb but to law and order.[39]

If this breakdown of government and civil society (or of 'native survival systems' as Santos puts it) can happen in a country like the US there is not much hope in weaker States. Indeed, when Hurricane Stan, 'a category one hurricane, entered Mexico from the Atlantic' on 4th October 2005, 'moving slowly southwest across the country and triggering storms further south in Central

America' it was clear by the second day that '[A]t least 162 people died throughout the region, most buried under mudslides or drowned by rivers converted into raging brown floods' and unleashing 'large quantities of rain capable of devastating this largely poverty-stricken area'. It is significant that 'Greenpeace blamed rampant deforestation for exacerbating the disaster'.[40]

Environmental refugees are not the only refugees who cannot be helped by resource-allocation alone. There are also refugees 'who stay put and "migrate" only because the political conditions in which they used to live "migrate" themselves'.[41] We may call them 'quasi-refugees'. As Santos explains, '[O]ver 25 million Russians who live outside Russia became minorities overnight when the USSR ceased to exist.'[42] Since it happened there, 'it is not farfetched to predict new situations of standstill migration in other parts of the world, in Africa, in India, in China and so on'. The point is that a reform proposal that is based on resource-allocation will not work in a situation where there is no territorial sovereignty. That is true not only of the 'failed state scenario' that we have examined in previous chapters. It is also true of those who are seeking 'ecological asylum' and those who are 'quasi-refugees' because while their political conditions have migrated they have not. As Santos, observes, '[U]nlike other forms of refugee situations, the fate of refugees is here determined by the weakness or even by the breakup of territorial sovereignty'.[43] Territorial sovereignty is at risk in cases both of environmental refugees and of 'quasi-refugees'.

Those such as Hathaway and Neve who advocate a system of resource allocation often do so in reliance on the work of Michael Walzer, who states that nations may give preference to applicants who are cultural 'relatives' of the host population.[44] From Walzer's belief that 'the impulse for communitarian exclusion can be defended',[45] Hathaway and Neve develop a protection structure for refugees that they believe will be reconcilable to the national interests of Northern states.[46] They conclude that the special moral claim of refugees to integration in a new community is not only suspect, but leads to an infringement of the right to return, thus implicating the morality of modern refugee reforms that emphasize integration.[47] They argue that the present refugee regime is ineffective because the grant of asylum often becomes a route to permanent immigration,[48] and because the monetary burdens of refugee admission are not fairly apportioned among nations.[49] They suggest, therefore, that the grant of asylum should not ordinarily imply permanent residence, that a new international system should promote viable repatriation,[50] and that states should share a common, but not particularized, responsibility to respond to refugee-creating situations. In short, they view the current system of unilateral, undifferentiated obligations as unfair and ultimately unsustainable.[51] Instead they argue that states should allocate the burdens and responsibilities for admitting and aiding refugees among themselves. To achieve these objectives, Professor Hathaway had originally proposed setting up a strengthened international organization, which would replace the United Nations High Commissioner for Refugees (UNHCR). Under Hathaway's original proposal, this organization would oversee firm assurances from state parties that they would either contribute financially or accept their fair share of refugees. However, both authors now argue, as a result of a five-year collaborative research project, for a re-tooling of the UNHCR's role in protecting refugees. They argue that the UNHCR should coordinate and supervize subglobal associations of governments and non-governmental actors charged with protecting refugees.[52] The problem, as will be discussed below, is that Hathaway and Neve's proposal for the UNHCR would weaken the role of a supervisory agency in maintaining proper international standards and leave ultimate discretion to the states.[53]

SPECIFIC CRITIQUES OF HATHAWAY AND NEVE'S PROPOSALS

Hathaway and Neve's proposed refugee paradigm suffers from two practical and theoretical flaws. First, their paradigm is discriminatory because it proposes a system under which wealthy (Northern) states can continue to discriminate against poorer (Southern) states without any particularized obligations to accept all victims of human rights abuses regardless of their country of origin. More seriously, it is racially or ethnically discriminatory because they also propose to permit Northern states to discriminate against refugees from Southern states on grounds that they are functionally, culturally and geographically dissimilar. This looks dangerously like an 'us' and 'them' philosophy.

Second, Hathaway and Neve confine their paradigm to those technically considered to be refugees, as so defined by the *Refugee Convention*, even though it is widely recognized that the *Refugee Convention* fails to cover an increasing number of the world's refugees today. They do not consider the many so-called economic migrants who cannot make a living in their home country because of environmental changes caused by the policies of the rich countries. These people are all too frequently just treated as immigrants seeking to enter a rich country illicitly for work. Any reform such as the one advocated by Hathaway and Neve needs to consider the immigration/migration element of refugee law. This is not least because refugees are only a component of all migrants. They fit into a specific, albeit highly distinctive, category of general state immigration law. The relationship between immigration, migration and refugees could be just as important as asylum *per se* in developing long-term reforms to the refugee regime. Indeed, State practice in refugee law is unlikely to change favorably unless its practice on immigration also changes at the same time. Otherwise, states will always view refugees as back-door migrants. Accordingly, whereas I do not disagree with Hathaway and Neve about ends, I do disagree with them about the means. The authors believe that refugee rights can only be augmented if, given their relationship to asylum, they are treated as being qualitatively different from immigration rights. But, this book has been devoted to showing that this distinction is arbitrary and cannot in any event be realistically made today in relation to the bulk of the world's refugee population. I believe that their approach is bound to founder in the *realpolitik* of international state practice, and that unless we take a more favorable approach towards free movement rights generally in a global economy, we will not strengthen refugee rights. The following section considers these two criticisms in turn.

A Framework of 'Common but Differentiated Responsibility'[54] among States

Current responsibility for refugees, although purportedly shared by all nations, is differentiated and lacks particularized obligations.[55] In 1991, there was an earlier reform proposal by Hathaway involving a plan to use a new supervisory international body to assign such obligations in the form of quotas.[56] However:

> in response to the unequivocal insistence of contributors from the South, the whole notion of 'refugee quotas' [was] dropped based on concerns that 'refugee commodification' might ensue ...[57]

Hathaway and Neve's recent proposal discards the idea of the supervisory body in favor of maintaining the UN as the body responsible for refugee movements. Also, their proposal allows states to negotiate their responsibilities for aiding refugees.[58] What they say now may not be open to the objection against the concept of quotas which has been abandoned. It is, however, open to the equally serious objection that it also allows racial, religious or cultural discrimination by permitting Northern states to weight asylum claims in favor of refugees who are functionally compatible, culturally affiliated, or geographically proximate to their own populations.[59] This is especially given that their scheme would not obligate Northern states to share the burdens of migration by admitting ethnically and culturally diverse refugees.[60] Thus, their proposal would further weaken the obligations of Northern states to accept victims of human rights abuses from all parts of the world, and would allow richer nations to pass the most difficult burdens of housing refugee populations onto others. Indeed, unlike the scheme Hathaway proposed in 1991, Hathaway and Neve's latest proposal, whilst now emphatically rejecting quotas of admission, does maintains the strict distinction between human and financial burdens, as a route to a more equitable paradigm of refugee policy. Hathaway's letter to me explained:

> Quite essential to the morality of my model as presently proposed is a disaggregation of (human) 'responsibility sharing' from (fiscal) 'burden-sharing ...' No state can simply 'trade off' money for the duty to provide asylum under our model, *because the Art. 33 duty of non-refoulement will continue to apply in all cases to all countries.* Responsibility sharing, in other words, will only be possible under conditions of scrupulous – and much more effectively monitored – respect for human rights.[61]

However, this distinction is likely to be impracticable. The rich nations of the North will manipulate it in circumstances where they do not themselves want to take on any more refugees from the South. Thus, notwithstanding the proposed fiscal arrangement, financially needy nations are likely to feel compelled to accept the best deal that the Northern states or the UN are able to broker for them. The poorer nations will, as Hathaway and Neve themselves acknowledge, end up accepting responsibility for all refugees who may be deemed their cultural relatives.[62] Further, notwithstanding the human responsibilities that Hathaway and Neve propose, the Northern countries inevitably will escape having to assume the wider burdens of human settlement because of the existence of the three subsidiary factors of functional compatibility, cultural harmony and geographical proximity. This resulting inconsistency suggests that the institutionalization and regulation of responsibility-sharing in the manner advocated by Hathaway and Neve will be a practice that is honoured more in the breach than in the observance by powerful Northern states.

This is worrying because already the rich countries of the modern world use increasingly popular techniques of dealing with mass migration, such as the use of 'safe havens',[63] 'containment'[64] or 'temporary protection'[65], which represent a weakening in the robust international commitment[66] to the right to asylum, which is the hallmark of refugee status.[67] It is well known that they do not advance refugee rights. In *The Price of Indifference*, the late Arthur Helton, pointed to the recent evidence which suggested that efforts at internal protection have had mixed results. His conclusion was that under international law, providing access to the territory of any asylum state will continue to be the primary form of protection.[68] This is unsurprising given that under the current international system and in the past, richer nations have wrongly avoided and unilaterally imposed the burdens of admitting refugees onto less powerful nations.[69] For example, after the Gulf war, the international community kept potential refugees in a 'safe haven' in Northern Iraq when Turkey closed its borders to Iraqi Kurds.[70] During the Bosnian conflict, the international community effectively contained hundreds of thousands of Bosnians in 'safe havens' in Bosnia-Herzegovina after European states imposed visa controls to prevent their entry into truly safe countries.[71] In 1994, when Hutus fled their homes in Rwanda after the Rwandan Patriotic Front assumed power, French troops directed the flow of Hutus not to France, but to crowded and violence-ridden camps in southwestern Rwanda and Zaire.[72] All such practices are a violation of Paragraph 31 of the UNHCR Guidelines on International Protection which states that:

[W]here internal displacement is a result of 'ethnic cleansing' policies, denying refugee status on the basis of the internal flight or relocation concept could be interpreted as condoning the resulting situation on the ground and therefore raised additional concerns.[73]

The violation of UNHCR Guidelines is unlikely to diminish under schemes of burden-sharing based on resource-allocation. States farther away from refugee producing regions (i.e. in the North) can, and likely will, direct a combination of fiscal transfers and residual resettlement opportunities to states in the South so that refugees will remain in the South.[74] Judicial policy is already in some countries taking this line by degrading the very concept of a 'safe haven' by linking it with the possibility of 'internal relocation' for refugees. In 2003, the court of Appeal in Britain said in relation to the right to refugee status under the *Refugee Convention* that:

> consideration of the reasonableness of internal relocation should focus on the consequences to the asylum-seekers settling in the place of relocation instead of his previous home[75]

and that this:

> involves a comparison between the conditions prevailing in the place of habitual residence and those which prevail in the safe haven, having regard to the impact that they will have on a person with the characteristics of the asylum-seeker.[76]

This is deeply disturbing. Are a people who have been raped, murdered and ethnically cleansed 'in their place of habitual residence' to be denied international surrogate protection by being placed in an internal 'safe haven' because the particular 'characteristics of the asylum-seeker' mean that they are used to regular human rights deprivations? In one recent case in the UK, the appeal tribunal in 2005 held that an immigration adjudicator had found that there was 'complicity by the government of Sudan in a campaign of ethnic cleansing in the Darfur region' but astonishingly held that:

> There is nothing in the UK law to support the assertion in paragraph 31 of the UN-HCR Guidelines on International Protection that if there has been a policy of 'ethnic cleansing' acceptance of the viability of internal relocation condones that policy or could be interpreted as condoning that policy. We do not accept it is legitimate to claim that governmental or governmental supported action amounting to persecution directed against an individual or group because of their ethnicity leading to their being displaced to another area in their country must lead to an entitlement to international protection as refugees even if, in the area to which they are displaced, there is no real risk of being persecuted.[77]

The appeal tribunal's conclusion was that:

> [I]f they are safe elsewhere in Sudan it cannot be the responsibility of the international community to give them refuge merely because of the abhorrent nature of the policy which has driven them from their homes.[78]

Unfortunately, this formulation is directly counter to the UNHCR Guidelines that this 'raised additional concerns'.

In the circumstances, it is interesting that Hathaway and Neve advocate their proposed shift to burden-sharing through resource allocation on the grounds that it would allow powerful governments to 'buy their way out' of providing refuge do not realize that there is 'very little left to buy'.[79] Yet, this is simply not true if the record of recent years is anything to go by. In 2005, only 40,000 Iraqis applied for asylum in Europe, despite the fact that with the 'on-going War' there are more than 600,000 Iraqi refugees still outside Iraq.

Indeed, Europe has repatriated 'an estimated 55,000 Iraqi refugees' in 2005 'as the War and its fallout caused a new displacement of tens of thousands of Iraqis and long-term refugee residents in the country'.[80] This raises another moral imperative. Western intervention through military action is surely responsible in some degree for the ungovernable state of countries like Iraq and Afghanistan. Previously, these were closed communities with closed borders under Saddam Hussein and the Taliban. The effect of western intervention, however morally justifiable, has transformed closed societies into open societies but with porous borders. The rise in refugees from these countries is something for which the West must bear some responsibility. Hathaway and Neve assume that states act out of self-interest, and thus believe that the above-mentioned combination of fiscal transfers and residual settlement opportunities is the most practical way to reform the refugee regime.[81] Indeed:

> [m]ore fundamentally, there is no inherent wrong in most refugees being protected in their region of origin if the decision to afford protection there follows logically from a good-faith application of ... responsible sharing criteria ...[82]

Given the North's history of unilaterally and improperly off-loading most of its refugee obligations onto the South, it is difficult to see why the system Hathaway and Neve propose is not inherently wrong. There is no reason, moreover, to assume that they will carry out their proposals in good faith. If the standards of functional compatibility, cultural harmony and geographic proximity that Hathaway and Neve suggest are applied, those poor countries will maintain the disproportionate housing of refugee burdens. In short, the purported equity of Hathaway and Neve's proposal is based upon the institutional entrenchment of a separate but equal paradigm that makes it inherently inequitable for the populations of the South. Indeed, the failure of Northern states to abide by their obligations to aid refugees in the past cannot be ignored so easily in any practical proposal for reform. Effective long-term policy should not, and cannot, in the long run, ignore Northern states' previous failure to honour their obligations to refugees, unless it is met with the installation of a free and uninhibited modern system.[83]

The Theory of Functional Compatibility, Cultural Harmony, and Geographical Proximity in Equitable Responsibility Sharing Allocations[84]

Thus, it is clear from above that the essence of the discriminatory feature of Hathaway and Neve's proposal lies in the provisions that deal with 'responsibility sharing' between states. These state that:

> First and foremost, responsibility sharing allocations should be predicated on a careful assessment of implications for physical security. Second, functional compatibility between refugees and their potential host communities is of vital importance. Third, attention should be paid to cultural harmony ... Fourth, geographical prox-

imity between the state of asylum and the country of origin is desirable to allow for ongoing contact between refugee and stayee communities, and ultimately to facilitate repatriation.[85]

The authors preface these with the remark that the assessment of physical security is a 'first and foremost' requirement. Nevertheless, I believe that the international community's response toward the Iraqi Kurds, Bosnian Serbs and Rwandan Hutus[86] and the continuing plight more recently of asylum-seekers from Iraq and Afghanistan (as seen in previous chapters) amply demonstrates how easily the first requirement can be subverted, in the guise of the latter three – that is, in the *realpolitik* of modern international relations. The latter three requirements are likely to lead cumulatively to ethnic and cultural discrimination by affluent Northern states against Southern states by keeping out refugees from the South programmatically.[87] Even though a publicly regulated and managed international system implies fairness, it will not provide refugees from the poorer South with equality and thus will not promote the values of universal justice.[88] This can have serious implications for international refugee law. It must not be forgotten that the *Refugee Convention 1951* was itself a consequence of the refusal in the 1930s by some Western European states to admit Jewish refugees fleeing from Nazi Germany. International refugee policy must never be undermined in this way again. Permitting states to respond differently to refugees of different ethnic origins will countenance the degrading and inhuman treatment of individuals and violate international law.[89] Yet, under Hathaway and Neve's program, most refugees will be physically protected only within their region of origin (where they are culturally 'related'). Such an outcome is unacceptable. When a state has the resources to grant asylum, it is inherently immoral for that state to deny asylum on grounds that are morally irrelevant, such as race, ethnicity and culture, as these are not within the control of victims of human rights abuses. Indeed, even exclusionists such as Charles Hyde have long regarded any form of racial, ethnic, cultural or geographical discrimination as 'tokens of arrogance'[90] because discrimination can have a deleterious effect on comity and good relations.

These considerations acquire heightened importance when it is remembered that most Northern states have applied their refugee laws and policies in a discriminatory manner throughout the twentieth century. After 1918, post war peace treaties acknowledged that millions of people would be residing as minorities in culturally, linguistically or religiously alien environments.[91] Nevertheless, the League of Nations treaties did not provide effective protection to minorities. First, the minority protections in the treaties were imposed only on a few selected states and the Great Powers were not bound by similar obligations. Second, the treaties guaranteed only what by that time had come to be viewed as traditional minority rights of religion, language and cultural activities, without implying any broader economic or political autonomy. Third, the purported 'self-determination' of certain nationalities was dependent on the dictates of the Great Powers, with minorities being 'permitted to lobby in Paris, but not to vote at home'.[92] Initially, Western nations enlisted the aid of private agencies to address the emerging burdens of refugee systems,[93] but international efforts at realizing an equitable solution to refugee needs did not succeed.[94] Immediately before World War II, for example, states in Western Europe and in North America began to resist receiving Jews and other culturally diverse refugees.[95]

Sadly, this experience did not teach the international community to be wary of ethnic and cultural discrimination. The Western world continues to turn away refugees who wish to escape repression and ill treatment. For example, European states in the 1990s subjected Bosnian refugees to group-based status determinations and temporary protection. The European states gave Bosnian refugees weaker protections than previous groups of refugees who enjoyed the protections of the *1951 Convention*.[96] Even Germany, which has had a better record of refugee admissions over the last 10 years than many other nations, granted only 59 asylum requests from Bosnian nationals in 1993 and denied asylum to another 1,913 Bosnian applicants, many of whom were fleeing the 'ethnic cleansing' of Serb forces.[97] Many of these fleeing Bosnians had better claims than many refugees who had fled from Communist Eastern Europe and had received asylum under the *1951 Convention*. Whereas refugees from communist Eastern Europe were routinely admitted during the Cold War,[98] Bosnian refugees were routinely denied entry to European countries. The same is now happening with Iraqi, Afghani and Sudanese refugees.

Events in the current decade confirm that the rich countries of the North are not going to accept a proportionately fair share of the world's refugees today. In fact, since the 1990s, refugee policy has entered an era of increased restrictionism. By the turn of this century, immigration and refugee policy has become an ever more politically explosive issue in the West today. The political salience of immigration and refugee policy means that politicians seeking democratic election can ill afford to ignore these issues. Indeed, the fate of politicians is often wrapped up in them. Two recent examples in Europe suffice to explain this. First, in the Dutch elections on 6 May 2002, a writer and politician, Pim Fortuyn, was murdered in the build up to May 15 2002 general elections. Fortuyn took a racist anti-migration stand. His slogan was 'Holland is full'.[99] Polls tipped his party to 'win 28 of the 150 seats'.[100] According to this, since he would win about 19 per cent of parliament seats, he would secure a possible place in the coalition government. His party in the event, however, fell short by just two seats, winning 26 seats or 17 per cent of the total votes cast.[101] Similarly, in the 2002 French Presidential National Elections, the extreme right wing candidate Jean-Marie Le Pen adopted an anti-immigration stance. He promised to immediately end immigration and expel all immigrants and refugees from France.[102] Le Pen surprised everyone by coming second in the first round. He defeated the formidable incumbent Prime Minister, Lionel Jospin.[103] In the event, however, he suffered a devastating defeat at the hands of Jacques Chirac in the final round. In both countries, however, the resilience and potency of the immigration issue was there for all to see. National policies are being changed as a result of this. Nowhere is this more clear than in the case of Australia.

Until a few years ago, asylum seekers could arrive by boat to land in Australia where their asylum claims could be processed. On 26 August 2001, an unauthorized boat arrived carrying 438 people in a Norwegian-registered container ship, MV Tampa. A dispute arose between Australia and Norway. Australia insisted that the asylum seekers should be returned to Indonesia from where they had originally come. Norway insisted that Australia should take them in. This is because the asylum seekers' ultimate destination was Australia. A standoff ensued. Legal action was taken.[104] In the end, a 'Pacific solution' was adopted. Under this, asylum seekers were no longer allowed to set foot offshore. Boats were to be intercepted at sea. Asylum seekers were to be transported to neighbouring Pacific states such as Nauru and Papua New Guinea (PNG). There, their claims would be processed. The intention of the Australian Government was to prevent illegal immigration[105] and it was to obstruct 'queue jumpers'.[106]

The point is, however, that even those found to be genuine refugees are not automatically admitted into Australian territory anymore.[107] They can be sent to other states. These states will admit them as refugees. Australia is able to share its burden in this way.[108] Ireland responded by promising to take 150 refugees.[109] New Zealand promised to take in 50.[110] These are tiny undertakings. As of February 2002, there were 446 detainees in Manus Island in PNG and 1,180 in Nauru.[111] As with the elections in Holland and France, the Tampa saga arose against the backdrop of Australian elections. Before August 2001, Prime Minister Howard's government was way behind in the opinion polls. When on September 11, just hours before the terrorist attacks in the USA, Justice North of the Federal Court, handed out the first decision in the Tampa case, brought by the Victorian Council for Civil Liberties, 'attention focussed on the fact that the majority of the boat people were Afghan nationals seeking asylum from the detested Taliban regime'.[112] The initial sympathy that the boat people aroused quickly dissipated. Once it was recognized that they were Muslims from Afghanistan, and the US Government claimed that the attacks on the twin towers came from Afghanistan, they were seen as potential terrorists. Many Australian respondents who were polled considered the boat people increased the risks of terrorism.[113] For Prime Minister Howard, the turn of events could not have been better. He was able to secure a third term in office, having benefited significantly from the Tampa saga.

Nevertheless, what Canberra now does is to incur financial costs for its asylum seekers. Those specific states that cooperate with them, such as PNG and Nauru are offered financial packages.[114] These specific states then agreed to Canberra's request to use their territories as asylum processing points. Following the Tampa saga, Nauru was paid 15 million Australian Dollars and PNG 10 million Australian Dollars. Poor countries, faced with such huge financial inducements, ended up prostituting themselves.[115] Canberra also bears all financial costs including provision of food, medicines, construction of makeshift detention camps and any other incidental costs. After Tampa, the Australian Government moved to push legislation through parliament:

to validate the actions taken by the Australian authorities in the course of the Tampa affair and to radically strengthen the powers of the Australian authorities to intercept and detect potential asylum seekers.[116]

What is interesting is, that Australia has not only set a precedent for other Northern states to emulate, by the determination of asylum claims being undertaken offshore, it has also set a very bad example for poor southern countries. It is well known that the vast majority of the world's refugees are confined to the poorest nations in the world. Africa alone hosts 80 per cent of the world's refugees. It was always wrong for the weaker nations to assume the lion's share of the world's humanitarian obligation. For example, one of the world's poorest countries, Tanzania, hosted refugees between 565,000 and 830,000 refugees compared to the USA – the richest country in the world – which during 1993 and 1995 hosted between 620,000 and 630,000 asylum seekers.[117] Yet, after the Tampa affair, African countries too, began to turn away refugees.[118] Already, in 1993 and 1994 when the genocide occurred in Burundi and Rwanda, Tanzania had closed its borders to prevent entry of hundreds of thousands asylum seekers relying on the US Interdiction Program, which prevented Haitian asylum seekers from landing on US soil. Similarly after the Tampa case, the Pakistani leader, General Pervez Musharraf, actually wondered out why if a wealthy state like Australia could refuse to admit less than a handful of boat people, a poor state like Pakistan, already over burdened with refugees should admit more.[119] Indeed, by the end of 2001, Pakistan hosted 2.2 million refugees. Australia only had 21,000 refugees.[120] Clearly, therefore, poorer countries are now following the bad examples of the West. These examples, from both the developed and the under-developed world, comprise living proof that contrary to Professor Hathaway's well-intentioned letter to me that, 'No state can simply "trade off" money for the duty to provide asylum under our model ...' the facts on the ground show that this is precisely what is happening today under a system of resource-allocation that was pioneered by Australia, but is now unscrupulously followed by an ever-increasing number of both rich and poor countries world-wide.

The Use of Temporary Protection[121]

In the circumstances, it hardly needs stating that just as with 'Safe havens', so also a reliance on a system of 'temporary protection', which is also propounded by Hathaway and Neve, would be an arbitrary, capricious, and a highly discriminatory policy to follow in countries with democratic human rights traditions. Temporary protection is also sometimes called temporary refuge, temporary asylum, or temporary safe haven.[122] Refugees who receive temporary protection are called *de facto* refugees. Some prominent writers and refugee law activists have criticized the concept on the grounds that it is simply one more clever technique in a battery of transparent devices, akin to detention and denial of work permits, to limit migrants access to the rights and remedies established by the Convention.[123]

The US adopted this practice in their policies relating to Haitian and Cuban refugees.[124] Its essential discriminatory effect, however, arises from the recognition by Peter Schuck, who made his somewhat similar proposals about the same time as Hathaway and Neve, that temporary protection is a:

> desirable strategy from the perspective of industrialized states' narrow self interest. It is a way to keep refugees safely (in both senses) in the Third World from which most of them come, thereby alleviating the pressures to grant them permanent resettlement in the First World.[125]

Indeed, many Northern states that have substantial capacity to absorb refugees now also go one step further and offer temporary protection in the territory of a third state over which they exert influence. An example of this practice occurred when President Clinton announced on July 5, 1994 that Haitians fleeing by boat would be provided a 'safe haven' at Guantanamo, Cuba, but that none would be resettled into the United States.[126] This policy was a disaster. By August 13, 1994, a total of 15,775 Haitians were housed at Guantanamo,[127] but on that day, a number of them rioted in protest against unsatisfactory conditions.[128] Difficulties in the Guantanamo camps only subsided when the Haitian military government relinquished power to President Aristide on October 15, 1994.[129]

Peter Schuck, just as Hathaway and Neve, has also considered the 'moral implications' of a system by which Northern states provide temporary protection in other lands, and the possibility that such a policy 'would allow and encourage states to traffic in human beings – and desperately vulnerable human beings at that – and that this offends common morality',[130] but denied that this would be immoral. He argued that this critique assumes the existence of:

> a more rational system that allocates them according to some exalted principle of justice. In reality, of course, the existing refugee system does not even pretend to approach such an ideal.[131]

On the other hand, the late Joan Fitzpatrick considered the US treatment of Haitian boat people quite differently. Fitzpatrick argued that:

> as with temporary protection in Europe, these offers of minimal safety are presented without an option both to persons who are Convention refugees, as well as to persons fleeing generalized violence or repression.[132]

What is interesting is that Hathaway and Neve recognize that the treatment of refugees in other contexts, under programs of temporary protection, has been no different.[133] Thus, it seems that even in a concept as transient as 'temporary protection', the distinction between refugees and immigrants that Hathaway and Neve maintain begins to break down.

The point is that by granting only temporary protection, states are denying refugees the full range of rights that refugees received in the past. Yet, Hathaway and Neve do not find this problematic because they argue that

the grant of asylum is inherently temporary. In this, they ignore the historical fact that in the Cold War era, refugees who fled communist-bloc countries were routinely granted permanent residency and even citizenship in host countries.[134] Now, Northern states no longer grant refugees full rights because they wish to encourage repatriation.[135] Today, host states do not want to bear the costs of immigration, when that immigration is essentially by culturally diverse peoples from outside Europe. In this, they fail to recognize that the cultural discrimination that they now espouse violates minority rights.[136] Yet, the West needs to be sensitive to this because the idea of minority rights has gained rapid currency since Will Kymlicka wrote his classic work *Multicultural Citizenship*.[137] This asserted that many liberal theorists have failed to acknowledge sufficiently the existence of states that are multinational, with a diversity of societal cultures, languages and national groups.[138] Most national minorities resist integration into the common culture and instead seek to protect their distinct existence by consolidating that societal culture.[139] However, by condoning the theory of temporary protection, Hathaway and Neve allow the use of deterrent devices that immorally preserve cultural homogeneity in both home and host countries.[140] This practice is indefensible and must be addressed in any long-term solution to the problem of international migration.

The Recourse to Repatriation

One of the most touted policy initiatives in modern refugee law since the end of the Cold War is repatriation. International refugee law allows for 'voluntary' repatriation but not 'forced' repatriation. The distinction is not always as clear-cut since governments often manage to induce people to leave. Hathaway and Neve also advocate repatriation as a necessary part of temporary protection. However, given the recent pattern of international responses to refugee flows, most Northern countries are more likely to repatriate refugees from the poorer South who are ethnically and culturally different from their populations.[141] Since repatriation corresponds to temporary protection, this will remain true whether the repatriation is 'voluntary' or mandatory. In either case the specific aim of temporary protection is to facilitate repatriation. This is made plain in Hathaway's letter in which, as he explained to me, both voluntary and non-voluntary repatriation may be used:

> Voluntary repatriation is preferred for a host of human rights and humanitarian reasons; it should be vigorously pursued *when and if* conditions warrant, and with full respect for refugee self-determination. However, *if* the cessation requirements of the refugee definition are honestly met (fundamental and durable change of circumstances that eradicates the basis of the claim to refugee status), repatriation – as a matter of international law – need not be voluntary. It must, however, not infringe the human rights of the persons to be repatriated, and (as a matter of logic) will be more viable if the facilitative and supportive system I outline is put in place.[142]

Once again, this is unrealistic. The practice of the Northern refugee-receiving States suggests that they are unlikely to be terribly concerned with according 'full respect for refugee self-determination' or to worry about whether 'the cessation requirements of the refugee definition are honestly met'. In fact, human rights organizations and religious groups oppose repatriation because, like deportation, it is a significant use of state authority against an individual.[143] Indeed, when on 1st September 2005, the European Commission adopted, in the words of EU Commissioner Frattini 'an important and comprehensive package of concrete measures in the field of immigration and asylum', given 'the need to end illegal stay in order to maintain the integrity of our migration policy' it included the 'use of coercive measures'.[144] For refugees, removal invariably means a return to conditions of poverty and insecurity. Even if repatriation is considered voluntary, it may be suspect in the circumstances described by Hathaway in fully being able to protect human rights, as it could just as easily be coercive. It is true that Hathaway and Neve advocate 'viable repatriation', but they do not clarify whether they mean voluntary or mandatory repatriation.[145] Mandatory repatriation may be appropriate in some cases,[146] but a system that formalizes repatriation will also send the wrong signals to states that admit refugees. In fact, voluntary repatriations could easily become coerced repatriations in situations where the host community does not make efforts to integrate refugees.

THE NEGLECT OF THE IMMIGRATION/MIGRATION DIMENSION OF REFUGEE LAW

It has been consistently argued in this work that the distinction between refugees and economic migrants is not always viable in situations where hundreds of thousands of people in the world today are fleeing from the effects of misguided governmental policies or natural disasters culminating in famine, starvation, and grinding poverty. As Santos has remarked the world's condition today often 'turns the question of the voluntary or involuntary nature of the migration into a macabre exercise'.[147] Yet, Hathaway and Neve continue to adopt the traditional and classical position that:

[i]n principle, refugee protection is not about immigration. It is intended to be a situation-specific human rights remedy: [w]hen the violence or other human rights abuse that induced refugee flight comes to an end, so does refugee status.[148]

This observation leads them to the conviction that:

[w]e can no longer insist on either the routine, permanent integration of all refugees, nor expect all governments, whatever their circumstances, simply to receive and provide quality protection to all refugees who arrive at their territory.[149]

It is interesting to note that Hathaway and Neve insist upon this distinction even though other non-refugee immigrants may be routinely admitted, given the "pull" of employment'[150] and labor demands, and even though they believe that there is no 'major difference between refugees and economic immigrants with regard to their economic prospects'.[151] The rigid distinction between refugees and other immigrants that Hathaway and Neve maintain is inconsistent with this conviction. Despite Hathaway and Neve's insistence to the contrary, all immigrants, not only asylum-seeking refugees, may place new and heavy burdens on host countries. Like asylum, immigration is recognized as placing 'new pressures on traditional welfare states'. Many immigrants cannot provide for themselves without assistance from the state.[152] For this reason, I believe that refugee protection could be promoted more effectively by linking it to the protection of immigrants and of immigration rights in general. Refugees and immigrants both are likely to suffer some of the problems of common migration in the receiving state.

Indeed, in reality, governments who face rising immigration and asylum claims may not make this distinction between refugees and immigrants.[153] The recent evidence in Europe that we have set out above, in relation to the electoral gains by politicians like Jean-Marie Le Pen and the late Pim Fortuyn, leave no doubt that this distinction is not even being explained by politicians, and still less understood by their electorates, in the some of the leading democracies of the North. In most countries there is a link in official governmental policy-making between voluntary and involuntary migrants. There is indeed a practical link between the two. This link between immigration policies in general and refugee law in particular is so certain that in the 1970s, when many European countries had lax immigration controls, refugees did not always apply for asylum when seeking refuge. Instead, 'many refugees from the Third World entered Europe either as immigrant workers or as students, which was then made possible by loose immigration controls'.[154]

What this, therefore, suggests is that it is far more effective in the long-term to focus on the liberalization of immigration policy in general. If Hathaway and Neve are fundamentally interested in a workable paradigm, then it is inconsistent for them to ignore a link that the Northern states themselves maintain. Indeed, it is not fortuitous that countries with liberal refugee policies, such as Sweden[155] and Denmark,[156] invariably also have liberal immigration policies.[157] All the evidence is that where immigration policies have been flexible, refugee policies have been flexible as well. The categories of asylum eligibility are completely arbitrary for this very reason. Indeed, contrary to conventional belief, asylum law in the post-war era has not only been applied to what may be termed 'political refugees', but has been extended to other, quite unrelated situations as well. For example, under the US *Refugee Relief Act* of 1953, the definition of a 'refugee' embraced:

> any person in a country or area which is neither Communist nor Communist-dominated, who because of persecution, fear of persecution, natural calamity, or military operations is out of his usual place of abode and unable to return thereto, who has not been firmly resettled, and who is in urgent need of assistance for the essentials of life or for transportation.[158]

Although 'transportation' and the 'essentials of life' (whatever that may mean) may be in the best traditions of an enlightened asylum law, as a matter of policy it would be impossible to provide these things without a basis in enlightened immigration policy. Asylum law then, in every practical sense, is the handmaiden of immigration policy. In 1958, the US Congress once again demonstrated the arbitrary nature of asylum policy by passing legislation to provide for 1,500 visas:

> to nationals or citizens of Portugal, who because of natural calamity in the Azore Islands subsequent to September 1, 1957, are out of their usual place of abode in such islands and unable to return there, and who are in urgent need of assistance for the essentials of life.[159]

Amendments made to US policy in 1965 set out 'to repeal the national origin quota provisions' of the existing law 'and to substitute a new system for the selection of immigrants to the United States'[160] by establishing a '[p]ermanent provision ... for the conditional entry of up to 10,200 refugees annually'.[161] Like the policies above, these amendments focused on a variety of political and non-political reasons for granting asylum. They allowed entry not only to people fleeing from either communist oppression or racial, religious, or political oppression in 'any country within the general area of the Middle East' but also to 'persons uprooted by catastrophic natural calamity ... who are unable to return to their usual place of abode'.[162]

Fundamentally, these examples are a testament not to the liberal asylum policies of the US at the time, but to its highly flexible immigration policy, without which its particular asylum policies could never have been affected. In fact, the 'general area of the Middle East' was meant to include the huge part of the under-developed world between and including Libya, Turkey, Pakistan and Ethiopia.[163] Indeed, as a result of flexible immigration policies, the refugee category was expanded to:

> provide relief in those cases where aliens have been forced to flee their homes as a result of serious natural disasters, such as earthquakes, volcanic eruptions, tidal waves, and in any similar natural catastrophes.[164]

It is worth asking why the provision of relief was proper in relation to 'volcanic eruptions' and 'tidal waves' 30 years ago but is not deemed to be so today, when environmental disasters are officially understood to be causing 'environmental refugees'. It is not because environmental disasters are any less common today It is surely only because the United States, like other developed countries around the world, has in the intervening period, tightened its immigration controls, with the unavoidable concomitant negative effect on its once-revered refugee policy. Yet, the amendments to its policies in the 1950s and 1960s are little known and little discussed in the context of refugee policy analyses today. The result is that when distinguished commentators call for a new international policy on forced migrations, they fail to develop the earlier traditions of US policy of this period.[165]

In the circumstances, distinguishing between refugees and other immigrants promotes a false view of the nature of modern migration at a time when this distinction is more blurred than it has ever been before. Refugees and economic migrants come from similar political, economic and environmental backgrounds. In my view, since distinguishing between refugees and migrants may be difficult, refugee rights can better be protected if they are seen in the context of the rights of other migrants, while still preserving their specific relationship to asylum, which remains unique to refugees. Otherwise, the failure to address this dimension will mean that refugees will continue to be subjected to a political and social climate in which immigrants are treated as unwelcome. This is clear if we examine a number of regional arrangements which set out to regulate migration generally. Regional agreements, such as the *Dublin Convention*[166] in Europe, the US-Cuba Joint Communiqué on Migration,[167] and the Comprehensive Plan of Action for Indo-Chinese Refugees in Thailand and Malaysia,[168] are more concerned with restricting migratory population movements than they are with specifically identifying refugees. What this suggests is that the technical distinction between refugees and other immigrants is of limited practical use if states themselves fail to observe it. The distinction may or may not be normatively better, but it needs to be addressed as a matter of practical necessity if a long-term refugee policy is to be implemented successfully.

A NEW PARADIGM FOR REFORM?

What is needed, therefore, is an approach to refugee law that makes connections between refugee law and general immigration rights, and integrates immigration law and refugee law into human rights laws, in the context of more general rights to free movement. This integration will both bolster the *Refugee Convention* and strengthen the rights of refugees as immigrants. Such an approach is warranted today at the beginning of the twenty-first century because of the world-wide socio-cultural approaches that have transformed most societies into pluralistic multi-cultural communities. Democratic pluralism is here to stay. Traditionally, the processes of law and policy-making have neglected the changes in a society's culture, instead attributing major shifts in world society to political and economic forces.[169] In reality, changes in culture have played a greater role in altering perceptions and catalyzing social movements such as women's rights, gay rights and minority rights than political or economic forces.[170] Current approaches to culture in the law are also limited by the idea that culture represents the mores and modes of behavior of narrow, politically powerful elites.[171] Legal discourses must recognize that this narrowly constructed world outlook is no longer appropriate because culture reflects a broader social base. Law and policy-makers must recognize and reflect the importance of more pluralistic and less ethnocentric forces in today's diverse world society.[172]

Lawmakers then, must learn to develop their understanding of refugee law not only through an understanding of modern migration policy concerns, but also through an appreciation of today's globalized and de-territorialized world where draconian restrictions on free movement rights are either counter-productive or contrary to the long-term interests of dynamic societies, or simply do not work. When enacted, the *Refugee Convention* was discriminatory because its drafting reflected only the regional concerns of Western European and North American countries, who hoped to aid people displaced by the Second World War and dissidents escaping communist regimes during the Cold War.[173] The Convention installed a regime limited to the regional concerns of its drafters.[174] As a result of the *Refugee Convention*'s narrow provisions, western countries did not make efforts to admit refugees from the horrors of wars in India, Palestine, China and Korea.[175] These examples suggest that ethnocentric basis of refugee law makes it inadequate for a future where poverty, drought, and ethnic and civil wars are displacing entire populations in developing countries.[176]

Immigrants bring cultural diversity to host nations, thus challenging the traditional concept of the nation-state.[177] Migration is making the traditional notion of an ethnically and culturally integrated and homogenized nation obsolete. This is because a nation is 'a community of people, whose members are bound together by a sense of solidarity, a common culture, a national consciousness' whereas '[a] state is a legal and political organisation, with the power to require obedience and loyalty from its citizens'.[178] Today '[t]here are few, if any, nation-states in the world whose population reflects an entirely homogeneous ethnic, cultural community to the exclusion of all others'.[179] Globalization has led to an emergence of new immigration patterns and new routes for the flow of capital,[180] new North-South relations over markets and the environment,[181] or new geo-political re-alignments following the breakup of post-Cold War and post-colonial states in the former Soviet bloc.[182] Although globalization is generally associated with the global integration of financial markets,[183] it also affects public health,[184] environmental protection,[185] information,[186] and culture.[187] Polarization of the global economy encourages both legal and illegal immigration and places pressure on receiving governments to control their borders.[188] Reform of refugee policy cannot ignore these considerations. Moreover, globalization dissolves the distinction between a states' domestic and foreign policies, forcing policy makers in all regions of the world to address wider global concerns.[189] The shortage of workers is as much of an issue in the developed world as is the rise in international migration. The revolution in computers and communications technology has rapidly globalized financial markets, information and culture,[190] obliterating the distinction between national and international competitors. It is perfectly true that economic globalization has placed renewed pressures on national border control, as the inequalities between Northern and Southern countries have given a fresh impetus to both legal and illegal immigration.[191] Yet, these challenges have to be met in the context of a globalized world that offers fewer opportunities for individual states to restrict migration, especially in the context of the need for more workers.

Some European nations have adopted regional agreements to prevent non-European people from entering their territories,[192] and the *Dublin* and *Schengen* agreements became particularly well known examples of this,[193] as did other discriminatory resettlement programs and safe country policies.[194] Refugee funding provided by the UN and its agencies shows favoritism toward Northern states: the UN has allocated more funds to refugee protection in Europe than to Africa, Asia and the Middle East combined, even though these regions contain three times as many refugees as Europe.[195] By 1995, the UNHCR was spending more on its residual material assistance and other programs in the former Yugoslavia than it was spending to help the 1.7 million Rwandan refugees in Burundi, Tanzania and Zaire.[196] The UN's different response to the Bosnian and the Rwandan refugee crises also reflected its biases.

We should adopt a variety of mediations and brokering techniques in regional conflicts including assistance and asylum programs. As the primary intergovernmental organization responsible for refugee protection, the UNHCR must be reformulated with an eye toward recognizing the diversity of migration flows, in any solution-oriented system for migration reform.[197] When the UN General Assembly promulgated the UNHCR's enabling statute in 1950, it used language synonymous to that of the *Refugee Convention*.[198] The *Refugee Convention* is not geared towards the needs of the South, and therefore neither is the UNHCR's charter. In addition, the UNHCR's governing structure and operating budget often compromise its independence. The UNHCR is funded primarily by voluntary donations from a few developed countries, which dominate the agency's decision making.[199] Other forces can contribute to the UNHCR's ineffectiveness: although Article 35 of its charter requires state parties to cooperate with the UNHCR and to assist it in its duty to supervise the application of the Convention, the Commissioner does not have the power to compel states to cooperate on refugee problems.[200] Accordingly, the UNHCR must be reformulated if it is to meet the demands of the massive flows of migration around the world. Historically, the UNHCR has effectively pressured states to grant asylum to needy refugees.[201] In the future, it must be afforded the resources to facilitate and encourage states to grant asylum to persons who deserve it.

The UNHCR is well equipped to do so. Between 1959 and 1975 the UN General Assembly gradually expanded the mandate of the UNHCR to include and cover protection for migrants who are not strictly refugees within the meaning of the *Convention*.[202] In 1959, *General Assembly Resolution 1388* authorized the grant of asylum to the large number of Chinese refugees who were entering Hong Kong by instructing the UNHCR to use its 'good offices' to assist 'refugees who do not come within the competence of the United Nations'.[203] In 1961, the General Assembly requested that the UNHCR help protect civilians fleeing African countries engaged in struggles for independence against refoulement, even though these migrants were not strictly within the definition of the original mandate.[204] The General Assembly in 1965 abandoned its formal distinction between refugees who were within and without the UNHCR's mandate, in order to extend protection to persons seeking refuge.[205] Again, in 1975, the General Assembly authorized the UNHCR to assume responsibility for persons who were not 'Convention refugees', but who were in 'analogous' situations resulting from man-made events beyond their control.[206]

The UN can facilitate this process further by inquiring into every situation no matter what its refugee impact is on the North. Thus, the UN can consider such factors as the level of acculturation and assimilation, the migration experience, the language spoken, the race and country of origin, the political and religious ties of the ethnic group, and the strengths and positive coping strategies. Only then can the UN reformulate how best to facilitate refugees' reception into a host country, whether than host country is a neighbouring one or a country in western Europe. Such an approach has far better chances of preserving the dignity and human rights of fleeing populations than formal agreements on burden-sharing.

The Overlap of Immigration and Migration in Human Rights Law

In this section, I want to develop the thesis that the incremental recognition of the rights of those other migrants is a necessary prerequisite to the effective long-term protection of the particular rights of present-day asylum-seekers, since both groups are vulnerable to the perverse effects of nativism and xenophobia upon national and international policy-making. The problem may be caused by the increased ease of travel from regions hitherto having restricted access, increasing insecurity in the developing world, or the failure of states to police their borders effectively. I want to argue that to succeed over time, the reform of refugee law must be a specific component within a broader system of immigration rights. State responses to refugees cannot realistically change unless they are tied to state responses to immigration as a whole. Even the European Commission does not doubt that 'asylum cannot be artificially separated from immigration policy in general'.[207] European press coverage, moreover, links the concern over immigration with the concern over refugees with little difficulty, given present public anxiety over the arrival of new migrants.[208] Hathaway and Neve explain why it is in the interests of refugees to be considered as separate from immigration policy, and yet part of human rights:

> It is in the interest of refugees to affirm that refugee protection is a human rights remedy, which should be separated from immigration policies. When refugees are grouped together with all other manner of migrants, be they legal or illegal, skilled or unskilled, law-abiding or undesirable, the fundamental distinction between refugees and other migrants, namely the involuntary nature of the refugees journey, is lost. Advocates have demanded that governments take steps actively to remind the public that refugees are not like other immigrants because they have been forced to flee their homes. A commitment to temporary protection, backed up by policies that will normally lead to repatriation, would help separate refugee protection from immigration policy in general, thereby restoring the focus of attention to the human rights basis of refugees' presence in host countries.[209]

Yet today, as we have already observed, people are migrating for many reasons other than a 'well-founded fear of persecution', as conventionally understood.[210] Commentators have recognized that:

[o]ften it is difficult to distinguish between 'economic' immigrants and refugees. Fleeing oppression is a more reasonable decision when you are anxious to improve your economic status, and when you believe that you will succeed in the country of refuge.[211]

Insisting on applying the *Refugee Convention*'s standards to all migrants will not solve the international problem of migration with which governments ultimately are concerned.[212] This is not to argue that refugees are not a very distinctive group of involuntary migrants deserving of asylum. Rather, refugees are not the only group of migrants who are making similar claims of entry, residence and protection upon national governments.

For that reason, it pays to look at refugees in the context of a general right to free movement for all migrants. Some states in the European Community already view refugees in this broader context.[213] Hathaway and Neve's proposal that 'separat[ing] refugee protection from immigration policy in general'[214] will provide for the 'human rights basis of refugee presence in the host countries'[215] is unconvincing because the human rights are not indivisible. If discrimination is promoted at one end, it becomes difficult to suppress it at the other. For this reason, the protections of both groups must be equally augmented, the growth of which affects the human rights of one group as much as the other.

The way forward is to apply the human rights remedy to all migrants who are either residing in, or are subject to the jurisdiction of, a foreign state. States must be required to respect the human rights of all migrants without regard to race, ethnicity or cultural concerns.[216] States may distinguish between voluntary migrants and involuntary ones, but must recognize the ambiguity of the line between voluntariness and desperation, and should attempt to expand the category of refugees beyond that of the 'persecuted' to include all 'victims' of misgovernment, lost opportunities and artificial disasters.[217] States should minimize this ambiguity by strengthening the application of human rights norms of equal treatment, non-discrimination, parity and justice to all immigrants, while perhaps easing the entry process for some kinds of migrants (such as refugees) more than for others. Proposals for the expansion of the right to refugee status, such as the one advanced by Andrew Shacknove that:

[r]efugee status should only be granted to persons whose government fails to protect their basic needs, who have no remaining recourse other than to seek international restitution of these needs, and who are so situated that international assistance is possible.[218]

will only prove possible in the context of a comprehensive policy that takes account of all migrants.

It is in this context that Hathaway and Neve's suggestion to consider refugees separately from other migrants does not make sense in light of the paradigm that they propose. If their argument is that among migrants, refugees have a unique moral claim to receive refuge, then a paradigm that severely hedges those rights by such stipulations as 'temporary refuge', 'absence of full community membership' and 'voluntary repatriation', is incongruent with that higher moral claim. Indeed, under Hathaway and Neve's paradigm, short-term immigrants, such as work permit holders or missionaries, might be allowed to remain permanently after the expiry of their leave,[219] while refugees fleeing from far more long-term national catastrophes would not. Accordingly, what the international community needs is a regime that clearly prohibits states from discriminating against refugees from such underprivileged areas as the south and incorporates the rights to freedom of movement accorded by other international human rights instruments. A new regime will allow us to move to the position of a principled adoption of a norm of non-discrimination and equal opportunity and equal protection in international law. Because such a norm is already installed in modern human rights law, this ultimately is the best way of incorporating refugee law into human rights law.[220]

Yet, by contrast, Hathaway and Neve reject the current debate among observers of international relations and human rights law who are questioning the dominance of Northern states. Instead, they adopt an approach that is 'reconcilable to Northern countries' self-interest'[221] and:

> simply accepts the reality that the vast majority of the world's refugees do remain in the South, and that their needs are often poorly met, while grossly disproportionate sums of money are spent on *non-entreé* practices and assessing the protection needs of the small minority who reach the North.[222]

Such an approach edifies the status quo, grounded in Hathaway's earlier belief that 'refugee law is fundamentally a means of reconciling the national self-interest of powerful states to the inevitability of involuntary migration'.[223] It is within such constraints that Hathaway first set out in 1991 to 're-orient the reform movement toward an alignment of refugee law with international human rights law', and to request that the current regime 'refocus[] on the restoration of the refugee's right to community membership', so that 'a binding system of inter-state obligation [is] enacted to ensure temporary asylum'.[224]

Given the development of human rights law since 1948, such an approach is retrograde. Existing protections should be strengthened rather than compromised by the recalcitrance of Northern governments. The solution is to bring together the international laws of refugees and of human rights. The latter should not be compromised in order to make the former more palatable to Northern states. After all, the failure of refugee law over the last half century has occurred because refugee law has never been properly incorporated into international human rights law. Thus, not only the *Refugee Convention*, but also mainstream human rights instruments such as the *Universal Declaration of Human Rights* (UDHR) or the *International Covenant on Civil and Political Rights* (ICCPR), fail to provide fleeing populations with the positive human rights of asylum, admission and protection from interdiction at sea.[225]

Integrating Refugee Law into Human Rights Law

So we end this book largely how we started it. We must emphasize and re-emphasize the principles of international morality. Refugee law should be reformed by strengthening and enforcing the provisions of the *Refugee Convention*, which refer to the international moral norms of dignity, integrity and security.[226] The *Refugee Convention* was designed to require states to determine a person's status as a refugee and then to confer the benefits specified in the *Refugee Convention* to all persons classified as refugees.[227] Today states are flouting the spirit of the *Refugee Convention* by denying the benefits of the *Refugee Convention* before they carefully determine whether a person is eligible for refugee status.[228] For example, states are ignoring the principle of non-discrimination, restricting access, denying food, shelter and healthcare to members of particular populations based on their prior determination that members of those populations will not qualify for refugee status regardless of circumstances.[229] This practice highlights the need to strengthen the *Refugee Convention*.[230] The *Refugee Convention* contains rights of dignity that are essential to the maintenance of human rights in the application of refugee law. The non-discrimination provisions of the ICCPR[231] and the *International Covenant on Economic and Social Rights* (ICESCR)[232] complement and provide force to the rights set forth in the *Refugee Convention*. Because refugees are among the most exposed and vulnerable members of society, the failure to accord them rights of dignity is particularly troubling. The norm of non-discrimination runs throughout the human rights conventions. For example, Article 3 of the *Refugee Convention* guarantees that refugees shall receive all *Convention* rights regardless of their race, religion or country of origin.[233] Similarly, Article 26 of the ICCPR entitles all persons to the equal protection and equal benefit of the law.[234] Article 2(2) of the ICESCR declares that state parties should ensure that all persons subject to their jurisdiction receive the equal benefit of the ICESCR.[235]

We cannot carry on ignoring the fact that the diversionary tactics states are using to weaken the protections accorded to refugees violate international human rights law. Article 20 of the *Refugee Convention* requires states to grant all refugees national treatment in access to rationing systems.[236] Refugees need material assistance such as food, shelter, health care and clothing, when they first arrive in another country.[237] Further, Articles 21, 23 and 24 of the *Refugee Convention* provide that a refugee lawfully living in a state is entitled to the same access to public housing, public assistance and social security as a state's nationals.[238] Articles 9, 11 and 12 of the ICESCR provide similar protections.

The *Refugee Convention* also protects refugees' freedom of movement and freedom of association. Many fleeing populations either want to 'associate' with family members who have settled in a state to which they are seeking entry, or want to seek asylum in the territories of former colonial powers (e.g., Britain, France and other European countries). Article 26 grants refugees lawfully in the territory of an asylum state the same freedom of movement that is available to aliens generally. Article 27 provides that refugees who do not have valid travel documents have an absolute right to be issued identity papers.[239] The ICCPR's provisions on freedom of movement and freedom of association correspond to the *Refugee Convention*.[240] Article 15 of the *Refugee Convention* provides refugees who reside lawfully within the territory of an asylum state the same right to freedom of association that states grant to most favored nationals of a foreign country.[241]

Similarly, the *Refugee Convention* protects freedom of religion and conscience as a basic right of dignity and subjects both freedoms to the principle of non-discrimination. Article 4 of the *Refugee Convention* guarantees refugees the same rights to freedom of religion accorded to the nationals of the asylum state.[242] Likewise, Article 18 of the ICCPR protects freedom of thought, conscience and religion, subject to the limitations necessary to protect public safety, order, health, morals, or the fundamental rights and freedoms of others.[243]

The international community should assume humanitarian responsibility for the refugee crisis developing around it. This requires a new normative order which recognizes both the changed nature of refugee movements as well as the changed nature of the modern state. The new normative order must recognize that the plight of refugees infringes their human rights, even before any state assumes political responsibility for them. This will involve rejecting the traditional concept of state sovereignty on which Hathaway and Neve base their proposed reforms. This is not a heretical position. As Louis Henkin has argued:

> [t]he international community should reject by its refugee law, as it has by its human rights law generally, the notion that states maintain exclusive power over entry and presence in their territory as the very essence of their national sovereignty.[244]

Yet, as Santos has remarked:

> [A]s things stand now, no international consensus has been reached on the possible terms of a compromise between the principles of international human rights applicable to nationals and non-nationals and to legal and illegal aliens, on the one hand, and the principle of territorial sovereignty, on the other. In other words, no international migration regime has come into existence.[245]

The international refugee regime must establish the rights of refugees as human rights and recognize a legal right to asylum as an aspect of the fundamental right to life and liberty.[246] The international system must recognize that the *Universal Declaration*, the covenants, and other human rights instruments apply to refugees as to all human beings who are or become subject to a state's jurisdiction in any manner [and that this] includes displaced persons and those in safe havens; it includes so-called 'boat people' on the high seas. And it applies to countries of first asylum as to all other states.[247] The principles of equality and equal treatment together with non-discrimination, which form the basis of the *Refugee Convention*, must receive the highest priority in future policy considerations. Otherwise, the human rights of refugees will mean little more in the future than they do today.

The international community must accept responsibility for causing the international disorder that is generating the refugee crisis.[248] This means accepting that military action in Afghanistan, Iraq, and possibly Iran has consequences that cannot be easily ignored if the interests of international order are to be safeguarded. Hathaway and Neve also attempt to develop a theory of international collective responsibility for the international disorder that generates refugee crisis, but in their scheme the shape of modern refugee law should be parallel to root causes of intervention, rather than something that can be traded off against it.[249] The international community must be held morally accountable more directly for failing to enforce the human rights responsibilities of states and for failing to assume responsibility to provide remedies for refugee flows. Nonetheless, holding the international community responsible will not in itself solve the current problems of global migration if states remain as reluctant to intervene as they were in the case of the Bosnian Muslims[250] in the 1990s, and as reluctant to intervene in Sudan or Zimbabwe today. As Professor Hathaway's letter to me recognized, only through multi-state responsibility can:

> [a] political system [assume] collective responsibility for addressing human rights violations in Bosnia, Rwanda, and Haiti, [and] . . . collective responsibility for the failure to end such violations and for the consequences of such failures.[251]

Human rights violations in the treatment of migrants threaten international order, just as other major human rights violations seriously threaten to international peace and security. Because the Security Council can intervene to prevent and remove threats to international peace,[252] it should be able to intervene to protect refugees. The UN's current failure to act forcefully to protect refugees reflects the cultural incompetence of the members of the Security Council, who view the problems of far-off developing nations as remote. As the UN Special Rapporteur in the Former Yugoslovia noted in 1994:

> The first safe area was not authorized until ... almost six months after the Special Rapporteur had made his recommendation. The safe areas in ... Sarajevo in particular are for the most part dramatically overcrowded, short of basic food and medical resources and [subject] to indiscriminate shelling and military attacks. UNPROFOR has been unable to ensure the safety of those areas. To a large extent they have become 'safe' only on paper.[253]

Thus, the Special Rapporteur recommended that 'human rights concerns be given priority in the peace process regarding Bosnia and Herzegovina'. In so doing, he reiterated his request for expansion of the 'safe area' concept and emphasized the need for both the international community and the parties to the Bosnian conflict to recognize the rights of flight and asylum.[254] Reform proposals today must not exacerbate the marginalism of refugee law, and should instead securely place the protections of refugee law within the international human rights movement.

To this end, it is time for the international community to leave behind outdated notions of state sovereignty and to promulgate a right to migrate as a critical component of international peace and world order. International law and practice show that the international community has the capacity to undertake such a reform.[255] The UDHR sets forth a norm of universal equal opportunity and protection for all members of the global community.[256] Member states of the UN have undertaken to engage in 'joint and separate action in co-operation with'[257] the United Nations to help achieve fundamental human rights and socioeconomic development. A good example of how states can, within international frameworks, cooperate in the admission of aliens is provided by the 1974 World Population Plan of Action, which developed new methods to facilitate human migration.[258] This instrument was the result of the 1974 World Population Conference in Bucharest, which urged governments to facilitate migration and help reunite families. The plan urged countries affected by significant numbers of migrant workers to conduct bilateral or multilateral consultations with a view to harmonizing policies that influence these movements.[259]

Similarly, the *1980 Brandt Commission on North-South Issues* demonstrated the importance of human migration as a component of global development.[260] It called for developed countries to liberalize their immigration laws and policies to facilitate migration. Scholars such as Stanley Hoffman, writing at the time that the *Commission* released its report, broadly endorsed its policy objective.[261] Hoffman argued that, 'it remains the duty of each country to open its own borders as widely as possible [to refugees], without looking for excuses or waiting for others to act'.[262] With respect to migrant workers, Hoffman argued that 'there is a moral duty on host states not simply to get rid of the foreign work force when a recession hits, nor to apply retroactive measures in order to thin its ranks'.[263] As the foregoing discussion illustrates, the expansion of refugee rights will succeed if the international community demands respect for the dignity and human rights of all migrants from the governments of foreign states. 'The ideal would be … that any person should be able to enter any country he might choose.'[264] The realities of global development require an immigration policy based on this ideal and on the fundamental rights of migrants to leave, stay and return, particularly with regard to those countries with whom individual migrants have particular close ties, whether racial or historical.

CONCLUSION

Any reform proposal today must be evaluated in the context of the failure of wealthy nations to fulfill their responsibility to admit refugees. The ever-widening regional conflicts of the world today suggest that the wider international community should bear a greater responsibility. For example, group interventions are often vetoed by one nation, with disastrous consequences. Yet, these situations should inform our sense of responsibility and duty in the resolution of conflict situations world-wide. When we consider the added impact of globalization on the paradigm of the conventional nation-state, we see how hollow the protection of narrow domestic national interests can be. This chapter has tried to make a clear case for the enfranchisement of refugee rights. These rights must be safeguarded if the international community can claim to be making a commitment to international human rights law in the twenty-first century. They are also necessary as a basis for a functional global community that relies on the unifying concepts of universal equal access, opportunity and open societies. A system of burden sharing must not be so one-sided as to impose disproportionate and discriminatory burdens on Southern states.

This chapter has also attempted to demonstrate that human rights discourse must develop a theory of immigration rights that includes refugee rights as a specific component of a broader system of rights. Such integration will be more effective and realistic than an approach that focuses only on the movement of refugees into foreign territories. Currently, the human rights element of refugee law is misunderstood because it is separated from broader considerations of immigration policy.

Even if states have the rights to exclude some aliens some of the time, international law must maintain the distinction between rightful and wrongful exercise of that power.[265] As a valid proposition of international law, exclusionary propositions are immoral and impractical, and ought to be rejected. Refugee policy and other pressing migration issues today cannot be confronted directly because of the questionable basis of the exclusionary proposition. Until exclusionary tactics are eliminated, the international community must insist that aliens – including refugees – be rejected only for the most extreme and valid of reasons, subject only to strict criteria such as public policy, public security and public health.[266]

NOTES

1   *The Convention Relating to Status of Refugees*, opened for signature, July 28, 1951, art. 1A(2), 189 U.N.T.S. 137 (entered into force April 22, 1954).

2   *Protocol Relating to the Status of Refugees*, opened for signature, January 31, 1967, art 1(3), 19 U.S.T. 6223, 606 U.N.T.S. 267 (entered into force October 4, 1967).

3   See Arthur C. Helton, 'Essay: The Role of International Law in the Twenty-First Century: Forced International Migration: A Need for New Approaches by the International Community', 18 *Fordham Int'l L.J.* 1623, 1627 (1995).

4   See James C. Hathaway and R. Alexander Neve, 'Making International Refugee Law Relevant Again: A Proposal for Collectivized and Solution Oriented Protection', 10 *Harv. Hum. Rts. J.* 115, 203 (1997). A system of burden-sharing, in this context, apportions different roles to different states. Instead of hosting refugees, wealthy nations may provide monetary support to poorer host nations.

5   See 2 Atle Grahl-Madsen, *The Status of Refugees in International Law* 3, 7 (1972). The effect of burden-sharing within the European Union, where it has proceeded further than anywhere else, is that refugees are allowed to apply for asylum only in the first member state they enter or in the state that issued their visas. Refugees may not travel to other European Union member states and apply for asylum in those states. These procedures were established by two accords: the *Convention Determining the State Responsible for Examining Applications for Asylum Lodged in One of the Member States of the European Communities*, June 15 1990, arts. 4–8, 30 I.L.M. 425 [hereinafter *Dublin Convention*] and the *Convention Applying the Schengen Agreement of 14 June 1985 Between the Governments of the States of the Benelux*

Economic Union, the Federal Republic of Germany and the French Republic, on the Gradual Abolition of Checks at their Common Borders, June 19, 1990, ch. 7, art. 30, 30 I.L.M. 84, 95–100 (1991) [hereinafter *Schengen II*]. These accords significantly reduced the ability of asylum-seekers to choose where to apply for asylum and made it more difficult for refugees to apply for asylum in countries with more liberal asylum laws. Thus, these accords replaced the individual will with the will of states. See Tom Casey, 'Europe 1992 – Closing the Doors', *STUD.* 48, 52 (1991), cited in James C. Hathaway, 'Harmonizing for Whom? The Devaluation of Refugee Protection in the Era of European Economic Integration', 26 *Cornell Int'l L.J.* 719, 726 n.45 (1993).

6   See Jeffrey A. Hart, Comments on 'Changing Sovereignty Games and International Migration', 2 *Ind. J. Global Legal Stud.* 171, 173 (1994).

7   See Aristide R. Zolberg *et al.*, *Escape from Violence: Conflict and the Refugee Crisis in the Developing World* v (1989). The authors observe that regional ethnic strife has created a refugee flow that is 'widely perceived as an unprecedented crisis', ibid.

8   Some feel that state practice is whittling away refugee protections. Those who want to expand traditional refugee protections, such as Aristide R. Zolberg, Astri Suhrke and Sergio Aguayo, argue that the definition of refugee should be expanded to include 'victims' of societal and international violence in addition to the 'activist[s]' and 'target[s]' who are currently protected. See *id.*, at 30–31. Others define the problem as one of numbers and not definitions because 'the Geneva system of 1959 is not fit to cope with large refugee movements'. Kay Hailbronner, 'Temporary and Local Responses to Forced Migrations: A Comment', 35 *Va. J. Int'l L.* 81, 92–3 (1994). Somewhat pragmatically, Peter Schuck recently has opted for the broadest connotation to characterize individuals who have fled their country for one reason or another and believe that they cannot or should not return to it in the near future, although they may hope to do so if conditions permit.
    Peter H. Schuck, 'Refugee Burden Sharing: A Modest Proposal', 22 *Yale J. Int'l L.* 243, 244 n.1 (Summer 1997).

9   *Convention Relating to Status of Refugees, supra* note 1, art. 1A(2). Article 1A(1) of the *1951 Convention* defined refugees as persons considered refugees under the 'Arrangements of 12 May 1926 and 30 June 1928 or under the Conventions of 28 October 1933 and 10 February 1938, the Protocol of 14 September 1939 or the Constitution of the International Refugee Organization'. *Id.* art. 1A(1). In addition, Article 1B gave State Parties to the Convention the option to restrict their commitment to persons displaced by 'events occurring in Europe'. ibid. art. 1B.

10 As Hathaway has observed, '[t]here is a pervasive belief that the cultural and racial heterogeneity which accompanies immigration jeopardizes European identity and solidarity'. James C. Hathaway, *Harmonizing for Whom?, supra* note 5, at 720.

11 *Convention Relating to the Status of Refugees, supra* note 1, art. 1(A)(2).

12 Ibid.

13 See Joan Fitzpatrick, 'Revitalizing the 1951 Refugee Convention', 9 *Harv. Hum. Rts. J.* 229, 253 (1996).

14 See, e.g., Rosemary Byrne and Andrew Shacknove, 'The Safe Country Notion in European Asylum Law', 9 *Harv. Hum. Rts. J.* 185, 185–6 (1996); Joan Fitzpatrick, *supra* note 13, at 231; Hathaway and Neve, *supra* note 4, at 119 n.7. The United Nations High Commissioner for Refugees (UNHCR) has described voluntary

repatriation as 'the ideal solution to refugee problems'. See Report of the Executive Committee of the Programme of the United Nations High Commissioner for Refugees on the Work of its Forty-Fifth Session, U.N. GAOR, 49th Sess. at 10, para. 19(v), UN Doc. A/Ac.96/839(1994) [hereinafter Executive Committee Report].

15   Permanent admission is clearly difficult in the case of an entire displaced population. According to the UNHCR:

> [i]n a number of conflicts today, displacement of people is not the by-product of war but one of its primary purposes. In the face of this grim reality, encouraging permanent resettlement of refugees can mean abetting forcible expulsion. In a setting such as Bosnia and Herzegovina, it is important to keep alive the idea of return in order to avoid collaborating, however unwillingly, in the crime of 'ethnic cleansing'.

United Nations High Commissioner for Refugees, *The State of the World's Refugees 1993: The Challenge of Protection* 41 (1993).

16   For example, in the 12 months after Britain imposed fines on airline carriers that brought foreigners to Britain without visas, the number of asylum applications filed at British airports fell by 50 per cent. Peter Kessler, 'Jet Set Refugees', 88 *Refugees* 35 (1992); see also Érika Feller, 'Carrier Sanctions and International Law', 1 *Int'l J. Refugee L.* 48 (1989).

17   The 'safe country notion' in European refugee law highlights this strategy. See Byrne and Shacknove, *supra* note 14, at 200–201.

18   Santos, ibid., at p.226.

19   See James C. Hathaway, 'Reconceiving Refugee Law as Human Rights Protection', 4 *J. Refugee Stud.* 113, 113–31 (1991).

20   Hathaway and Neve, *supra* note 4.

21   *Reconceiving International Refugee Law* (James Hathaway (ed.), 1997).

22   Letter from James Hathaway, Osgoode Hall Law School of York University, to Satvinder Juss 2 (Jan. 25, 1998) (on file with author) [hereinafter 'Letter from Hathaway'].

23   Satvinder S. Juss, 'Toward a Morally Legitimate Reform of Refugee Law: The Uses of Cultural Jurisprudence', *Harvard Hum. Rts Jnl* (Vol. 11, 1998) pp.311–354. It is to be noted that humanitarian law has an undisputed moral basis. The European Commission has determined that the European Convention on Human Rights, like the Convention on Genocide, has a humanitarian character whose object was to 'safeguard the very existence of certain human groups' and to 'endorse the most elementary principles of morality'. European Commission of Human Rights, Report, 15 *Hum. Rts. L.J.* 215, 228 (1994). See also European Convention for the Protection of Human Rights and Fundamental Freedoms, opened for signature Nov. 26, 1987, Doc. no. H(87)4 1987, E.T.S. 126, reprinted in 27 I.L.M. 1152 (entered into force Feb. 1, 1989). Arguably, this observation applies to all humanitarian rules of international law, yet scholars have given little consideration to the morality of migration processes. On the other hand, the immorality of current refugee practices is evident in the handling of the recent Iraqi Kurdish crisis in 1991, which provides a useful lens through which to evaluate current reform proposals. See *infra* text accompanying note 60. As Dennis Gallagher of the Refugee Policy Group has observed:

> [T]he Kurdish case was a clear example of refugees fleeing danger and being rejected at the frontier. Rather than affirming refugees' right to seek asylum,

the international community affirmed its own right to establish conditions allowing repatriation by citing a threat to international peace and security.

Dennis Gallagher, 'Durable Solutions in a New Political Era', 47 *J. Int'l Aff.* 429, 440 (Winter, 1994).

24 In his response to a draft of this chapter, Hathaway said:

> Fundamentally, I do not dispute the moral attractiveness of the alternative paradigm you posit. Rather, our disagreement is about whether that paradigm is, or ever could become, part of international law (I believe not). Your study is an eloquent plea in the tradition of critical legal studies. My own work, in contrast, is essentially a neo-pragmatic attempt to reconcile critical analysis to what I believe to be real and unchangeable constraints of international law and relations. My assessment is that your alternative proposal – premised on the proclamation of a general human right to migrate at will – can never succeed in the real world. In my view of ethicality – in which criticality must be tempered by considerations of feasibility – it therefore fails the test of moral legitimacy.

Letter from Hathaway, *supra* note 22, at 1. The reader may also consider the arguments for equal opportunity and protection, already made in the international forum. See *infra* text accompanying notes 189–90.

25 Hathaway and Neve, *supra* note 4, at 117.
26 Ibid. at 139, 163–5.
27 Hathaway and Neve state:

> We argue for an openness to reform of the mechanisms of refugee law on purely instrumentalist grounds. Reform makes sense not because temporary protection and shared responsibility are necessarily better than permanent protection and particularized responsibility, but as a means to counter the withdrawal of states from their protective responsibilities.

Ibid., at 155 (emphasis added).
28 Ibid. at 137–38, 206.
29 As Hathaway and Neve state:

> The approach advocated here simply accepts the reality that the vast majority of the world's refugees do remain in the South, and that their needs are often poorly met, while grossly disproportionate sums of money spent on non-entrée practices and assessing the protection needs of the small minority who reach the North. Better protection in the regions of origin, which we believe will flow from a principled sharing regime, will benefit the overwhelming majority of refugees.

Ibid., at 207 (internal citation omitted).
30 As Hathaway and Neve observe, 'it is presently politically unwise to insist that states permanently enfranchise all refugees. Such a stance holds refugees hostage to a major project of social transformation', ibid. at 139 (emphasis added).
31 Hathaway and Neve note clearly that '[n]ativism, and even racism, have undoubtedly shaped the refugee policies of many governments'. Although they recognize that it is 'important to promote a breaking down of irrational fears of

foreigners and, in particular, a credible understanding of the democratic limits to communal closure', they also observe that requiring states to enfranchise all refugees permanently would entail a 'major project of social transformation' and for this reason opt for 'solution-oriented temporary protection'. ibid. at 138–39.

32 See ibid., at 204.

33 Hathaway and Neve suggest that in such cases 'other states will of necessity be called upon to receive refugees'. ibid. at 206. These invariably will be the poorer states adjoining existing refugee-producing territories.

34 See *Environmental Refugees: The Case for Recognition*, available at http://www. neweconomics.org/gen/z_sys_PublicationDetail.aspx?PID=159.

35 See Paul Brown, 'Refugee Warning to Global Polluters', *The Guardian*, 30th September 2003.

36 Santos, *op.cit.*, at p.234.

37 Santos, *op.cit.*, at p.226.

38 M. Woehlcke, *Environmental Refugees*, Aussenpolitik, 43(3), 1992, pp.287–8.

39 Andrew Hagan, 'A journey in the South', *London Review of Books* (Vol. 27, No. 19, 6th October 2005, pp.3–12) at p.6.

40 Jo Tuckman, 'The deadly aftermath of a hurricane called Stan', *The Guardian* (7th October 2005) at p.20.

41 Santos, *op.cit.*, at p.226–7.

42 Santos, *op.cit.*, at p.227.

43 Santos, *op.cit.*, at p.227.

44 See *id.*, at 183. Walzer shows how the protection of refugee rights in practice today cannot be separated from the dominant state practice of the exercise of partisan immigration policies. Although Walzer regards refugees as having a special entitlement to be taken into a national community because the 'need ... for membership' is a 'non-exportable good', he also takes the view that '[t]he liberty that makes certain countries possible homes for men and women ... is also non-exportable'. See Michael Walzer, *Spheres of Justice: A Defense of Pluralism and Equality* 48–9 (1983). This being so, '[t]hese goods can be shared only within the protected space of a particular state' where preferential admission policies can be enacted. *Id.*

45 The sovereign states' right to close its borders is fundamental because the

> distinctiveness of cultures and groups depends upon closure and, without it, cannot be conceived as a stable feature of human life. If this distinctiveness is a value, as most people (though some of them are global pluralists, and others only local loyalists) seem to believe, then closure must be permitted somewhere.

Ibid., at 39. Even when 'necessitous strangers' seek asylum, under Walzer's theory, a state may fulfill its obligation by exporting its superfluous wealth to assist them. ibid., at 47.

46 See Hathaway and Neve, *supra* note 4, at 206.

47 Drawing upon the paradigm of Gervase Coles, Hathaway considers that except:

> in the case of intractable situations of human rights abuse, where the norm of temporary refuge must at some stage be converted to permanent residency, the special moral claim of refugees to integration in a new community is ... suspect, and may indeed constitute an infringement of the refugee's right to

be restored to full membership in her own society. This position opens the door to renewed analysis of the morally acceptable options to address the claims of refugees.

Hathaway, 'Reconceiving Refugee Law', *supra* note 19, at 125.

48   Hathaway and Neve, *supra* note 4, at 117, 140, 142, 209–10.

49   Hathaway and Neve observe that '80 per cent of the world's population is already protected in the less developed world'; that the 'wealthy governments contribute less than US $1.2 billion each year to address the needs of … refugees remaining in the South'; and that 'Africa alone shelters nearly double the number of refugees protected in all of Europe, North America, and Oceania combined'. They hold that under the scheme they propose, 'the criteria identified here are likely to mean that most refugees will be physically protected within their region of origin'. ibid. at 146, 153, 191–2, 205 (internal citation omitted).

50   Ibid., at 117, 140, 171–2, 210. Hathaway and Neve's views on 'voluntary repatriation' resemble those of Coles, who first argued that states have a 'serious responsibility to take whatever measures [are] possible … to enable people who have fled its territory to return', failing which 'it would institutionalize exile at the expense of the fundamental rights of the individual to return to his country and to enjoy his basic human rights'. See G. Coles, *Placing the Refugee Issues on the New International Agenda* 10 (1990), cited in Hathaway, *Reconceiving Refugee Law, supra* note19, at 116–17.

51   Hathaway and Neve propose 'to shift away from particularized duties and toward substantially greater collectivized protection efforts'. Hathaway and Neve, *supra* note 4, at 143. Hathaway and Neve refer to this as 'a framework of common but differentiated responsibility among states'. See ibid. at 118. As this chapter argues, the collectivized effort they propose would continue to place the majority of the burden on poor Southern states.

52   See ibid. at 196–201.

53   Hathaway originally drew inspiration for this from Garvey's effort to link the pursuit of human rights aims to politically pragmatic processes. Garvey advocates a requirement that states that create refugee flows compensate states that grant asylum to refugees. To oversee compliance, Garvey proposes establishing an international supervisory institution. See G. Garvey, 'The New Asylum Seekers: Addressing Their Origin', in *The New Asylum Seekers: Refugee Law in the 1980s: The Ninth Sokol Colloquium on International Law* 188 (David A. Martin (ed.), 1988), cited in Hathaway, *Reconceiving Refugee Law, supra* note 19, at 118–19. Although Garvey acknowledges that many refugee-producing states may lack the means to make proper restitution, he believes that some involvement of the state of origin is essential for a constructive resolution of the refugee problem because 'international law is respected where it represents mutual political interests or fear of political sanction'. See ibid.

54   Hathaway and Neve, *supra* note 4, at 201.

55   See, e.g., ibid. at 210.

56   See Hathaway, 'Reconceiving Refugee Law', *supra* note 19, at 128–9.

57   Letter from Hathaway, *supra* note 22, at 2.

58   Hathaway's advocacy of negotiation has grown stronger since he published his first article in 1991. See generally Hathaway, 'Reconceiving Refugee Law', *supra* note 19; Hathaway and Neve, *supra* note 4.

59   See, e.g. Hathaway and Neve, *supra* note 4, at 204.

60   Hathaway and Neve refer to the need for 'functional compatibility between refugees and their potential host communities', and state that 'attention should be

paid to cultural harmony'. They explain that '[t]he existence of ethnic, religious, or other bonds between refugees and the population of a particular host state is often indicative of a situation in which refugees are most likely to be most readily accepted'. ibid. at 204.

61   Letter from Hathaway, *supra* note 22, at 2 (emphasis in original). See also Hathaway and Neve, *supra* note 4, at 206–207.

62   Hathaway and Neve, *supra* note 4, at 146, 153, 191–2, 205.

63   See T. Alexander Aleinikoff, 'Safe Haven: Pragmatics and Prospects', 35 *Va. J. Int'l L.* 71, 74 (1994). 'Safe havens' have the effect of internalizing refugees by keeping them within their area of origin. Under UN Security Council Resolution 688, the UN created what may be viewed as the first 'safe haven' by insisting that Iraq allow immediate humanitarian assistance to Kurdish enclaves, and halt repression of Kurdsih populations, in Northern Iraq. As the events described in the text above illustrate, however, this measure did not adequately protect the Kurds. UN Sec. Council Res. 688, April 5, 1991. See also Jane E. Stromseth, 'Iraq's Repression of its Civilian Population: Collective Responses and Continuing Challenges', in *Enforcing Restraint: Collective Intervention in Internal Conflicts* 77, 88–93 (Lori F. Damrosch (ed.), 1993). The 'safe haven' concept was later applied in Bosnia-Herzegovina, when the U.N. felt that the existence of safe havens would help NGOs provide more humanitarian aid and greater protection of human rights. See European Consultation on Refugees and Exiles ('ECRE'). *Report of ECRE Bi-annual General Meeting* (Berlin April 23–25, 1993). The EC documents state that displaced people should be encouraged to stay in the 'nearest safe area to their homes' with the provision of assistance to enable this. See Council of Europe, *Contribution to the CSCE Human Dimension Seminar on Migration, including refugees and displaced persons* (Warsaw, Apr. 20–23, 1993)(Apr. 14, 1993). See also Danièle Joly, 'The Porous Dam: European Harmonization on Asylum in the Nineties', 6 *Int'l J. Ref. L.* 159, 162 (1994), citing Jochen Blascke, 'Refugees and Turkish Migrants in West-Berlin', in *Reluctant Hosts: Europe and its Refugees* (Danièle Joly and R. Cohen (eds), 1989).

64   'Containment' comprises deterrent, exclusionary and diversionary measures. The paradigmatic example of containment is the US and Cuban governments' Migration Accord, which seeks to contain populations fleeing from Cuba and create channels for orderly migration of Cubans by limiting all irregular migration flows. See 'The US-Cuba Joint Communique on Migration', 5 *US Dep't St.* Dispatch 603 (Sept. 12, 1994). A similar strategy has been used to control the migration of people from Indochina. See Stem A. Bronee, 'The History of Comprehensive Plan of Action', 5 *Int'l Refugee L.* 534 (1993). In his study, Peter Schuck has argued that '[t]he CPA resettlement program provides a useful study of the conditions under which burden-sharing can succeed'. Schuck, *supra* note 8, at 254. Containment would appear to be the hallmark of contemporary refugee policy since, according to Joan Fitzpatrick, 'large numbers of persons with unadjudicated but potentially valid, claims to political asylum have been funneled either into off-shore temporary refuges or into temporary protection schemes in European states'. Joan Fitzpatrick, 'Flight from Asylum: Trends Toward Temporary 'Refuge' and Local Responses to Force Migrations', 35 *Va. J. Int'l L.* 13, 65. For a detailed discussion of containment see Andrew Shacknove, 'From Asylum to Containment', 5 *Int'l J. Ref. L.* 516 (1993).

65   'Temporary protection' has become a fundamental norm of the modern refugee regime. The idea dates back at least to 1979, when the UN Executive Committee concluded that 'in cases of large-scale influx, persons seeking asylum should always receive at least temporary refuge'. See *Report on the Thirtieth Session of the*

Executive Committee of the High Commissioner's Programme, 30th Sess., UN Doc. A/AC.96/572, para. 72(2)(f) (1979). In 1981 the UNHCR emphasized this idea again, arguing that temporary protection provided support for the principle of non-refoulement. See *Addendum to the Report of the United Nations High Commissioner for Refugees*, UN GAOR, 36th Sess., Supp. No. 12A, at 18, UN Doc. A/36/12/Add.1 (1981).

66　For example, even 'temporary refuge', which is the most 'pragmatic and flexible method' of dealing with mass flow of migration, diminishes existing rights. See Executive Committee Report, *supra* note 14, paras. 19(r), 19(s). As the UNHCR said in 1993, 'there are fears that temporary asylum, while broadening refugee protection, may also weaken it' because it 'eases pressure on governments to apply the [Refugee] Convention along with its wide range of economic and social rights'. UNHCR, *supra* note 15, at 41.

67　See Joly, *supra* note 54, at 179–83.

68　Arthur Helton, *The Price of Indifference* (OUP, 2002) at chapter 6.

69　Hathaway and Neve recognize that:

> [t]he North has thus far acted unilaterally, to the detriment of both refugees and the Southern countries that shoulder the resultant responsibilities and burdens of protection.

See Hathaway and Neve, *supra* note 4, at 205. The United States has engaged in this discriminatory behavior as well. Under the Reagan and Bush administrations in 1982 and 1992, the US intercepted Haitian refugees at sea and returned them to Haiti. See generally Bill Frelick, 'Haitian Boat Interdiction and Return: First Asylum and First Principles of Refugee Protection', 26 *Cornell Int'l L.J.* 675 (1993), cited in Hathaway and Neve, *supra* note 4, at 122 n.18. In 1994, the US refused to accept Cuban refugees who tried to flee to the US by boat. The US Coast Guard placed the Cuban refugees in refugee camps in Panama and Guantanamo Bay. See Tim Johnson, 'US Troops Wary on Moving Cubans', *Seattle Times*, Jan. 31, 1995, at A11.

70　See Katherine A. Wilkens, 'How We Lost the Kurdish Game', *Washington Post*, Sept. 15, 1996, at C1.

71　See Mikhael Barutciski, 'The Reinforcement of Non-Admission Policies and the Subversion of the UNHCR: Displacement and Internal Assistance in Bosnia-Herzegovina (1992–94)', 8 *Int'l J. Refugee L.* 49, 74–5, 85 (1996).

72　See 'Zaire Expels 3,500 Refugees from Rwanda Border Camp', *N.Y. Times*, Aug. 22, 1995 at 2. See also Hathaway and Neve, *supra* note 4, at 137.

73　*Internal Flight or Relocation* (UNHCR 23rd July 2003).

74　Hathaway and Neve recognize that '[a]s refugee populations originate disproportionately in the South, most refugees will remain in the South under a workable responsibility sharing plan, and Northern states might be viewed as 'buying their way out' of an obligation to provide refuge'. Hathaway and Neve, *supra* note 4, at 205.

75　*AE and FE v. Secretary of State for the Home Department* [2003] INLR 475. CA per the Master of the Rolls, at para 67.

76　Ibid., at para 24.

77　*AE (Relocation-Darfur-Khartoum an option) Sudan CG* [2005] UKIAT 00101 (d. 3 May 2005) AIT at *para 14*.

78　Ibid., at para 15. Also now see, *LM (Relocation-Khartoum-AE reaffirmed) Sudan* [2005] UKIAT 00114 (30 June 2005). See also, Johann Hari, 'The century's first genocide is nearly over', *The Independent*, (4th October 2005) at p.31, who concludes that, 'Darfur's holocaust is a bleak demonstration of how little the world's most powerful institutions are motivated by basic human morality'.

79 Hathaway and Neve rightly recognize that 'the developed world has already off-loaded most obligations onto the South, without paying anything for the privilege'. However, they state that 'the difference between the status quo and what we propose is ... not so much where refugees will be protected, but the equity of the conditions under which that protection will be provided'. Ibid. at 206.

80 *Said Mohammed v. SSHD*, Refusal Letter (at para 11) dated 21st June 2005, HO Ref: M1078895, App. Ref: AA/06019/2005, Heard in Walsall on 28th Sep 2005.

81 Hathaway and Neve explain:

> There is ... no quid pro quo that could induce the North to dismantle all barriers to access and to grant temporary protection, much less routine permanent admission, to all refugees who arrive at its borders. Ready access to durable asylum in the North is simply not on the table, and an approach to refugees law reform that assumes otherwise is bound to fail. Ibid.

82 Ibid.

83 Good faith is a part of international law. See Michael Virally, 'Review Essay: Good Faith in Public International Law', 77 *Am. J. Int'l L.* 130 (1983) (reviewing Elisabeth Zoller, *La Bonne Foi en Droit International Public* (1977)). Since discriminatory treatment on racial, ethnic and cultural grounds has been regarded even by exclusionists as a 'token[] of arrogance', the role of good faith suggests that even if States have the right to exclude some of the aliens some of the time, the distinction between rightful and wrongful exercise of that power must be emphatically maintained in international law as a matter of international order. See Charles C. Hyde, *International Law Chiefly as Interpreted and Applied by the United States* 216, 218 (2d rev. ed. 1947).

84 Hathaway and Neve, *supra* note 4, at 204.

85 Ibid (footnotes omitted).

86 See *supra* text accompanying notes 60–62.

87 Hathaway and Neve, *supra* note 4, at 204 (internal citations omitted). Note also that Rosemary Byrne and Andrew Shacknove observe that Hathaway's earlier proposals were based on the assumption that 'refugees would not have the liberty to seek asylum in the State of their choice, but would rather be afforded protection within a culturally, racially, politically or otherwise affiliated State'. Byrne and Shacknove, *supra* note 14, at 197 n.48 (internal citations omitted).

88 No public system should countenance discrimination, whether in its terms or in its effect. See Hathaway, 'Reconceiving Refugee Law', *supra* note 19, at 128. See also Hathaway and Neve, *supra* note 4, at 204 (calling for functional compatibility between refugees and their potential host communities). In the case of post colonial societies, the cultural compatibility may be a root cause of contention; for example, Africans may assert special rights to receive asylum from their European former colonial masters, but find it denied on the grounds of cultural compatibility.

89 See the 1973 East African Asians Case, in which the European Commission of Human Rights held that UK legislation designed to prevent Asian citizens of the UK from gaining entry, after their continued residence in East Africa became difficult, was racially motivated and therefore tantamount to degrading and in-

human treatment. Despite its importance, the decision was only made public in 1994, 20 years later. *East African Asians v. United Kingdom*, App. Nos. 4403/70-4419/70, 4422/70, 4423/70, 4434/70, 4443/70, 4476/70-4478/70, 4486/70, 4501/70, 4526/70-4530/70, 78-A, reprinted in 15 *Hum. Rts. L.J.* 215 (1994).

90   See HYDE, *supra* note 83, at 216, 218.

91   See United Nations Sub-Commission on Prevention of Discrimination and Protection of Minorities, Treaties and International Instruments Concerning the Protection of Minorities, 1919–1951, paras. 2–12, U.N. Doc. E/CN.4/Sub.2/133 (1951).

92   Hurst Hannum, *Autonomy, Sovereignty, and Self-Determination* 55 (rev. ed. 1996).

93   G.A. Res. 428, U.N. GAOR, 5th Sess., Supp. No. 20, at 46, U.N. Doc. A/1775 (1950).

94   See Michael R. Marrus, *The Unwanted: European Refugees in the 20th Century* 122–207 (1985).

95   Ibid.

96   See Morten Kjaerum, 'Opinion: Temporary Protection in Europe in the 1990s', 6 *Int'l J. Refugee L.* 444, 450–56 (1994).

97   See Ulrike Davy, 'Refugees From Bosnia and Herzegovina: Are They Genuine?', 18 *Suffolk Transnat'l L.J.* 53, 63–4 (1995).

98   Ibid. See also Fitzpatrick, *supra* note 13, at 241 n.52. For a discussion of Germany and Europe, see Gerald L. Neuman, 'Buffer Zones against Refugees: Dublin, Schengen, and the German Asylum Amendment', 33 *Va. J. Int'l L.* 503.

99   See *BBC News*, 'Obituary: Pim Fortuyn', available at *BCC News* website at http://www.bbc.co.uk.

100   See *CNN.com*, 'Dutch Election on Despite Murder', available at *CNN News* website at http://www.cnn.com.

101   Ibid.

102   See Hugh Schofield, 'Profile: Jean-Marie Le Pen', available at *BBC News* website at http://www.bbc.co.uk.

103   See *BBC News*, 'Profile: Lionel Jospin', available at *BBC News* website at http://www.bbc.co.uk.

104   See the case of, '*Victorian Council for Civil Liberties Incorporated v. Minister for Immigration and Multicultural Affairs* [2001] FCA 1297, 11 Sept. 2001, which was overruled later by Minister for *Immigration and Multicultural Affairs and others v. Victorian Council for Civil Liberties Incorporated and others* [2001] FCA 1329, (18 Sept. 2001). A final appeal to the High Court took place in the case of Minister for *Immigration & Multicultural Affairs and others v. Victorian Council for Civil Liberties Incorporated and others* [2001] FCA 1865 (21 Dec. 2001). Note, that the asylum seekers were euphemistically referred to Justice North in the first case on 11 September 2001 as 'rescuees' to denote a neutral term.

105   See Department of Immigration, Multicultural and Indigenous Affairs, 'Offshore Processing Arrangements', Fact Sheet No. 76, 14 January 2003, on the number of 'unauthorized' boats that had been stopped from reaching mainland Australia since the Tampa's case.

106   This is meant to refer to those people who have not lost their asylum applications offshore. 'They jump the queue by entering the country first and then applying for asylum. Australia has set aside only 12,000 asylum spaces per annum. This means that for every boat person currently in refugee status, one position less is available for genuine asylum seekers who are, both applying from offshore … waiting patiently, in the minister's mind at least, in some squalid and crowded

[refugee] camp'. See B. Mares quoted by 'US Committee for Refugees, Australia. See 'Change: Australia's New Approach to Asylum Seekers', http://www.refugees.org/downloads/australia.

107   See Oxfam Community Abroad, 'Adrift in the Pacific: The implications of Australia's Specific Refugees Solution' (2002) 15.

108   The refugee convention has a fundamental principle of 'burden sharing', which is cleared from its preamble which states that, 'the grant of asylum may place unduly heavy burdens on certain countries', so that 'international cooperation' is necessary in order to 'distribute' the load.

109   See *Oxfam Report*, above, at 11.

110   See ibid at 50.

111   See Department of Immigration, Multicultural and Indigenous Affairs, 'Offshore Processing Arrangements', Fact Sheet, No. 76, 2 January 2002.

112   See Mary Crock and Ben Saul, 'Future Seekers: Refugees in Australia' (Sydney, Federation Press, 2002, who state that the September 11 attacks could not have come 'at a worst time for Australia's boat people' at page 38.

113   Ibid.

114   See Kalinga Seneviratne, 'Rights: Australia Set to Back Down on Refugee Policy', available at *Oneworld.net* website at http://www.oneworld.net/article/frontpage/104/3.

115   See Mark Metherell and Michell Grattan, 'Pacific Solution "treats nations like prostitutes"', available at the *Sydney Morning Herald* website at http://www.smh.com.au/.

116   See Crock and Saul supra at 38. The legislation that was passed comprised migration amendment (excision from migration zone) Act 2001, migration amendment (excision for migration zone) (consequential provisions act (Cth), 2001; migration amendment (excision for migration zone) act, (Cth) 2001; migration legislation amendment act (no. 6), (Cth), 2001; migration legislation amendment act (no. 1), (Cth) 2001; migration legislation amendment act (no. 5), (Cth) 2001; border protection 'validation and enforcement powers' act, (Cth) 2001; and migration legislation amendment (judicial review) act, (Cth) 2001.

117   See *UNHCR, Statistical Year Book*, supra, at 87.

118   See Bonaventure Rutinwa, 'The End of Asylum? The Changing Nature of Refugee Policies in Africa', (2002) 1 and 2 (21) *Refugee Quarterly Survey*, 12 at 33.

119   Quoted by Mark Baker, 'Pakistan Leader's Swipe at Australia's Refugee Ban', http://old.smh.com.au/news/0110/24/national/national4.html who states of General Musharraf that he said that, 'hundreds of thousands of refugees want to cross over into Pakistan and our dilemma is we already have about 2.5 million refugees here. ... Compare this, when you think of Australia not accepting even 200 (Tampa) refugees. So a poor country, an economically weak country like Pakistan cannot really accept refugees over this great figure of 2.5 million'.

120   See US Committee for Refugees, 'Worldwide Refugee Information: Country Report', Pakistan, 2002, http://www.refugees.org/world/countryrpt/scasia/pakistan.htm. Also see USCR, For Worldwide Refugee Information: Country Report, Australia, 2002, http://www.refugees.org/world/countryrpt/easia-pacific/australia.htm respectively.

121   See Report on the Thirtieth Session of the Executive Committee of the High Commissioners Program, *supra* note 65, at para. 72(2)(f) 'in cases of large-scale influx, persons seeking asylum should always receive at least temporary refuge'.

122   See Schuck, *supra* note 8, at 265 n. 84.

123 See Fitzpatrick, *Flight from Asylum*, *supra* note 64, at 16–18.
124 See Harold Hongju Koh, 'America's Offshore Refugee Camps', 29 *U. Rich. L. Rev.* 139 (1994).
125 Schuck, *supra* note 8, at 265–6.
126 See US Committee for Refugees, 'Haiti', in *World Refugee Survey – 1995* 180, 181 (1995).
127 See Updates, XV:7 Ref. Rep.14, 15 (July 26, 1994).
128 See 'Haitians Riot at Guantanamo as Tensions Mount', XV:8 *Ref. Rep*.11, 12–13 (Aug. 19, 1994).
129 See John Kifner, 'Aristide, In a Joyful Return, Urges Reconciliation in Haiti', *NY Times*, Oct. 16, 1994, at A1. See also generally, Guy S. Goodwin-Gill, 'The Haitian Refoulment Case: A Comment', 6 *Int'l Refugee L.* 103 (1993); Arthur C. Helton, 'The United States Government Program of Intercepting and Forcibly Returning Haitian Boat People to Haiti: Policy Implications and Prospects', 10 *N.Y.L.Sch. J. Hum. Rts.* 325 (1993).
130 Schuck, *supra* note 13, at 296.
131 Ibid.
132 Fitzpatrick, 'Flight from Asylum', *supra* note 64, at 20.
133 See Hathaway and Neve, *supra* note 4, at 126–8.
134 Indeed, Gervase Coles has criticized the previous 'exile bias' of refugee law. See Gervase Coles, 'Approaching the Refugee Problem Today', in *Refugees and International Relations* 373, 390–92 (1989). This bias is clear in Sarah Collinson's account of refugees fleeing from the former communist eastern bloc countries during the 1950s and 1960s. As Collinson observes, 'the Western states offered refuge to these groups in an almost automatic fashion ('presumptive refugee status'), even though the majority would not have been able to make a case for refugee status according to a strict interpretation of the 1951 Convention'. See Sarah Collinson, *Beyond Borders: West European Migration Policy Towards the 21st Century* 66 (1993).
135 As Danièle Joly observes, '[t]emporary protection and temporary stays will enable States to allow entry while continuing to pander to some sections of the electorate demanding immigration controls'. See Joly, *supra* note 63, at 187.
136 Since the 1980s, Northern states have made their asylum policies even more restrictive. At one time, 'in Europe and North America granting asylum was equivalent to accepting refugees permanently'. Dennis Gallagher, *supra* note 23, at 437. Hathaway and Neve observe that the Refugee Convention:

> while it links the duration of refugee status to the continuation of risk in the refugee's home state ... says nothing about how best to make repatriation a viable form of solution. This lapse reflects the Cold War-era pessimism that refugees would never return home.

Hathaway and Neve, *supra* note 4, at 171.
137 Will Kymlicka, *Multicultural Citizenship: A Liberal Theory of Minority Rights* (Oxford Political Theory Series 1995).
138 Ibid., at 11.
139 Ibid., at 10. The study of 'group' rights in this respect, as distinct from 'individual' rights is controversial. See Juha Räikkä, 'Is a Membership-blind Model of Justice False by Definition?', in *Do We Need Minority Rights?*, 3–16 (International Studies in Human Rights Vol. 46, Juha Räikkä (ed.), 1996).
140 Leading activists and scholars agree that deterrent devices are actually designed

to promote cultural homogeneity. See Byrne and Shacknove, *supra* note 14, at 197.

141   In Europe, this is seen in the 1991 Dublin Convention and Schengen II accords. See *supra* note 5. In North America this is seen in the US's responses to the Haitian boat people. See *supra* text accompanying notes 126–9.

142   Letter from Hathaway, *supra* note 22, at 3.

143   Satvinder Juss, 'Administrative Justice and the Carltona Principle', *Oxford J. Leg. Stud.* 142 (1993).

144   EU Commissioner Fratini on migration and asylum policies: see Press conference 1st September 2005 at http://www.statewatch.org/news/newsfull.htm. According to EU Commissioner Frattini, 'The package adopted today comprises of measures constituting the two sides of the same coin: coherent, fair, efficient and credible European asylum and immigration policies'.

145   Hathaway and Neve, *supra* note 4, at 172.

146   As Hathaway and Neve maintain, '[b]ecause refugees are admitted on the basis of necessity, it cannot legitimately be asserted that they should routinely be entitled to stay in the host state once the harm in their own country has been brought to an end'. ibid. at 140. They later observe that '[w]hether voluntary or mandated, return to the country of origin in conditions of safety and dignity is an important means to continually regenerate asylum capacity'. Ibid. at 172.

147   Santos, *op. cit* at p.226.

148   Ibid. at 117.

149   Ibid.

150   Julian L. Simon, *The Economic Consequences of Immigration* 51 (1989).

151   Ibid. at 314.

152   James A. Morone and Janice M. Goggin, 'Health Policies in Europe: Welfare States in a Market Era', 20 *J. Health Pol., Pol'y & L.* 557, 561 (Fall 1995).

153   Hathaway recognizes this overlap when he states at the outset of his proposals that 'governments increasingly believe that a concerted commitment to refugee protection is tantamount to an abdication of their migration control responsibilities'. Hathaway and Neve, *supra* note 4, at 117.

154   Joly, *supra* note 63, at 162. Hathaway and Neve's premises are all the more inconsistent in having recognized this line and observing that today '[t]he termination of most labor-based immigration has put real pressure on the asylum process, now the only legal mechanism to come to Europe available to most foreigners'. See Hathaway, 'Harmonizing for Whom?', *supra* note 5, at 721.

155   Sweden has opposed today's common policy of the European Union countries that unless a person faces a risk that 'is individual in nature and is encouraged or permitted by the authorities,' that person will not qualify as a refugee. Hathaway and Neve, *supra* note 4, at 121.

156   Byrne and Shacknove commend Denmark's appeal procedure for asylum decision. As they note, Denmark's procedures focus on 'the quality of first instance interviews; the impartiality of decision-makers; and the quality of language interpretation and fact-finding'. See Byrne and Shacknove, *supra* note 14, at 225.

157   See Satvinder Juss, *Immigration, Nationality and Citizenship* 2 (1993).

158   Quoted in S. Rep. No. 89-748, at 17(1965), reprinted in 1965 U.S.C.C.A.N. 3328, 3335.

159   Act of Sept. 2. 1958, Pub. L. No. 85–829, 75 Stat. 1712 (1958), cited in S. Rep. No. 86-1651 at 36 (1960), reprinted in 1960 U.S.C.C.A.N. 3124.

160   S. Rep. No. 89-748, *supra* note 158, at 3328.

161   Ibid. at 3334.

162 Act of Oct. 3, 1965, Pub.L. No. 89-236, 79 Stat. 911, repealed by Refugee Act of 1980, Pub. L. No. 96-212, 94 Stat. 102.

163 Ibid.

164 S. Rep. No. 89-748, *supra* note 158, at 3335.

165 For example, the insightful reforms suggested by Arthur C. Helton and by Zolberg *et al.* (see *infra* note 212) overlook the liberal categories of US asylum law in the 1950s and 1960s, although these categories resemble those advocated by Helton and Zolberg.

166 *The Dublin Convention*, like the *Second Schengen Agreement*, contains rules for determining a 'responsible state' which agrees to process an applicant for asylum from a country outside the European Community. The *Convention* addresses only procedural aspects of asylum, but is part of a wider package designed to make the asylum policies of European Community members more consistent. By doing so, the *Convention* aims to restrict the entry of 'aliens' into the member state of the European Community. *Dublin Convention*, *supra* note 5; Schengen II, supra note 5.

167 See 'US-Cuba Joint Statement on Migration', 6 *Dep't. St. Dispatch* 397 (1995).

168 See Office of the United Nations High Commissioner for Refugees: International Conference on Indo-Chinese Refugees, Declaration and Comprehensive Plan of Action, U.N. GAOR, 44th Sess., Plenary Meetings, Annex, at 10, U.N. Doc. A/44/523 (1989).

169 See Martin Jacques, 'Cultural Revolutions', *New Statesman*, Dec. 5, 1997, at 24.

170 See Alan Dawley, Struggles for Justice 228–31 (1991). Dawley, in a new interpretation of the making of modern America, traces the group struggles involved in the nation's rise to power by probing the dynamics of social change. He observes how the end of the First World War 'created new views' about women's suffrage, 'anticolonial agitation', and a 'new morality'. Ibid.

171 The idea was first propounded by the Italian socialist thinker Antonio Gramsci (1891–1937), one of the most creative and original thinkers within the Marxist philosophical tradition, whose important prison writings, 'Civil Hegemony', have defined the doctrine of hegemony in the fields of political science, sociology and aesthetics, as well as defining the role of arts in popular culture for subsequent generations. See Stuart Sim, Gramsci, Antonio, in *Biographical Dictionary of Twentieth-Century Philosophers* 283–5 (Stuart Brown *et al.* (eds) 1996). Gramsci emphasized the importance of ideas as instruments for change, arguing that that the ruling class controlled the masses because the masses had internalized the social, cultural and moral values of the ruling class. Through education and the promulgation of cultural change, revolutionaries could assure a dominant position. ibid. See also James D. Wilkinson, *The Intellectual Resistance in Europe* 4–7, 230–34 (1981).

172 Citizens of the world must 'look at [themselves] in [their] infinite variety'. E.A. Hiebel, *The Law of Primitive Man: A Study in Comparative Legal Dynamics* 10 (1954). Although technology and ease of travel have enhanced the importance of cultural pluralism, the idea is not new and has been expressed widely in the field of legal anthropology. See generally Bronislaw Malinowski, *Crime and Custom in Savage Society* (1926); Karl Llewelyn and Edward Adamson Hoebel, *The Cheyenne Way* (1941); Max Gluckman, *The Judicial Process among Barotse of Northern Rhodesia* (1955); Paul Bohannan, *Justice and Judgment Among the Tiv* (1957).

173 Joan Fitzpatrick notes that, unlike today's interpreters of the Refugee Convention, the drafters focused on 'the need to assimilate persons displaced in Europe by the Second World War and the ensuing regime changes in Eastern Europe'. Fitzpatrick, *supra* note 13, at 232–3.

174   See Gil Loescher, *Beyond Charity: International Co-operation and the Global Refugee Crisis* 61–2, 71–2 (1993). See also Protocol Relating to the Status of Refugees, *supra* note 2, art 1(3).

175   See Loescher, *supra* note 174, at 61–2, 71–2. See also *Protocol Relating to the Status of Refugees, supra* note 2, art 1(3).

176   Drawing attention to the shift in the locus of refugee-producing territories from the European cross-border flows of half a century ago, to the African, South- and South-East Asian, Middle Eastern and Caribbean flows that began in the 1960s, 1970s and 1980s, Peter Schuck recently has observed that '[r]efugee emergencies have become so endemic that the rhetoric of crisis today is as likely to numb as it is to energise'. See Shuck, *supra* note 8, at 244.

177   This is because immigrant groups are invariably minorities and, as Hurst Hannum notes, 'the concept of "minorities" does not fit easily within the theoretical paradigm of the [modern] state, whether that state is based on the individual social-contract theory of Western democracies or the class-based precepts of Marxism'. Hannum, *supra* note 92, at 71.

178   Hugh Seton-Watson, *Nations and States: An Enquiry into the Origins of Nations and the Politics of Nationalism* 1 (1977).

179   See Hannum, *supra* note 92, at 26.

180   Ibid. at 189–91.

181   Carol J. Greenhouse, 'Democracy and Demography', 2 *Ind. J. Global Legal Stud.* 21, 23 (1994).

182   Ibid.

183   See Gordon R. Walker and Mark A. Fox, 'Globalization: An Analytical Framework', 3 *Ind. J. Global Legal Stud.* 375, 377, 380 (1996).

184   See David P. Fidler, 'The Globalization of Public Health: Emerging Infectious Diseases and International Relations', *Ind. J. Global Legal Stud.* (1998) (on file with Harvard Human Rights Journal).

185   Jeffrey Dunoff, 'From Green to Global: Toward the Transformation of International Environmental Law', 19 *Harv. Envtl. L. Rev.* 241 (1995).

186   See Fred H. Cate, 'Global Information Policymaking and Domestic Law', 1 *Ind. J. Global Legal Stud.* 467 (1994).

187   See generally, Benjamin R. Barber, *Jihad vs. McWorld* (1995).

188   See Jeffrey A. Hart, 'Comments on Changing Sovereignty Games and International Migration', 2 *Ind. J. Global Legal Stud.* 171, 173 (1994).

189   This is particularly the case now in relation to public health. See Seth F. Berkeley, 'AIDS in the Global Village: Why US Physicians Should Care About HIV Outside the United States', 268 *J. Am. Med. Assoc.* 3368, 3369 (Dec. 16, 1992); George A. Gellert *et al.*, 'The Obsolescence of Distinct Domestic and International Health Sectors', 10 *J. Pub. Health Pol'y,* 421 (1989), cited in Fidler, *The Globalization of Public Health, supra* note 184, at 15.

190   See Walker and Fox, *supra* note 183, at 382.

191   See Hart, *supra* note 188, at 173.

192   In 1992, the Immigration Ministers of the European Community adopted the London Resolutions, which effectively institutionalized the 'safe country of asylum' notion in European refugee policy. An asylum seeker from a 'safe country of asylum' is one who comes from a country in which he or she is safe from prosecution and to which safe return is deemed possible. Although not legally binding, the London Resolutions are to be incorporated into national law as soon as possible. See European Communities, The Council, Conclusions of the Meeting of the Ministers Responsible for Immigration (London, Nov. 3– Dec. 1, 1992), Doc. 10579/92 IMMIG.2. There are three documents to the London

Resolutions: 'The Resolution on a Harmonized Approach to Questions Concerning Host Third Countries'; the 'Resolution on Manifestly Unfounded Applications for Asylum'; and the 'Conclusions on Countries in Which There is Generally No Serious Risk of Persecution', cited in Byrne and Shacknove, *The Safe Country Notion in European Asylum Law, supra* note 14, at 191 n. 24. Rosemary Byrne and Andrew Shacknove have observed that 'the London Resolutions establish that the return of asylum-seekers to a safe country of asylum obviates any obligation of Member States to investigate the merits of a claim to refugee status as required by the Dublin Convention'. See ibid. at 192.

193   The coordinated approach inherent in the harmonization of immigration policies in these two instruments imposes a systematic duty, for example, to impose visa requirements, underwritten by the imposition of carrier sanctions, on the nationals of those less-developed countries that generate refugees. Any country that wants to accede to the Schengen Agreements, and thereby acquire unrestricted freedom of movement for their citizens within the Community, is obliged to adopt the same stringent visa and border controls. See Hathaway, *Harmonizing for Whom?, supra* note 5, at 724. As a result, Italy, Spain, Portugal and Greece all were required recently to adopt such controls as a 'condition precedent' to accession to 'Schengenland'. Ibid.

194   Byrne and Shacknove write that '[w]estern Europe shortsightedly treats certain States, including Poland, the Czech Republic, Hungary, Croatia and Slovenia, as buffers against asylum-seekers from elsewhere in Eastern Europe, the Balkans, the Middle East, and Africa'. Byrne and Shacknove, *supra* note 14, at 215.

195   Report of the United Nations High Commissioner for Refugees, U.N. GAOR, 49th Sess., Supp. No. 12, Table 1, at 10, U.N. Doc. A/49/12 (1994).

196   See Hathaway and Neve, *supra* note 4, at 141. In fact, Hathaway observes that the disparities were far greater because agencies other than the UN assisted with relief work in the former Yugoslavia, bringing the total international contribution there to $514,800,000, as compared to only $183,597,500 in Burundi, Tanzania and Zaire. See id. at 141 n.111, (citing Report of the United Nations High Commissioner for Refugees, UN GAOR, 51st Sess., Supp. No. 12, paras. 82, 169, and Table 1, UN Doc. A/51/12 (1996)).

197   See generally Juss, *Discretion and Deviation in the Administration of Immigration Control, supra* note 157, at 5.

198   See G.A. Res. 428, U.N. GAOR, 5th Sess., Supp. No. 20, 325th plen.mtg. at 46, U.N. Doc. A/1775 (1950).

199   See James C. Hathaway, 'A Reconsideration of the Underlying Premise of Refugee Law', 31 *Harv. Int'l L.J.* 129, 161 (1990). See also Edward Epstein, 'United Nations Role Coping with Refugee Crisis', *S.F. Chron.*, Apr. 6, 1992, at A10, suggesting that a budget cut and a sharp increase in the number of refugees has forced the UNHCR to rely heavily upon assistance from states of origin. See also William Dullforce, 'Refugee Agency in Disarray After Chiefs Resignation', *Fin. Times*, Oct. 30, 1989, at 4, referring to the elimination of controls on spending leading to failure to be efficient in allocating decision making power. See also Cindy Schiner, 'The Superhero of World at War', *The Guardian*, May 16, 1995, at 10.

200   See P.D. Maynard, 'The Legal Competence of the United Nations High Commissioner for Refugees', 31 *Int'l & Comp. L.Q.* 415, 416 (1982).

201   See, e.g., G.A. Res. 2039, U.N. GAOR, 20th Sess., Supp. No. 14, at 41, U.N. Doc. A/6014 (1965) (eliminating the distinction between those refugees within and those without the UNHCR's mandate); G.A. Res. 1673, U.N. GAOR, 16th Sess.,

Supp. No. 17, at 28, U.N. Doc. A/5100 (1961) (extending the organ's competence to those for whom the UNHCR could extend its 'good offices').

202 See Luise Drüke, *Preventive Action for Refugee Producing Situations* 246–8 (1990).

203 See G.A. Res. 1388, U.N. GAOR, 14th Sess., Supp. No. 16, at 20, para. 2, U.N. Doc. A/4354 (1959).

204 See G.A. Res. 1673, U.N. GAOR, 16th Sess., Supp. No. 17, at 28, U.N. Doc. A/5100 (1961).

205 See G.A. Res. 2039, U.N. GAOR, 20th Sess., Supp. No. 14, at 41, U.N. Doc. A/6014 (1965).

206 See G.A. Res. 3454, U.N. GAOR, 30th Sess., Supp. No. 34, at 92, U.N. Doc. A/10034 (1975).

207 In the forward to the Communication from the Commission of the European Communities to the Council and the European Parliament on Immigration and Asylum Policies, the Commission speculates that asylum, rather than immigration in general, became the focal point for harmonized restrictive measures because asylum-seekers formed the most visible portion of irregular migration into and out of the Union. The Commission asserted that asylum cannot be artificially separated from immigration policy in general, and that harmonization must be pressed much further. See Foreword to the *Communication from the Commission to the Council and the European Parliament on Immigration and Asylum Policies*, COM(94)23 at 1A.

208 'European electorates expect their governments to maintain a tough immigration policy, and that is very difficult to combine with a generous asylum policy'. Edward Mortimer, 'Behind Closed Doors', *Fin. Times*, Oct. 28, 1992, at 21.

209 Hathaway and Neve, *supra* note 4, at 152.

210 This is a standard that refugees have to satisfy under the *1951 Refugee Convention*. See *supra* text accompanying note 11.

211 Simon, *supra* note 150, at 314.

212 Thus, Arthur C. Helton argues that 'a new international regime concerning forced migration is needed'. Helton, *supra* note 3, at 1627. Zolberg *et al.* argue that all 'victims', and not just activists and targets of violence, should be given asylum. Zolberg *et al.*, *supra* note 9, at 30–31.

213 See *supra* notes 154–5 and accompanying text.

214 Hathaway and Neve, *supra* note 4, at 152.

215 Ibid.

216 The extent of this protection may differ from one kind of migrant to another. Thus a foreign worker may be required to apply for a work permit before entry, but also to renew his work permit. An asylum-seeker may be allowed to meet less rigorous standards of entry and documentary verification.

217 See, e.g., Arthur Helton, *supra* note 3, at 1627; Zolberg *et al.*, *supra* note 1, at 30–31; Fitzpatrick, *supra* note 13, at 240.

218 Andrew E. Shacknove, 'Who is a Refugee?', *Ethics* 274, 284 (Jan. 1985).

219 Consider, for example, the situation in the United Kingdom, where holders of a work permit 'for more than four years may be considered for indefinite leave' and thereby no longer need to obtain work permits. Also, immigrant 'ministers of religion, missionaries and members of religious orders', among others, need not obtain work permits in order to maintain legal employment. David Jackson, *Immigration Law & Practice* 291, 301 (1996).

220 See Louis Henkin, 'An Agenda for the Next Century: The Myth and Mantra of State Sovereignty', 35 *Va. J. Int'l L.* 115, 118 (1994).

221 Hathaway and Neve, *supra* note 4, at 206.

222   Ibid. at 207.

223   Hathaway, *Reconceiving Refugee Law, supra* note 19, at 113.

224   Ibid.

225   See *supra* text accompanying note 13, and section under 'Temporary Protection'.

226   See generally Universal Declaration of Human Rights preamble, adopted Dec. 10, 1948, G.A. Res. 217A (III), 3 U.N. GAOR, at 71, U.N. Doc. A/810 (1948) reprinted in 43 *Am. J. L. Supp.* 127 (1949) (discussing norms behind the argument).

227   As is well known, the Convention was originally drafted to deal with the population displacement that arose from World War II. To maintain the Convention's original spirit, its ambit has been extended to other war-related persecution. See Fitzpatrick, *supra* note 13, at 241–2.

228   For example, German adjudicators often denied asylum to victims of ethnic cleansing and rape from former Yugoslavia. In 1993, Germany granted only 58 asylum requests out of 1,913 on the grounds that, due to the general conditions of war, applicants' predicaments were no different from those suffered by most other individuals in their home country. See Davy, *Refugees from Bosnia and Herzegovina, supra* note 97, at 53.

229   As Fitzpatrick notes, if the same stringent requirements had been applied in the 1950s and 1960s to Cold War asylum seekers as are applied today, 'many ballet dancers and athletes would not have been able to transfer their loyalties ...'. See Fitzpatrick, *supra* note 13, at 238. For example, Turkey closed its border to Iraqi Kurds and European states imposed visa controls upon Bosnian Serbs, even though both of these population flows included refugees who met Convention standards for non-refoulement and protection.

230   Ibid., As Henkin observes:

> [h]alf a century of human rights law has washed away notions that how a state treats its inhabitants is nobody else's business ... International law is now responding to human rights violations inside states through a variety of institutions, including committees, commissions, courts, and tribunals, even the General Assembly and the Security Council, and by a number of means, reaching even to collective economic sanctions and military intervention.

Henkin, *supra* note 220, at 118.

231   *International Covenant on Civil and Political Rights*, 999 U.N.T.S. 171, G.A. Res. 2200A, U.N. GAOR, 21st Sess., Supp. No. 16, U.N. Doc. A/6316 (1966) [hereinafter 'ICCPR'].

232   *International Covenant on Economic, Social, and Cultural Rights*, 999 U.N.T.S. 3, G.A. Res. 2200 A, U.N. GAOR, 21st Sess., Supp. No 16, U.N. Doc. A/6316 (1966) [hereinafter 'ICESCR'].

233   *Convention Relating to the Status of Refugees, supra* note 1, art. 3.

234   See ICCPR, *supra* note 231, art. 26.

235   See ICESCR, *supra* note 232, art. 2(2).

236   *Convention Relating to the Status of Refugees, supra* note 1, art. 20.

237   Ibid.

238   Ibid., arts. 21, 23, 24.

239   Ibid, arts. 26, 27.

240   See ICCPR, *supra* note 231, art. 12 (freedom of movement), 22 (freedom of association).

241 *Convention Relating to the Status of Refugees, supra* note 1, art. 15.
242 Ibid. art. 4.
243 See ICCPR, *supra* note 231, art. 18.
244 Henkin, *supra* note 220, at 118.
245 Santos., *op. cit*, at p.222.
246 See ibid., at 119.
247 Ibid.
248 Henkin writes:

> [T]he international community needs to develop international responsibility for refugees as it has recognized responsibility for human rights generally ... There needs to be an increased awareness that large refugee flows result from massive human rights violations and from the failure of the international system to deter, prevent, or terminate those abuses. Ibid.

249 See Letter from Hathaway, *supra* note 22, at 3.
250 See text at p.20 and 31 *supra*.
251 See Letter from Hathaway, *supra* note 22, at 3.
252 See UN Charter, ch. VII, art. 39.
253 See *Sixth Periodic Report on the Situation of Human Rights in the Territory of the Former Yugoslavia*, Submitted by Mr. Tadeusz Mazowiecki, at 46, para. 296, U.N. Doc. E/CN.4/1994/110 (1994). [hereinafter Mazowiecki].
254 See Mazowiecki, *supra* note 253 at 19, para. 94.
255 See *supra* text accompanying footnote 230.
256 *Universal Declaration of Human Rights, supra* note 226.
257 UN Charter, *supra* note 252, arts. 55, 56.
258 See *Population Plan of Action*, U.N. Doc. E/CONF. 60/WG/L.55/Att.3 (1974) reprinted in 71 Dep't State Bull. 440, 447 (1974).
259 See ibid. at 448.
260 *Independent Commission on International Development Issues, North-South, A Programme for Survival* 108–12 (W. Brandt *et al.* (eds), 1980).
261 Stanley Hoffman, *Duties Beyond Borders: On the Limits and Possibilities of Ethical International Politics* 224–5 (1981).
262 Ibid.
263 Ibid. at 225.
264 Rona Aybay, 'The Right to Leave and the Right to Return: The International Aspect of Freedom of Movement', 1 *Comp. L. Y.B.* 121, 125 (1977).
265 The definitive American opinions of the late nineteenth century are *The Chinese Exclusion Case*, 130 U.S. 581 (1899) and *Fong Yue Ting*, 149 U.S. 698, 707 (1893). These opinions, which give Congress the right to exclude aliens, 'qualified the excludability of aliens by citing international legal authority to the effect that a state can exclude aliens only when they present a danger to the peace and security of the country'. James A.R. Nafziger, 'The General Admission of Aliens Under International Law', 77 *Am. J. Int'l L.* 804, 828 (1983).
266 This is the standard of exclusion set in Article 48(3) of the Treaty of Rome. See Satvinder Juss, *Immigration, Nationality and Citizenship, supra* note 157, at 111.

8 Migration and Global Development

INTRODUCTION

In *Peoples and Empires*, Anthony Pagden wrote that:

> [T]he cultures of most of the world's races, if not all, are shaped by prolonged periods of migration, and many of the stories we tell ourselves about our pasts, and our futures, are tales of peregrination.[1]

The movement of peoples has been historically so widespread that it has a strong claim to being recognized as a 'civil right' in much the same way as freedom from 'tyranny' and 'direct abuse' is today is regarded as a civil right. Since travel enables one to escape inhuman and oppressive conditions, like other civil rights, free movement enables one to achieve the equalization of opportunity. This is best explained by Roger Nett, who writes that, 'the right of people to equal opportunities is rather clearly the underlying theme of all civil rights today' quite simply because people have become conscious that the purpose of such things as 'free speech, religion, and the right to vote' is 'to make possible a life that would otherwise be denied, and that it is in this sense that we are most likely to define justice today'.[2] But does an argument for greater free movement rights overstate this case? Not so, according to Roger Nett, who writes a system of open migration is preferable today because:

> The main and most concrete advantage to all societies, however, is that a major type of social waste would begin to dry up. Adding open migration to the basic human rights would be a giant step, perhaps the biggest we could now seriously imagine, toward providing a functional basis for doing away with situational inopportunity *at relatively low world cost*. Any other social device for doing the same, including *laissez faire*, would probably cause much more dislocation and entail more effort. By eliminating one primal cause of poverty and involuntary subordination, it would allow individuals to rise by their individual energies and give hope of real betterment to untold numbers where little now exists. All of this might be done by changing only one key factor. The social waste referred to is of two parts; one is the loss of contributions to overall human purposes – talent for science, production, higher humanistic efforts – from people who are so disadvantaged that they spend

269

virtually all their time and energies just maintaining life. The other is the amount of concrete effort, including emotional energy, spent by those who try to contain the former. It is hardly possible to measure the costs of all the different kinds of re-action, which may well include undeclared and cold wars and more generally non-cooperation, where cooperation could reasonably be hoped for.[3]

Conventional individual human rights have not alleviated the violation of basic rights to be free from hunger and poverty. In Africa, for example, two-thirds of the people lack access to safe water.[4] Less than half the children attend primary school.[5] Africa is a shameful example of absolute poverty on our planet. Even in the booming economies of East and Southeast Asia, half the people still lack access to safe water and basic health care.[6] More than a decade ago in 1991, the United Nations Development Programme's *Human Development Report 1991* stated that of the world's current population of 5.3 billion, over 1 billion live in absolute poverty; some 180 million children, 1 in 3, suffer from serious malnutrition; and 1.5 billion are deprived of primary health care.[7] Nearly 3 million women die each year from immunizable dis-eases.[8] About half a million women die each year from causes related to pregnancy and childbirth.[9]

Yet, a decade later and into the new millennium, this situation has not improved at all. If anything, it has gone from bad to worse. Moreover, the prognosis is that it will continue to worsen. On 8th July 2003, the widening gulf between developed and the under-developed world was revealed, when the UN announced that in 1990s, while the developed world was booming economically, more than 50 countries suffered falling living standards. The UN's annual *Human Development Report 2003* reported a rise in poverty for more than a quarter of the world's countries. The lethal combination of famine, HIV/Aids, conflict and failed economic policies were reversing de-velopment trends. The situation was particularly grim in sub-Saharan Africa and the countries of the former Soviet Union that emerged as fledgling states at the end of the Cold War. Fifty-four countries saw their average income decline in the 1990s. Twenty countries saw the clock turn back in human development, with declining income, life expectancy, and literacy.

The UN's millennium development goals of halving the number of people living on less than a dollar a day, of achieving a two-thirds drop in mortality for under-fives, of ensuring universal primary education, and of halving the number of people without access to safe drinking water, would not now be met by the year 2015, but the year 2147. It would be 2165 before child mortal-ity was cut by two-thirds. The UN found that 30,000 children still die of preventable diseases every year. Some 500,000 women a year, one for each minute, die in pregnancy and childbirth. An even more staggering figure is the number of children who died of diarrhoea in the 1990s, which was 13 million, which was more than all the people lost to armed conflict since World War II. The decline in life expectancy in particular demonstrated the North/South divide in living standards. Life expectancy in Norway, which stood at the top of the UN's league table for human development, is 78.7 per cent (only four children in 1,000 do not survive), there is a 100 per cent literacy rate, and annual income is just under $30,000 (about £18,200). On the other hand, in Sierra Leone, a newborn child will be lucky to reach 35 years of age (363 children in a thousand do not even reach their fifth birthday), and has a two in three chance of growing up illiterate, and lives on $470 a year. In Zimbabwe, life expectancy has actually gone backwards. In the 1970s life expectancy in Zimbabwe was 56 years. It is now just 33 years. By contrast, life expectancy in the United Kingdom rose from 72 to 78.2 years.

For this reason, the UN's 2003 *Report on Human Development* had two very important observations to make. First, contrary to those who had argued that the 'tough love' policies of the 1980s and 1990s have spawned a growing new middle class, the world became ever more divided between the super-rich and the desperately poor. The richest 1 per cent of the world's population (around 60 million) now receive as much income as the poorest 57 per cent. The income of the richest 25 million Americans corresponds to 2 billion of the world's poorest people. In 1820, Western Europe's *per capita* income was only three times that of Africa. In the 1990s, however, it had rocketed to more than 13 times as high. Secondly, although the events of September 11th had created a 'genuine consensus' that poverty was the world's problem, the one-size-fits-all liberalization agenda foisted on poor countries was not working. Market reforms were not enough. Liberalizing the economy was not enough. What was needed was an interventionist strategy. As the UN's 2003 *Report on Human Development* said, 'Over the past 20 years too much development thinking and practice have confused market-based economic growth with *laissez faire*'. What the West needed to do now was to tear down trade barriers, dismantle its lavish subsidy regimes, provide deeper debt relief and double aid from $50 billion to $100 billion a year. It is this that would provide the resources for investment in the basic essentials of development, namely, health, education, clean water and rural roads.[10] Yet, as it becomes increasingly clear that in future most of the world's wars will be fought over resources – from oil to water – the importance of world development to international peace must also be recognized. Widespread regional squalor and destitution will lead to instability, breed terrorism, and obstruct development. Peace and international development are inextricably intertwined. As the General Assembly said in 1987, 'international peace and security were essential elements for the full realization of human rights including the right to development'.[11] This was echoed some years later by the UN General Secretary Boutros Boutros-Ghali, who said in 1994, that development itself is the most secure basis for peace.[12] In turn, it is also clear as India's Justice Bhagwati, said in 1995, that 'peace, both nationally and internationally, is essential for development'.[13]

In this chapter, I will first consider how globalization has made the reception of foreign migrants technically easier for national polities to countenance. Second, I will consider how human rights law can be augmented to include the right to development as a specie of 'Third-Generation Solidarity Rights'. Third, I will consider how the insightful observations and recommendations of the *International Development Sixth Report on Migration and Development* published in July 2004, make out a practical case for bringing all the foregoing together under one rubric. It makes out a case for how migration can be used to prosper, to escape insecurity and poverty, and to move in response to opportunity. It thus leaves no doubt that the issues of human rights, development, and the economic growth in the developed world are indivisible and inseparable. Fourth, I consider a recent European Commission report of 2005 which suggests that Western governments, by rushing to introduce populist measures to restrict immigration, are sacrificing long-term economic prosperity for short-term electoral gain. Fifth, I will consider a European Commission Green Paper, *'Confronting demographic change: a new solidarity between generations'*, which warned of a shrinking workforce in the European Union in the next 20 years. I will also consider the 2004 report of the *European Foundation for the Improvement of Living and Working Conditions* which reaches the same conclusions. Finally, I will consider the case for a new paradigm of migration analysis and a new theory for migration, which I refer to as a 'development theory' based on the understanding of migration that cannot be divorced from the wider international system of economics and politics which shapes the lives of poor people. I will effectively suggest that given that there has never in history been a society with economic prosperity but a declining population, what Western Europe needs to do is to both allow for freer immigration to its borders and actively encourage human rights and political reform in the developing world.

MIGRATION AND THE GLOBAL CITIZEN

Already by the end of the closing years twentieth century, the advent of globalization meant that there was talk of a 'borderless world'. This was a world of transnational corporations led by the USA, Europe and Japan, together with the newer economies of the South East, which in the future 'will be ensuring the free flow of information, money goods and services as well as the free migration of people and corporations'. It was said that '[T]raditional governments will have to establish a new single framework of global governance'.[14] It did not stop there. Talk of the 'globalized world' led to talk of a 'post-national citizenship' extolled as a 'new and more universal concept' but interestingly, 'one whose organizing and legitimating principles are based on universal personhood rather than national belonging'.[15]

This notion of a 'post-national citizenship' comes most notably from Yasemin Soysal. She argues that 'world-level pressures towards more expanded individual rights have led to the increasing incorporation of foreigners into existing membership schemes'. The effect of this extension of membership beyond national systems has been that of 'making national citizenship less important'.[16] Soysal maintains that the territorially bounded nation-state with which we are so familiar was the dominant form for only about 100 years from the mid-nineteenth to the mid-twentieth century, and the emergence of universal personhood is eroding the territorially bounded nation-state. The 'post-national belonging' that she espouses is firmly based on universal human rights laid down in conventions and declarations of supra-national bodies like the UN, and which are being slowly incorporated into the constitutional fabric of nation-states. It is also true that the UN in one of its documents, when stating that the world should 'focus attention explicitly on global citizenship' takes the 'starting point' the ideal that 'all human beings have certain fundamental rights' which are 'codified in the Universal Declaration which had been made concrete by ignoring national borders'.[17] However, what of states that do not make such incorporation? And, what of states that do make the incorporation but do not follow such universal standards? Is it still meaningful to say that universal human rights form the basis of such 'post-national belonging'? It would appear not. It seems that the concept of 'post-national belonging' is far better advanced on the basis of an inter-connectedness and inter-dependency between world societies and communities. In a practical sense it is this more than anything else that makes for our sense of universal personhood. It is an awareness of the stranger who is no longer the 'other' that makes for a feeling of global citizenship. It is this sense of community that is different from the sense of community we feel with kith and kin.

Yet, it is trite that a 'citizen' is also always a 'national' implying his membership also of a nation. In this way, citizenship is universalistic and above cultural differences, but only because it is grounded in the context of a nation-state which itself is based on cultural specificity.[18] This is what is said to make one 'nation' different from another nation. It extols the virtues of a 'national culture'. Yet, the concept of a national culture itself is contested today. Traditional definitions, such as that of Seton-Watson, of describing a nation as 'a community of people, whose members are bound together by a sense of solidarity, a common culture, a national consciousness'[19] are inapposite descriptions for most nations of the world. Similarly, traditional definitions of a nation are also arguably obsolete. Thus, Connor defines a nation as 'a group of people who *believe* they are ancestrally related'.[20] Anthony Smith's more elaborate description is equally inapplicable when he explains that:

> A nation can therefore be defined as a named human population sharing an historic territory, common myths and historical memories, a mass, public culture, a common economy and common legal rights and duties for all members.[21]

The existence of disparate ethnic groups in a polity give rise today to the idea of homogenous nation-states. Robert Reich has even questioned the existence of a national society given that there is no longer a national economy. Reich, who served as US Secretary for Labour in President Clinton's first administration, wrote that 'the idea that the citizens of a nation shared responsibility for their economic well-being' was closely linked to the rise of the democratic nation-state'[22] and that since 'almost every factor of production – money, technology, factories, and equipment – moves effortlessly across borders, the very idea of a national economy is becoming meaningless'.[23] Global citizenship is in the ascendancy because national citizenship looks increasingly difficult to sustain as a meaningful idea. There is today, in the words of Schnapper, 'the *weakening of civic feeling* and *of political bonds*' and 'nothing to guarantee that the modern democratic nation will in future have the capability of *maintaining the social bond*, as it has done in the past', with the result that it is increasingly, 'impossible for democracies to demand of their citizens to defend them with their lives'. The breakdown in these historic bonds is such that today, 'the individuals and their interests have taken the place of the citizens and their ideals'.[24]

In this sense, if a 'nation' is to mean anything it is to mean a community of willing members functioning as a political unit simply because it is their common desire to do so. It is in this way that, as Schnapper explains, the nation can be understood only as essentially a 'political project' that transcends the tension between universalism and particularism.[25] Castles and Davidson argue that a 'theory of citizenship for a global society must be based on the separation between nation and state'. They argue for:

> a new type of state that is not constituted exclusively or mainly around the nexus of territoriality and belonging. Citizenship should ... not be connected to nationality ... citizenship should be a political community without any claim to common cultural identity.[26]

The question is, of course, what this 'political community' is to be. Although, Castles and Davidson argue for 'a new notion of state borders' and for a 'notion of porous borders',[27] there is arguably room here to make the concept of a political community even more elastic so as to embrace the entire world community and to fully embrace the notion of a global citizenship.

According to Santos, one of the most exciting modern writers, the world system today is based on 'unequal exchanges' between different peoples, leading to such global hardships as 'war, starvation, oppression, and ecological disaster' because it is deliberately based on an 'ahistorical knowledge' of world history which 'benefits the countries that have benefited from the unequal exchanges'. Santos, makes a case for this imbalance in the world system to be redressed by calling for 'new cosmopolitan politics'.[28] Relying on the ideas of Hegel, Santos advocates for 'a new subaltern cosmopolitanism' where the use of modern science as a tool for the making of 'distinctions, divisions and discriminations' for the so-called progress of knowledge is ended, with its resultant demise of social differences based on scientific distinctions 'which in turn engendered subordination'. What is interesting about Santos is the way in which he calls for a learning from '[t]ransnational Third Worlds of people' with their 'transnational Third worlds of knowledges' as this is 'one of the epistemological prerequisites of cosmopolitan politics'[29] the significance of which lies in their cosmopolitanism. Santos is strongly of the view that '[w]henever transnational migration is forced upon people, there is no justification to distinguish between nationals and non-nationals'.[30] In my view, the case is stronger than divesting oneself of an 'ahistorical knowledge' in favour of 'new cosmopolitan politics' (though that is by no means insignificant), given that the claims for Western responsibility in the economic devastation of Africa, resulting from colonial and continuing post-colonial exploitation of that continent, have in the past decade been growing louder.[31] The international community can lift the barriers to migration from the Third World, allowing them to enter and work for periods of time, in a way that is to the mutual advantage of both regions. The alternative is expensive, wasteful, and globally unfair.

This call for a 'new cosmopolitan politics' also appears to be behind the developing idea of a 'global citizenship'. After the first Gulf war ended, Richard Falk, who held considerable influence with the UN in the 1990s, argued for global citizenship on the grounds that, 'the global citizen … adheres to a normative perspective' and that economic integration, awareness of the limits to global resources and transnational militancy were reinforcing that development.[32] As he explained 'an African baby is a powerful symbol of the vulnerability and solidarity of the species as a whole'.[33] Falk could see no hope of a commitment even to regional parliaments without adequate economic, social and cultural investment in the global constituency.[34] This is also the sense in which the Global Commission understands the term when it recommends that the UN create a representative Forum of Civil Society, end the Security Council veto, consider a system of civil petition, and ultimately establish a people's chamber that controls the globe democratically.[35]

Global inequalities are terrifyingly huge. Unlike richer countries, mortality rates show that there is a greater chance of dying under the age of 5 years in poor countries. Richer countries have a life expectancy of 80 years as against 54.4 years in poor countries. In richer countries over 90 per cent of the children go to secondary schools as against fewer than 20 per cent in poor countries.[36] In fact, in both Africa and Latin America, real minimum wages fell by 50 per cent in the 1980s. Health and education were badly affected. In the 42 poorest countries of the world, the expenditure on health fell by 50 per cent. At the same time, the resource transfer to poor countries fell from 43 billion dollars in 1981 to 33 billion dollars in 1988. The result is that comparative income gaps have escalated. The average *per capita* income is now 58 times higher in an advanced country than in the least developed countries where over half the world's population live on 5.6 per cent of world income.[37] Globalization is not necessarily making things better. The Global Commission referred to a 'relentless growth' in the number of the 'absolute poor' which, by 1993, had already reached 1.3 billion.[38] Yet, the problem is how to develop the idea that all human beings have certain fundamental rights. The challenge is both theoretical and practical. I will deal with both below.

MIGRATION AND THIRD-GENERATION SOLIDARITY RIGHTS

Global resources are not being redistributed in a way that facilitates the access of people to those resources. Some people have access to those resources, but other people do not. If human rights law is all about developing 'a normative vocabulary that facilitates both the framing of claims and the identification of the rights holder'[39] then the task at hand is how to best make out such a case here. Karel Vasak divided human rights into three categories of first, second and third 'generation'. The term 'generation' is not meant to indicate a hierarchical listing of rights. This would be antithetical to the concept of human rights. All human rights are inter-related, indivisible, and inter-dependent.[40] A priority of one right could be an impediment to the realization of other rights.[41] The term 'generation' is designed only to suggest a theory that seg-regates certain human rights groups.[42] 'First generation' rights consist of political and civil rights. 'Second generation' rights consist of social, economic and cultural rights. 'Third generation' rights consists of a range of rights to economic and social development, the right to a clean environment, the right to peace, and the right to own the common heritage of mankind.[43] These rights correspond to the French Revolution ideals of libertè, egalitè, and fraternitè.[44] The first generation of civil and political rights are often referred to 'as rights of liberty or negative rights in that they require states to refrain from interfer-ing in citizens private life'.[45] The second generation of economic, social and cultural rights, however, require the State to create conditions for their protec-tion and fulfillment so that the government has to provide these rights. This is clear from the *International Covenant on Economic, Social and Cultural Rights 1966*, which requires the State to intervene to provide these rights by ensuring that there is equal enjoyment of these rights by all members of society.[46] Third-generation rights of solidarity go further still because they recognize and require co-operative mutual support, common action, mutual responsibility and shared risks. They require community input and shared activity.[47] The ideologists of the French Revolution promoted solidarity rights as a central value of actions at the international level.[48]

Solidarity rights are predicated on community involvement. Without com-munity involvement there cannot be solidarity rights. The question is what is the Community? Community is both local, national and international. This is because solidarity is unachievable without mutual support and partnership at a global scale. It is this which makes solidarity a key feature of third genera-tion rights. Solidarity is co-operative mutual support, universal brotherhood, respect for others, peace and justice. Universal values of social justice, global equity and international stability are promoted by these rights. Solidarity rights are antithetical to nationalism, racism and an abuse of power. Accord-ingly, these rights require purposeful action to address the needs and rights of the disadvantaged. They require strong engagement and intensified co-operation between governments, the business sector, and civil society generally, to ensure effective implementation.[49] Two outstanding questions about 'third-generation solidarity rights' are however, whether they are ca-pable of being legally formulated and if so, whether they are collective or individual rights.

As to the first question, in 1984, Philip Alston observed that a large number of disparate 'third-generation solidarity rights' were increasingly being pro-pounded. These rights ranged from the right to sleep and the right to social transparency to the right to coexist with nature and the right to tourism.[50] Alston considered whether the United Nations could or should adopt sub-stantive criteria that would have to be satisfied for the recognition of any new human right. He concluded that, given the present intergovernmental setting, such an approach was unworkable.[51] Accordingly, he proposed that certain procedural requirements should be met, such as the formal acknowledgment of an intention to accord recognition; a detailed analytical study by the Secretary-General; comments by governments; examinations by a specialist committee; and the formal endorsement by both the UN Commission on Human Rights and the General Assembly.[52] Two years later in 1986, the General Assembly responded by adopting the principles that states should 'bear in mind' in developing human rights instruments:

> a) Be consistent with the existing body of international human rights law; b) Be of fundamental character and derive from the *inherent dignity and worth of the human person*; c) Be sufficiently precise to *give rise to identifiable and practicable rights and obligations*; d) Provide, where appropriate, realistic and effective implementation machinery, including reporting systems; e) Attract broad international support.[53]

Yet, even if it is possible to argue that solidarity rights are 'of fundamental character' and derive 'from the *inherent dignity and worth of the human person*' and are also 'sufficiently precise to *give rise to identifiable and practicable rights and obligations*', an additional question is whether these rights are collective or individual rights. This question has made the very concept of solidarity a highly contested one. Some African writers believe that they are collective rights with attendant benefits to the individual.[54] As collective rights, they are to:

> be regarded as *sui generis*. They are not individual, but collective; they belong to groups, communities or peoples. When the group secures the rights in question, then the benefits rebound to its individual constituents and are distributed as individual rights.[55]

But other Western writers hold to the view that 'collective rights are always ultimately destined for individuals, they are *ipso facto* ... individual rights'.[56] The right to environment can be one such example. The individual alone as a self-governing entity can exercise the right to a clean environment. Whereas the individual is at liberty to pursue his environmental goals without the intervention of arbitrary government, his collective rights in international law, which are designed to further his rights as an individual, can only have meaning if exercised in community with others.[57]

Clearly, therefore, solidarity rights benefit the individual, however they may be formulated, because they protect individual rights by promoting that individuals development status, through both individual and collective action. It is, however, the collective action that gives solidarity rights its particular qualitative status. Collective action best ensures development status for the individual at all levels of society. This brings us to the right to development. Alexander Leaf has observed that '[t]oday every country seems to be rushing to promote economic growth' because of 'the current population explosion and the desire of people everywhere to improve their standard of living'.[58] Yet, as a human right, the right development is much broader than the promotion of economic growth.

The right to development is principally understood as a collective right. Yet, it represents both individual and group demands for wealth, enlightenment, peace and happiness. It incorporates within it, both the personal individual opportunity for a better standard of living, as well as the group demand for the positive economic development of society that makes the realization of personal ambitions a realistic objective. The United Nations *World Conference on Human Rights in Tehran* in 1968 first discussed the relationship between human rights and development and it was the United Nations Commission on Human Rights in 1977 that first recognized the right to development.[59] Initially, the right to development was seen as an economic right for developing countries, and emphasis was placed very much on the material aspect of the right.[60] Yet, there were early recognitions that development could not just be confined to material development. After all, the right to development has its foundations in the natural law idea that every individual is entitled to life and well being.

A UN Study on Development in 1960–1964 observed that 'One of the greatest dangers in development policy lies in the tendency to give to the more material aspects of growth an overriding and disproportionate emphasis'.[61] The 1969 *Declaration on Social Progress and Development* referred to 'the continuous raising of the material and spiritual standards of living of all members of society ... in compliance with human rights and fundamental freedoms'.[62] The focus changed decisively during the era of the United Nations Third Decade for Development, and especially under *UN Resolution 35/56* in 1980 which set out a new Development Plan, emphasizing human dignity and the participation and equal distribution of the benefits resulting from the Development Plan.[63] The definition of Johan Caltung states that development '... stands for the development of human beings and not for the development of countries ...'.[64] This was an acknowledgment that society must respond more effectively to the non-material needs of individuals, so that '[T]he ultimate goal of development is to improve and enhance human well-being and the quality of life of all people'.[65]

In 1986 that the United Nations General Assembly first enshrined the right to development in *Declaration on the Right to Development*.[66] The *Declaration* is a shining affirmation in international law of solidarity rights because it was passed not just to protect human rights as conventionally understood, but also to solve 'international problems of an economic, social, cultural or humanitarian nature'.[67] Human rights cannot be achieved without development policy. In the same way, development policy cannot be achieved without human rights.[68] The *Lome Convention of 1989* declared that 'development policy and co-operation are closely linked with respect for and enjoyment of fundamental human rights'.[69] This is unsurprising given that interdependence and indivisibility of all human rights is now well known.[70] This Declaration recognized that any violation of civil, political, economic social and cultural rights runs counter to the very spirit of the right to development. Since development is 'centred on man' this must entail 'respect for and promotion of all human rights'.[71] In 1993, *The Vienna Declaration* then provided that '... the human person is the central subject of development'.[72] There is no doubt that radical reforms will have to be undertaken in the realization of economic, social and cultural rights if a satisfactory and satisfying level of development is to be achieved. Some years later, the *Copenhagen Declaration on Social Development* in 1995, left no doubt how the right to development was to be understood, when it declared that, '... societies must respond more effectively to the material and spiritual needs of individuals, their families and the communities in which they live throughout our diverse countries and regions'.[73] Well-being cannot be achieved without basic human rights since, as the *Commission on Human Rights* said in 1999, 'A prosperous community of slaves who do not have civil and political rights, will not be regarded as a society with well-being'.[74]

These principles are a natural conclusion from the *Declaration on the Right to Development* which first legalized this right in 1986. The right to development is declared in Article 1 of as 'an inalienable human right' and is linked to the 'right of peoples to self-determination'.[75] We are reminded in Article 2 that 'the human person is the central subject of development' and 'all human beings have a responsibility for development' with states having the 'right and the duty to formulate appropriate national development policies'.[76] The duty extends, however, beyond the borders of national states because under Article 3, States have the primary responsibility for the creation of national and international conditions favourable to the realization of the right to development.[77] Article 4 goes even further and states that:

> sustained action is required to promote more rapid development of developing countries. As a complement to the efforts of developing countries, effective international cooperation is essential in providing these countries with appropriate means and facilities to foster their comprehensive development.[78]

The legal obligation to solve 'international problems of economic' and especially of a 'humanitarian nature' is absolute and wide-ranging. Article 8 states that 'all necessary measures for the realization of the right to development', including 'equality of opportunity for all in their access to basic resources, education, health services, food, housing, employment and the fair distribution of income'[79] must be taken.

Indeed, as an instrument for the attainment of global justice, it is very far reaching. It also requires that '[a]ppropriate economic and social reforms should be carried out with a view to eradicating all social injustices'[80] so that development '... aims at the constant improvement of the well being of the entire population and of all individuals ...'.[81] Governments and nations throughout the world should commit themselves to the enhancement of human development and share their responsibilities in a spirit of global partnership in a common cause because development '... involves the well-being of the people involved'.[82] This is because the objectives of development policy must be to enable people to live satisfying lives. World society must, accordingly, eliminate or reduce the major sources of social distress and instability for the family and for society. The goal of the international community must be the well-being of mankind.

The focus in 1995 of the *Copenhagen Declaration on Social Development* on explicitly non-material objectives must mean that co-operation at the international level is needed to eliminate or reduce such phenomena as poverty, social inequality, illiteracy, unemployment, malnutrition, hunger, war, insecurity, environmental degradation, and violation of basic human rights. For the first time, international development policy is formulated in general, rather than limited economic terms, to a embrace a range of human needs and aspirations. Development is a holistic phenomenon. It is to do with the desire of human beings to find fulfillment in life, through education, culture and an enhanced quality of life. Indeed, according to the economist Fredrick Harbison, the development of the spirit and human potentiality comes before material and economic development.[83]

The *Copenhagen Declaration* is also the first time that there is a clear recognition that the objective of wealth creation is not an end in itself but a means to the end of advancing the quality of life of all people. This has the following consequences. First, development means the well-being of people. It means recognition of their desire to be free from deprivation and a recognition of their desire to develop their capabilities and skills. This is clear from Article 10 of the Declaration which is formulated in terms of 'the needs, rights and aspirations of people' when it states that:

> By this Summit we launch a new commitment to social development in each of our countries and new era of international co-operation between Governments and peoples based on a spirit of partnership that puts the needs, rights and aspirations of people at the center of our decisions and joint actions.[84]

Second, it is clear from that same provision that the reference to 'a spirit of partnership' and 'joint actions' is a reference to strengthening international co-operation. Economic prosperity is a means for enhancing communications, human mobility, increased trade, and the opening up of new borders and opportunities, so that everyone everywhere can develop. The disparities are huge. The developed countries spend $1 billion every day on agricultural subsidies, more than the entire gross domestic product of sub-Saharan Africa.[85] A liberalizing of these subsidies would go a long way in aiding the farmers of the Third World countries and would thereby aid in economic, social and political development.

International effort is called for since it is only by these means that poverty, unemployment, illiteracy and social exclusion can be eliminated as a social evil. It is joint action by the international community that alone will facilitate greater social stability, peace, and security and reduce inequality between the developed and the underdeveloped nations of this world. There is therefore a new strategy at a global level that reflects a sense of solidarity between nations. The Copenhagen Declaration is the first time that the coalition of all national and international actors was required for the implementation of the phenomenon of development. In this way, development strategy can be used in such a way as to enhance productive investments, increase trade and capital flows, promote scientific progress through technological developments, and maximize the availability of resources. On the other hand, a world of hunger, poverty, and under-development is an impediment to a sustainable development strategy. In this way, the right to development contains the kernal of all other human rights. Development is a process for the benefit of mankind. If these rights are implemented, they will help eliminate social imbalances in society and the world at large, as well as have a critical effect on social stability and the development and viability of many struggling nations.

It is unsurprising, therefore, that Mohammed Bedjaoui has said of the right to development that:

> It is the alpha and omega of human rights, the first and last human right, the beginning and the end, the means and the goal of human rights, in short it is the *core right* from which all others stem …[86]

International law cannot, he maintains, ignore the principle of dignity of man, and 'it can no longer be reduced to a collection of dry techniques' especially if it 'puts at risk the basic moral values of the human race'.[87] Bedjaoui argues that, because of the 'negative consequences of the colonial experience and the reticence of the former colonial powers to recognize obligations towards the peoples concerned', the single most important objective of the right to development is to establish an obligation for wealthier countries to provide financial and other types of assistance to poorer countries.[88] This view is not without basis. Leading international lawyers, Philip Alston and Gerard Quinn have written that there are three provisions in the *Declaration of the Right to Development* that can be interpreted as giving rise to an obligation by richer states to provide assistance to poorer states. The first is connoted by the phrase 'individually and through international assistance and cooperation, especially economic and technical'.[89] The second is rooted in the provision in Article 11(1) requiring State Parties to take appropriate steps to ensure the realization of an adequate standard of living. The third is found in the provision in Article 11(2) requiring State Parties to take 'individually and through international cooperation', relevant measures concerning the right to be free from hunger.[90]

Alston and Quinn argue that during the preparatory phase of these provisions, 'it was accepted by virtually all delegations that the developing states would require some form of international assistance if they were to be able to promote effectively the realization of economic and social rights', but that this obligation did 'not extend much, if at all, beyond that general proposition'.[91] Yet, there is no evidence to show that when it comes to international migration the obligation for international assistance does extend beyond general propositions. Indeed, in the context of migration, the right to development has today not just a moral, but a practical imperative as the *International Development Sixth Report on Migration and Development* in 2004 shows.

THE *INTERNATIONAL DEVELOPMENT SIXTH REPORT ON MIGRATION AND DEVELOPMENT*

'The history of migration' according to the British Parliament's *International Development Sixth Report on Migration and Development* published in July 2004[92] 'is the history of peoples' struggle to survive and to prosper, to escape insecurity and poverty, and to move in response to opportunity'. The result is that 175 million people worldwide, or just under 3 per cent of the total population of the world, live outside their country of birth.[93] In what is one of the best things ever written on managing international migration, this *Report* first observes that:

> [M]igration may be the exception rather than the rule, but it is increasing. It is already very important – in terms of economics and politics, domestically and internationally – because of the links it establishes between countries.

The *Report* then sets out to debunk a number of key 'migration myths', such as that migration is a 'problem'; that international migration causes a 'brain drain' for developing countries; and that Britain is 'being flooded by asylum seekers and refugees'.[94]

What is most refreshing about the *Report* is its premise that today:

> the challenge is to *manage migration* so that when people choose to migrate their experience, and that of the people they leave behind, is positive; the benefits are maximized; the costs are minimized; and both the costs and the benefits are shared equitably between home and host societies.[95]

However, it is unclear how far the *Report* would want the developed states to be involved in 'managing migration' as we shall see later. Nevertheless, the *Report* recognizes that the relentless process of globalization has not benefited everyone in the world and so adopts 'a development perspective' and considers the challenge of population flows and the resources that people often remit, could be used 'to deliver benefits in terms of poverty reduction in developing countries and thereby to make globalization work for the poor'.[96]

In this way, the focus of the *Report* is squarely on determining 'equitable and development-friendly outcomes from migration'. In this respect it does not draw a distinction between voluntary and involuntary migrants or between economic migrants and refugees. It recognizes that it is not embarking on an easy task. This is because although it is well known that migration produces costs and benefits, it is the distribution of these costs and benefits which adds yet more complexity. Migration may be a global phenomenon, but different people, in different places, have different stories to tell. When these people decide to move, they will weigh up the costs and benefits of migration differently too.[97] The *Report* observes how:

> from Hargeisa, Somaliland, the dominant story may be one of civil war, a struggle for independence, refugees and their gradual return, and the vital role which migrants' remittances play in sustaining their home country.

On the other hand, as the *Report* notes, the story may be different 'from Nairobi, Kenya, that of a capital city receiving economic migrants from rural areas, and economic migrants and refugees from neighbouring countries, all in search of a better life'. Yet again:

> from the UK, the stories are of increased cultural diversity, a health service dependent on foreign-born nurses and doctors, but also of desperate attempts to enter the UK in the back of lorries, and of workers exploited by gangmasters and dying in the sands of Morecambe Bay.

These are all narratives that we have considered to a greater or lesser extent in this book. However, the *Report* is critical of what it perceives to be an imbalanced approach to international migration, pointing out that the majority of narratives are about the impact of such forms of migration on the richer developed world: 'Too rarely in the UK is the narrative about the impacts on developing countries themselves.'[98]

These findings are consistent with the *International Development Sixth Report on Migration and Development* which highlighted the opportunities from migration and from the resource flows which migration can generate. As it observed, even a slight relaxing of restrictions on the movement of workers – such as increasing the proportion of migrants in developed countries' workforce to just 3 per cent – would deliver global gains of $150 billion per year, some of which could be spent on poverty reduction.[99] Should there be even more radical liberalization this would offer 'economic gains which far exceed those which a successful conclusion to the World Trade Organization's (WTO) "Development Round" might achieve'.[100] As the *Report* makes clear, the current volume of remittances sent home by international migrants is estimated to be $93 billion per year. If the unrecorded remittances were to be added to this, then the total amounts to perhaps a staggering $300 billion that international migrants themselves are sending back to their home countries.[101] This stands in stark contrast to the total global aid of $68.5 billion per year. The opportunities are clear to both migrants and host societies should they wish to avail themselves of them. As the *Report* resoundingly declared:

> Migrants have the chance to employ their energies and enterprise in pursuit of a better life. Host societies have the opportunity to benefit from an influx of skills. Home societies can benefit from resources remitted by people who have moved away, and from the return of migrants, armed with new skills and ideas.[102]

This accordingly, is a trail-blazing and seminal report, the contents of which deserve to be much better known than they have been to-date. It leaves no doubt that whether we like it or not we are today all 'global citizens'. We are all inter-dependent. We must work to advance the principles of international solidarity. We can no longer just say: Why should we be concerned about global as opposed to national interests? The answer is simple. Global and national interests do not as easily divide any longer as they once might have done. But there are opportunities too, from migration and from the resource flows which migration can generate. The *Report,* for this reason, observes that:

> [W]e broadly support the 'managed migration' approach: the UK should be neither a fortress nor an open house.[103] It seems to us that on balance, migration is economically beneficial to the UK, but not by a huge amount.[104]

Yet, as has been argued consistently in this book, economic imperatives are not the only imperatives in the management of international migration. As the *Report* points out:

> decisions about the desirable level of migration into the UK cannot be made on the basis of economics alone. There are important social, cultural and political costs and benefits to consider, and there are important distributional questions about which economic and social groups reap the benefits or suffer the costs of migration.

It is for this reason that it concludes that '[U]ltimately, decisions about migration are more a matter of values than of economics'. As such, the choice is 'not a choice between wealth and poverty' and nor just about the sort of country that one desires to inhabit 'but it is also about the sort of world that one wants to live in, and the relationship of one's country to the world'.[105] The *Report,* which is quoted extensively hereafter, is most useful in that it provides access to statistics on current trends in migration, analysing the political economy which causes movement and ways in which it can be harnessed for a common good.

THE NEEDS OF THE DEVELOPED WORLD

In early 2005, a European Commission Green Paper *Confronting demographic change: a new solidarity between generations,* warned of a shrinking workforce within the European Union.[106] The *European Commission Report* stated that within the next 20 years, a drastic slump in birth rates combined with an ageing population will undermine Europe's prosperity, unless immigration is encouraged. As European workers' age and birth rates lag across the Continent, the document, published on 17th March 2005, holds out the spectre of a demographic time-bomb and a widening gap between the European Union and the United States. It states that the fertility rates in Europe is 'insufficient to replace the population' and adds that '[n]ever in history has there been economic growth without population growth'. In addition to recommending that life should be made easier for parents in Europe, the Green Paper also controversially concludes that 'ever larger migrant flows may be needed to meet the need for labour and safeguard Europe's prosperity'. The *Report* shows that between now and 2025, the population of the European Union will grow slightly from the current figure of 458 million to 469.5 million, although this 2 per cent rise is because of immigration. But by 2030 that figure will fall to 468.7 million. Between 2005 and 2030, the number of working-age people (between 15 and 64 years) will fall by 20.8 million, or 6.8 per cent, while the number of those over 65 will more than double, growing by a total of 40 million. By contrast the population of America will increase by more than a quarter between 2000 and 2025.[107]

What is clear from other recent reports is that immigration from the European Union countries will not be able to fill the void. A report published in 2004 by the *European Foundation for the Improvement of Living and Working Conditions*[108] shows the potential extent of migration from the acceding and candidate countries towards the European Union to be minimal. On 1st May the ten Eastern European countries of the Czech Republic, Estonia, Cyprus, Latvia, Lithuania, Hungary, Malta, Poland, Slovenia and the Slovak Republic, became members of the European Union. Governments of the existing EU member states were concerned that there might be high levels of migration from the accession countries into existing member states, and that adverse economic consequences would follow, such as the immigration of low-paid and unskilled workers leading to increased unemployment increased pressure on the social welfare system increased competition for public housing; increased levels of crime, and increased tensions within multicultural society. There were fears that whilst unemployment levels in the accession countries might be reduced by the emigration of low-skilled workers, highly skilled qualified workers from the existing EU countries might emigrate causing a 'brain drain' to take place.

Using information based on attitudes to three questions, namely, (1) general inclination to migrate, (2) basic intention to migrate, and (3) firm intention to migrate, the study[109] predicted that across the whole of the European Union only 1.1 million people (approximately 1 per cent of the population of the accession and candidate countries) would migrate over the next 5 years. The survey did not, unfortunately, distinguish between short-term and long-term migration, so it is very possible most people simply wanted to embark on 'circular migration', leaving home, working in another country, and then returning back home. Bulgaria and Romania showed the highest migration potential. Most migrants from any of the countries would be highly qualified. Up to 2–3 per cent of a country's graduates would be coming from another accession country. Thus, the typical migrant was expected to be young, single, and well-educated or a student of higher education – precisely the sort of person that most studies have found to be essential for Europe's future prosperity. Both acceding and candidate countries would face a 'youth drain' of 2–5 per cent of the youngest age group over the next 5 years. There would also be a 'brain drain' of 3–5 per cent of those with higher education and over 10 per cent of students over the same period. As noted above, the study has not distinguished between long-term and short-term migrants, so it is possible that most would not want to stay permanently.

What was remarkable about the research was the finding that unemployment was less a factor in the decision to migrate than expected. Only 2 per cent of the unemployed expressed a firm intention to migrate, with the highest figures being in Turkey, Bulgaria, and Estonia. Even so, although no single or overall reason for migration was found, employment and financial motives were significant factors. Thus, there was an overwhelming desire among migrants to better themselves. Low income, however, could only be identified as statistically significant in Turkey, where both high and low income influenced decisions to migrate, as did income differentials. In Poland, men were more likely to migrate than women, younger people were more likely than older people to migrate, and the unemployed (or those fearing unemployment) were more likely to migrate than those in secure employment. In this respect, potential migrants from Poland were not dissimilar to those from Turkey.

This is a good example of how conceptual categories such as 'push' and 'pull' factors help us to understand migration. As the *International Development Select Committee* states a number of studies have shown that the 'push' factors are useful in explaining how migrants may be motivated to leave a place for reasons ranging from the economic and demographic (poverty, unemployment, low wages, high fertility rates, lack of basic health and education), to the political (conflict, insecurity, violence, poor governance, corruption and human rights abuses), the social and cultural (discrimination on the basis of ethnicity, religion, gender or caste), and the environmental (harvest failure, resource depletion, and natural and/or man-made disasters).[110] However, the 'pull' factors are also at work here because, as we have seen, the *European Commission Report* has concluded that falling birth rates in Europe mean that 'ever larger migrant flows may be needed' and there are therefore, perceived economic opportunities here for migrants from the accession countries, which an increasingly global media has imparted to them. As with migrants generally, it is clear that these migrants are also attracted by the possibility of employment, better standards of living, greater opportunities for personal and professional development. To that extent, it matters not whether their journey takes them to a nearby town, to the capital city, to a neighbouring country, or to a distant land.[111]

What this demonstrates is that migrants are motivated by various combinations of 'push' and 'pull' factors against a background of transport and other costs.[112] Migration can often begin as a result of push factors, such as lack of work in the case of the European accession countries (or such calamities as drought in many under-developed countries). However, the 'push' factors often take over when migrants return with stories of a better life elsewhere, and family networks which link home and host regions are established.[113] On the other hand, it is also the case that migration may be initiated following a community, such as the Eastern European accession countries, making contact with, and learning more about, the outside world[114] – which in this case would be the wider western European community. What the example of the European accession countries does show, however, is that although identifying push and pull factors does shed some light on the reasons for migration, there are actually a constellation of factors at work here. For this reason, 'it is perhaps more useful to see migration as one of the options which poor people and households have for managing their risks and sustaining their livelihoods'.[115] This is because '[I]f people felt that their current place of residence provided them with adequate chances for secure lives, free of poverty, and with the prospect of improvement, then they would not feel forced to move' and that '[A]chieving this is a matter of improving the prospects for sustainable development in developing countries' together with 'ensuring that the right structures – of governance, for education, for health – are in place'.[116] When it comes to policy-making, therefore, what is required is '[U]nderstanding migration as part of the range of poor people's livelihood options', as such an understanding has important implications for policy' not least of which would be that '[M]igration and migrants should not be seen as problems to be dealt with'. This is because the simple fact is that, '[M]igrants are people trying to improve their lives and must be treated accordingly'.[117]

Even so, what is most significant about the report of the *European Foundation for the Improvement of Living and Working Conditions*, is its conclusion that existing EU member states would be 'hardly affected' by the impact of migration from the accession and candidate countries. Also significant was the finding that most migrants would return back to their countries once economic and social conditions began to improve in the new member states (as it is bound to do). In the existing EU countries the impact on the labour market and on housing conditions was expected to be limited. On the other hand, the existing EU countries could expect to gain a 'high quality supply of young, qualified, and mainly unmarried people, which should improve its short-term economic and its long-term socio-economic base through an improved demographic structure'.

A DEVELOPMENT THEORY OF MIGRATION

International Migration is a collective process based on fundamental social changes in society. Various social-scientific paradigms have been devised by migration scholars.[118] They have sought insights from fields as diverse political science, psychology, law, geography, sociology, demography and history. Migration studies is accordingly an interdisciplinary vocation. Three main approaches have emerged: neo-classical economic equilibrium theory, the historical-structuralist theory, and migration systems theory.[119] But I would argue that it is time for a 'Development Theory' of migration based on principles of international solidarity, universal human rights, and the notion of the global citizen. Such an approach is entirely consistent with the outlook of the *International Development Sixth Report on Migration and Development*. It is ethical as well as just to both sides.

The *neo-classical economic equilibrium theory* has been used largely by demographers, geographers and economists.[120] It is based on the work of the nineteenth century geographer, Ravenstein, who developed the first systematic theory on migration by developing statistical laws,[121] based on the so-called 'push-pull' factors. The theory suggests that people move from densely populated to sparsely populated areas; or from low-wage to high wage societies; or that population movements correspond to fluctuations in the business cycle. The 'push-pull' factor lies in the people being attracted away from one area to another. This tradition of migration has been criticized as bearing little relation to reality because it is individualistic and ahistorical.[122] It is based on the idea of the 'immigration market' whereby, in the words of Borjas, 'competing host countries make "migration offers" from which individuals compare and choose' before deciding whether to leave or remain in their countries of origin with the result that '[n]eo-classical theory assumes that individuals maximize utility: individuals 'search' for the country of residence that maximizes their well-being …'.[123] This is an overly simplistic view of migration which can hardly ever be explained in terms of individual action alone. It cannot explain the current population movements and nor can it help to predict future migratory movements.[124] As Castles and Miller point out, it is hardly ever the poorest people in the least developed countries who move to the richest countries but 'people of intermediate social status from areas which are undergoing economic and social change'.[125] Moreover, some of the most densely populated parts of the world, like Britain and Germany, are countries currently of immigration. This is to say nothing of the fact that certain populations go to particular countries, regardless of whether it is the most profitable country for them to go to. Algerian migrants have traditionally gone to France and people from Surinam have gone to the Netherlands.[126]

The *historical-structural theory* arose in the 1970s with intellectual roots in Marxist political economy. This approach emphasizes the unequal distribution of power in the world economy from economic and political standpoints. The requirements of cheap labour for capital are met by powerful groups being able to facilitate migration.[127] The exploitation of resources makes for uneven development in the world economy. The rich become richer and the poor ever more poor. According to the adherents of this theory, the neo-classical approach is inadequate because it lays such great store on free human choice, whereas in reality most migrants have very little.[128] Individual migrants are constrained in reality by the inequality of power and resources between different countries and the use of entry restrictions placed on non-citizens.[129] The historical-structuralist approach was useful in providing an explanation for the mass recruitment of labour by capital. It took into account the long legacy of colonialism. It accounted fully for the regional inequalities of societies. Further, it offered a critique of the 'push-pull' theories of an earlier generation, as providing an explanation only for the voluntary migrations of individuals before 1914, principally in the context of European migration to the America. The recruitment of labour by capital, however, was a more widespread modern phenomenon, ranging from the factories of Germany to the infrastructure projects of Australia such as the Snowy Mountain Hydro-Electric Scheme. Labour migration was a pivotal device used forging domination between the major economies of western capitalism and the underdeveloped world. Yet, it was only a matter of time before when the historical-structuralist approach too began to be criticized for its inadequacies. Why was it, it was asked, that labour migrants became permanent settlers in certain countries? Why was it, if the power of capital and the interests of the Western world was so dominant, that their migration policies broke down so completely and so unexpectedly? Critics charged that if the neo-classical approach took insufficient account of the historical causes of migration and of the role of the state in migration, the historical functional approach took too great an account of the interests of capital, giving insufficient regard to the interests, motivations and actions of both individuals and groups. In short, both theories were one-sided. It was in this context that a third theory emerged.

Migration systems theory advanced the notion that migratory movements mostly arise from pre-existing links between the sending and receiving countries, based on such connections as colonization, political influence, trade, investment or cultural ties.[130] As such, it takes much greater account of collective action, institutional factors, international relations and political economy. In the words of Fawcett and Arnold, there is in evidence here, 'state-to-state relations and comparisons, mass culture connections and family and social networks'.[131] This theory is most useful in the context of comparative research. When two or more countries exchange migrants there is in existence a migration system. Regional migration systems are analyzed such as the South Pacific or West Africa,[132] but different regions may also be linked by a migration system, such as the Caribbean and Western Europe, or North Africa and France. In my earlier work, I have described the 1950s immigration of colonial immigrants to Britain by observing that '[t]he British policy of favouring colonial immigrants' was 'based on a common bond of citizenship and the continuance of post-independence links overseas'.[133] Sassen even observes that the Korean and Vietnamese migrations to the USA were both the result of long-term US military involvement in those countries.[134]

According to the migrations system approach, any migration can therefore be explained on the basis of interacting macro- and micro-structures. Macro-structures are those structures that refer to large-scale institutional factors. One such factor is as the political economy of the world market. Over the last 500 years, the world economy has become ever more integrated with increased production, distribution and exchange and this has impacted on migratory movements.[135] Another factor is international relations. Industrialized economies do not readily admit migrants, but seek to control the entry of workers and refugees into their territories. Where such migration takes place, states often play a role in sending and receiving migrants.[136] They will often take steps to promote migratory movements.[137] Other macro-structure factors are interstate relationships, and the laws, structures and practices established by the states of sending and receiving countries to control migration settlement.

Micro-structures are those structures that set up networks, practices and beliefs of the migrants themselves. These networks are informal. They are often socially developed by the migrants themselves. They are developed so that migrants can help travel, arrive, integrate and settle themselves in host communities. The networks involve personal relationships, family and household patterns, friendship and community ties, mutual help in economic and social matters. Bourdieu and Wacquant have referred to this as 'social capital'.[138] They help bind 'migrants and non-migrants together in a complex web of social roles and interpersonal relationships'.[139] The phrase 'chain migration' has often been used to explain this behaviour.[140] Castles and Miller state that:

[t]oday many authors emphasize the role of information and "cultural capital" (knowledge of other countries, capabilities for organizing travel, finding work and adapting to a new environment) in starting and sustaining migratory movements.[141]

Micro-structures can be quite decisive in formulating immigration patterns. Asian migration, for instance, is usually undertaken not by individuals but by families.[142]

Whichever of these migration models are adopted, it is clear that if Governments are to make migration deliver benefits then policies need to be based on a sound understanding of the complex relationship between migration and development.[143] This is not least because the United Nations Population Division estimates that 175 million people currently live outside their country of birth, represents in absolute terms, an increase of 100 million since 1965. Yet, in percentage terms this is only an increase from 2.3 percent to 2.9 percent of the world's total population over the last 40 years.[144] As the *International Development Sixth Report on Migration and Development* makes clear, however, although 'it may well be the case that many more people would like to migrate, …there is currently … no "tidal wave" about to crash on the shores of the UK or the developed world as a whole'.[145] Some 60 percent of the world's international migrants live in the developed world, and 40 percent in the developing world. In Europe, there are 56 million migrants living. In Asia, there are 50 million, and in North America there are 41 million international migrants.[146]

Yet, what is interesting is that refugees comprise only 16 million people, around nine per cent of the international migrants. This is because refugees are overwhelmingly to be found in developing countries. In this respect, the richer developed world of the North has a disproportionately lesser burden to shoulder. Thus, Asia is home to 9 million; Africa to 4 million; and the developed world as a whole is home to only 3 million. What is even more disconcerting is that developing countries also house most of the 25 million Internally Displaced Persons (IDPs) who, as we have seen in Chapter 5, are defined as people who have been forced to leave their homes, but who are not classified as refugees because they have not crossed over a national border.[147] What the current theories of migration do not do – and what the current figures on international migration overall fail to do – is capture the vast scale of migration that also takes place within countries. In India for instance, there are estimated to be 200 million temporary and seasonal migrants, and within China there are 120 million internal migrants.[148] These are huge numbers and a testament to the importance of migration for people in search of safety and security.

The migration between the rich world and the poor world not only establishes links between the South-north regions but it also has important implications for development and poverty reduction in developing countries themselves.[149] However, any understanding of international migration must recognize also that migration is not primarily a south-north phenomenon.[150] It is a fact not sufficiently well highlighted that most migration, and in particular the migration of the poor, takes place within and between developing countries.[151] Many countries in south-east Asia, for example, are heavily dependent on cheap migrant labour from neighbouring countries[152]. We saw an example of this in chapter 1 when we discussed the example of Malaysia which in expelled 380,000 impoverished Indonesian foreign workers – much to its cost! In the same way, international migration from Vietnam between 1994 and 1999 of 300,000 pales into insignificance when compared to the 4.3 million people who migrated within Vietnam over the same period.[153] Indeed, urbanization in many developing countries is only possible because it is fed by large volumes of rural-urban migration.[154]

Temporary migration is also much overlooked as an outstanding feature of much of international migration. It needs to be remembered that 'a very high proportion of migrants, and perhaps even the majority, migrate on a temporary basis'. This phenomenon occurs from the smallest countries to the biggest and even occurs on an international scale. They will do so either for a number of years before returning home, or they will migrate to and fro each year.[155] This has important implications for Western Europe which often harbours worries about immigrants entering to work, but then not leaving. It is well known, for example, that in relation to the workforce in the Dominican Republic, many Haitians go backwards and forwards between there and their home country.[156] It is also well known that in India, poor people's lives have long been characterized by regular temporary, circular, and seasonal migration, with people moving in response to opportunities for agricultural work, or for off-farm rural employment in construction and services.[157]

The *International Development Sixth Report on Migration and Development* reminds us how on a global scale even, '[M]uch south-south migration, especially temporary, circular and seasonal migration, falls between the cracks, with migration unrecorded and migrants undocumented'. The losers here are not the receiving countries who benefit from the labour of migrant workers, but the casual migrants themselves. Their lack of documentation, together with their absence of protective legal frameworks, contribute to such migrants having few rights, leaving them vulnerable to exploitation, in a land where they are largely invisible to policy-makers.[158] In short, any understanding of international migration needs to be fully cognizant of the multi-faceted nature of migration, including temporary, circular and seasonal migration, within and between developing countries, as well as from south to north. For contemporary liberal democratic societies any ethical, just and fair management of migration should be based on policies that aim to deliver development and poverty reduction in the world today. As such, they should rid themselves of the assumption that migration is a rare occurrence, a south-north phenomenon, or a one-off event.[159]

What this points to, I would suggest, is a new paradigm of migration analysis and a new theory for migration. There are two reasons for this, both of which are based on the understanding of migration that 'cannot be divorced from the wider international system of economics and politics which shapes the lives of poor people'. Thus, a 'small farmers' ability to survive on the land may be damaged by the dumping of subsidized agricultural produce by the

EU, and the provision of food aid in kind by the USA'.[160] The result is that 'with this livelihood option closed off, they may face little choice other than migration to the capital city, or perhaps, if they have the resources, to the developed world'. What is important for the wider international community is that:

> in seeking to manage or respond to migration, policy-makers in the developed and developing world should consider carefully the impacts of a range of other policies, on issues including aid, trade, investment, arms exports, climate change, human rights, corruption and governance.[161]

The first specific reason for a development theory of migration is that this international system of economics and politics makes a nonsense of the usual distinctions often drawn, in the words of the *International Development Sixth Report on Migration and Development*, 'between types of migrants (voluntary or forced), between their motivations for moving (economic or non-economic), and between 'push' and 'pull' factors in motivating migration'.[162] This is based on the facile notion that 'voluntary migrants choose to move; forced migrants do not' and that 'economic migrants move to gain access to resources or to improve their employment opportunities, whereas non-economic migrants move to escape persecution'. The argument runs that 'migrants responding to push factors are leaving places where life is a struggle, migrants responding to pull factors are moving to places where they think they might prosper'.

Yet, whereas it is the case, as the *International Development Sixth Report on Migration and Development* suggests, that making distinctions between migrants and their motives is necessary in order to ensure that refugees fleeing political persecution are afforded protection and asylum, the fact is that 'people who move often have multiple motives',[163] and the fact is that 'the places from which they move often have multiple problems – a lack of economic opportunities and political instability – linked by the common thread of poor governance'.[164] The result is that most movements of 'forced' or 'voluntary' migrants is often difficult to rationalize in such a straight-forward way because 'forced migrants may retain some choice as to where they flee; voluntary migrants may be escaping depths of poverty and insecurity which give little room for choice'. Indeed, 'economic migrants may be fleeing persecution as well as poverty'. The result is that although, 'policy-makers may seek clarity ... the line between voluntary and forced migration and economic and non-economic migrants is frequently blurred'.[165]

The second specific reason for a development theory of migration is that the current international system of economics and politics is such that the poor and the destitute of the world, who most need to better their lot by taking up the opportunity of working in a rich country, are the least likely to migrate to rich a country. This is because migration requires resources and the poor of the world lack resources. They are bereft of finance. They do not have access to the social networks and social capital which help to make migration possible.[166] For this reason, the poorest people tend not to migrate. If they do migrate they do not migrate far.[167] In the words of the New Economics Foundation:

although international travel is cheaper and more accessible than at any other time in history, the cost of a plane or train ticket is still well beyond the reach of the majority of the world's population.[168]

The reality of international migration is that generally only those with access to financial resources and social networks make for long-distance migrants. This consigns the poor to migrate only locally.[169] The *International Development Sixth Report on Migration and Development* describes the fact that poor people tend not to migrate internationally in aggregate terms as the phenomenon of the 'migration hump'.[170] What the migration hump shows is that where there are low levels of development there is little migration, but that with rising development income levels, there is a corresponding rise also in migration. Since it takes time for increased income levels and consumer demand to translate into increased domestic production and opportunities for employment,[171] people gradually become more able to migrate. What is interesting is that migration continues to rise with income levels until an income threshold is reached.[172] Migration then starts to taper off once this threshold is reached because the domestic economy begins to offer people opportunities at home.[173] There are both European and non-European examples of this phenomenon. In the 1960s and 1970s, Spain and Portugal saw rapidly increasing levels of out-migration as their position began to rise up the migration hump. When in the 1980s and 1990s they passed over the hump, net outward migration decreased and has now been reversed.[174] A very similar pattern has been followed in Italy and South Korea.[175]

What is important about the migration hump phenomenon is that it raises some very important issues for policy which, in my view, can best be solved by the adoption of a development theory in migration studies. If the poorest do not migrate, or do not migrate far, then 'it cannot be assumed that policies which help migrants will also help the poor'.[176] Therefore, it is necessary not overlook the impact of migration on those left behind in developing countries. Furthermore, the developed countries cannot expect to forestall an increase in immigrants to their shores by reducing poverty in developing countries. This is because according to the migration hump, if the international community is overly successful in reducing poverty, there will be an increased out-migration from developing countries to the developed world.[177] It is for this reason that the *International Development Sixth Report on Migration and Development* suggests that the answer lies in the West pursuing a wider agenda of development of the kind that we have discussed above, because:

... there may be aspects of development – democracy, good governance, gender equality – which developed countries might promote, and which might have the effect of reducing the push factors that encourage migration, leading to a situation where migration is an informed choice rather than a desperate option.[178] Improving governance is of the utmost importance; better governance would make some migrants less desperate to leave, and – by encouraging migrants to remit and perhaps to return – would also make that migration which does take place more development-friendly. This is primarily the responsibility of developing country governments.

All of this points to a policy of 'circular migration' enabling the better off people in a country to migrate, earn money, make remittances to poorer relatives at home, and then return back, but in the process alleviating the lot of their country. This is not least because migration can impact upon development and poverty. Thus, recent research by the World Bank suggests that as little as a 10 per cent increase in the share of migrants in a country's population, will result in a 1.9 per cent decline in the share of people living on less than $1 per day.[179] Consequently, the benefits of migration can be harnessed to improve the livelihoods of people even when migration does not directly involve the poor.[180] It does not as the *International Development Sixth Report on Migration and Development* suggests, point to the adoption of a policy of 'managed migration'.[181] This is because 'managed migration' neither controls immigration and nor does it meet the needs of national economy in a cost-effective way. In 2004 Beverley Hughes, the British Home Office Immigration Minister, talked about adopting 'world-wide solutions' to migration, pointing out that 'What we have been trying to argue for some time – and I think this is beginning to get through – is the need for managed migration and for better refugee solutions worldwide'. She went onto explain how in Britain (as in the developed world generally) 'We are vastly short of vital workers such as teachers, nurses and even policemen.' As she explained a programme of 'managed migration' would enable Britain to announce that it will take in a certain number of economic migrants each year.[182]

Yet, as the *Report* of the *Migration Commission* of the Royal Society of Arts (RSA) in its year long investigation into the needs of British industry, made clear in November 2005 – and of which I declare I was a member – 'managed migration' has failed both to control the number of overall migrants because of the existence of irregular migration, and to meet the labour demand of British employers in a cost-effective way: '[S]ignificant irregular migration is the sign that government has failed in its policy – it has lost control of the number of new entrants'. As it explains, such has been the failure of this new policy that the government was only 'saved by entry to the European Union of the eight new accession states, and its decision to allow their citizens to work in Britain rather than postponing this as much of the Union did', because 'it implicitly granted an amnesty to the citizens of the eight already working irregularly in the UK' and also 'vastly extended the domestic labour market to include the eight so that those who might have migrated irregularly before without this change, could now do so legally'.[183] According to the Migration Commission of the RSA, '[T]he authors of Managed Migration must have known that it would fail because almost certainly non of them believe manpower planning can be made to work, especially in an open economy'. Its conclusion is damning in that, '[I]rregular migration was the precondition for allowing Managed Migration to work at all, and yet irregular migration was also the measure of the policy failure'.[184] In fact, '[M]anaged Migration by failing to recruit sufficient low-skilled workers, lends itself to the general loss of control or even knowledge – more and more economic activity slips below the level of the statistically recorded into the black economy'.[185] In this respect, it is salutary to bear in mind the example of Mexico *vis-à-vis* America. As one witness to the US Congressional Committee on the US-Mexican relations said in 1990:

[A]s our people become older, the problem will not be to find jobs for people but people for jobs. For many years, Mexico, with its relatively young and expanding population will complement and balance our own as well as provide a formidable defence to attacks on our position in world markets.[186]

Thus, the enthusiasm for 'managed migration' by the *International Development Sixth Report on Migration and Development*, in its otherwise excellent report, would appear to be misguided in these respects.

To conclude, we need a new 'Development Theory' of international migration because just as socialism, which worked in theory but not in practice, globalization too has its shortcomings. Theoretically, increased global trade should reduce poverty. The reality is different. First, foreign investment into the least developed countries has not alleviated hardship for ordinary people. Free markets have not been better than control of the economy by dishonest, profligate and unscrupulous officials working in inflexible, centralized governments. Thus, although the World Bank and the International Monetary Fund (IMF) often insisted on privatization of public services as a condition of loans or grants, these services were subsequently usually taken over by foreign firms and not by local businesses. The result often was that privatization made the poor pay more for water, more for education, and more for healthcare, than before. African countries were often criticized for having too little globalization, rather than too much, and so in the 1990s many of them liberalized their economies as required. The result is not the alleviation of hardship. Most of these countries have found themselves falling even further back in the provision of basic amenities than before. Privatizing state run services has not been a panacea. The infrastructure has been debilitated, with inadequate transport, electricity services and the like. The lot of the people, from skill levels to basic health, has not improved. Second, rising prosperity in the G8 countries has not acted as a *sine qua non* for increased prosperity in the under-developed world. Instead, what the openness to global markets has done for the poor world is to impoverish and destroy the few sectors of the economy, such as subsistence farming, that just about worked. Third, in much the same way as socialism was wrecked by the rapacious avariciousness of its trailblazers, so too has globalization been crippled by those at its forefront, namely, by big business and the powerful governments of rich nations. This is hardly surprising. Big business is, after all, concerned with maximizing profits, and rich countries with winning votes. What is surprising is the less than whole-hearted commitment to free trade. Just as the Soviet elite only gave lip-service to the ideals of equality and justice, so too free marketeers demand the removal of government subsidies elsewhere while supporting their own farmers at $350 a year, which is more than seven times what the aid for the developing world. Free marketeers demand an end to tariffs, but then retain their own barriers to manufactured products, at a cost of $700bn a year to the developing nations. And, most devastatingly for the world's poor, free marketeers insist on the free movement of capital, but set strict limits on the free movement of labour. Yet, globalization is damaged by the restrictions on free movement. If the richer countries really wanted to alleviate hardship, to increase prosperity, and to bring real benefits of globalization to bear in the poorer world, there is no better way to do that than to lift the barriers to control in the developed world. Globalizing the free movement of people across the world would enable vastly more people in the under-developed world to improve themselves and their people. Money earned in rich countries would flow back as remittances back home to relatives in poorer countries. Already, it is clear that the single most effective method of help for the world's poor is money sent home by workers from overseas. These remittances often amount to more than the total export earnings for their countries. They vastly exceed what the developed world gives by way of aid to the under-developed world. At the same time, big business and multinationals would be forced to improve working conditions in Africa and Asia for fear that workers in those countries would set out to find work in the developed world. That would be true globalization with a truly globalized market, rather a neo-colonialist framework enabling the greedy and the powerful to do as they want.

CONCLUSION

The ideas presented in this concluding chapter may appear to be radically unnatural. Yet, they are only so to the intellectually hide-bound. The truth of the matter is that it is the restrictions on free movement that the developed free world has pursued for the better part of a hundred years that are unnatural and radical. It has taken the economic and demographic changes that appear to be ready to engulf us in the new millennium to remind us how greater free movement is the most natural of all human activities. Nearly half a century ago, in 1971 Roger Nett asked:

> Do we have any knowledge of how an open system of world migration might work? We have limited cases. One might think of free movement of people within the British system. A clearer example, however, is within the United States of America, where people have, and have had, the right of free movement since slavery was abolished more than a century ago. Here we have a fair-sized experiment to see how free movement operates in one instance. It works surprisingly well on one subcontinent anyway. When there is a drought in one region, as in the dust-bowl days of the 1930s, people move to another region, and opportunities are somewhat equalized. When clumsy state officials or demagogues disrupt a school system, teachers move to another state. This has a corrective effect on state policies or, if it does not, enriches the states which have better policies or more to offer. But perhaps the best modern example is that of the European Union which allows free movement in the interests of jobs and welfare. Imagine what it would be like if everybody were kept within the boundaries of his own state, and you have a fair picture of most of the rest of the world today![187]

Despite this classic and irrefutable formulation in favour of an expanded right to free movement, it remains true that free movement rights are generally resisted in the developed world. Yet, the important question that is posed by the *International Development Sixth Report on Migration and Development* is how to incorporate migration policies aimed at delivering development and poverty reduction into general policies of immigration control. For developed countries, the policy-making focus can no longer be specifically on the costs and benefits to the receiving state of migration. The Goal 8 of the *Millennium Development Goals* (MDGs) reminds us, that the international community has to establish a global partnership for development in the pursuit of the internationally-agreed MDGs, with the result that focus has to be on the longer-term aim of a general poverty reduction in developing countries. In this way policy-makers will have to remember that their national policies have global repercussions.

Today the expectations from a right of free movement go far and wide. Free movement is the catalyst for the realistic achievement of a right to development. For that, there will need to be fresh thinking. The relationship of the international right to development, as enshrined by the General assembly in the *Declaration on the Right to Development*, to an individual's right to migrate has not thus far been analyzed. There are certainly provisions in that *Declaration* that bear further scrutiny from this angle. The *Declaration* does not just address human rights but broader international problems, including those of a cultural and humanitarian nature, and development rights are in specific recognition of the fact that the 'human person is the central subject of development' with the purpose being to ensure equality of opportunity in the basic resources and a fair distribution of income.[188] What is, however, clear is that the global community can no longer determine global policy on the basis of particular own interests neglectful of others, if only because its own interests are inextricably intertwined with the interests of others less fortunate – but who inhabit the same world.

NOTES

1 Anthony Pagden, *Peoples and Empires* (London, Weidenfeld & Nicolson, 2001), see inside cover.
2 Roger Nett, 'The civil right we are not ready for: The Right to Free Movement of People on the Face of the Earth', 81 *Ethics*, 212, at 216 (1971).
3 Roger Nett, ibid., at p.228.
4 United Nations Development Programme, 1991 *Human Development Report* 2 (1991).
5 *Loc. cit.*
6 *Loc. cit.*
7 *Loc. cit.*
8 *Loc. cit.*
9 *Loc. cit.*
10 Quoted from Larry Elliot, 'The Lost Decade', *The Guardian*, 9th July 2003 at p.1.
11 General Assembly Resolution on the *Alternative approaches and ways and means*

within the United Nations system for improving the effective enjoyment of human rights and fundamental freedoms (7 December 1987).

12   Boutros Boutros-Ghali, Secretary General of UN, *An Agenda for Development*, 1995 A/48/935 (6th May 1994), UN, New York, 1995, see Introduction at para 3.

13   *Copenhagen Declaration on Social Development* (March 1995), Copenhagen, Denmark, Art. 5.

14   K. Ohmae, *The Borderless World* (New York: Harper Collins, 1991), at pp.xii–xiii.

15   Yasemin Soysal, *The Limits of Citizenship: Migrants and Postnational Membership in Europe* (Chicago: University of Chicago Press, 1994), at p.1.

16   Ibid., at p.29.

17   The UN document in full argues as follows: 'Perhaps the time has come ... to focus attention explicitly on *global citizenship*. This does not mean striking out in a new direction, but rather pursuing more deliberately a process that is already under way. The starting point was "... recognizing that all human beings have certain fundamental rights" ... codified in the Universal Declaration which as been made concrete by ignoring national borders as "... demands for human rights have been taking precedence over claims to national sovereignty"': See, UNRISD. *States of Disarray: The Social Effects of Globalization* (London, United Nations Research Institute for Social Development, 1995), at pp.168–70.

18   Steven Castles in Stephen Castles and Alastair Davidson, *Citizenship and Migration* (Macmillan, 2000), at p.12.

19   H. Seton-Watson, *Nations and States* (London, Methuen, 1977), at p.1.

20   W. Connor, 'From tribe to nation', *History of European Ideas* 13, 1 /2 (1991), at p.6 (quoted from D.P. Moynihan, *Pandemonium: Ethnicity in International Politics* (Oxford, OUP. 1993) at p.1).

21   A.D. Smith, *National Identity* (London, Penguin, 1991), at p.14.

22   R. Reich, *The Work of Nations: Preparing Ourselves for the 21st Century Capitalism* (London, Simon & Schuster, 1991), at p.18.

23   Reich, *op. cit.* (1991), at p.8.

24   D. Schnapper, *la communaute des citoyens: sur l'ide'e moderne de la nation* (paris: Gallimard, 1994), at p.11 (translated by Steven Castles in Stephen Castles and Alastair Davidson, *Citizenship & Migration* (Macmillan, 2000) at p.1).

25   Schnapper, *op.cit.* (1994) at pp.83–114.

26   Steven Castles in Stephen Castles and Alastair Davidson, *Citizenship & Migration* (Macmillan, 2000) at p.24.

27   *Loc. cit.*

28   'The history of the world system is a history of unequal exchanges that are at the roots of the war, starvation, oppression, and ecological disaster that force people to migrate. Modern science has managed to separate the knowledge of this history from the history of this knowledge. For this reason, modern historical knowledge is ahistorical. Because this ahistorical knowledge benefits the countries that have benefited from the unequal exchanges, modern science is intrinsically territorial. To that extent, it is as great an obstacle to the development of a new cosmopolitan politics as the nation-state itself. Short of such a new subaltern cosmopolitanism, neither the needs nor the differences of transnational migrants can be properly addressed. As things stand now, the needs of migrants have been codified and ranked by criteria of nationality and territoriality that are inherently biased against them, while their differences have been codified and ranked by a hegemonic form of knowledge that cannot understand them except by what they are not': See, Boaventura de Sousa Santos, *Toward a New Legal Common Sense* (2nd edn., 2002, London, Butterworths) at p.234.

29 'Hegel conceived of modern science as a form of knowledge that progressed by distinctions, divisions and discriminations. He oversaw the fact that, in the real world, rather than calling for a philiosophical *Aufhebung* (*suppression* or *sublation*), that form of knowledge became articulated with the modern state, whereupon scientific distinctions became social differences, which in turn engendered subordination. Subordinate transnational movements are movements of knowledges that have been suppressed and marginalized. Transnational Third Worlds of people are also, and they feed on each other. Learning from them, learning from the South, is one of the epistemological prerequisites of cosmopolitan politics'. See, Boaventura de Sousa Santos, *Toward a New Legal Common Sense* (2nd edn., 2002, London, Butterworths), at p.234.

30 Ibid., at p.233.

31 See Issa G. Shivji, 'The Concept of Human Rights in Africa', 43 (1989) at 29–33. Also see Makau wa Mutua, 'The Banjul Charter and the African Cultural Fingerprint: An Evaluation of the Language of Duties', 35 *Va. J. Int'l. L.* 340, 378 (1995). Also see, Satvinder Juss, 'The Coming of Communitarian Rights: Are Third-Generation Human Rights Really First-Generation Rights?', *International Journal of Discrimination & the Law* (1998) vol. 3, pp.159–80. Further, Bill Morris, as the Transport and General Workers' Union leader in Britain, argued that 'Resources have been pillaged and plundered in so many parts of the world. You can't take out the minerals, you can't take out the resources, you can't exploit everything that's going and then turn the people away', see, Jack Ashley, 'Britain's best-known trade unionist wants managed migration, and will help the Lib Dems to fight privatization', *New Statesman*, 10th September 2001 pp.18–19 at p.18.

32 Quoted from Castles and Davidson, *op. cit.*, at p.225.

33 R. Falk, 'The Making of Global Citizenship', in B. van Steenbergen (ed.) *The Condition of Citizenship* (London: Sage, 1994), at pp.131–3.

34 *Loc. cit.*

35 Global Commission, *Our Global Neighbourhood: Report of the Commission on Global Governance* (Oxford Univ. Press, 1995) at pp.255–6, Chap. 7 (quoted from Castles and Davidson at p.223).

36 Y. Bradshaw and M. Wallace, *Global Inequalities* (California: Pine Forge, 1996), at Chapter 2. Also see, P. Streeten, 'Governance of the global economy', in *Globalization and Citizenship: an international conference*, 9–11 December (Geneva: United Nations Research Institute for Social Development, 1996).

37 D. Turk, 'How World Bank – IMF policies adversely affect human rights', *Third World Resurgence* (1993) at pp.17–18. Also see, M. Khor, Globalization: implications for development policy', *Third World Resurgence* (1996) pp.15–22.

38 Global Commission, *Our Global Neighbourhood: Report of the Commission on Global Governance* (Oxford Univ. Press, 1995) at pp.21–3.

39 Satvinder Juss, 'The Coming of Communitarian Rights: Are Third-Generation Human Rights Really First-Generation Rights?', *International Journal of Discrimination & the Law* (1998) vol. 3, pp.159–80, at p.174.

40 See P. Hoffman, 'Globalize this! Respect for Human Rights' ACT79/003/2003, 3rd World Social Forum at http//web.amnesty.org/aidoc/aidoc_pdf.nsf/index/ ACT790032003ENGLISH/$File/ACT7900303.pdf. Also see, UNDPI in Armenia at http://www.undpi.am/new/page5.html. Also see, D. Ayton-Shenken, 'The Challenge of Human Rights and Cultural Diversity', at http//:www.un.org/ rights/dpi1627e.html.

41 A. Sengupta, 'Realizing the Right to Development', in *Development and Change* (Blackwell Publishers, Oxford; vol. 31, No. 3, June 2000), at p.556.

42   See, the United Nations Educational, Scientific and Cultural Organization (UNESCO), Working Group of the Standing Committee of the International Non-Governmental Organizations, Symposium on the Study of New Human Rights: The Rights of Solidarity: 'The Rights of Solidarity: An Attempt at Conceptual Analysis' at 2, U.N. Doc. SS-80/Conf.806/5 (1980). Also see, J. Downs, 'A Healthy and Ecologically Balanced Environment: An argument for a Third Generation right', *Duke J. Comp. & Int'l L.* (vol. 3, 1993), at p.364.

43   Karel, Vasak, 'A 30-year struggle, The sustained efforts to give force of law to the Universal Declaration of Human Rights', *Unesco Courier* 29 (1977) at p.29.

44   J. Downs, 'A Healthy and Ecologically Balanced Environment: An argument for a Third Generation right', *Duke J. Comp. & Int'l L.* (Vol. 3, 1993) at p.364. Also see, Philip Alston, 'Conjuring Up New Human Rights', *op. cit* at p.613.

45   J. Downs, ibid., at p.364. Also see, N.T. Saito, 'Beyond Civil Rights: Considering "Third Generation" International Human Rights Law in the United States', *University of Miami Inter-American Law Review* (vol. 28, 1996–97), at p.392. Also see, B. Weston and B. Murray, 'Encyclopaedia Britannica: Human Rights', University of Iowa Centre for Human Rights at http://www.uichr.org/features/eb/weston4.shtml.

46   Karel Vasak, 'Pour une Triosieme Generation des Droits del' homme', in *Studies and Essays International Humanitarian Law and Red Cross Principles of Jean Pictet* (Christophe Swinarski (ed.), 1984), at pp.837–9.

47   J. Downs, 'A Healthy and Ecologically Balanced Environment: An Argument for a Third Generation right', *Duke J. Comp. & Int'l L.* (vol. 3, 1993), at p.364.

48   Keles Rusen, 'Biopolitics as a tool for Sustainable Solidarity', Faculty of Political Sciences at Ankara University, at http://business.hol.gr/~bio/HTML/PubS/VOL5?html/kel_tur.htm.

49   J. Downs, 'A Healthy and Ecologically Balanced Environment: An Argument for a Third Generation right', *Duke J. Comp. & Int'l L.* (Vol. 3, 1993), at p.364. Karel Vasak, 'Pour une Triosieme Generation des Droits del' homme', in *Studies and Essays International Humanitarian Law and Red Cross Principles of Jean Pictet* (Christophe Swinarski (ed.), 1984), at pp.837–9. Philip Alston, 'Conjuring Up New Human Rights: A Proposal for Quality Control', 78 *Am J. Int'l L.* (1984) 607.

50   Philip Alston, 'Conjuring Up New Human Rights: A Proposal for Quality Control', 78 *Am J. Int'l L.* (1984) 607.

51   *Loc. cit.*

52   *Loc. cit.*

53   G.A. Res. 120, U.N. GAOR 3d Comm., 41st Sess, 97th mtg. U.N. Doc. A/41/878 (1986) at 351, 352.

54   See for example, M.W. Mutua, 'The Banjul Charter and the African Cultural Fingerprint: An Evaluation of the Languages of Duties', *Va J. Int'l L* (Vol. 35, 1995, p.340), at p.342. Also see, I.G. Shivji, *The Concept of Human Rights in Africa* (1989), at p.3.

55   R. Kiwanuka, 'The Meaning of "People" in the African Charter of Human and People's Rights', *Am. J. Int'l L* (Vol. 82, 1988), at p.85.

56   L. Sohn, 'The New International Law: Protection of the Rights of Individuals Rather than States', *Am. U.L. Rev.* (1982), at p.48.

57   See US National Security Council, Position of Indigenous Peoples, University of Minnesota Human Rights Library at: www1.umn.edu/humanrts/usdocs/indigenousdoc.

58   Alexander Leaf, 'Potential Health Effects of Global Climatic and Environmental Change', 321 *New Eng. J. Med.* 1577, at 1581 (1989).

59   See H.J. Steiner and P. Alston, *International Human Rights in Context* (1ˢᵗ edn., Oxford, 1996), at p.1111.
60   W.W. Rostow, *Les etapes de la corissance economique* (Paris, Le Suil, 1963) cited at G. Tsaltas, *The Right to Development as a Human Right* (Marangopoulos Foundation for Human Rights, Sakkoulas, Athens, 1988), at p.238.
61   UN Doc. E/3347/Rev. 1, para 90 (1960) *Five-year Perspective*, 1960–64.
62   *Declaration on Social Progress and Development*, General Assembly (1969) (Preamble Part ii).
63   *Resolution 35/56*, General Assembly 1980, UN GAOR Supp. (No.48) at 106, UN Doc. A/35/48 (1980) at para 42.
64   Cited at Ved P. Nanda, 'The Right to development under International Law – Challenges Ahead', *California Western International Law Journal* (Vol. 15, 1985), at p.431.
65   Secretary General, *Agenda for Development*, Policy Framework, B. Social Development, at para. 92.
66   *Declaration on the Right to Development*, U.N. GAOP 3ʳᵈ Comm., 41ˢᵗ Sess., 97ᵗʰ mtg. U.N. Doc. A/Res/41/128 (1986).
67   Ibid., at Article 2.
68   Thus, a 1999 study of the Commission of Human Rights concluded that the realization of civil, political and economic, social and cultural rights 'form an essential basis for the right to development': see, *Commission on Human Rights* (Fifty-sixth session) E/CN.4/1999/WG.18/2 (27ᵗʰ July 1999) Study on the current state of progress in the implementation on the Right to Development, submitted by Mr. Arjun K. Sengupta, at para 28.
69   Fourth ACP-EEC Convention, signed in Lome on 15ᵗʰ December 1989, text printed in, The Courier (No. 120, March–April 1990) ACO 70, (Developing Countries in Africa, Caribean and the Pacific) Art. 5(1).
70   See *Ksentini Report* UN Doc. E/CN.4/s UB.2/1994/9, at p.59 para 244.
71   *Lome Convention 1990, op. cit.* at p.12.
72   *Vienna Declaration of the World Conference on Human Rights* (10ᵗʰ June 1993) Part 1, at para 10.
73   *Copenhagen Declaration on Social Development*, World Summit for Social Development (adopted March 1995, in Copenhagen, Denmark), at Article 3.
74   *Commission on Human Rights* (Fifty-sixth session) E/CN.4/1999/WG.18/2 (27ᵗʰ July 1999) 'Study on the current state of progress in the implementation on the Right to Development', submitted by Mr. Arjun K. Sengupta, at p.17 para 54.
75   Ibid., at Article 1.
76   Ibid., at Article 2.
77   Ibid.,at Article 3.
78   Ibid., at Article 4.
79   Ibid., at para 8.
80   *Loc. cit.*
81   *Declaration on the Right to Development*, A/RES/41/128 (4ᵗʰ December 1986) ANNEX.
82   A/52/436, 8ᵗʰ October 1997, *Fifty-second session*, Agenda item 97(a) and 99(b): see Chairmans' Introduction at p.3.
83   Fredrick Harbison, 'Human Development and Financial Project' (1963) *Significance: Social and Educational Biases Human Development: Concepts*, at http://google.com.
84   *Copenhagen Declaration and Program of Action*, World Summit for Social Development, adopted in 6–12 March 1995, Denmark.

85   Volker Turk, 'The Role of UNHCR in the development of international refugee law', in Frances Nicholson and Patrick Twomey (eds) *Refugees Rights & Realities: Evolving International Concepts and Regimes* (CUP, 1999), at p.154.

86   Mohammed Bedjaoui, 'The Right to Development', in *International Law: Achievements and Prospects* (1991) 1177, at 1182 (emphases added).

87   Mohammed Bedjaoui, 'Some Unorthodox Reflections on the "Right to Development"', cited in F. Snyder and P. Slinn, *International Law of Development* (Abingdon Professional Book, 1987) at p.87. The principle of dignity is well recognized in the statement that 'The development process must promote human dignity. The ultimate aim of development is the constant improvement of the well-being of the entire population on the basis of its full participation in the process of development and a fair distribution of the benefits therefrom': see, GA, 'International Development Strategy for the Third Development Decade'.

88   Mohammed Bedjaoui, 'The Right to Development', in *International Law: Achievements and Prospects* (1991) 1177, at 1182 (emphases added), at p.1182.

89   Philip Alston and Gerard Quinn, 'The Nature and Scope of States Parties' Obligations Under the International Covenant on Economic, Social and Cultural Rights', 9 *Hum. Rts. Q.* (1987) 156, at p.186. Also see, Philip Alston, 'Revitalising United Nations Work on Human Rights and Development', 18 *Melb. U.L. Rev.* (1991) 216, at 218 and 220.

90   *International Covenant on Economic, Social and Cultural Rights*, G.A. Res. 2200, UN. GAOR, 21st Sess, Supp. No. 16, U.N. Doc. A/63/6 (1966) at art. 11(2).

91   Alston and Quinn, *supra.*, at p.188.

92   *International Development Select Committee* (Sixth Report) (HC 79 session 2003–4) published in July 2004 (hereafter the *Report*). See also http://catalogue.bized. ac.uk/redirect?url=http%3A%2F%2Fwww.publications.parliament.uk%2Fpa% 2Fcm200304%2Fcmselect%2Fcmintdev%2F79%2F7902.htm&rec=1089297454-7620&log=bized.

93   *International Development Select Committee* (Sixth Report) (HC 79 session 2003–4) published in July 2004, *op. cit.*, see Ev 211 [International Organization for Migration (IOM) memorandum].

94   *International Development Select Committee* (Sixth Report) (HC 79 session 2003–4) published in July 2004, ibid.

95   *International Development Select Committee* (Sixth Report) (HC 79 session 2003–4) published in July 2004 , *op. cit.*, see Ev 247 [Oxfam memo]. See also Philip L. Martin, *Sustainable Migration Policies in a Globalizing World*, International Institute for Labour Studies, International Labour Organization, March 2003. Available at http://www.ilo.org/public/english/bureau/inst/download/migration.pdf.

96   Her Majesty's Government (HMG), 'White Paper on International Development, Eliminating World Poverty: Making globalization work for the poor', 2000 – see http://www.dfid.gov.uk/policieandpriorities/files/whitepaper2000.pdf; Ev 124 [DFID memo]; Q 21 [Masood Ahmed, Director General for Policy and International, DFID]; Ev 169 [Centre on Migration, Policy and Science (COMPAS) University of Oxford memo]; Ev 205 [International Institute for Environment and Development (IIED) memo)]; Catherine Barber, 'Making Migration "Development-Friendly"', Unpublished MA dissertation, 24 March 2003 – copy placed in House of Commons library.

97   Highlighting the fact that people assess migration differently, Newsweek suggested that: 'The migrant worker is many things to many people. For conservative politicians and Trade Union organisers in industrial countries, he is the illegal migrant – who deserves a one way ticket back to whatever country he came from.

For immigration advocates and business groups, he is a vital pillar of today's globalized economic order, whether a legal resident of his new country or not. For the political leaders of developing countries, he is a modern day "hero" who sends home a hefty portion of his paycheque to help support his family members and keep his old community afloat' (*Newsweek International*, 19th January 2004).

98   *International Development Select Committee* (Sixth Report) (HC 79 session 2003–4) published in July 2004, ibid. at paras 3–4 at p.2.

99   Terrie L. Walmsley and L. Alan Winters, 'Relaxing the Restrictions on the Temporary Movement of Natural Persons: A Simulation Analysis', Centre for Economic Policy Research Discussion Paper No. 3719, 4 Nov 2002, p.3. Available at: http://www.gtap.agecon.purdue.edu/events/Board_Meetings/2003/docs/Walmsley_Mobility.pdf.

100 Dani Rodrik of Harvard University states that 'liberalizing cross-border labor movements can be expected to yield benefits that are roughly 25 times larger than those that would accrue from the traditional agenda focusing on goods and capital flows'. Dani Rodrik, 'Feasible Globalizations', John F. Kennedy School of Government Working Paper Series RWP02-029, July 2002, pp.19–20. See http://ksghome.harvard.edu/~.drodrik.academic.ksg/Feasglob.pdf.

101 World Bank, 'Global Development Finance: Harnessing cyclical gains for development', 2004. Available at http://www.worldbank.org/prospects/gdf2004/.

102 *International Development Select Committee* (Sixth Report) (HC 79 session 2003–4) published in July 2004, *op. cit.* at para 4 adopting Ev 247 [Oxfam memo].

103 The Prime Minister, Tony Blair, 'Controlled Migration', speech given at the London Business School, hosted by the CBI, 27 April 2004. Available at http://www.labour.org.uk/tbmigrationspeech/.

104 *International Development Select Committee* (Sixth Report) (HC 79 session 2003–4) published in July 2004 *op. cit.* Q 32 [Sharon White, Director, Policy Division, DFID].

105 *International Development Select Committee* (Sixth Report) (HC 79 session 2003–4) published in July 2004 *op. cit.*, at para 6 on p.3.

106 Green Paper *Confronting demographic change: a new solidarity between generations* [COM (2005) 94 final], Also available at http://europa.eu.int/scadplus/leg/en/cha/c10128.htm.

107 Stephen Castle, 'Fall in population threatens economic future of Europe', *The Independent*, 18th March 2005, at p.24.

108 The full report can be found at www.eurofound.eu.int/publications/EF03113.htm.

109 Samples of 1000 people in accession and candidate countries were asked identical questions and their attitudes recorded.

110 *International Development Select Committee* (Sixth Report) (HC 79 session 2003–4) published in July 2004, *op. cit.*, at para 16 at p.7, referring to Ev 140 [Anti-Slavery International (ASI) memo]; Ev 128 [DFID memo]; Ev 229 [New Economics Foundation memo]; Ev 193 [The Corner House memo]; Ev 260 [Refugee Studies Centre memo]; Q 289 [Heaven Crawley, AMRE Consulting].

111 *International Development Select Committee* (Sixth Report) (HC 79 session 2003–4) published in July 2004, *op. cit.* at para 16 at p.7, referring to Q 365 [Agnes Kumba Dugba Macauley]; Ev 140 [ASI memo]; Ev 276 [Unlad Kabayan memo].

112 *International Development Select Committee* (Sixth Report) (HC 79 session 2003–4) published in July 2004, *op. cit.* at para 21 at p.9, referring to Ev 205 [IIED memo]; Q 56 [Richard Black, University of Sussex]; Q 205 [Mr Winston Cox, Deputy Secretary General of the Commonwealth].

113   *International Development Select Committee* (Sixth Report) (HC 79 session 2003–4) published in July 2004, *op. cit.*, at para 21 at p.9, referring to Q 56 [Dr Priya Deshingkar, Research Fellow on the DFID-funded Livelihoods Options Project, India, Overseas Development Institute (ODI)].

114   *International Development Select Committee* (Sixth Report) (HC 79 session 2003–4) published in July 2004, *op. cit.*, at para 21 at p.9, referring to Q 54 [Ronald Skeldon, University of Sussex].

115   *International Development Select Committee* (Sixth Report) (HC 79 session 2003–4) published in July 2004, *op. cit.*, at para 21 at p.9, referring to Ev 232 [ODI memo]; Ev 205 [IIED memo]; Ev 125 [DFID memo]. See also Arjan de Haan, Migrants, 'Livelihoods and Rights: The relevance of migration in development policies', DFID Working Paper No. 4, Feb 2000, p.i. Available at http://62.189.42.51/DFID-stage/Pubs/files/sdd_migwp4.pdf.

116   *International Development Select Committee* (Sixth Report) (HC 79 session 2003–4) published in July 2004, *op. cit.*, at para 21 at p.9, referring to Q 371 [Agnes Kumba Dugba Macauley].

117   *International Development Select Committee* (Sixth Report) (HC 79 session 2003–4) published in July 2004, *op. cit.*, at para 21 at p.9, referring to Q 71 [Priya Deshingkar, ODI].

118   D.S. Massey, J. Arango, G. Hugo, and J.E. Taylor, 'Theories of international migration: review and appraisal', in *Population and Development Review* (Vol. 19, 1993). Also see, D.S. Massey, J. Arango, G. Hugo, and J.E. Taylor, 'An evaluation of international migration theory: the North American Case', in *Population and Development Review* (Vol. 19, 1994).

119   G. Hugo, *The Economic Implications of Emigration from Australia* (1993, Canberra: Australian Government Publishing Service), at pp.7–12.

120   See for example, J.A. Jackson, *Migration* (ed.) (1969, CUP).

121   E.G. Ravenstein, 'The laws of migration', *Journal of the Statistical Society* (Vol. 48, 1885). Also see, E.G. Ravenstein, 'The laws of migration', *Journal of the Statistical Society* (Vol. 52, 1889).

122   See R. Cohen, *The New Helots: Migrants in the International Division of Labour* (1987, Aldershot, Avebury) at pp.34–35; A.R. Zolberg, 'The next waves: migration theory for a changing world', in *International Migration Review* (Vol. 23, Issue 3, 1989) at pp.403–405.

123   G.J. Borjas, 'Economic theory and international migration', *International Migration Review* (Vol. 23, Issue 3, 1989, Special Silver Anniversary Issue), at p.461.

124   S. Sassen, *The Mobility of Labour and Capital* (CUP, 1988); M. Boyd, 'Family and Personal Networks in Migration', *International Migration Review* (Vol. 23, Issue 3, 1989, Special Silver Anniversary Issue); A. Portes and R.G. Rumbaut, *Immigrant America: A portrait* (Univ. of Calif. Press, Los Angeles, 1990).

125   S. Castles and M.J. Miller, *The Age of Migration* (Palgrave Press, 2nd edn., 1998), at p.21.

126   Given the criticism, Stark has suggested the 'new economics of labour migration' suggesting that because markets rarely work in an ideal way as suggested by the neo-classicists, one has to factor in the chances of secure employment, the availability of capital for entrepreneurial activity, and the need to manage risk over long periods: see, O. Stark, *The Migration of Labour* (Blackwell, Oxford, 1991).

127   S. Castles and G. Kosack, *Immigrant Workers and Class Structure in Western Europe* (OUP, 1985); R. Cohen, *The New Helots: Migrants in the International Division of Labour* (1987, Aldershot, Avebury); S. Sassen, *The Mobility of Labour and Capital* (CUP, 1988).

128 G. Hugo, *The Economic Implications of Emigration from Australia* (Australian Government Publishing Service, Canberra, 1993).

129 A.R. Zolberg, 'The next waves: migration theory for a changing world', in *International Migration Review* (Vol. 23, Issue 3, 1989).

130 For example consider the migration of Mexicans to the USA in Portes and Rumbaut 1990 at pp.224–30.

131 Fawcett and Arnold (1987, 456–7).

132 see Kritz, Lin and Zlotnik, 1992.

133 S. Juss, *Immigration, Nationality and Citizenship* at p.6.

134 S. Sassen, 1988 at pp.6–9.

135 Portes and Borocz (1989), at p.626.

136 Dohse (1981); Bohning (1984) Cohen (1987) Fawcett (1989) Mitchell (1989) Manfrass (1992).

137 Zolberg (1989) at p.408.

138 Bourdieu and Wacquant (1992), at p.119.

139 Boyd (1989), at p.639.

140 See Price (1963), at pp.108–10.

141 Castles and Miller, at p.25.

142 Hugo, *The Economic Implications of Emigration from Australia* (1993, Canberra: Australian Government Publishing Service), at pp.7–12.

143 For useful overviews of migration and development see: IOM, *The Migration-Development Nexus*, 2003; Christina Boswell and Jeff Crisp, *Poverty, International Migration and Asylum*, Policy Brief No.8, United Nations University – World Institute for Development Economics Research, 2004; Kathleen Newland, *Migration as a Factor in Development and Poverty Reduction*, Migration Policy Institute, 1 June 2003; Kimberley Hamilton, *Migration and Development: Blind faith and hard-to-find facts*, Migration Policy Institute, 1 Nov 2003; IOM, International Migration and Development: *The potential for a win-win-situation*, June 2003; Ronald Skeldon, 'Migration and Poverty', *Asia-Pacific Journal*, Vol. 17(4) pp.67–82, 2002.

144 Some of the increase from 1985 to 2000 is accounted for by the dissolution of the USSR – new borders and countries have been established; people who have not moved find themselves classified as 'international migrants'.

145 *International Development Select Committee* (Sixth Report) (HC 79 session 2003–4) published in July 2004, *op. cit.*, at para 13 at p.6, referring to Q 57 [Professor Ronald Skeldon, Member, University of Sussex Development Research Centre on Migration, Globalization and Poverty].

146 *International Development Select Committee* (Sixth Report) (HC 79 session 2003–4) published in July 2004, *op. cit.*, at para 14 at p.6, referring Ev 124 [Department for International Development (DFID) memo].

147 *International Development Select Committee* (Sixth Report) (HC 79 session 2003–4) published in July 2004, *op. cit.*, at para 14 at p.6, referring to Ev 249 [Oxfam memo].

148 *International Development Select Committee* (Sixth Report) (HC 79 session 2003–4) published in July 2004, *op. cit.*, at para 14 at p.6, referring to Ev 124 [DFID memo].

149 *International Development Select Committee* (Sixth Report) (HC 79 session 2003–4) published in July 2004, *op. cit.*, at para 15 at p.7, referring to Ev 78 [Professor Richard Black, Director, University of Sussex Development Research Centre on Migration, Globalization and Poverty].

150 *International Development Select Committee* (Sixth Report) (HC 79 session 2003–4)

published in July 2004, *op. cit.*, at para 15 at p.7, referring to Q 4 [Masood Ahmed, DFID].

151　*International Development Select Committee* (Sixth Report) (HC 79 session 2003–4) published in July 2004, *op. cit.*, at para 15 at p.7, referring to Ev 124 [DFID memo]; Ev 228 [New Economics Foundation (NEF)].

152　*International Development Select Committee* (Sixth Report) (HC 79 session 2003–4) published in July 2004 *op. cit.* at para 15 at p.7, referring to Ev 276 [Unlad Kabayan memo].

153　*International Development Select Committee* (Sixth Report) (HC 79 session 2003–4) published in July 2004, *op. cit.*, at para 15 at p.7, referring to Ev 212 [IOM memo].

154　*International Development Select Committee* (Sixth Report) (HC 79 session 2003–4) published in July 2004, *op. cit.*, at para 15 at p.7, referring to Ev 206 [IIED memo].

155　*International Development Select Committee* (Sixth Report) (HC 79 session 2003–4) published in July 2004, *op. cit.*, at para 16 at p.7, referring to Q 64 [Dr Ben Rogaly, Member, University of Sussex Development Research Centre on Migration, Globalization and Poverty].

156　*International Development Select Committee* (Sixth Report) (HC 79 session 2003–4) published in July 2004, *op. cit.*, at para 16 at p.7, referring to Ev 155 [Catholic Institute for Institutional Relations (CIIR) memo].

157　*International Development Select Committee* (Sixth Report) (HC 79 session 2003–4) published in July 2004, *op. cit.*, at para 16 at p.7, referring to Ev 232 [Overseas Development Institute (ODI) memo]; Ev 206 [IIED memo]; Ev 125 [DFID memo].

158　*International Development Select Committee* (Sixth Report) (HC 79 session 2003–4) published in July 2004, *op. cit.*, at para 16 at p.7, referring to Ev 210 [IIED memo]; Ev 224 [Joint Council for the Welfare of Immigrations (JCWI) memo].

159　These are generally the premises of the *International Development Select Committee* (Sixth Report) (HC 79 session 2003–4) published in July 2004, *op. cit.*

160　*International Development Select Committee* (Sixth Report) (HC 79 session 2003–4) published in July 2004, at para 22, *op. cit.*, see Q 118 [Cecilia Tacoli, IIED].

161　*International Development Select Committee* (Sixth Report) (HC 79 session 2003–4) published in July 2004, *op. cit.*, at para 22.

162　*International Development Select Committee* (Sixth Report) (HC 79 session 2003–4) published in July 2004 at para 18, *op. cit.*, Ev 124 [DFID memo].

163　*International Development Select Committee* (Sixth Report) (HC 79 session 2003–4) published in July 2004 at para 19, *op. cit.*, Ev 260 [Refugee Studies Centre memo].

164　*International Development Select Committee* (Sixth Report) (HC 79 session 2003–4) published in July 2004 at para 19, *op. cit.*, see, Ev 124 [DFID memo]; Q 297 [Dr Heaven Crawley, Director, AMRE Consulting and formerly Associate Director, IPPR]. See also Stephen Castles, Heaven Crawley and Sean Loughna, States of Conflict: Causes and patterns of forced migration to the EU and policy responses, The Institute for Public Policy Research (IPPR), 2003.

165　Ev 272 [UNHCR memo]; Ev 124 [DFID memo]; Q 288 [Anita Bundegaard, Co-ordinator for Durable Solutions, UNHCR].

166　*International Development Select Committee* (Sixth Report) (HC 79 session 2003–4) published in July 2004 at para 23, *op. cit.*, see, Ev 234 [ODI memo]; Ev 186 [Childhood Poverty Research Centre memo].

167　*International Development Select Committee* (Sixth Report) (HC 79 session 2003–4) published in July 2004 at para 23, *op. cit.*, see, Ev 273 [UNHCR memo].

168   *International Development Select Committee* (Sixth Report) (HC 79 session 2003–4) published in July 2004 at para 23, *op. cit.,* see, Ev 228 [NEF memo].

169   *International Development Select Committee* (Sixth Report) (HC 79 session 2003–4) published in July 2004 at para 23, *op. cit.,* see, Ev 205 [IIED memo]; Q 56 [Ben Rogaly, University of Sussex].

170   *International Development Select Committee* (Sixth Report) (HC 79 session 2003–4) published in July 2004 at para 24, *op. cit.,* see, Richard Adams and John Page, International Migration, Remittances and Poverty in Developing Countries, World Bank Policy Research Working Paper No. 3179, Dec 2003, p.1. See http://econ.worldbank.org/files/31999_wps3179.pdf.

171   *International Development Select Committee* (Sixth Report) (HC 79 session 2003–4) published in July 2004 at para 24, *op. cit.,* see, Ev 125 [DFID memo].

172   *International Development Select Committee* (Sixth Report) (HC 79 session 2003–4) published in July 2004 at para 24, *op. cit.,* see, Ev 125 [DFID memo]. The income level at which migration begins to decrease is not clear. Recent World Bank research – see footnote 53 in the report – gives a threshold of $1630 in 1995 dollars. In their memo, the Joint Council on the Welfare of Immigrants suggest a threshold of $4000 in 1985 dollars, but points out that Mexico, with a per capita income of $7000, is still a migrant-sending country (see Ev 220).

173   *International Development Select Committee* (Sixth Report) (HC 79 session 2003–4) published in July 2004 at para 24, *op. cit.,* see, Ev 220 [JCWI memo].

174   *International Development Select Committee* (Sixth Report) (HC 79 session 2003–4) published in July 2004 at para 24, *op. cit.,* see, Q 57 [Richard Black, University of Sussex].

175   *International Development Select Committee* (Sixth Report) (HC 79 session 2003–4) published in July 2004 at para 24, *op. cit.,* see, Philip Martin, *NAFTA and Mexico-US Migration Policy Options in 2004*, Paper for the IRPP Conference on North American Integration April 1–2 2004, 8 Feb 2004, p.10. See http://www.irpp.org/events/archive/apr04/martin.pdf.

176   *International Development Select Committee* (Sixth Report) (HC 79 session 2003–4) published in July 2004 at para 25, *op. cit.,* see, Q 82 [Richard Black]; see also Uma Kothari, *Migration and Chronic Poverty*, Chronic Poverty Research Centre Working Paper No. 16, Institute for Development Policy and Management, University of Manchester, March 2002. Available at http://www.chronicpoverty.org/pdfs/MigrationJun-02.pdf.

177   *International Development Select Committee* (Sixth Report) (HC 79 session 2003–4) published in July 2004 at para 25, *op. cit.,* see, Ev 220 [JCWI memo]; Q 57 [Richard Black, University of Sussex]; Timothy J. Hatton and Jeffrey G. Williamson, 'Demographic and Economic Pressure on Emigration out of Africa', *Scandinavian Journal of Economics*, Vol. 105 (January 2003), pp.465–86.

178   *International Development Select Committee* (Sixth Report) (HC 79 session 2003–4) published in July 2004 at para 25, *op. cit.,* see, Sharon Stanton Russell, Migration and Development: Reframing the international policy agenda, Migration Policy Institute, 1 June 2003, paragraph 3. Available at http://www.migrationinformation.org/Feature/display.cfm?ID=126.

179   *International Development Select Committee* (Sixth Report) (HC 79 session 2003–4) published in July 2004 at para 26, *op. cit.,* see, Richard Adams and John Page, International Migration, Remittances and Poverty in Developing Countries – see footnote 53 in the report.

180   *International Development Select Committee* (Sixth Report) (HC 79 session 2003–4) published in July 2004 at para 26, *op. cit.,* see, Ev 212 [IOM memo].

181   *International Development Select Committee* (Sixth Report) (HC 79 session 2003–4)

published in July 2004, *op. cit.*, see Ev 247 [Oxfam memo]. See also Philip L. Martin, *Sustainable Migration Policies in a Globalizing World*, International Institute for Labour Studies, International Labour Organization, March 2003.

182   See 'Relishing the next ride on the Westminster rollercoaster', *The Guardian*, Monday 1st March 2004.

183   See 'Policy Responses', at para 4.2, at p.10.

184   See 'Policy Responses', at para 4.2, at p.12.

185   See 'The Migrant', at para 5, at p.10.

186   See 'Policy Responses' at para 4.2, at p.10.

187   Roger Nett, ibid, at p.227.

188   *Infra.*, at pp.29–30.

Select Bibliography

Aleinikoff, A., 'Safe Haven: Pragmatics and Prospects', 35 *Va. J. Int'l L.* 71, 74 (1994).

Allen, J., *A History of Political Thought in the Sixteenth Century* (Methuen ed. 1960), pp.412–13.

Alston, P., 'Conjuring Up New Human Rights: A Proposal for Quality Control' 78 *Am J. Int'l L.* (1984) 607.

Alston, P., 'Revitalising United Nations Work on Human Rights & Development', 18 *Melb. U.L. Rev.* (1991) 216.

Alston, P. and Quinn, G., 'The Nature and Scope of States Parties' Obligations Under the International Covenant on Economic, Social & Cultural Rights', 9 *Hum. Rts. Q.* (1987) 156.

Arboleda, E., 'Refugee Definition in Africa and Latin America' (1991) 3 (2) *Int'l J. of Refugee Law* 185.

Aybay, R., 'The Right to Leave and the Right to Return: The International Aspect of Freedom of Movement', 1 Comp. L. Y.B. (1978), pp.121, 122.

Bach, S., 'International migration of health workers: labour and social issues' (ILO, Geneva, July 2003) at http://www-ilomirror.cornell.edu/public/english/dialogue/sector/papers/health/wp209.pdf.

Bagshaw, S., 'Internally Displaced Persons at the 54th Session of the United Nations Commission on Human Rights' (1998) 10 (3) *International Journal of Refugee Law* 548.

Barutciski, M., 'The Reinforcement of Non-Admission Policies and the Subversion of the UNHCR: Displacement & Internal Assistance in Bosnia-Herzegovina (1992–94)', 8 *Int'l J. Refugee L.* 49, 74–5, 85 (1996).

Bedjaoui, M., 'Some Unorthodox Reflections on the "Right to Development"', cited in F. Snyder and P. Slinn, *International Law of Development* (Abingdon Professional Book, 1987), p.87.

Bhabha, J., 'European Harmonization of Asylum Policy: A Flawed Process', 35 *Va. J. Int'l. L.* 101 at 102.

Bhabha, J., 'Internationalist Gatekeepers?: The Tension Between Asylum Advocacy and Human Rights' *Harv. Hum. Rts Jnl.* (vol. 15, Spring 2002), p.155.

Bhagwati, J., 'Borders Beyond Control', *Foreign Affairs*, vol. 82, No. 1, January/February 2003, p.99.

Bhagwati, J., *In Defense of Globalisation* (OUP, 2004), p.218.

Bigo, D., 'Polices en resaux. L' experience europe'enne' (1996, Paris, Presses de Science Po).

Black, R., and Robinson, V., (eds) *Geography and Refugees: Patterns and Processes of Change* (Belhaven Press, 1993).

Bohning, W.R., 'Integration and Immigration Pressures in Western Europe', 130(4) *Int'l. Labor Rev.* 445, 451–2 (1991).

Borchard, E., *The Diplomatic Protection of Citizens Abroad or the Law of International Claims* (1915), pp.46–8.

Borjas, G.J., 'Economic Theory and International Migration', *International Migration Review* (vol. 23, Issue 3, 1989, Special Silver Anniversary Issue), p.461.

Bradshaw Y., and Wallace, M, *Global Inequalities* (California: Pine Forge, 1996).

Bruderlein, C., *The Security Council at the Crossroads: Towards More Humane and Better Targeted Sanctions*, at 7 & nn. 26–7 (U.C. Berkeley, Inst. Of Gov't Stud., Working Paper No.15, 1999) available at http://www.igs.berkeley.edu/publications/workingpapers/99-15B.pdf.

Brierly, J., 'The Law of Nations' (6th edn., 1963), p.276.

Bronee, S.A., 'The History of Comprehensive Plan of Action', 5 *Int'l Refugee L.* 534 (1993).

Bunting, M.M, 'Regime change, European-style, is a measure of our civilisation' *The Guardian*, 26th September 2005: see m.bunting@guardian.co.uk.

Byrne, R. and Shacknove, A., 'The Safe Country Notion in European Asylum Law', 9 *Harv. Hum. Rts. J.* 185, 185–6 (1996).

Callovi, G., 'Regulation of Immigration in 1993: Pieces of the European Community Jig-Saw Puzzle', 26 *Int'l. Migration Rev.* 353–4 (1992).

Carens, J., 'Aliens and Citizens: The Case for Open Borders', *Review of Politics,* 47 (1987) 251.

Castles S. and Davidson, A., *Citizenship & Migration* (Macmillan, 2000).

Castles, S. and Miller, M., *The Age of Migration* (Palgrave / St. Martins Press, 2nd edn, 1998).

Cohen, R., *The New Helots: Migrants in the International Division of Labour* (1987, Aldershot, Avebury).

Cohen, R., 'Exodus Within Borders: The Global Crisis Of Displacement' (May 31, 2001, see http://www.brookings.edu).

Coles, G., 'Background Paper for Asian Working Group on the International Protection and Displaced Persons', p.83 (unpublished, 1980).

Collinson, S., 'Beyond Borders: West European Migration Policy Towards the 21st Century', (London: RIIA) (1993).

Connolly, William E., *The Terms of Political Discourse* (2nd ed., Princeton University Press, 1983).

Connor, W., 'The Political Significance of Ethno-Nationalism Within Western Europe', in Abdul Said and Luiz R. Simmons (eds.), *Ethnicity in an International Context* (New Brunswick, N.J.: Transaction Books, 1976), pp.111–12.

Davy, U., 'Refugees From Bosnia and Herzegovina: Are They Genuine?', 18 *Suffolk Transnat'l L.J.* 53, 63–4 (1995).

Deng, F.M., 'The International Protection of the Internally Displaced' (1995) Special Issue, *International Journal Of Refugee Law* 74 at 76.

Deng, F.M., 'The Global Challenge of Internal Displacement', *Journal of Law & Policy* (Vol. 5, 2001) p.144.

Dillon, M., 'The Scandal of the Refugee: Some Reflections on the "Inter" of International Relations and Continental Thought' in David Campbell and Michael Shapiro (eds) *Moral Spaces: Rethinking Ethics and World Politics* (Minneapolis, University of Minnesota Press, 1999).

Dolan, C., *Policy Challenges for the New South Africa, Southern African Migration: Domestic and Regional Policy Implications* (Workshop Proceedings, 14, Centre for Policy Studies, Johannesburg, 1995, pp.53–4).

Donner, J.P.H., 'Abolition of Border Controls', in *Free Movement of Persons in Europe, Legal Problems and Experiences*, p.5 (Henry G. Schermers *et al*, eds., 1991).

Downs, J., 'A Healthy and Ecologically Balanced Environment: An argument for a Third Generation right', *Duke J. Comp. & Int'l L.*, (vol. 3, 1993), p.364.

Drumbel, M.A., 'Waging War Against The World', 22 *Fordham Int'l L.J.L.* 122, 126 (1998).

Dummett, M., *On Immigration and Refugees* (London, Routledge, 2001).

Ely, J.H., *Democracy and Distrust* (Harvard, 1980) pp.178–9.

Environmental Refugees: The Case for Recognition, available at http://www. neweconomics.org/gen/z_sys_PublicationDetail.aspx?PID=159.

Falk, R., 'The Making of Global Citizenship' in B. van Steenbergen (ed.) *The Condition of Citizenship* (London, Sage 1994), pp.131–3.

Feller, E., 'Carrier Sanctions and International Law', 1 *Int'l J. Refugee L.* 48 (1989).

Fiore, P., *International Law Codified and its Legal Sanction* (E. Borchard trans. 1918) p.42.

Fitzpatrick, J., 'Flight from Asylum: Trends Toward Temporary "Refuge" and Local Responses to Forced Migrations', 35 *Va. J. Int'l L.* 13, 65 (1994).

Fitzpatrick, J., 'Revitalizing the 1951 Refugee Convention', 9 *Harv. Hum. Rts. J.* 229, 253 (1996).

Fitzpatrick, J., *Human Rights Protection For Refugees, Asylum Seekers, and the Internally Displaced Persons: A Guide to International Mechanisms and Procedures* (New York, Transnational Publishers, 2002), p.5.

Frelick, B., 'Haitian Boat Interdiction and Return: First Asylum and First Principles of Refugee Protection', 26 *Cornell Int'l L.J.* 675 (1993).

Galbraith, J.K., *The Nature of Mass Poverty* (Harvard University Press, 1979), p.7.

Gallagher, D., 'Durable Solutions in a New Political Era', 47 *J. Int'l Aff.* 429, 440 (Winter, 1994).

Gellner, E., *Culture, Identity, and Politics* (CUP, 1987).

Ghosh, B., *Huddled Masses and Uncertain Shores: Insights into Irregular Migration* (Martinus Nijthoff, 1998).

Gibney, M., *The Ethics and Politics of Asylum* (CUP, 2004).

Global Commission, *Our Global Neighbourhood: Report of the Commission on Global Governance* (Oxford University Press, 1995).

Glover, S., Gott, C., Loizillon, A., Portes, J., Price, R., Spencer, S., Srinivasan, V., and Willis, C., 'Migration: An Economic and Social Analysis' (Home

Office *RDS Occasional Paper* No 67, 2001), at http://www.homeoffice.gov. uk/rds/pdfs/occ67-migration.pdf.

Goodwin-Gill, G.S., 'Non-Refoulment and the New Asylum Seekers' (1986), 26(4) *Virginia J. Intl. L.* 897.

Goodwin-Gill, G.S., *The Refugee in International Law* (2nd edn., Oxford, Clarendon Press, 1996), p.2.

Grahl-Madsen, A., *The Status of Refugee in International Law* (1966), p.191.

Guild, E., The Legal Elements of European Identity: EU Citizenship and Migration Law (Kluwer Law International, The Hague, 2004).

Haddad, E., 'Who is (not) a Refugee?' (European University Institute, Florence, June 2004) (EUI Working Paper SPS No. 2004/6) at www.iue.it.

Hailbronner, K., 'Non-refoulment and "Humanitarian" Refugees: Customary International Law or Wishful Legal Thinking?' (1986), 26(4) *Virginia J. Intl. L.* 857, p.887.

Hailbronner, K., 'Temporary and Local Responses to Forced Migrations: A Comment', 35 *Va. J. Int'l L.* 81, 92–3 (1994).

Hannum, H., *Autonomy, Sovereignty, and Self Determination: The Accommodation of Conflicting Rights* (Rev. Ed. 1990).

Hannum, H., Autonomy, Sovereignty, and Self-Determination 55 (rev. ed. 1996).

Hansen, R., 'Asylum Policy in the European Union', *Geo. Immgr. L.J.* (vol. 14, 2000, pp.779–800).

Harris, N., *The New Untouchables* (I.B. Taurus, London, 1995).

Harvey, C.J., 'Talking about Refugee Law', *Journal of Refugee Studies* (OUP., vol. 12, No.2, 1999), pp.101–33.

Hathaway, J.C., 'Reconceiving Refugee Law as Human Rights Protection', 4 J. Refugee Stud. 113, (1991).

Hathaway, J.C., *The Law of Refugee Status* (Butterworths, 1991).

Hathaway, J.C., 'Harmonising for Whom? The Devaluation of Refugee Protection in the Era of European Economic Integration', 26 *Cornell Int'l L.J.*, 719, at 722, fn. 21 (1993).

Hathaway, J.C., and Neve, R.A., 'Making International Refugee Law Relevant Again: A Proposal for Collectivized and Solution Oriented Protection', *Harvard Human Rights Journal*, Vol. 10, 152 (1997).

Helton, A.C., 'The Role of International Law in the 21st Century: Forced International Migration: A Need for New Approaches by the International Community', 18 *Fordham Int'l L.J.* 1623 (May 1995).

Helton, A.C., *The Price of Indifference* (OUP, 2002), chapter 6.

Henkin, L., 'An Agenda for the Next Century: The Myth and Mantra of State Sovereignty', 35 *Va. J. Int'l L.* 115, 118 (1994).

Hollifield, J., *Immigrants, Markets & States* (Harvard University Press, 1992).

Hugo, G., *The Economic Implications of Emigration from Australia* (Australian Government Publishing Service, Canberra, 1993).

Hugo, G., *The Economic Implications of Emigration from Australia* (1993, Canberra: Australian Government Publishing Service), pp.7–12.

Human Development Report 2004, 'Cultural liberty in today's diverse world' (published for the United Nations Development Programme, OUP, 2004).

Huysmans, J., 'The European Union and the Securitization of Migration', *Journal of Common Market Studies* (2000, vol., 38, No. 5), pp.751–71.

Hyndman, P., 'Refugees under International Law with Reference to the Concept of Asylum' (1986) 60 *Australian L.J.* 148, p.150.

International Development Select Committee (Sixth Report) (HC 79 session 2003–4) published in July 2004 (hereafter "the Report"). See also http://catalogue.bized.ac.uk/redirect?url=http%3A%2F%2Fwww.publications.parliament.uk%2Fpa%2Fcm200304%2Fcmselect%2Fcmintdev%2F79%2F7902.htm&rec=1089297454-7620&log=bized.

Jacobsen, D., *Rights Across Borders* (Baltimore, John Hopkins University Press, 1996).

Johnson, K.R., 'Open Borders?' 51 *UCLA Law Review* 193 (2003), pp.193–265.

Joppke, C., 'Why Liberal States Accept Unwanted Immigration' http://muse.jhu.edu/journals/world_politics/v050/50.2joppke.html (pp.266–93).

Joly, D., 'The Porous Dam: European Harmonization on Asylum in the Nineties', 6 *Int'l J. Ref. L.* 159, 162 (1994).

Juss, S.S., *Immigration, Nationality, and Citizenship* (Mansell, London, 1993).

Juss, S.S., 'Administrative Justice and the Carltona Principle', 2, Oxford J. Leg. Stud. 142 (1993).

Juss, S.S., *Discretion & Deviation in the Administration of Immigration Controls* (Modern Legal Studies Series, Sweet & Maxwell, London, 1997).

Juss, S.S., 'The Coming of Communitarian Rights: Are Third-Generation Human Rights Really First-Generation Rights?', *International Journal of Discrimination & the Law* (1998) vol.3, pp.159–80.

Juss, S.S., 'Toward a Morally Legitimate Reform of Refugee Law: The Uses of Cultural Jurisprudence' *Harvard Hum. Rts Jnl* (vol. 11, 1998) pp.311–354.

Juss, S.S., 'Cultural Competence and the Law of Mental Health' in Bhui and Olajide, *Mental Health Service Provision for a Multi-Cultural Society* (Saunders, London, 1999), pp.102–17.

Juss, S.S., 'Abandoning Vires-Based Review', The King's College Law Journal (vol. 13, Part 2, 2002), pp.239–53.

Kaldor, M., 'Armageddon Myths' *New Statesman*, 26th May 2003, pp.48–9.

Kalin, W., 'The Guiding Principles on Internal Displacement – Introduction', 10 *International Journal of Refugee Law* 557, 559– 560 (1998).

Kaye, R., 'British Refugee Policy in 1992: The Breakdown of A Policy Community', 5(1) *J. Refugee Stud.* 47, 57 (1992).

Keane, D., 'The Environmental Causes and Consequences of Migration: A Search for the Meaning of "environmental refugees"' 16 *Geo.Int'l Envt'l.Rev.* 209.

Keely, C.B., and Russell, S.S., 'Responses of Industrial Countries to Asylum Seekers', 47 J. *Int'l Aff.* 399, 402 (1994).

Kibreab, G., 'Environmental Causes and Impact of Refugee Movements: A Critique of the Current Debate', 21 *Disasters* 20–38 (1977).

Kiwanuka, R., 'The Meaning of "People" in the African Charter of Human and People's Rights' *Am. J. Int'l L* (vol. 82, 1988), p.85.

Klare, K., 'Legal Theory and Democratic Reconstruction: Reflection on 1989', *U. Brit. Colum. L. Rev.* (1991) vol. 35, 69, p.100.

Kneebone, S., (ed), *The Refugees Convention 50 Years On* (Ashgate Publishing Limited, Aldershot, 2003).

Koh, H.H., 'America's Offshore Refugee Camps', 29 *U. Rich. L. Rev.* 139 (1994).

Kostakopoulou, T., '"The 'Protective Union"': Change and Continuity in Migration Law and Policy in Post-Amsterdam Europe' *Journal of Common Market Studies* (2000, vol. 38, No. 3), pp.497–518.

Kunstler, J.H., *The Long Emergency* (Atlantic Books, 2005).

Kymlicka, W., *Multicultural Citizenship: A Liberal Theory of Minority Rights* (Oxford Political Theory Series 1995).

Lavenex, S., 'The Europeanization of Refugee Policies: Normative Challenges and Institutional Legacies' *Journal of Common Market Studies* (2001, vol. 39, No. 5, pp.851–74), p.869.

Legomsky, S.H., 'Why Citizenship?' *Va Jnl. of Int'L Law* (vol. 35, No.1, Fall 1994, pp.279–300).

Legomsky, S.H., 'Immigrants, Minorities, and Pluralism: What kind of society do we really want?', 6 Willamette J.Int'l and Disp. Reosl. 153 (1998).

Lillich, R.B., 'Sovereignty and Humanity: Can They Converge?' in Atle Grahl-Madsen and Jiri Doman (eds.), *The Spirit of Uppsala* (Berlin and New York: De Gruyter, 1984), p.413.

Loescher, G., 'The European Community and Refugees', 65 *Int'l. Affairs*, 617, 619 (1989).

Loescher, G., 'Refugee Movements and International Security', 28 (Adelphi Papers No. 268, 1992).

Magner, T., 'Does a failed state country of origin result in a failure of international protection? A review of policies toward asylum seekers in leading asylum nations', *Georgetown Immigration Law Journal* (Summer 2001, 15) p.703.

Martin, D.A, *The Refugee Concept: On Definitions, Politics and the Careful Use of a Scarce Resource*, in H. Adelman (ed.), *Refugee Policy* (York Lane Press, Toronto, 1991).

Massey, D.S., Arango, J., Hugo, G., and Taylor, J.E., 'Theories of International Migration: Review and Appraisal', in *Population and Development Review* (vol. 19, 1993).

Massey, D.S., Arango, J., Hugo, G., and Taylor, JE.,'An Evaluation of International Migration Theory: The North American Case' in *Population and Development Review* (vol. 19, 1994).

Massey, D.S., et al., *Worlds in Motion: Understanding International Migration at the end of the Millennium* (Oxford, 1998).

Masters, S.B., 'Environmentally-Induced Migration: Beyond a Culture of Reaction', 14 *Geo.Immigr.LJ* 855 (2000), p.872.

McDougal N., and Reisman, W., *International Law in Contemporary Perspective*, 925 (1981).

McGregor, J., *Refugees and Environment in Geography and Refugees: Patterns and Processes of Change*, 159 (Richard Black and Vaughan Robinson eds., 1993).

Mignolo, W., 'The Many Faces of Cosmo-Polis: Border Thinking and Critical

Cosmopolitanism' in Breckenridge, Pollock, Bhabha and Chakrabarty (eds) *Cosmopolitanism* (Durham, Duke University Press), pp.157–87.

Moore, J., 'From Nation State to Failed State: International Protection from Human Rights Abuses by Non-state Agents' 31 *Columbia Human Rights Law Review*, 81, pp.96–7 (1999).

Morton F.L., and Knopff, R., *The Charter Revolution and the Court Party* (Broadview Press, Peterborough, Ontario, 2000).

Muntarbhorn, V., 'Protection and Assistance for Refugees in Armed Conflicts and Internal Disturbances' (1988) 265 *Int'l Rev. of the Red Cross* 351.

Mutua, M.W., 'The Banjul Charter and the African Cultural Fingerprint: An Evaluation of the Language of Duties', 35 *Va. J. Int'l. L.* 340, (1995).

Myers, N., 'Environmental Refugees in a Globally Warmed World', *BioScience* (vol. 43, December 1993), p.11.

Nafziger, J.A., 'A Policy Framework for Regulating the Flow of Undocumented Aliens into the United States', 56 *Or. L. Rev.* 63, at 86–7 (1977).

Nafziger, J.A., 'The General Admission of Aliens Under International Law', 77 *AJIL* (1983), pp.804–47.

Nanda, V.P., 'The Right to Development under International Law – Challenges Ahead' *California Western International Law Journal* (vol. 15, 1985), p.431.

Nett, R., 'The Civil Right we are not Ready for: The Right to Free Movement of People on the Face of the Earth', 81 Ethics 212, at 216 (1971).

Nozick, R., *Anarchy, State and Utopia* (Oxford: Basil Blackwell, 1974).

Odhiambo-Abuya, E., 'Refugees and Internally Displaced Persons: Examining Overlapping Institutional Mandates of the ICRC and the UN High Commissioner for Refugees', 7 *Sing. J. Int'l & Comp. L.* 236, p.244.

Ohmae, K., *The Borderless World* (New York: Harper Collins, 1991).

Oppenheim, L., *International Law* (8th edn., Lauterpacht, 1955), pp.675–6.

Pankhurst A, *Resettlement and Famine in Ethiopia: The Villagers' Experience* (Manchester University Press, UK, 1992).

Perluss, D., and Hartman, J.S., 'Temporary Refuge: Emergence of a Customary Norm', (1986) 26 *Virginia J. of Int'l L.*551, pp.597–8.

Plender, R., 'The Legal Basis of International Jurisdiction to Act with regard to the Internally Displaced' (1994) 6 (3) *International Journal of Refugee Law*, 345.

Portes, A., and Rumbaut, R.G., *Immigrant America: A Portrait* (University of California Press, Los Angeles, 1990).

Ravenstein, E.G., 'The Laws of Migration', *Journal of the Statistical Society* (vol. 48, 1885).

Ravenstein, E.G., 'The Laws of Migration', *Journal of the Statistical Society* (vol. 52, 1889).

Rawls, J., *A Theory of Justice* (Cambridge, Mass. Harvard University Press, 1971).

Reich, R., *The Work of Nations: Preparing Ourselves for the 21st Century Capitalism* (London, Simon & Schuster, 1991).

Roberts, A., 'Destruction of the Environment during the 1991 Gulf War', *Int'l Rev. of the Red Cross*, 1992, p.538.

Rubio-Marin, R., *Immigration as a Democratic Challenge: Citizenship and Inclusion in Germany and the United States* (CUP, 2000).

Ruddick, E.E., 'The Continuing Constraint of Sovereignty: International Law, International Protection, and the Internally Displaced' (1997) (77) (2) *Boston Univ.L.R.*429.

Rutinwa, B., 'The End of Asylum? The Changing Nature of Refugee Policies in Africa', (2002) 1 and 2 (21) *Refugee Quarterly Survey*, 12 at 33.

Saito, N.T., 'Beyond Civil Rights: Considering "Third Generation" International Human Rights Law in the United States', *University of Miami Inter-American Law Review* (vol. 28, 1996–97), p.392.

Santos, B de Sousa, *Toward a New Legal Common Sense* (2nd edn., 2002, London, Butterworths), p.226.

Sarooshi, D., *International Organisations and Their Exercise of Sovereign Powers*, (OUP, Oxford Monographs in International Law, 2005).

Sassen, S., *The Mobility of Labour and Capital* (CUP, 1988); M. Boyd, 'Family and Personal Networks in Migration', *International Migration Review* (vol. 23, Issue 3, 1989, Special Silver Anniversary Issue).

Sassen, S., *The Mobility of Labour and Capital* (CUP, 1988).

Sassen, S., *Guests and Aliens* (New Press, 1999).

Satz, D., 'Equality of What among Whom? Thoughts on Cosmopolitanism, Statism, and Nationalism' in Shapiro and Brilmayer (eds) *Global Justice* (New York, NYU Press), pp.67–8.

Schnapper, D., *la communaute des citoyens: sur l'ide'e moderne de la nation* (Paris: Gallimard, 1994).

Schermers, H.G., 'Human Rights and Free Movement of Persons: The Role of the European Commission and Court of Human Rights', in Henry G. Schermers *et al*, eds. *Free Movement of Persons in Europe, Legal Problems and Experiences* (1991), pp.235, 237.

Schuck, P.H., 'Refugee Burden Sharing: A Modest Proposal', 22 Yale J. Int'l L. 243, 244 n.1 (Summer 1997).

Select Committee on International Development (Sixth report; Session 2003–04) Published by the House of Commons on 29th June 2004. See http://www.publications.parliament.uk/pa/cm200304/cmselect/cmintdev/79/7902.htm Ev 211 [International Organisation for Migration (IOM) memorandum].

Sengupta, A., 'Realising the Right to Development' in *Development and Change* (Blackwell Publishers, Oxford; vol. 31, No. 3, June 2000).

Seton-Watson, H., *Nations and States* (London, Methuen, 1977).

Shacknove, A., 'Who is a refugee?' *Ethics* (vol. 95, 1985) pp.274–84.

Shacknove, A., 'From Asylum to Containment', 5 *Int'l J. Ref. L.* 516 (1993).

Shah, P., *Refugees, Race and the Concept of Asylum* (London, Cavendish Publishing, 2000), pp.31–34.

Shivji, I.G., 'The Concept of Human Rights in Africa', 43 (1989), pp.29–33.

Simon, J.L., *The Economic Consequences of Immigration* (Blackwell Press, 1989).

Smith, A.D., *National Identity* (London, Penguin, 1991).

Smith, J.P. and Edmonston, B., *The New Americans: Economic, Demographic and*

Fiscal Effects of Immigration (National Academy Press, Washington DC, 1997).

Sohn, L., 'The New International Law: Protection of the Rights of Individuals Rather than States' *Am. U.L. Rev.* (1982), p.48.

Solomon, H., 'Who is an Illegal Immigrant?" (*Published in African Security Review Vol 5 No 6, 1996*), p.3 (a Senior Researcher, Human Security Project, Institute for Defence Policy, quoting from his earlier research).

Soysal, Y., 'The Limits of Citizenship: Migrants and Postnational Membership in Europe' (Chicago: University of Chicago Press, 1994).

Spellman, W.M., *The Global Community* (Sutton Publishing Limited, 2002).

Stark, O., *The Migration of Labour* (Blackwell, Oxford, 1991).

Steingraber, C.J., and Niggli P., *The Spoils of Famine: Ethiopian Famine Policy and Peasant Agriculture, Cultural Survival Inc* (Cambridge MA, 1988).

Sternberg, V., 'The plight of the noncombatant in civil war and the new criteria for refugee status', 9 *Int'l J. of Refugee L.* 169, 178 (1977).

Streeten, P., 'Governance of the Global Economy', in *Globalisation and Citizenship: An International Conference*, 9–11 December (Geneva: United Nations Research Institute for Social Development, 1996).

Sztucki, J., '"Who is a Refugee?" The Convention Definition: Universal or Absolute?', in Frances Nicholson and Patrick Twomey (eds) *Refugee Rights and Realities: Evolving International Concepts and Rregimes* (Cambridge, CUP, 1999), p.64.

Teitelbaum, 'Political Asylum in Theory and Practice', 76 The Public Interest, 74, pp.77–8 (1984).

Turk, D., 'How World Bank – IMF policies adversely affect human rights', *Third World Resurgence* (1993).

Turk, V., 'The Role of UNHCR in the development of international refugee law' in Frances Nicholson and Patrick Twomey (eds) *Refugees Rights & Realities: Evolving International Concepts & Regimes* (CUP, 1999), p.154.

Vasak, K., 'A 30-year Struggle: The sustained Efforts to Give Force of Law to the Universal Declaration of Human Rights' *Unesco Courier* 29 (1977), p.29.

Vernant, J., *The Refugee in the Post-War World* (London, Allen & Unwin, 1953), p.5.

Virally, M., 'Review Essay: Good Faith in Public International Law' 77 *Am. J. Int'l L.* 130 (1983).

Walker, K., 'Defending the 1951 Convention Definition of Refugee', *Geo.Immigr. L.J.* (vol. 17, p.597).

Walzer, M., *Spheres of Justice: A Defence of Pluralism and Equality* (Oxford. 1983).

Weiner, M., *The Global Migration Crisis: Challenge to States and to Human Rights*, (Harper Collins, New York, 1995).

Weis, P., *Nationality & Statelessness in International Law* (Hague, Martinus Nijthoff, 1956).

Weston B., and Murray, B., *Encyclopaedia Britannica: Human Rights*, University of Iowa Centre for Human Rights at http://www.uichr.org/features/eb/weston4.shtml.

Whitaker, E., 'The Schengen Agreement and its Portent for the Freedom of Personal Movement in Europe', 6 *Geo. Immigr. L.J.*, 191, 219 (1992).

Winder, R., *Bloody Foreigners* (London, Little Brown, 2004), p.198.

Woods, J.N., 'Travel That Talks: Towards First Amendment Protection of Freedom of Movement' *George Washington Law Review* (Vol. 65, 1996) pp.106–29.

Zartman, W., 'Introduction to Collapsed States: The Disintegration and Restoration of Legitimate Authority' (in William Zartman, ed., 1995).

Zetter, R., 'Labelling Refugees: Forming and Transforming a Bureaucratic Identity', *Jnl of Ref. Std.* (vol. 4, issue 1, 1991), pp.39–62.

Zolberg, A.R., 'The Next Waves: Migration Theory for a Changing World', in *International Migration Review* (vol. 23, Issue 3, 1989).

Zolberg, A.R., Suhrke, A., and Aguayo, S., *Escape from Violence: Conflict and the Refugee Crisis in the Developing World* (Oxford, 1989).

Index

Note: numbers in brackets preceded by *n* are note numbers.